HAVE I GOT IT RIGHT GOD

You may say you know God; but does He know of you?

Not every one that saith unto me, Lord, Lord, shall enter into the kingdom of heaven; but he that doeth the will of my Father which is in heaven.

Many will say to me in that day, Lord, Lord, have we not prophesied in thy name? and in thy name have cast out devils? and in thy name done many wonderful works? And then will I profess unto them, I never knew you: depart from me, ye that work iniquity.

Why do ye also transgress the commandment of God by your tradition? but in vain they do worship me, teaching *for* doctrines the commandments of men. For the time will come when they will not endure sound doctrine;

Take heed to thyself that thou be not snared by following them

And he shall speak *great* words against the most High, and shall wear out the saints of the most High, and think to change times and laws: . .. and they shall be given into his hand until a time and times and the dividing of time. …

And the great dragon was cast out, that old serpent, called the Devil, and Satan, which deceiveth the whole world: … and causeth the earth and them which dwell therein to worship the first beast!

Here is the patience of the saints: here *are* they that keep the commandments of God, and the faith of Jesus.

BY ROGER LEE

HAVE I GOT IT RIGHT GOD

ACKNOWLEDGEMENTS

I thank all those people who I encountered on my journey to find God or Him to be pleased with me. Who tolerated my discussions on the subject of this book. Who through their reasoning and objections inspired me to find biblical and other true answers to share with others who may have the same reasoning or objections. Though I think I have been thorough, if you are not convinced and have other reasons to those covered, do not hesitate to contact me with them at my details given in the book.

God Bless you all.

PREFACE

All Christians believe in the same God; the one and only of all creation. Whether named Yahweh or Jehovah. The true God of the whole human race, whether Jew, Christian, Muslim, Gentile or other. Then why the differing beliefs between denominations, from where and when did they come? Should the same God not have a universal standard to be met to get His ultimate prize for which we all aim; heaven or immortality? Then why according to the sentiments in Luke 13:24 of all those "seeking" few will be able to enter in?

Because satan has used the Trojan horse deception. Bringing apparent "gifts" into God's true method. The Trojan horse was portable on wheels; likewise satan makes his deceptions to fit each believer's weakness. They can adapt their believe of God into what appeals to them. This book, though primarily focusing on the major deception of satan will also cover some of the others in the hope of informing Christians of some facts, of which most are unaware. It is a study book not a novel and I recommend you read and re-read it with a highlighter to mark the pages or scripture quotations. The scriptures are at the back in the Glossary to save you carrying your bible. As God says in Hosea 4:6 "my people are destroyed for lack of knowledge: because thou has rejected knowledge I will also reject thee". Lack of knowledge destroys. The devil comes to destroy by keeping you away from know- ledge; so lack of knowledge is ungodly. 1Jhn 3:8 Jesus came to destroy work of devil as is the aim of this book by giving you knowledge. The truth will set you free of the untruth bondage of the devil. We serve who we follow, truth or lie, God or the devil. With this knowledge, you can decide whether to obey God in the manner He prescribes or not. As will seen, just as in human legislation, ignorance is no excuse. I assume the facts contained will inflict some spiritual cuts to some, to others welcomed information they may never have come across. The cuts are to heal as a physician not a butcher. The information is to vindicate not condemn. To restore readers to God who may be like the lost sheep of Israel following customs against God's real way. Though some bible texts may be quoted more than once; this is unavoidable when the same text is of benefit under two different points or topics. Remember the apparent Trojan "gift" destroyed them. I hope you find its contents valuable.

INTRODUCTION

Those of you familiar with the bible, would know Jesus said some hard things to people. Many could not take what he said and left following Him. For example, Matt 10:34-38, Luke 9:57-62, 13:1-5 and 14:25 "Think not that I am come to send peace on earth: I came not to send peace, but a sword. For I am come to set a man at variance against his father, and the daughter against her mother, and the daughter in law against her mother in law. And a man's foes shall be they of his own household. He that loveth father or mother more than me is not worthy of me: and he that loveth son or daughter more than me is not worthy of me. And he that taketh not his cross, and followeth after me, is not worthy of me. Luke 9:59 And he said unto another, Follow me. But he said, Lord, suffer me first to go and bury my father. Jesus said unto him, Let the dead bury their dead: And another also said, Lord, I will follow thee; but let me first go bid them farewell, which are at home at my house. And Jesus said unto him, No man, having put his hand to the plough, and looking back, is fit for the kingdom of God. Luke 9:2 And Jesus answering said unto them, Suppose ye that these Galileans were sinners above all the Galileans, because they suffered such things? Luk 13:3 I tell you, Nay: but, except ye repent, ye shall all likewise perish. Or those eighteen, upon whom the tower in Siloam fell, and slew them, think ye that they were sinners above all men that dwelt in Jerusalem? I tell you, nay: but, except ye repent, ye shall all likewise perish. Luk 14:25 And there went great multitudes with him: and he turned, and said unto them, If any man come to me, and hate not his father, and mother, and wife, and children, and brethren, and sisters, yea, and his own life also, he cannot be my disciple. And whosoever doth not bear his cross, and come after me, cannot be my disciple.

Jesus was not concerned about gaining the support or following of "the multitude". He was looking for real followers, doers not hearers of His word. The multitude would be whittled down to the genuine. Today preachers of God's word stay clear of saying hard things in fear of loosing the multitude following, the size of the collection plate, offending others. They seek quantity rather than quality of members. Rather than getting followers to step up to the word of God, they bring the word of God down to suit the needs and desires of the people. They preach comfort rather than the whole truth. What people want to hear rather than should hear and hearers then think the comfort message is the truth. This book is not against the sincere preachers trying to bring people to God; but the pretenders and charmers. However, even the sincere ones can sincerely believe what is wrong. The followers of truth would prove their sincerity Though Paul tried to be all things to all people (1Cor 9:22) it was for "might by all means save some". He never corrupted or deviated from the word of God nor preached for his own financial gain, merely adapted (not changed) the message to personal levels. I heard a Christian radio show preacher stating he personally knows preachers of large television ministries, refusing to preach on or use the words sin, hell, salvation. They do not want to tell people they are sinning, risk going to hell, need to change to be saved, as it would give them an inferiority complex. Would offend them. Then what are the preachers there for? To prosper individually or as a church through collections? Is it not better to save one than none? Phil 3:18-19 (For many walk, of whom I have told you often, and now tell you even weeping, that they are the enemies of the cross of Christ: Whose end is destruction, whose God is their belly, and whose glory is in their shame, who mind earthly things). These same preachers, who maybe were once godly; but went astray with the wealth or concerns of the world, then ordain others to preach their same corrupted interpretations or write books etc which others believe. Today the concept is blessed are the prosperous. Was John the Baptist or Jesus wealthy compared to Herod and the like? Did Jesus give His blessing to the rich and healthy or the poor, blind, lame? In Mark 10:23 did Jesus not advise the rich man to give away his riches then added "how hardly shall they that have riches enter into the kingdom of God"? Did Jesus not say in Matt 11:11 of all men born of women, no one was better or worthy than John the Baptist? Yet he was poor. Do you or the world think you are godly because of prosperity? Does the bible not contradict this view?

As a religion, Christians have to suffer a lot of offensive ridicule, silencing legislation, blasphemy of their God and more. So why as individuals should they get any more offended when told the truth? Luke 12:40 Be ye therefore ready also: for the Son of man cometh at an hour when ye think not.… Who then is that faithful and wise steward, whom his lord shall make ruler over his household, to give them their portion of meat in due season? Blessed is that servant, whom his lord when he cometh shall find so **doing**.

Of course I do not wish to offend nor advocate offensiveness. However, one should not be offended by the word of God. So how can I put a point across to you without offending? Do not look at the delivery but the message. The motives are in love (Pro 13:24; Heb 12:6,7; Rev 3:19 chastening is sign of love from one who cares). 2Ti 4:2 "Preach the word; be instant in season, out of season; reprove, rebuke, exhort with all longsuffering and doctrine. 2Ti 4:3 for the time will come when they will not endure sound doctrine; but after their own lusts shall they heap to themselves teachers, having itching ears; 2Ti 4:4 And they shall turn away *their* ears from the truth, and shall be turned unto fables". 3Jo 1:4 I have no greater joy than to hear that my children walk in truth. Do not make up your mind until reading its entirety. Christians seem to want the encouraging texts that pats them on the back, tell them they are doing well, have met the heavenly standards even if they have not. Personally, would prefer being told where I am going wrong not what I have done right as that does not need fixing; but he devil has implanted in us thoughts of resentment when correction comes. Finding fault in the delivery, or calling it judgement. It is the winner that gets the prize not the hardworking second best and we ought to strive to get in at the narrow winners' gate. Better I get into heaven adhering to rebuke than not change due to praises.

I began this book as a letter to a newspaper that printed an article stating church attendance was on the increase. My letter stated that, though the increase was a good thing, it was a shame almost all Christians follow customs rather than God's word. Doing the most abominable thing(s) to Him in the belief they are worshipping Him. As a result, I estimate 99% of Christians would end up the very place they wish to avoid, hell. That includes the seemingly most devoted. The Bible talks of the majority always getting it wrong ("as for me and my house Jos 24:15) and advises not to follow them ["…all the world …worshipped the dragon. And deceiveth them that dwell on the earth…" (see Rev 13:3,4,12-14 in the Glossary)]. As I began to write why and speak to Christians in my travels I decided to add and respond to the many excuses I heard. Others may have the same excuses as read in a book, learnt from a pastor or other source. I hope you give the contents deep thought, as it is written with a sincere wish to bring more Christians to God, our creator.

First, let me remind you for what Christians are aiming. To get to be with God in heaven or paradise according to your specific belief on the topic. To be in the presence of the One so pure and unadulterated. For this you have to be the same to be in His presence. Remember Moses having to take off his shoes when on holy ground, protect his eyes as God moved past. How Aaron and the priests had to wash and wear special clothing of specific material used solely in His presence and, of course, why Jesus had to be conceived by Immaculate Conception. Thus by then we are to have no imperfections. We have proved ourselves worthy by our disobedience and life on earth where we forsook everything as pleasures of lust, greed, envy etc for the one incomparable reward. "The kingdom of heaven is like unto a merchant man, seeking goodly pearls: Who, when he had found one pearl of great price, went and sold all that he had, and bought it" (Matt 13:45-46).Not everyone would make that sacrifice. Some may think and try to have it all. Use arguments to convince themselves they are doing the right thing, especially if that has become the way of the world. Others may prefer the here and now rather than seek or believe there is anything better. Believing the deception of the master deceiver, satan. His deception being so subtle and finely tuned that even the very elect would be deceived (if that was possible) (Mark 13:22).

Satan has gone as far as to set up a parallel Christian religion where he is god, the angel of light (2 Thes 2:4, 2 Cor 11:14-15). Has copied all the components of the true system by having a false Christ, prophets, teachers, churches, bible and method of worship. These are illustrated later. They could very possibly be versed in scripture better than you. They would quote the bible to appear as angels of light bringing you the truth. Remember it was scripture satan used even against Jesus. The same against Eve in the garden and, even though Eve knew and recognised the mis-quote of what God said, she was still fooled into sinning. [Gen 3:1-3 "Now the serpent was more subtle than any beast of the field, which the LORD God had made. And he said unto the woman, Yea, hath God said, Ye shall not eat of **every tree** of the garden? And the woman said unto the serpent, "We may eat of the fruit of the trees of the garden: **But** of the fruit of the tree, which is in the midst of the garden, God hath said, Ye shall not eat of it, neither shall ye touch it, lest ye die"]. What deception has he used on you? Pride, stiff neck, closed ears, laziness, intolerance, keeping you busy, dependant on this or that…?1 John 2:15-16 "love not the world, neither the things that are in the world. If any man love the world, the love of the father is not in him. For all that is in the world, the lust of the flesh and the lust of the eyes and the pride of life is not of the father but is of the world" .I.e. latest T.V, computer or phone game or gadget home furnishing, keeping up with the Jones'.

Such is the similarity, it is almost impossible to know which system you are in, true or false, God's or satan's. As a precaution I would suggest doing as God commanded even if you do not fully understand His reasons. "To obey is better than sacrifice" (1st Sam 15:22); prayers, good intentions etc. Do what you know worked for those in the bible, for Abraham, Moses, David, Jesus and others. That is hard evidence. Not new reasoning, customs, modern way of life. "Not everyone that say onto me Lord, Lord, shall enter into the kingdom of heaven; but he that **do** the will of my father which is in heaven" (Matt 7:21). Mat 13:9 When any one hearth the word of the kingdom, and understandeth it not, then cometh the wicked one, and catcheth away that which was sown in his heart. This is he which received seed by the way side. Mat 13:20But he that received the seed into stony places, the same is he that heareth the word, and anon with joy receiveth it; Mat 13:21Yet hath he not root in himself, but dureth for a while: for when tribulation or persecution ariseth because of the word, by and by he is offended. Mat 13:22He also that received seed among the thorns is he that heareth the word; and the cares of this world, and the deceitfulness of riches, choke the word, and he becometh unfruitful.

As all satan had to do was impose a custom contrary to God's way. Ban ownership of scripture, kill by persecution and legislation under the banner of a church, those owning or spreading the true way. Then after a relatively short time, say 100 – 200 years, the true system would be lost (except to a few faithful). Subsequent generations would follow the false custom and even come up with justification for those customs. They would interpret bible text to fall in line with those new customs and beliefs. This is what took place and why most Christians are on the wrong road and will never reach the prize of heaven they seek. Fortunately , records exist of the early post Christ and apostle period, of the reformation, Spanish inquisition etc so that diligent seekers can discover the origins of the customs they keep. One aspect of the "root" mentioned in Matt 13:21 could be lack of historical grounding. No depth in your research. Taking the easy way of believing what others say, because they were given a title by who knows who and you placed your salvation on their guidance. "The cares of this world and deceitfulness of riches" of Matt 13:22 could be those who, as many have said to me, do not do exactly as God said, because they feel they cannot keep to God's ways. Because that was old times, things have changed, moved on, become more modern, the world of today operates on a different cycle. My guidance, Luk 13:24"Strive to enter in at the straight gate: for many, I say unto you, will seek to enter in, and shall not be able". Note this applies to those "seeking" entry. Devout Christians. Mat 7:13"Enter ye in at the straight gate: for wide is the gate, and broad is the way, that leadeth to destruction, and many there be which go in thereat." Therefore, know biblical history, it would liberate you from mental slavery of custom and lies. The truth will set you free to worship God as He intended and commanded. Your redemption depends on it.

Then we have preachers who advocate the wealth and riches Christian; serving God and mammon (Matt 6:24). They seek financial pledges, contributions etc to their ministry in exchange for a pray, blessing or good fortune just like indulgences offered by Catholic Church in the 16th century, to which Martin Luther objected. Did any prophet,

Jesus or apostle sell a blessing? No. Was John the Baptist or Jesus rich compared to Herod, tax collectors and others? No. Did Jesus give blessing to the rich or poor, blind and lame or healthy? What did God's people say when offered financial reward for blessings and what happened to those who sort any such reward? The Godly refused any reward for God's work as in 1Kings 13:8. In Num 22:17-18,22; 23:8; 31:8,16; Deu 23:5; Jos 24:10 we read of Balaam trying to gain reward for cursing God's people. God killed him. In 2Kings 5:15-16, 20-27 Elisha heals Naaman of leprosy and refused any reward. His servant went and took a reward and got the leprosy. In Acts 8:9,18-20 Peter rebukes baptized sorcerer for "thinking the gift of God may be purchased with money". God does not require nor take reward; Deu 10:17. As Jude 1:4,11,17 confirms ungodly men have crept into Christianity "turning the grace of God into lasciviousness". Quoting bible text for more money, better suits, cloths and property than they would receive doing a day's work in the commercial labour market. you trying to be a Christian for riches, good fortune or physical healing? If so your motivation is flawed. Matthew 6:31-33 says take no thought what you shall eat, drink or wear, God knows what you need. Seek first the kingdom of God and His righteous-ness and everything else you need (not desire) will be added unto you. Joh 6:27 Labour not for the meat which perisheth, but for that meat which endureth unto everlasting life, which the Son of man shall give unto you: for him hath God the Father sealed.

Blessing are to make receivers believe in God and His ability, not bring financial reward to anyone. Everything belongs to God. He created and owns all (Acts 17:25). He does not need your money only your obedience. Anyone asking for your money in exchange for prays or a blessing is not of, nor from God. There has always been the ungodly claiming to serve God who fit into this text from Micah "The heads thereof judge for reward, and the priest thereof teach for hire and the prophets thereof divine for money". Did Jesus not make the ultimate sacrifice, His life and did He not give it freely? Did He not say to his apostles in Mat 10:8 "heal the sick, cleanse the lepers, raise the dead, cast out devils, **freely ye have received, freely give".** So these false preachers have no mandate to charge for blessings or request any financial contribution.

People are turning God's laws into a science or an art. God's laws are as those of nature, they are discovered; maybe through scientific observation or experiments; but do not change as gravity. One can like or dislike art, poetry, the use of words. 2+2= 4 in any language, religion or denomination. So it is with God's way. One for all regardless of intellect, gender or creed. God's people are of one denomination: others are of demonation. God cannot allow our intellectual input into His formulae to do with whether we get into heaven or follow Him. If He allowed our reasoning in one small part, then each individual would use their way of thinking to come up with their concocted belief based on their rational. An intelligent person will come up with one level of thinking and a less intelligent with another. Later someone else may develop a previous theory and take it further away from God. Just like in the European Union or verdict in a court trial whereby one member has the power of veto against the others' majority decision, nothing gets done. So God has made it simple. Regardless of intelligence. Obey.

IS THERE A GOD.

In a word, an emphatic YES. Christians know that; so this short section is for the sceptics. The evidence for there being a God of creation far out weighs the alternative theories to the extent that more and more scientist are reaching that conclusion. For every theory the sceptics concoct they are disproved by the numerous gaps within them and assumptions on which they are based. Even Darwin, the father of the evolution theories was left in doubt in his older years. One of the gaps being how something can come from nothing. A basic contradiction of scientific principles. Even if starting from the hypothesis that first there were gases in space; what is the origin of these gases?

One of the latest theories being that the big bang was formed by certain gases, in specific proportions, coincidentally coming and then tightly compressing together at a certain point, to reach a temperature similar to that of the sun before exploding into the big bang from whence came the universe. One can see the gaps. The gases have to be of a specific type, quantities and mixture, all meeting at one pin head of a point etc. Gases expand and disperse, not contract. Also there are so many stars, universes, galaxies each of which were formed by the one off coincidence. Billions of dollars have been invested to recreate this scenario whereby a container can be made to withstand the huge temperature needed. The nearest they have got is getting as much energy out as they have put in. They can not do once which was apparently done thousands of times by the claimed coincidence. The sun creates all this energy without the smoke and other undesirables. Not one part of creation can the scientist recreate only manipulate.

These scientist simply rebel against the evidence of God. For the ordinary person one only has to look at nature to see God. Human's individual finger prints, eye scans, D.N.A. How, for example, an insignificant seed can be eaten and that is the end of it. Yet placed in the ground can yield a solid very tall oak tree with roots going one way and hard wood another. Its Trunk of one colour, soft leaves of another and pods of yet another. It sucks up water against gravity, through an intricate system ending in veins on the leaves. Every creature and item of creation is evidence of an intelligent designer of the universe. To the scientists they have even more bewildering evidence from their own calculations. Of all the weigh of matter in the universe, when it was made. Trillions of grains of sand, trees, rocks etc; if the universe had one more or less grain of sand it would not have exist. Either exploding or contracting on itself. I do not know how they work that out; but that is their findings. The complexity of a single human cell is said to have more going on in it than rush hour in New York. Not just the thousands of people going various directions; but their mobile and other phone conversations, train and car travel etc . Yet about twenty of these cells can fit on a pin head. The universe is so finely tuned that if you imagine a radio dial with two billion miles of tuning range, one centimetre turn either to the right or left would cause it to either explode or contact. There are numerous statistical analogies all stating any other option; but an intelligent designer God is impossibility. These atheist scientists with their own propagating agenda even stretch or some may say falsify evidence in support of their agenda. The Christian and Hebrew bible together with ancient literature of other religions believe the Genesis creation event as reiterated in John 1:3 "All things were made by him and without Him was not anything made that was made". Heb 1:2 Hath in these last days spoken unto us by *his* Son, whom he hath appointed heir of all things, by whom also he made the worlds. The more these scientists find out while trying to "remake the wheel" already made by God, the more they discover they do not know and cannot explain. They now know that the human body has the same chemical properties as the earth as told in Genesis Gen 2:7 "And the LORD God formed man *of* the dust of the ground, and breathed into his nostrils the breath of life; and man became a living soul". Jer 17:5 thus saith the LORD; cursed *be* the man that trusteth in man, and maketh flesh his arm, and whose heart departeth from the LORD. Ecc 3:11 He hath made every *thing* beautiful in his time: also he hath set the world in their heart, so that no man can find out the work that God maketh from the beginning to the end. Rom 1:20 For the invisible things of him from the creation of the world are clearly seen, being understood by the things that are made, *even* his eternal power and Godhead; so that they are <u>without excuse</u>: Rom 1:21 Because that, when they knew God, they glorified *him* not as God, neither were thankful; but became vain in their imaginations, and their foolish heart was darkened. Rom 1:22 professing themselves to be wise, they became fools,   As Christians we know who is really behind the rebels. Some say the Bible was written by man. This is wrong, it was written by God, recorded by man who also recorded the human history parts.

WHO IS GOD

Most humans of all civilizations acknowledge a force greater than them. This force or being they term God. Whether some call the force nature or other name, they refer to the creator. Most turn to this creator, invisible yet stronger than them, for sympathy and help in times of desperation. There are many biblical names for the creator. For the purpose of this booklet I shall use two of the most common, Yahweh or Jehovah. The Jews held the creator in the highest esteem that they would not even pronounce His name out of respect. The foundation and origin of this God is found in the bible. Though they may differ on the characteristics of this God, the Jews, Christians and Muslims all recognise Him as the God in their bible or bible equivalent. He created the universe and mankind as narrated in Genesis. However, the characteristics of the Christian God differs from the one they call Allah in the sense the Christian's is loving, humans can have a personal relationship with Him as did Adam and He provides an attainable plan of salvation. Some people refer to Jesus as Jehoshua (pronounced Isuyah) and claim the Romans used "Jesus".

Many non believers have tried to disprove the bible; but have failed. From whatever angle the task is approached it fails by their own accepted standards of evidence. Whether from a legal, forensic, investigative, archaeological, or statistical. They only believe in what they can see or understand. Not seeing something or someone does not necessarily mean they do not exist. At one point in time the world was thought to be flat. It is known the bible characters existed from historical records found. These records span centuries and were written by various persons in different time zones and different countries. For example the predictions spoken of in the book of Daniel 2 regarding forthcoming empires were written centuries before the empires came about and the book found. The predictions about Jesus, where and of whom He would be born, the manner of His birth and death were again written by many in various centuries, centuries before Jesus was actually born. These prophecies were not vague; but very specific. Down to being crucified as a criminal yet His legs not be broken like other criminals, cloths not ripped, and rising from the dead. History confirms he existed; though some limit Him to a mere good mortal. When he was born and teaching He was able to refer back to these centuries' old predictions the story of Lots wife turning to a pillar of salt in Gen 19:26 can be confirmed by historical records. There was for centuries a peculiar formation of crumbling rock associated with the account. Josephus (Antiquities 1.11.4) declared he had seen it day. Clement of Rome, Irenaeus, and Benjamin of Tudela also saw it in his day. The fire and brimstone accounted in Gen 19:24 has been confirm by astronomers who say a trace of the event as regards meteorites falling in that vicinity in that year has been left in space similar to how an aeroplane leaves a trail of smoke behind it. In short, the bible has been proven to be authentic. The instructions and guidance given within by God are found to be the best way to deal with man's problems.

For example, societies could not exist without the moral code of God as described in the bible. If murderers were not punished and some rule of law adopted to protect the weak, the strongest would survive and rule as a tyrant. They would always be weary of challenges and eventually be killed by a younger stronger person. Today's legal system includes disobedient juveniles, adultery, divorce, theft and murder. All these are covered in the ten commandments of Exodus 20. Inventions would not flourish if one's investment was not protected. No one would spend their time or money inventing something for another stronger one to simply come and take it. Lastly, quarantining or cutting out an illness is still practiced thousands of years after instructed by God. Whether in the human body or say dampness in a building. Male circumcision is now medically known to prevent many illnesses as well as abstention from pork.

Some people excuse following God's ways by saying he gave me a brain and common sense to use. That is true; but he did not give you them to use validating nor rationalising His commands. In spiritual things we take God at His word and obey. As He says Job 38:4 "Where wast thou when I laid the foundations of the earth? declare, if thou hast understanding".

So we have a God who created all of which we know and the universe of which we do not really know. An all knowing God with foresight to give instructions on how to exist. What else could we know about this God? In truth we may never know His full potential. We could not even comprehend a fraction of Him much less for me to try and put it into words. What I would like to say however, is reiterate some of His characteristics found in the bible. We did not evolve from a monkey or similar as those denying God would like us to believe. Humans are wonderfully made in His image our complexity is simplicity to Him. No individual is cloned or has another exactly like them. Even twins are distinguishable in some physical manner, finger prints and DNA. He made you and there is no other like you. Knows every hair on your head and has a plan for each individual which is best for them. He is constantly calling us back to His plan. The contents of the Bible is one of love, how He will do anything to save YOU and reserve you for the better things He has planned for YOU. (This book is to encourage you to get onto that plan). Mostly, He is love. Far beyond what we can comprehend as pure 100% love to the last degree. Sin and Him cannot co-exist. In His presence sin would melt long before coming into His presence like a candle getting close to the sun. Christians should know the story of Moses in God's presence. God having to hide Moses in the cleft of a rock, cover his eyes and only barely see the back of Him as He manifestly passed by. How Moses' face shown so bright when descending from the mount that a cloth had to be put over his face.

As to His longsuffering, almost endless mercy and time given us to repent of our sins and recognise Him is another concept we really do not comprehend. We say the words; but really have little idea. For all He has done for us as humans, giving us all things for our existence, beauty, pleasure. As individuals, family, friends, emotions and freewill which we constantly use against Him. Yet, even yet He holds out a loving hand willingness to do the extreme to show His love. Despite constantly talking to us, sending messengers whom we ignore if not kill, yet he paid the last price. Manifesting in human form (sending His son), suffering and have us kill His outstretched hand. That is love beyond any humans' sacrifice. If we truly understood we would want to reciprocate this love by living our lives as a living sacrifice to Him. To the sick, He is a healer; lonely a companion, broken hearted a comforter; needy a provider. Most importantly, He can change lives and the heart of those who accept Him, His will, His timing. So how can we be that living sacrifice? By obeying His will as prescribed in His commandments. Christians are aware God has an enemy, satan one of God's created angels who of his free will turned rebellious. Envious of God he is working to deceive the world about God by any means possible. This is why God is misrepresented, misunderstood and misinterpreted and blamed for things caused by satan who is the total opposite to God. God is good, satan evil. God is pure truth, satan lies deceives and is selfish. God creates, satan takes., God is love, satan is not., God's message is one of salvation and saving men (Luk 9:56 For the Son of man is not come to destroy men's lives, but to save *them), satan's to destroy us.*

God requires people to honestly and without reservation seek Him out, the only true God. Then work with Him to give all people a chance to know Him and experience the new life (Joh 17:3 And this is life eternal, that they might know thee the only true God, and Jesus Christ, whom thou hast sent). Christians claim to believe in this God of the Bible, to love Him and His son Jesus, want to show this love by following His commandments, and yet find excuses not to do His will. Instead they follow customs of men instituted by the devil to take praise and recognition due to God for himself or make us keep his times rather than God's i.e New Year. He knows humans are creatures of habit and find it hard to break customs (Pro 26:11 As a dog returneth to his vomit, *so* a fool returneth to his folly). . Unfortunately he has ploys unknown to us to prevent many finding out the truth. . One being having the practice ongoing for so long many think that is how it always was. Changed their mentality to thinking any or their own standard of "goodness" would do. Fill their time with so much duties or pleasure of this world that they have no time for proper biblical research. Keeping them reading limited parts of the Bible either as "thoughts for the day", motivation or similar books so they do not wish to get to know the real God and His ways. Why be a Christian if you are not going to put God first. Could you make a "U" or are you addicted to what you are doing? How does a true Christian stand out from the kind person, or one who admires nature, believes in themselves or another form of god? One is a servant of whom or what they follow God, satan or self. If God instructs to do something and satan not to do it. Then according to whether you do it or not say to who you give your allegiance. It goes beyond believing who is right. One can believe something; but not do it. The believe is then vain. One does not believe what they know to be a lie, though one can believe a lie through being deceived. The devil has more belief in God and Jesus than most Christians following custom. Unlike them, he knows his deceits are lies, thus also the truth that Jesus is "the way, the truth, and the life: no man cometh unto the Father, but by me." John 14:6 Jam 2:19 Thou believest that there is one God; thou doest well: the devils also believe, and tremble." Luk 4:33-4 "in the synagogue there was a man, which had a spirit of an unclean devil, and cried…Jesus of Nazareth…I know thee who thou art; the Holy One of God" Yet the devil nor those who side with him definitely will not be saved in the new heaven and earth. They know and some believe the real understanding of scripture; but choose not to follow it and mislead you with false interpretations. So one has to do more than believe. They must also act in the properly in line with that believe.

What it is God's people are to do is the purpose of this book. An attempt to counter the counterfeiter. The devil's deception centres around who to worship, when and how, what happens after death from earth and deceptions regarding the penalty for disobeying God and / or lowering God's standard in our mind so we do not achieve it. Imagine a scale of minus ten to plus ten with you in the middle, the devil at minus ten and God's finish line at plus ten. As you try to cross God's finish line, the devil constantly tries to hinder you by pulling on a rope around your waist. The rope of worldly or selfish desires. All the devil has to do is stop you getting to No. ten. You can get as far as plus nine and yet end up with him in hell providing he gets you to break at least one. "whosoever shall break one of these least commandments …" is guilty of breaking all and will not get to heaven (Matthew and James 2:10). I am not saying grace does not play a part in us getting to No. ten, the finish line. 1Jo 1:9 "If we confess our sins, he is faithful and just to forgive us *our* sins, and to cleanse us from all unrighteousness". However, note one has to confess the sin in order to get forgiveness. If the devil can persuade us what we are doing is not a sin, God's standard has changed, been lowered, He is all love merciful etc so that we do not recognise our action as a sin.

We do not confess it, do not gain the cleansing and thus cannot be in God's presence at the end. The devil would have won you. It is therefore imperative you examine all your actions, customs and believes to get it right with God.

God gives us every chance as well as our freewill. By our failure to make the right research, decision and choice, we choose our fate.

WHAT GOD REQUIRES OF US

Unfortunately through one man (and Eve) exercising the freewill given to them, sin came into the world and affected all his descendants. Each subsequent human is born in that sinful state. The antidote is similarly through exercising that freewill given to each human. Rom 5:19 For as by one man's disobedience many were made sinners, so by the obedience of one shall many be made righteous. We can now choose for ourselves to obey God and blot out the disobedient stain of our earthly father Adam. Obeying God's directives to follow the One He sent (Rev 14:12 Here is the patience of the saints: here *are* they that keep the commandments of God and the faith of Jesus).

Here are just a few quotes from the bible on the topic. The rest are inserted throughout the book under other headings.

1King 2:3 And keep the charge of the LORD thy God, to walk in his ways, to keep his statutes, and his commandments, and his judgments, and his testimonies, as it is written in the law of Moses, that thou mayest prosper in all that thou doest, and whithersoever thou turnest thyself: Psa 103:17 But the mercy of the LORD *is* from everlasting to everlasting upon them that fear him, and his righteousness unto children's children; Psa 103:18 To such as keep his covenant, and to those that remember his commandments to do them. Psa 111:10 The fear of the LORD *is* the beginning of wisdom: a good understanding have all they that do *his commandments* his praise endureth for ever. Psa 119:97 MEM. O how love I thy law! it *is* my meditation all the day. Psa 119:98 Thou through thy commandments hast made me wiser than mine enemies: for they *are* ever with me. Deu 28:1 And it shall come to pass, if thou shalt hearken diligently unto the voice of the LORD thy God, to observe *and* to do all his commandments which I command thee this day, that the LORD thy God will set thee on high above all nations of the earth: also John 12:44, Acts 15:14, 17, 19 (God wishes humans, Jew or Gentile to turn to Him and keep His ways).

The Cracked Pot

A water bearer in India had two large pots, each hung on each end of a pole which he carried across his neck. One of the pots had a crack in it, and while the other pot was perfect and always delivered a full portion of water at the end of the long walk from the stream to the master's house, the cracked pot arrived only half full. For a full two years this went on daily, with the bearer delivering only one and a half pots full of water in his master's house.

Of course, the perfect pot was proud of its accomplishments, perfect to the end for which it was made. But the poor cracked pot was ashamed of its own imperfection, and miserable that it was able to accomplish only half of what it had been made to do.

After two years of what it perceived to be a bitter failure, it spoke to the water bearer one day by the stream. "I am ashamed of myself, and I want to apologize to you."

"Why?" asked the bearer. "What are you ashamed of?"

"I have been able, for these past two years, to deliver only half my load because this crack in my side causes water to leak out all the way back to your masters house. Because of my flaws, you have to do all of this work, and you don't get full value from your efforts." The pot said.

The water bearer felt sorry for the old cracked pot, and in his compassion he said, "As we return to the master's house, I want you to notice the beautiful flowers along the path."

Indeed, as they went up the hill, the old cracked pot took notice of the sun warming the beautiful wild flowers on the side of the path, and this cheered it some. But at the end of the trail, it still felt bad because it had leaked out half its load, and so again the Pot apologized to the bearer for its failure.

The bearer said to the pot, "Did you notice that there were flowers only on your side of your path, but not on the other pots side? That's because I have always known about your flaw, and I took advantage of it. I planted flower seeds on your side of the path, and every day while we walk back from the stream, you've watered them. For two years I have been able to pick these beautiful flowers to decorate my masters table. Without you being just the way you are, he would not have this beauty to grace his house."

Each of us has our own unique flaws. We are all cracked pots. But if we will allow it, the Lord will use our flaws to grace His Fathers table. In Gods great economy, nothing goes to waste. Don't be afraid of your flaws. Acknowledge them, and you too can be the cause of beauty. Know that in our weakness we find our strength.

SATAN'S PARALLEL "CHRISTIAN" SYSTEM

Jesus says in John 15:1, He is the "true vine" and His father in heaven is the husbandman. Meaning there is or are false vines. These are tendered not by God but satan.

As said in the introduction, satan, the master deceiver, has a parallel Christian system with that of the true system of Jehovah God "who art in heaven", the creator of all things. To God and God alone should be directed our praise and worship's system is loving, fair and open to build up and save us while not imposing on our freewill. The deceiver's, deceitful, bullying, working like a roaring lion (1 Pet 5:8) to destroy you life by any means. Purely for simplicity of hierarchy illustration (not in denial of the Holy Trinity) I will list Jesus next, followed by God's prophets, disciples, teachers, pastors, His church and sheep (us). For satan to exalt himself as god he desires and needs us to worship him. Maybe he thinks he can dethrone God. As an English saying goes "possession is 9/10th of the law. Possibly satan feels by gaining our worship he becomes god if not in theory at least by our practice and worship.

Two second year university theologian students got hold of an early draft of this book, which offered £1,000.00 to anyone and their friend who could disprove its content. They began by arguing irrelevancies such as whether God existed, is all loving, the flood etc. Eventually after much patience and frustration with them they got to the Sabbath using two main arguments a) The disciples plucking corn and b) Jesus healing, both on the Sabbath. During hours of email exchanges I was astonished they had not grasped the basic beliefs of or knowledge of Christianity. Mentioning the same to a friend a few months later, she explained how many non believers opposing Christianity, study theology with a view to disproving Christian beliefs. I then recalled some lectures I attended informing me of commercial songs with satanic lyrics and similar promotional artistry. Some of the singers having studied in part, about Christ and Christianity. I also recall television documentaries on satanic subjects showing Christian signs, such as the cross, Star of David, long black robes and others, being used for satanic meanings (although changed in some way, i.e. inverting the cross). I also spoke to a theology student from the prestigious Yale University of America. She also informed me that early Christian history (1st 400 years A.D.) is not part of theology studies at most universities or theology study centres. Studies start from after many pagan customs were amalgamated into Christianity and are limited.

Satan's false worship system (a counterfeit of Yahweh's the real one).

GOD   Thessalonians 2:4 Who opposeth and exalteth himself above all that is called God, or that is worshipped; so that he (satan) as God sitteth in the temple of God, shewing himself that he is God. I.e. satan putting himself in position as if he is the real God.

CHRIST   Mark 13:22For false Christs and false prophets shall rise, and shall shew signs and wonders, to seduce, if it were possible, even the elect (same as Matt 24:24) , Matt 24:5 for many shall come in my name saying, I am Christ and shall deceive many.

PROPHETS   Jer 14:14 The Lord said, the prophets prophesy lies in my name: I sent them not neither have I commanded them, neither spake onto them, they prophesy onto you false vision and divination, and a thing of naught, and the deceit of their heart. See also Jer 23:13-14, 21, 31-32 "For both prophet and priests are profane, yea in my house have I found their wickedness saith the Lord…): If satan cannot stop the true message reaching you, he will distraught it. In Acts 23:12, satan tried to use the church against Paul to stop his testimony and teachings getting out. Fighting like with like (i.e. fire with fire). Today we have Christian Spiritualist churches offering contact with the dead etc when the bible clearly states i.e. in Leviticus 20:27 "A man also or woman that hath a familiar spirit, or that is a wizard, shall surely be put to death: they shall **stone** them with **stone**s: their blood shall be upon them". , Zech 10:2. Matt 7:15 Beware of false prophets which come to you in sheep clothing.24:11many false prophets shall rise and shall deceive many. See also Luke 6:26.Rev 19:20 "and the beast was taken and with him the false prophet that wrought miracles before him with which he deceived them that had mark of beast and worshiped his image. 2 Corn 11:14-15 and no marvel; for **satan himself is transformed into an angel of light**; therefore it is no great thing if his ministers also be transformed as the ministers of righteousness: whose end shall be according to their works.: A test of God's prophets is not only must their prophesies come true (not by guess or being vague) but they must also coincide with all prior revelations and scripture. In N.T. Paul and John taught that the content of the message already received was the standard by which to judge any new message even if it came from an angel (Gal 1:8) or a spirit masquerading as God's Spirit (Eze 13:3)

PASTORS / TEACHERS   2Cor11.13 For such are false apostles, deceitful workers, transforming themselves into apostles of Christ. Jer 2:8 "the priest said not, where is the Lord? And they that handled the law knew me not: the pastors also transgressed against me, and the prophets prophesied by Baal, and walked after things that do not profit .Jer 12:10 Many pastors have destroyed my vineyard, they have trodden my portion under foot, they have made my pleasant portion a desolate wilderness. Jer 22:22 "the wind shall eat up all thy pastors" Jer 23:1-2 Woe be onto the pastors that destroy and scatter the sheep of my pasture! Saith the Lord. 2 Tim 4:3-4, Isaiah 43:27 Thy teachers have transgressed against me, 2 Peter 2:1 But there were false prophets among the people, as there shall be false teachers 2:3 and through covetous- ness shall with feigned words make merchandise of you i.e. being good speakers and sales men sell you to the devil knowingly or in ignorance. Some kings installed priests for a fee or their own purpose (i.e. 1 Kings 13:33), just like sorcerer in Acts 8:9 and 19 who wanted to buy the gift of the Holy Ghost for a price. See also Micah 3:11

CHURCH   Rev 2:9 "I know blasphemy of those who say are Jews but are not, but synagogue of satan". 2Kings 21:3-5, 23:5 burnt incense onto Baal, to the sun, moon and planets and to the host of heaven…. In house of the Lord. Some kings put idols etc in God's house and worshipped other gods there (2 Kings 17:33, 41; 17:16, 21:3-4).

MIRACLES   in Daniel 1:20 and Ex 7 – 12 it is seen pagan kings had numerous magicians. Pharaoh's magicians did the same miracles as Moses except for one which they said was only capable by God Ex 8:7, 12, 18, 22; Rev 18:23 "for by thy sorceries were all nations deceived." Rev 13:13 and he doeth great wonders, so that he maketh fire come down from heaven on the earth in the sight of men, Rev 13:14 And deceiveth them that dwell on the earth by *the means of* those miracles which he had power to do in the sight of the beast; saying to them that dwell on the earth, that they should make an image to the beast, which had the wound by a sword, and did live. There are other workers of sorcery in bible, fortune tellers etc.

GOOD FORTUNE / BLESSINGS   satan offered Jesus riches etc so he can give riches in exchange for your or as reward for others souls.

BAD FORTUNE   Satan brought bad things unto Job to make him turn against God as did other people to whom he did the same. Except Job was special and sincere. Satan can also make bad things happen to make us seek God. Then he sends false teacher and church to us to make us join his system in belief we are serving Yahweh. Keeps some there with happiness and what they want in worship. Being in his system mean you are his and will not get to where you intended. By the time you discover the deceit (on death) it will be too late. We only get one chance, he may only have to fool you or harden your heart and mind once.

FALSE CHRISTIANS   Though the Bible does not use this specific description, it does allude to this category numerous times in various ways, one example being Matt 7:21-23 "Not every one that saith unto me, Lord, Lord, shall enter into the kingdom of heaven; but he that doeth the will of my Father which is in heaven. Many will say to me in that day, Lord, Lord, have we not prophesied in thy name? and in thy name have cast out devils? and in thy name done many wonderful works? And then will I profess unto them, I never knew you: depart from me, ye that work iniquity".   These may want to be Christians, say they are, have a certain believe and faith in a person of the Bible called Jesus the son of God and may even be right in many of their beliefs. However, they refuse to walk as Jesus walked, do His and His fathers will and / or worship in both spirit and truth doing ALL things He commanded. They pollute His ways with customs of man or pagan systems or succumb to arguments that they can worship God as they like rather than as He prescribed. As the Bible puts it, having a form of godliness but do not endure sound doctrine. Turning away from the truth unto fables

Rev 3:15 I know thy works, that you are neither hot nor cold: I would prefer if you were hot or cold. Galatians 2:4 And that because of false brethren unawares brought in, who came in privily to spy out our liberty which we have in Christ Jesus, that they might bring us into bondage. The world consists of two religious systems God's and satan's. Good and evil. The two opposing systems are mentioned in Exodus, with

Moses representing God and the Pharaoh the other (satan's). Eze 28:1-6, 13-15 The word of the LORD came again unto me, saying, Eze 28:2 Son of man, say unto the prince of Tyrus, Thus saith the Lord GOD; Because thine heart *is* lifted up, and thou hast said, I *am* a God, I sit *in* the seat of God, in the midst of the seas; yet thou *art* a man, and not God, though thou set thine heart as the heart of God (refers to satan's aspirations) Eze 28:3 Behold, thou *art* wiser than Daniel; there <u>is no secret that they can hide from thee</u>: Eze 28:4 With thy wisdom and with thine understanding thou hast gotten thee riches, and hast gotten gold and silver into thy treasures: (he offers riches of this world as cannot offer life in the next) Eze 28:5 By thy great wisdom *and* by thy traffick hast thou increased thy riches, and thine heart is lifted up because of thy riches: Eze 28:6 Therefore thus saith the Lord GOD; Because thou hast set thine heart as the heart of God; Eze 28:13 Thou hast been in Eden the garden of God; every precious stone *was* thy covering, the sardius, topaz and the diamond, the beryl, the onyx, and the jasper, the sapphire, the emerald, and the carbuncle, and gold: the workmanship of thy tabrets and of thy pipes was prepared in thee in the day that thou wast created. Eze 28:14 Thou *art* the anointed cherub that covereth; and I have set thee *so*: thou wast upon the holy mountain of God; thou hast walked up and down in the midst of the stones of fire. Eze 28:15 Thou *wast* perfect in thy ways from the day that thou wast created, till iniquity was found in thee.

In and subsequent books of Exodus the two biblical systems that extend to today, are distinguished. God's and Baal's or other name given to anti-God (satan's). God's people were told not to worship host of heaven, i.e. sun, planets (2nd of Ten Commandments). Nor were they to seek contact with the dead through magicians, etc or make themselves out to be gods. Whereas the Egyptians did the contrary. Alexandra the Great adopted the Egyptian religion, made himself a god to be worshipped as such and, if my memory serves of an inscribed image I saw on the ancient Egyptian tombs, had himself ascending to heaven in a chariot (similar to cover of book). These practices and beliefs became the Roman's, before and after Christ. The early Roman Catholic Church, from which many of today's popular believes and customs came, carried forward these beliefs to today. Not many Christians know of this nor that they should return to how it ought to be. Matt 24:4 "Take heed that no man deceive you… for many shall come in my name". If satan cannot stop the true message reaching you, he will distort it. In Acts 23:12, satan tried to use the church against Paul to stop his testimony and teachings getting out. Today we have Christian Spiritualist churches offering contact with the dead etc when the bible clearly states i.e. in Leviticus 20:27 it states "A man also or woman that hath a familiar spirit, or that is a wizard, shall surely be put to death: they shall **stone** them with **stone**s: their blood shall be upon them".

INTERPRETING THE BIBLE

There are three points I wish to cover under this heading.

1. *The choice of bible version:*

i.e. King James version (KJV), New King James (NKJV), New International version (NIV), Living Translation etc .This is extremely important, the first and main place to start in acquiring the correct interpretation. I did not realise this until sharing this article with a fellow Christian in a library. His bible had three versions side by side. Asking him to look up 2 Chronicle 19:10, he came up with:

"In every case that comes before you from your fellow countrymen who live in the cities whether **bloodshed** or other concerns of the law, **commands**, decrees or ordinances, you are to warn them not to sin against the LORD; otherwise his wrath will come on you and your brothers. Do this and you will not sin". From the (**NIV**) which he, like many others prefer for the easier reading.

Now my (KJV) reads "And what cause soever shall come to you of your brethren that dwell in their cities, between **blood and blood**, between law and **commandment,** statutes and judgements, ye shall even warn them that they trespass not against the LORD, and so wrath come upon you, and upon your brethren: this do, and ye shall not trespass."

The NKJV reads: "Whatever case comes to you from your brethren who dwell in their cities, whether of **bloodshed** or offences against law or commandment, against statutes or ordinances, you shall warn them, lest they trespass against the LORD and wrath come upon you and your brethren. Do this, and you will not be guilty."

The Living Translation reads: "Whenever a case comes to you from fellow citizens in an outlying town, whether a **murder case** or some other violation of God's laws, **commands**, decrees, or regulations, you must warn them not to sin against the Lord, so that he will not be angry with you and them. Do this and you will not be guilty."

The background to the passage starts in 19:4 whereby King Jehoshaphat wants to bring the people "back unto the Lord God of their fathers". He sends out the Levites, who represented Gods word, to judge the people according to Gods word. "To judge in all controversies". Not having respect of person or taking gifts i.e. bribes. Now according to KJV verse 19 makes it clear they are to judge between a) All causes, between their brethren b) Between blood and blood i.e. family members just like the brother who came to Jesus In Luk 12:13 asking "Master, speak to my brother, that he divide the inheritance with me. To which Jesus replied "Man, who made me a judge or a divider over you?" c) Between Law and commandment as some may not know the difference (similar to many of today who think they are one and the same, similar or interchangeable). Some of the Jews of the bible made the same mistake in grouping them under the title "Law of Moses". d) Statutes and judgements.

If you were to look up the original Hebrew reference word translated as commandment

(H4687), law (H8451), statute (H2701) or judgement (H4941), you will be able to trace every occurrence where this word has been translated and see it is the same word or meaning being referred to in various places of the bible. For example in Exodus 24:12 God uses the same Hebrew words for commandment and law when He said to Moses "come up to me in the mount, and be there and I will give thee tables of stone and a law AND commandments which I have written; that though may teach them". Clearly two separate things. Different as God is not an author of confusion to use two words when one would do.

However, if you read the NKJV it has translated "blood and blood" into bloodshed and "commandment" into command. Now blood shed means shedding of blood either murder, manslaughter or such. Then where in the sentence, reflecting Jehosphaphat's instructions are those for family disputes, i.e. over inheritance, land etc? The New living Translation goes even further away from the intended meaning by actually calling it "murder" and the Good News bible says "homicide". I suppose such translations would think blood brothers means co-participants in a murder! Hebrew word translated as command elsewhere in the bible is reference H6680.It is used for example in Genesis 18:19, 27:8 and Ex 7:2.It relates to a general instruction of God or man. Differs essentially from the specific commandments given on Mount Sinai and is likely to cause people to sin against God by eroding its special purpose. There are other word changes in these versions that may cause misunderstanding. Unfortunately, due to the financial outlay in acquiring them, the owners may be unwilling to discard them. I would not recommend giving them to another (unless the benefit to that non Christian person having one is better than having none) as it may cause them to sin against God. As for denominations that produce their own versions of the bible, in my observations, they cannot be trusted to portrait the truth.

"Blood against blood" or "bloodshed". The original Hebrew word from which the translation is taken is Dham / da^m pronounced *dawm. Has an extensive explanation, which is summarised in one concordance as* From H1826 (compare H119); *blood* (as that which when shed causes *death*) of man or an animal; by analogy the *juice* of the grape; figuratively (especially in the plural) *bloodshed* (that is, *drops* of blood): - blood (-y, -guiltiness, [-thirsty]), + innocent. I met a Spanish Jewish family, the mother produced her bible with Jewish and English text side by side. Reading directly from the Jewish language she read "blood against blood" without any prompting or indication from me. Comparing the same to the English translation it read "homicide". She said she had not heard of homicide except via the title of a TV series! I think this confirms my original assertion that the KJV gives a better translation as, unlike the others, it allows for family disputes and is supported by Deu 17:8 If there arise a matter too hard for thee in judgment, between blood and blood, between plea and plea, and between stroke and stroke, *being* matters of controversy within thy gates: then shalt thou arise, and get thee up into the place which the LORD thy God shall choose. See also Duet 1:16, Luk 12:14; 1 Cor 6:6.

Requirements of God that His commandments be followed are deleted or rephrased in many bible cases so people will break them or at least one and sin against Him. Appendix H details some differences in bible versions. Further examples are,. A) Deut 11:13 in KJV reads "And it shall come to pass, if ye shall hearken diligently unto my commandments which I command you this day, to love the LORD your God, and to serve him with all your heart and with all your soul". Yet other versions i.e. NIV may say "if you faithfully obey the commands I am giving you today-to love the LORD your God and to serve him with all your heart and with all your soul-". KJV speaks of a "command" that God is giving "this day" that His commandments of the past are kept. The NIV has made it sound that "today" God is giving them a command to "love the Lord your God…". Nothing about what God has said in the past. It also changes the requirements of Christians to do one thing, "love" rather than ten as in the "Commandments" given in the past. The false translation could then be used to say God gave a new commandment of love to replace the old ten.

B) *Fornication*: From Strong's Dictionary: **G4202** πορνεία, porneia, *por-ni'-ah*. From G4203; *harlotry* (including *adultery* and *incest*); figuratively *idolatry*: - fornication. **G4203** πορνεύω, porneuō, *porn-yoo'-o*. From G4204; to *act* the *harlot*, that is, (literally) *indulge* unlawful *lust* (of either sex), or (figuratively) *practise idolatry*: - commit (fornication).

Many translations and as a result most Christians believe it is to do with sexual immorality as adultery. Some say fornication is to do with unmarried sexual immorality and adultery for married people. I think the aim of the change in use is to take away one's consciousness or importance of false god or idol worship. Break the first commandment "thou shalt have no other god before me". As Jesus said this is the first and greatest commandment. The bible is complete from start to finish about how God detest false god worship. Calling it an abomination and punishes those committing it. If there was one commandment we are not to break it is that one. If God used the word for false idol worship purposes; idolatry. Lusting after a false god like a harlot lusting after men; but man subsequently focused on the harlot analogy used and thus now translates it to a sexual nature, does not change God's intention. Does an apple become a chair because it is now called such? Does idolatry become adultery? Let us examine the bible.

In Matthew 5:32 & Matt 19:3 Jesus addresses the question of fornication and marriage. Note in 19:3 the question is to do with married people not unmarried "The Pharisees also came unto him, tempting him, and saying unto him, Is it lawful for a man to put away his wife for every cause". Jesus' reply states there is only one legitimate reason a man can put away his wife. That of fornication. Mat 5:32 "But I say unto you, That whosoever shall put away his wife, **saving (except) for** the cause of fornication, cause her to commit adultery: and whosoever shall marry her that is divorced committeth adultery. (Mat 19:9 And I say unto you, Whosoever shall put away his wife, **except** *it be* for fornication,.). If fornication and adultery are both sexual immorality and we substitute both for sexual immorality in Jesus' statement it would read … whosoever puts away his wife except for sexual immorality causeth her to commit sexual immorality! How can his action cause her to commit what she has already done?

If there is only one reason God would allow divorce is it not more likely it would be for the highest reason, worshipping another god. Would sex with another take higher ranking above recognising another god? If we then look at 2Chron 21:11 "Moreover he made high places in the mountains of Judah, and caused the inhabitants of Jerusalem to commit fornication, and compelled Judah *thereto" and Rev 2:20* "Notwithstanding I have a few things against thee, because thou sufferest that woman Jezebel, which call herself a prophetess, to teach and to seduce my servants to commit fornication, and to eat things sacrificed unto idols." We see it is to do with false god worship. As confirmed by Ezra 10:3. Eze 16:25-26. This now puts Acts 15:20 into perspective "But that we write unto them, that they abstain from pollutions of idols, and *from* fornication...". In other words no more worshipping false gods. Yet many bible translations have taken out "fornication" and replaced it with "sexual immorality" or "adultery".

C) Num 22:20 And God came unto Balaam at night, and said unto him, **If** the men come to call thee, rise up, *and* go with them; but yet the word which I shall say unto thee, that shalt thou do. Num 22:22 And God's anger was kindled because he went: and the angel of the LORD stood in the way for an adversary against him. Now he was riding upon his ass, and his two servants *were* with him. "IF" not in the NIV.

The history of post King James bible versions was not to assist readers in understanding God's word's through the bible; but take away certain biblical concepts from His message. Some being the pre-existence of Christ who conquered satan, His equality with God and the miraculous virgin birth and that Jesus really died on the cross or bled. This topic or listing all the subtle deceiving amendments in the ever changing bible versions is not the subject of this book and is only mentioned to direct bible students to the KJV (not even the NKJV) from which the enemy and his advocates want to keep you. In short, in Rev 22:18-19 God said whoever adds or takes away from His book shall be damned. Though many come to know God/Christ through these versions, they ought (or may need) to move onto the KJV for a full appreciation of God and how to serve Him. Some examples of the changes are: KJV says Jesus is the son, some change son to servant, word Lord in respect of Jesus is removed numerous times. Rev 22:14 in KJV "Blessed are they that do His commandments" changed to "blessed are they who wash their robes..." in some versions.

The KJV stood until the early 19th Century. Then there was a revision by two gentlemen Westcott and Hort. After the revised version, the first main reprint was the Jehovah Witness' old version in the early 19th Century. They for example removed Matt 16:3, Mark 9:46, Mark 16:19-20 (because Jesus appeared physically after the resurrection. A contradiction of their teaching). John 1:1, in NWT Jesus is "a god" rather than "God" as in KJV. John 8:1-11 omitted, Acts 8:37 omitted 1Joh 5:7 because Jesus and God are "one". Subsequent versions followed their example as regards the variances, either in the text or in the footnotes. What we have is so called scholars changing the bible to fit their understanding rather than try to understand it as it is and, when they cannot, simply admit it and await God's revelation if He thinks them deserving. Just like scientist who make recommendations based on findings over a small sample of the population only to be contradicted in future years as further scientist make more discoveries of God's mysteries.

For further research see a booklet titled New Versions and Old Heresies or a DVD titled Changing the Word, by Prof Walter Veith from Total Onslaught producers. In the New American Standard version there are 909 verses affected, Revised Version 788, New World translation 767, NIV, 695, Good News 614, Amplified 484, Douay 421 (Jesuits bible which was rejected by the Reformation), old Jehovah's Witnesses 120 (more in the present version now called New World Translation) and NKJ ignored the textus recepticus 1200 times. A list of some amendments is in Appendix H; but note for example Matt 17:21, 18:11 and Mark 7:16 being omitted in some editions of some bibles versions. For some reason a different edition of the same version may be different.

Lack of space does not allow me to show all the flaws in all the new bible versions so I will use the most popular NIV as an example of why all other versions except the KJV should be avoided, even the NKJV. Though the KJV may be harder to understand due to the old English used, I recommend raising your standard and learning to understand it. The problem with the world is standards are dropping, people are opting for the easier or quicker route. This allows satan in to deceive. In 2Pet 3:15-17 Peter warns about some things Paul wrote being "hard to understand" which those unlearned in proper theology, as are numerous of today's preachers including "bishops", twist the meaning "as they do the scriptures" but onto theirs and your "destruction" . Peter says the way is to do what knew from "before" i.e in the Old Testament. He calls these teachers "wicked" intentionally out to deceive you. This is the purpose of the new bible versions, to destroy Christians by polluting their water source.

Peter says believers should be "steadfast", doctrinally sound (v17). These wicked versions were not composed by doctrinally sound theologians who readily admit this in the preface to the NIV. Stating they wanted to wanted to publish a new Bible that was free of any sectarian bias (i.e., that wouldn't offend any particular religious group). So they got everybody together, compromised the Word of God, and published a perverted Bible that satisfied each group. Of course, there were no blood-washed, born-again, Christ-honoring, Hell-fire and damnation, Sin-hating, soul winning believers invited. Their STATED MAIN PURPOSE was not to preserve THE TRUTH; but rather, to publish a translation that was non-offensive to the participating religious denominations (i.e., WIDELY MARKETABLE). The NIV is as ecumenical as you can get (i.e., they all set aside their doctrinal differences in sinful compromise to further one-world religious unity). Biblically, God commands us to be divided by truth, rather than be united by error (2nd Corinthians 6:14-17). The Word of God magnifies TRUTH; whereas, the devil's crowd magnifies UNITY. Hundreds of words, phrases and even entire Bible verses were removed from the Word of God by the NIV.

The KJV Bible mentions the "Godhead" three times, the NIV has completely removed the word as it has with "propitiation". In fact, all of the following words have been removed: regeneration, mercyseat, Calvary, remission, Jehovah, immutable, devils, omnipotent, Comforter, Holy Ghost, Messiah, quickened, infallible, sodomite, fornication, trucebreaker winebibbers, carnal, slothful, unthankful, effeminate, backbiting, vanity, lasciviousness, whoredom, Lucifer, damnation, brimstone and the bottomless pit. One of the most blasphemous omissions in the NIV is in John 3:16 where Jesus is no longer proclaimed as the "only BEGOTTEN Son of God." "Jesus" has been removed in 38 places, "hell" in 40 and changes every mention of people "worshipping" Jesus to a mere "knelt"? . Yet the NIV is the most popular! Thank God for the King James Bible!

2nd Timothy 2:15 instructs each believer to "Study to shew thyself approved unto God, a workman that needeth not to be ashamed, rightly dividing the word of truth." Well, the NIV removes the word "study" from this verse. To no surprise, Paul's admonition against "science falsely so called" in 1st Timothy 6:20 is gone too, and there are no longer any fables to avoid. Of the 54 times "hell" is mentioned in the King James Bible, the NIV reduces it down to 14 times. The King James Bible states in 1Tim 3:16 that "GOD WAS MANIFEST IN THE FLESH"; but the NIV waters it down to... he was revealed in a body. In Philippians 2:6 of the NIV Jesus is no longer EQUAL with God; but rather, could not grasp equality with God. The NIV and others is Wicked! Vile! Blasphemy! Why would any caring Christian searching for the truth use it and others like it?

"Lest Satan should get an advantage of us: for we are not ignorant of his devices." 2nd Corinthians 2:11. Do you see what the devil has done to God's Word? satan only comes to kill, steal, and destroy (John 10:10). If the devil can't destroy the Bible, then he tries to change it, replace it with fables. The latest satanic ploy is the claim that several pagan religions outdate Christianity and that Christianity originated in ancient Egypt. The truth is that Abraham believed on the Lord for salvation in Genesis 15:6 (about 2,000 B.C.). Christianity was here from the Creation, which is evidenced by Abel's offering of a blood sacrifice to God (thus signifying his faith in the coming Savior). People were saved back in the Old Testament the same way we are today, by grace through faith in Jesus Christ (Ephesians 2:8,9). When Noah and his family walked off the ark, Christianity had no competition. It wasn't until men came together in UNITY that they corrupted themselves once again, that God segregated them across the earth in Genesis 11:9. So, Biblically, Christianity came before any pagan religions. It wasn't until 566 B.C. that Buddha arrived. Anyone who thinks Christianity didn't exist until the time of Christ is ignorant. Psalm 22 was written around 1000 B.C. by king David, prophesying the crucifixion of Christ. Acts 11:26, "And the disciples were called Christians first in Antioch." Notice that there were DISCIPLES of Christ before the term "Christian" came into being. Thus, there were followers of Christ throughout the Old Testament. Satan's greatest weapon is people's ignorance (2nd Corinthians 4:4). How tragic that even professed Christians today are woefully deceived concerning the Word of God. Is this not exactly what Jesus warned about in Mark

13:22. If professed Christians today are gullible enough to trade in their faithful King James Bible for a demonic counterfeit like the NIV, then where will Christianity be 10 years from now?

Romans 10:9 from the King James Bible, "That if thou shalt confess with thy mouth the Lord Jesus, and shalt believe in thine heart that God hath raised him from the dead, thou shalt be saved." Romans 10:9 from the NIV "That if you confess with your mouth, "Jesus is Lord," and believe in your heart that God raised him from the dead, you will be saved." I am not sure the Bible requires us to make Jesus our "Lord" to be saved, only trust Him as our Savior (John 14:6). Peter shows clear evidence of this when he professed, "Thou art the Christ, the Son of the living God" in Matthew 16:16. Peter never confessed "Jesus is Lord." Rather, Peter received Jesus as the Messiah. Genesis 15:6 simply states that Abraham, "...believed in the LORD; and he (God) counted it to him for righteousness." It is our faith upon Jesus as our Savior, because of the blood that He shed for our sins, that saves us (1st Peter 1:18,19). Making Christ the Lord of our life is a matter of Christian obedience; NOT Salvation. If one had to make Jesus the Lord of their life to be saved, then Lot, Samson and Solomon would fail. What about Ananias and Sapphira? What about the carnal Believers at Corinth? What about 1st Corinthians 3:15? If you believe that you have to do as little as give a cup of water to someone to be saved (Matt 25:35), you are mistaken. The blood of Christ is what takes our sins away (not just the death of Christ), see the "Sanctuary" section.

What Does the NIV, the Satanic Bible, and Gay Sex Have in Common? According to Wikipedia.org, the New International Bible (NIV) is the most popular Bible version today. The largest bible publisher, Zondervan, are owned by Harper Collins, who also publishes The Satanic Bible and The Joy of Gay Sex. Christian money is supporting these demonic publications. The Jehovah's Witnesses' New World Translation comes from same Greek manuscripts as does the NIV! The Jehovah's Witnesses' Interlinear Greek New Testament is based upon the corrupt Greek of Westcott and Hort, openly admitted in front of the publication. By the way, the owner of the exclusive printing rights to the NIV, Rupert Murdoch, was just made a Knight by the Pope. Murdoch had put the NIV under the same umbrella as the TV Guide, which he also owned.

Why would anyone use the NIV and similar? If you sincerely love the Lord Jesus Christ, who is God Almighty (John 1:1-3,14; 10:33; Colossians 1:16; 1st Timothy 3:16; Revelation 1:8), then you should not use these damned versions that violate the commandment not to add or take away from God's word.

See Appendix H for further examples of possible changes in your bible. I would recommend the KJV but be weary of the editor's commentary.

2. *Choice of commentary*:

Rather than giving or limiting their commentary to facts i.e. historical, archaeological or varied theological views on a text with the pros and cons of each view, some bibles or commentaries propagate singular or their own commentary or interpretation. This is wrong, as many readers will take the fact it is written in a book as being correct, will think the author knows best etc. Again while doing studies with a fellow Christian who used the NKJV, I was astonished to read some of the commentaries in her bible titled "Spirit Filled Life Bible for Students". It had a caption on the cover "Learning and Living God's Word by the Power of His Spirit". Here are some examples:

Mat 4:23-4 "And Jesus went about all Galilee, teaching in their synagogues, and preaching the gospel of the kingdom, and healing all manner of sickness and all manner of disease among the people. And his fame went throughout all Syria: and they brought unto him all sick people that were taken with divers diseases and torments, and those which were possessed with devils, and those which were lunatic, and those that had the palsy; and he healed them".

Their commentary on this text is "Jesus preached the "gospel of the kingdom" and He healed people of sickness and disease. He demonstrated and taught that the preaching of "the gospel of the kingdom" should be accompanied by signs and wonders. It means that kingdom power and authority will naturally flow from the lives of believers, and we need to be open to the Holy Spirit's prompting to move into the realm of the miraculous".

Now which specific words of verse 23-4 mention a third person having or should receive power? It is directions as these that lead people to manufacture a belief that they have power of tongues or other. That they should join a church where healing and miracles is a big part of the ministry. Rather than going to serve God, paying attention to Jesus' words of blessed are the meek, poor etc (Mat 5:3-12).Is it a matter of following signs and wonders? See section on miracle performing churches. Did Jesus give a sign to those who asked for one or did he say "no sign shall be given you except for Jonah"? Did he tell those he healed to go and shout from the rooftops or keep it to themselves?

KJV Mar 16:20"And they went forth, and preached every where, the Lord working with them, and

confirming the word <u>with</u> signs following. Amen." NKJV "And they went out and preached everywhere, the Lord working with them and confirming the word through the <u>accompanying</u> signs, Amen."

The commentary states 16:20 "God confirmed the preaching of His word with miraculous signs. The miracle that accompanied the disciples preaching confirmed to the people that the messengers were telling the truth. That God was backing up their message with supernatural phenomena. God continues to confirm His word today with signs and miracles. Although a sign in and of itself does not prove that something is of God, it does confirm the preaching of God's message as clearly presented in the bible. The gospel was never intended to be a presentation of words. It is to be confirmed by the miraculous."

If this is the case, then our belief is not based on faith but on the sight or experience of miracles. In which case there should be a world of miracles every day; assuming somewhere the gospel is being preached. By now it should have spread like wild fire and the whole world converted. I shall not list all the numerous times in the New Testament where the gospel was preached and no miracle occurred. You only have to read Acts or the other books. Brethren, heed the warning in Rev 18:23 for by thy sorceries were all nations deceived. Rev 13:14 deceiveth them that dwell on the earth by the means of those miracles which he had power to do in the sight of the beast; saying to them that dwell on the earth, that they should make an image to the beast Rev 16:14For they are the spirits of devils, working miracles, which go forth unto the kings of the earth and of the whole world, to gather them to the battle of that great day of God Almighty. Rev 19:20"And the beast was taken, and with him the false prophet that wrought miracles before him, with which he deceived them". These bible versions are setting people up to believe in satan or his "beast" representative when he comes as Christ using miracles as his proof (Rev 13:14; 16:14; 19:20)

That said, the differences in wording to which I wish to draw attention are with / through, following / accompanying. "With signs following" indicates a time difference. No indication of how long that time lapse is. "Through the accompanying signs" indicates simultaneously, together. The choice of words in previous verses makes the possibility of getting the correct interpretation even worse.

Matt 26:26-28NKJV (with KJV in bold where differs in meaning): And as they were eating, Jesus took bread, blessed and broke it, and gave it to the disciples and said, "Take, eat; this is My body." Then He took the cup, and gave thanks, and gave it to them, saying, "Drink from it, all of you (**drink ye all of it**). For this is my blood of the new covenant (**testament**), which is shed for many for the remission of sins."

The Commentary titled: God makes a new and final covenant with mankind. Firstly, can the author prophesise God's future actions to the extent they know or tells God not to make any future covenants with mankind? It goes on to say: "The Passover anticipated Jesus' sacrifice to establish God's new covenant relationship with men. Jesus used the Passover meal to explain the soon coming New Covenant. The old covenant with Moses written on tables of stone, would be fulfilled in Jesus. Christ's new covenant with mankind would make it possible for God's law to be written on tables of flesh (that is in human hearts), giving motivation from within. No longer would righteousness be determined by external demands. Now there can be genuine desire on the inside as Christ's spirit takes up residence within the believer. The righteous requirements of the law now can be fulfilled in us as God continually works within, "both to will and to do His good pleasure" (Phil2:13). Later, on the cross, Jesus' blood would be shed as a substitution payment for "the breaking of God's covenant laws" (sin). Jesus changes the meaning of the Passover cup so that it now represents this. The bread now represents his body, which would be given; the cup, His blood, which would be shed for the forgiveness of sins". (Heb 9:12/Rom 3:25)."

It is misrepresentations as these that make me think satan has changed God's bible, its texts and, where that would be too obvious, the teaching commentaries. The main biblical difference is the changing of the word **testament to covenant**. I shall deal with the correct interpretation using the word Testament, later in the "New Covenant" section. Here I shall deal with the misrepresentation. The subtle reasoning in the commentary is more dangerous as it could send its readers to hell for the following reasons. It links the word covenant and this event to the ten commandments, all the Laws, previous covenants i.e. that of circumcision, the rainbow etc, then abolishes them by claiming this new one replaces them all. As you will see on completion of reading this book, commandments, Laws, statutes, covenants and more are totally separate things not to be merged as one. That even if one is altered or cancelled, it still leaves the others binding on mankind and God, as they were generally two party agreements. Jesus had nothing to do with the fulfilling of the commandments as written on the tables of stone. These were the moral duties of mankind to God and fellow humans such as thou shalt have no other God, or thou shalt not kill. Surely, Jesus would not now be saying we can have more than one God or are permitted to murder etc. The commentary also states we are not bound by external demands of God. That the righteous requirements of the Law now can be "fulfilled". You will read from bible texts quoted, this is clearly not so. It is the "doers" of the Law and commandments that will be saved. The commentator uses words from the bible; but in the wrong place to confuse readers just like satan when he part quoted scripture to Jesus when He was hungry, in an attempt to get Jesus to succumb to his body weakness. As he does with our worldly lust and desires to take the easy way out. The word "fulfil" is related to prophesy: future events as the coming of a Messiah. The Law does not contain prophecy or the prediction of Jesus. They are not tied as the commentator has made them! Then he indicates that since "God continually works in us" we can blame God if we fail or sin! They quote Phil 2:13 which read v12 "… work out your own salvation with fear and trembling v13 for it is God which worketh in you both to will and to do of his good pleasure". If God working in us rather than we adhering to external factors, is a new replacement, how does one explain Matt16:15, 17 whereby God is working in Simon, a commandment and Law keeper? "But who do you say I am… blessed art thou Simon for flesh and blood have not revealed this to you but my father which is in heaven". I cannot be sure if the author is saying, due to Jesus' crucifixion, we can now sin as the payment has been made. He quotes Heb 9:12 and Rom 3:25.Again this topic is covered later; but these simply show Jesus replaced Lev 16.34 not the commandments, Laws, etc which existed and were binding when they were administered.

Mark 2:21-22 KJV (with NKJV variance in bold): No man also seweth a piece of (**unshrunk** used instead of **new**) new cloth on an old garment: else the new piece that filled it up taketh away from the old, and the rent is made worse. And no man putteth new wine into old bottles (wineskins): else the new wine doth burst the bottles, and the wine is spilled, and the bottles will be marred: but new wine must be put into new bottles.

Commentary: "Jesus warned that trying to tack the new gospel to the old, legalistic system of Judaism would be like patching an old garment with a new, unshrunk cloth, which would be ruined by the first wash. In addition the joy of the new message cannot be contained within Jewish legalism any more than fermenting wine can be held by brittle, old wineskins. This parable of Jesus is relevant today as it relates to the staleness of legalism of contemporary religious institutions. When the fresh spirit of God's grace is poured out, the old legalistic ways will not be able to contain what God is doing. In the same manner today, when God's spirit is poured out with fresh fire upon the church, the church must be able to contain the new thing that god is doing."

We can see this person is against the keeping of the commandments and everything on which God based His philosophy. The commentator is putting his biased view into the word of God, wrongly speaking for God and mis-directing readers. Where in the text is reference to legality against which the commentator repeats? Where is the time element, "first wash", mentioned as to when the new patch would tear the old garment? Where does it state that the Laws and commandments of the Old Testament cannot co-exist with any new additions? In other words, the new has no foundation. It just appears and floats around in people's hearts without any reference to structure, foundation, legal or moral format etc. The youth of today have no regard for anything older than them. Laws, principles etc which are "staleness" and too binding. Telling them what to do, they find fault with it and justification not to have any constraints. They think they know it all. This author speaks like one of the foolish women referred to by Job in 2:10.God has now changed His spirit to a "fresh" one and discarded the old. The God the bible says is the same yesterday, today and forever. Has the reader never studied God through His bible? His nature, legalistic makeup etc? Examples are given later. What is this new thing the author thinks God will be doing that believers and the church must prepare themselves to contain?

The text actually reminds me of Jesus' words in John 3:3 "Jesus answered and said unto him, Verily, verily, I say unto thee, Except a man be born again; he cannot see the kingdom of God". Could it not be the text is simply saying people have to put on a new belief in Him, a new desire to be saved, need to walk in the newness of life? Willing to give up any lustful desires of the world, take up their cross and follow Jesus?

Luke 17:21"Neither shall they say, Lo here! or, lo there! for, behold, the kingdom of God is within You"

Commentary states: "Simply put, a kingdom is a place where a king rules. The kingdom of God is wherever God reigns over the lives of His subjects. The kingdom of God is not visible because God is not visible. It is a spiritual kingdom not a visible one. Jesus gave us the Lord's prayer, a petition to God: "your kingdom come. Your will be done on earth as it is in heaven" (Matt 6:10).This prayer shows the priority Jesus gave to the kingdom of God. Can we not say that the kingdom of God will come on earth when the will of God is as respected here as it is in heaven, when the visible world totally reflects the invisible world? In the kingdom of God, everything is subject to Gods power, instantly with no question. In the visible world there is resistance to God's will. The kingdom of God is eternal. At the present time, it is an invisible kingdom here in our midst. Wherever there are those who honour Jesus, the King and wherever the Spirit of the king is, there is the kingdom of God." This could lead readers to think there is no kingdom of God for which to aim after death; it is here on earth and will be accomplished when everyone on earth subjects themselves to God's kingship ("will come on earth when the will of God is… At present time is an invisible kingdom here in our midst"). How does the author then explain texts as Jesus saying "I go to prepare a place for you…".Thess 4:17 "then we, which are alive and remain shall be caught up together with them in the clouds, to meet the Lord in the air: and so shall we ever be with the Lord". Or 2Peter 3:10?

3) *Read from the bible not into it.*

A fault of most reading the bible is that they do not know the difference between facts and information. They therefore read information as fact, make assumptions from the information and call it fact or proof or believe others interpretation as fact. An example of how people misread information as fact is a sentence may say "He left the party at 10pm and was in bed by midnight". From this some may state as fact his journey home was about two hours, and then went to bed as soon as he arrived home, or other assumptions. They do not consider he could have gone onto 5 other parties, lived one minute journey from the party so went home and looked at television for about two hours before bed or maybe slept in someone else's bed. It was assumptions as these that persons have given me as to 1) The feasts as mentioned in Exodus 23:14, Lev 23:16, 17, 33-36 being cancelled based on Acts 25:9-12. Their reasoning being, Paul refused to go to Jerusalem at the time of the Passover. than look at the information that Paul refused to be tried by the Jews .Especially in view of18:21 "But bade them farewell, saying, I must by all means keep this feast that cometh in Jerusalem: but I will return again unto you, if God will. And he sailed from Ephesus." Acts 20:16, 22; 21:11; 24:11 and 28:17"… though I have committed nothing against the people or customs of our fathers".

What we call the Last Supper of Jesus was the keeping of the Passover by Jesus [Mat 26:18].If it was to be cancelled, would Jesus not have said so at the dinner table or some other time? 2) The seventh day Sabbath was cancelled by Jesus because he healed on the Sabbath day and allowed his disciples to pluck corn from their stalks and eat the same on the Sabbath day. This is dealt with below. Jesus is lord of the Sabbath so that means it is cancelled. If a person is King over some land or country does that mean his kingship over or the land is cancelled. That any commands he had in place is cancelled even if a new king took over? No. Unless a separate sentence states that fact, one cannot assume it.

The above 3 sub-headings (choice of version, commentary and read out of bible) are examples of how a reader's perspective of God and what He requires of us can be changed using "the bible". Especially when those on whom we rely to teach us, pastors, succumb to the same deceptions. The deceiver does not have to deceiver each individual on a one to one basis, simply alter the source of our information and keep us too busy in choirs, bible study and other "church" or world activities to research the truth. A sentence that should, for example read "God is now here" can be changed to read "God is nowhere". Many pastors are given their title from growing up in and being taught by their church. Of those who may take a course in theology, even at

32

degree or doctorate level, it is not a requirement to know of the earliest periods of Christian history. At best, possibly a superficial knowledge. One cannot fully teach the bible without knowing Christian history. In particular the essential periods recording the merger of early "Jewish Christians" and pagan Rome's Sun and idol worshipers from where the pollution came. Many pastors give good sermons on parts of the bible; but mislead others by teaching handed down customs, lessons, understanding. They need to empty their vessel of pride, ego etc and learn the history. Failure would mean adding or taking away from the word of God, teaching others to break a commandment. Two of the warnings found in the bible.

BORN INTO A DENOMINATION

When born we are placed into a family, religion and even sometimes battles with others due to the history of our family or nation's connections. Those we cannot choose, yet many adults choose to be controlled by others. If they are told not to read something, they do not. Rather than read it for the information and make up their own minds. A circulated email said the best way to hide something from some people is to put it in a book, as they do not read. They can be told something is red when it is blue and believe it. Even the bible says one should 'try' and 'prove' what they are told by the "spirit". Studious people know to research all opinions (including alternative ones) otherwise they are in danger of being uninformed, holding someone else's view, biased or indoctrinated. Are you one of them? Do not be one of those who at their end say I should have, would have, if only. We do not have to follow an inherited worship system, belief, and customs of our family or the world. Christians should all be one denomination, Christians. Collectively or individually striving to do right in the sight of God not according to a particular denomination. Like the apostles, we may differ on minor views as when the end of the world may come; but not on following God's commandments. If you read the books of Kings and Chronicles you will see good kings followed bad ones and visa versa. Some set up worship customs, priests and places and caused the whole nation to follow them i.e. 2 Chron 11:15"And he ordained him priests for the high places, and for the devils, and for the calves which he had made." 2 Kings 21:3-5"For he built up again the high places which Hezekiah his father had destroyed; and he reared up altars for Baal (the devil), and made a grove, as did Ahab king of Israel; and worshipped all the host of heaven, and served them. And he built altars **in the house of the LORD**, of which the LORD said, In Jerusalem will I put my name. And he built altars for all the host of heaven in the two courts of the house of the LORD.2 king 21:9 "But they hearkened not: and Manasseh seduced them to do more evil than did the nations whom the LORD destroyed before the children of Israel."

If these happened in the past, how can you be so sure what you do today is not a similarly created practice?

Many believers of the Bible, Jews, Muslims and Christians follow customs sometimes doing the most abominable thing(s) to God in the belief they are worshipping Him.

When presented with the actual historical facts, they don't want to know. Preferring to remain in ignorance, quoting illogical hearsay why they should not listen to or read alternative opinions. They do it primarily through ignorance, following what pastors (or leaders) tell them, etc. The pastors who themselves are following centuries old customs, foolishly passing on false teachings. Just like the blind leading the blind. Secondly because they like it or it has become convenient. If one was to direct them to a history book or similarly informative literature they have the same excuses, not wanting to buy it, not wanting to read it because they were advised to only get teachings from their one or similar source, their church organisation or denomination. Thirdly, not wanting to debate what they have been told in case they are proven and have to admit to being wrong and doing wrong things. In other words they prefer to remain ignorant. As one saying goes the devil finds work for idle hands, another could be the devil has a place for ignorant minds. Lastly, some knowing the truth continue in their ways because their friends do it. Would you go to hell because your friends are there? Sooner or later you will be separated why not now? Follow Christ not company.

Some read the bible in part, only the New Testament, verses as directed etc. They may pick texts in support of their opinion not knowing of others. The bible must be read as a whole for the true guidance to be revealed. Isaiah 28:10 "For precept must be upon precept; line upon line, here a little, and there a little". Not many have read the bible in total, every word. Even fewer have read it in total several times, making notes or cross referencing verses. Any competent person of a task knows they can not become proficient like a professional sports person with one attempt, cannot pass an exam with one reading of study guides. To be competent or knowledgeable in any topic or task one has to study for themselves otherwise they can be misled, placing trust in others' word or opinion. We come to the judgement seat on our own efforts and understanding. Blaming others would not suffice. Hosae 4:6 "**My people are destroyed for lack of knowledge: because thou hast rejected knowledge, I will also reject thee,**". **satan comes to destroy by withhold you from knowledge. Anything or one that comes to destroy is not of God; therefore lack of knowledge is ungodly**.

It is a fallacy to believe that God forgives the ignorant with good intentions and this can be proven numerous times from the bible. Christians have no need to be ignorant. They have the bible, history and common sense. This should be sufficient to spurn one who really wants to serve God and end up with Him to compare and question what they are being taught with what others are teaching.

Ignorance is no excuse and sinning through the same is still a sin just like in worldly law, one is still guilty of a crime and receives punishment even if they did not know their act was against the law .In Lev 4:1, 5:1-2; 22:14; 15 Num 15:28 and other places some of the penalties for sins through ignorance are set out Exo 19:13 "There shall not an hand touch it, but he shall surely be stoned, or shot through; whether *it be* **beast** or man, it shall not live:"…Even the ignorant beast was not forgiven for its accident.

Of course one has to say sorry to God, repent and seek forgiveness and try their hardest not do that sin again. Whatever sin you may be committing must cease and repentance made and forgiveness sought. A good example of how ignorance is no excuse for going against God's word even in the belief you were doing His commandment is the story of a man of God in 1 kings 13:1-26. It is a story of a man of God, sent by God to deliver a message to King Jeroboam. After delivering the message he was instructed not to eat or drink anything offered by the king and to return to Judah a different way to that by which he went. Such was his favour with God that his request that God restores the king's hand which God had just dried up, was immediately granted. He correctly refused food offered him by the king and made his way back to Judah as instructed. However, a "prophet" (real of fake we are not told) came to the man of God, stating in v18 "I am a prophet also as thou art; and an angel spake unto me by the word of the LORD, saying, Bring him back with thee into thine house, that he may eat bread and drink water. But he lied unto him." The result for this disobedience regardless of belief and who gave him the message was a violent death at the jaws of a lion in v24. And when the lying prophet heard of the death he said in v26 "It is the man of God, who was disobedient unto the word of the LORD: therefore the LORD hath delivered him unto the lion, which hath torn him, and slain him, according to the word of the LORD, which he spake unto him." Note not even a man of God escaped for his disobedience which he believed was God's instruction given to him by one of God's prophets. Neither was it a sympathetic, humane death. Similarly with Moses' striking of the rock in Exo 17:6 and Numbers 20:8-12. God did not forgive him when he struck the rock twice instead of once. God did not excuse him because he had a lot to do leading and judging over such a multitude for so many years. Their moaning, rebellion, etc. Even Moses' father said the task was too much for him and persuaded Moses to appoint assistants. So being a "good" person is not sufficient, neither may be trying ones best in the belief you are God's words. One has to do the commandments of God as He directs not what we or others think He directs; no matter how good the intentions. Other examples are 2 Sam 6:6 Uzzah not knowing of the instruction given in Ex 27:7 tried to stop it falling. 1Sa 6:19 And he smote the men of Bethshemesh, because they had looked into the ark of the LORD, even he smote of the people fifty thousand and threescore and ten men: and the people lamented, because the LORD had smitten *many* of the people with a great slaughter. Lastly Saul's two sins in 1Sam 13 – 17 despite thinking and saying to Samuel he did obey God's commandments. Note 13:1, 5-6 Saul, God's anointed had only recently been made king, his army vastly outnumbered hid in fear (600 without weapon against "as people of the sand" heavily armed, well over 36,000 verses 5, 15 & 22), v8 Samuel failed to arrive and Saul's men were deserting, v8 he tried to please God and in desperation "forced" himself to make the offering Samuel should have made. That was his first sin. Jonathan won the battle, Saul vowed a fast to thank God; but Jonathan his son broke it. Saul wishing to do the honourable thing was willing to pay the price with his or his son's life as God identified. The people transgressed, Saul annoyed and wished to make amends for them v32-3. His second sin was disobeying 15:3; in 15:9 saving the "best" and "good" for God (is that your reasoning that you choose what to give God). Thereafter in v13 he says "I have performed the commandments of God", then it was the people (v15), I have, I have v 20. He earnestly believed he had done as commanded. To obey is better than sacrifice... for rebellion is sin..." (v22-3). V24-29 I am sorry "I have sinned… I pray thee pardon my sin and turn again with me that I may worship the Lord". On his knees he clung to Samuels skirt pleading again for pray and finally together worshipping God in v31. However, God had left him and his troubles began. The lesson of these scriptures is do as the bible clearly states not what you think or someone claiming to speak for God, even your pastor says.

Let us put one example to the test. About 99% of Christians worship on Sundays and 1% on Saturdays, why? The Saturday minority say they wish to keep all God's commandments as given in Exodus 20:1-17 including the fourth in 20:8, the Sabbath. The Sunday majority say they keep the other nine commandments; but as to the fourth, Jesus changed or cancelled the "law" and thus these commandments. Some say they are still bound to keep the fourth; but not on a particular day and so can keep the "Sabbath" on Sunday. Other excuses are, the commandments were only for the Jews, they wish to celebrate Jesus' rising from the dead on the Sunday, that the Apostles did it, they are now under grace not the law or any works, it is what is in their heart that counts, Jesus broke the Sabbath by healing on the Sabbath day or allowing His disciples to eat picked grain. etc. I shall deal with these and other excuses later. Also give my explanation of love and grace. For now, let us analyse whether they are right in God's eyes using three measuring tools. What the bible says, what history says and, only as a last supplement, common sense. In other words is God an unfair God. Did or does He have one standard of salvation for the Jews (which in today's society would make Him a racist) or those born before Jesus and another for those born after. Our second consideration after seeing the change was made by man not God, is whether it matters. If it does not, ask yourself, why would God institute a standard and requirement, kill people of old for breaking it, if it does not matter? Or is it because you may be one deceived by the prince of deceit and counterfeits? I suggest using a King James' bible, not the New King James or any other version due to the examples given above. Though other versions do retain the "blood against blood" words of 2Chron 19:10, they may have other errors. A free computerised version of KJV can be downloaded from www.e-sword.net to your mobile phone or computer. It would also give you the original Hebrew and Greek words with their meanings and uses from which our bible comes. Bible texts can be found quickly with a click of the mouse. Due to the above examples given and the possible dangers of reading commentaries, I would also advocate not reading them; but let the bible speak for itself. Ask your priest, reverend or vicar, to list all ten commandments (make sure & insist in order) with their relevant numbers as compared to Ex 20   Some denominations will find their denomination has omitted one and split another into two to keep the ten total. The bible does instruct not to call any man your spiritual "father". Neither would some denominations call their leaders "reverend" on the basis only God and Jesus should have our reverence. (This book is primary for Christians. History shows the Muslim religion which originally kept the bible (God's) Sabbath, has made a similar alteration to their day of worship. Research would also show greater flaws in their service to God whom they call Allah).

TEST ONE, HISTORY

There are 2 categories of law; moral and civil. Similarly, two different governing bodies, church and state, which should not be amalgamated. Otherwise the state would believe it could legislate and change God's moral laws. An act it has done and continues to try and do, i.e. in the Sunday observance laws, laws on sex such as age, gender and others. These are clearly against God's laws on the subjects.

History clearly records how the followers of Christ were persecuted, tortured and killed. Even non religious or non Christians know how the apostles and early Christians were persecuted. How, even before Jesus' birth, Jews were persecuted. Persecution continued during His lifetime and well after his death. It is known Jerusalem and other areas were under the control of the Romans. From the bible, shall start from Acts though Roman adversaries as Barabbas (Matt 27:21) and the question to Jesus in Matthew 22:17 whether taxes should be paid to the occupying forces of Rome should show there were hostility between the Jews and the Romans prior to Acts. Early Christians met and worshipped in catacombs for fear of death by the Romans. If one visits the ancient pagan temples in Egypt, they would see signs of the Christians meeting in secrecy there and defacing the pagan god symbols on the walls so that their worship would not be seen as to those deities.

For your insight and reasoning here are a few historical facts leading up to the merging of early Christians (converted Jews who believed Jesus was the Messiah) and the pagan Roman religious system. The bible records Paul's imprisonment and death as well as Peter's by inverted crucifixion.

Early Christians are Jew & Who Changed the Day.

The book of Romans was written about A.D. 56.The dispersion of the Jews led to a multitude of synagogues being established in the midst of heathenism throughout the Roman Empire. The Apostle Paul and many converts to Christianity had access to these synagogues. At that time the polytheistic religion of the Romans was becoming unpopular causing many to become proselytes to Judaism or began to worship the one true God (albeit in their perverted way).

Acts 8:1 At that time there was a great persecution against the church. Acts 10:28 It is an unlawful thing for a man that is a Jew to keep company or come unto one of another nation. Refers to Peter and Roman. It is a common practice of the devil to use man made laws to outlaw his followers from even listening to God's teachings. God did the same when He warned his people from mixing with other believers as they would be a snare to them. Biblical history proved this to be so. Yet Christians of today are taught and follow teachings of tolerance, let everyone do their own thing worshiping God in their way. Acts 11:19 preaching the word to Jews only (i.e. followers of festivals, Sabbaths etc).

Acts 10:45 and they of the circumcision which believed were astonished, as many as came with Peter, because that on the Gentiles also was poured out the gift of the Holy

Ghost. Circumcised being the Jews as was Peter. Acts 11:19 Now they which were scattered abroad upon the persecution that arose about Stephen travelled as far as Phenice, and Cyprus, and Antioch, preaching the word to none but unto the Jews only. Act 11:20 and some of them were men of Cyprus and Cyrene, which, when they were come to Antioch, spake unto the Grecians (Greeks, non Jews, Gentiles), preaching the Lord Jesus.

Acts 11:26 "and the disciples were called Christians first in Antioch".. Acts 12:1about that time Herod the king stretched forth his hands to vex certain of the church Act 13:14when they departed from Perga, they came to Antioch in Pisidia, and went into the synagogue on the Sabbath day, and sat down. Act 13:15And after the reading of the law and the prophets the rulers of the synagogue sent unto them, saying, Ye men and brethren, if ye have any word of exhortation for the people, say on.13:42 and when the Jews were gone out of the synagogue, the Gentiles besought that these words might be preached to them the next Sabbath. Act 13:44 and the next Sabbath day came almost the whole city together to hear the word of God. Act 13:46 Then Paul and Barnabas waxed bold, and said, It was necessary that the word of God should first have been spoken to you: but seeing ye put it from you, and judge yourselves unworthy of everlasting life, lo, we turn to the Gentiles. Act 13:47 For so hath the Lord commanded us, *saying*, I have set thee to be a light of the Gentiles, that thou shouldest be for salvation unto the ends of the earth. Act 14:1 And it came to pass in Iconium, that they went both together into the synagogue of the Jews, and so spake, that a great multitude both of the Jews and also of the Greeks believed. Act 15:5 But there rose up certain of the sect of the Pharisees which believed, Act 16:13 And on the Sabbath we went out of the city by a river side, where prayer was wont to be made; and we sat down, and spake unto the women which resorted thither. (Because there was no synagogue in the city.)16:20brought them to the magistrates, saying, These men, being Jews, do exceedingly trouble our city, Acts 16:21 And teach customs, which are not lawful for us to receive, neither to observe, being Romans. These show early Christians were Jews, merely believers of Christ. Hence they kept all previously kept Jewish laws and customs including the Sabbath Act 17:1when they had passed through Amphipolis and Apollonia, they came to Thessalonica, where was a synagogue of the Jews: Act 17:2Paul, as his manner was, went in unto them, and three Sabbath days reasoned with them out of the scriptures,17:17 Therefore disputed he in the synagogue with the Jews, and with the devout persons, and in the market daily with them that met with him. Act 18:2found a certain Jew named Aquila, born in Pontus, lately come from Italy, with his wife Priscilla; (because that Claudius had commanded all Jews to depart from Rome:) and came unto them. 18:4he reasoned in the synagogue every Sabbath, and persuaded the Jews and the Greeks.18:8 And Crispus, the chief ruler of the synagogue, believed on the Lord with all his house; and many of the Corinthians hearing believed, and were baptized Act 18:19 And he came to Ephesus, and left them there: but he himself entered into the synagogue, and reasoned with the Jews. 18:21 But bade them farewell, saying, I must by all means keep this feast that cometh in Jerusalem: Act 18:28he mightily convinced the Jews, and that publickly, shewing by the scriptures that Jesus was Christ. Act 21:20 And when they heard *it*, they glorified the Lord, and said unto him, Thou seest, brother, how many thousands of Jews there are which believe; and they are all zealous of the law: Act 21:24 Them take, and purify thyself with them, and be at charges with them, that they may shave *their* heads: and all may know that those things, whereof they were informed concerning thee, are nothing; but *that* thou thyself also walkest orderly, and keepest the law. The strict Judaziers who insisted Gentiles also had to be circumcised in order to get salvation were against Paul teaching otherwise (Acts 15:1). They tried to accuse him of teaching against keeping the laws and commandments. Paul was advised to show that this was not the case. That he was simply saying circumcision profitteth nothing to a Gentile as regards gaining salvation through faith in Jesus Christ.

Act 21:26 Then Paul took the men (who had been purified according to the law), and the next day purifying himself with them entered into the temple, to signify the accomplishment of the days of purification, until that an offering should be offered for every one of them.. Act 24:5we have found this man a pestilent fellow, and a mover of sedition among all the Jews throughout the world, and a ringleader of the sect of the Nazarenes: Act 24:11that thou mayest understand, that there are yet but twelve days since I went up to Jerusalem for to worship. Act 24:12 And they neither found me in the temple disputing with any man, neither raising up the people, neither in the synagogues, nor in the city:

Act 24:14But this I confess unto thee, that after the way which they call heresy, so worship I the God of my fathers, believing all things which are written in the law and in the prophets: v21Except it be for this one voice, that I cried standing among them, Touching the resurrection of the dead. Act 25:8he answered for himself, Neither against the law of the Jews, neither against the temple, nor yet against Caesar, have I offended any thing at all. In other words the only difference between Paul's teachings and that of the Jews conforming to the law was that of the resurrection of the dead and faith in Jesus Christ the expected Messiah. Verse 19 But had certain questions against him of their own superstition, and of one Jesus, which was dead, whom Paul affirmed to be alive. Acts 26:4-8should it be thought a thing incredible with you, that God should raise the dead? Acts 26:22 witnessing both to small and great, saying none other things than those which the prophets and Moses did say should come.

Some persons say they don't care about or wish to know about history when deciding how and when to worship God. It is like saying

I don't care if this man killed my family, I will still make the same mistake as my family did. As stated below about Moses crossing the Red Sea by aeroplane when planes were not invented at that time. It is the same with today's reasons not to adhere to the fourth commandment. Until one searches historical records, they will continue believing satan's propaganda. Lies enter our minds, can take hold, change our belief, from whence cometh our actions. All satan has to do is sow a lie. Maybe 50% will believe and 50% may not. But every time he tells that lie, maybe by dressing up the reasoning for it, 50% of the remainder succumb to it. The more one hears the lie from various sources, one believes unless they have researched in the right place and know the truth. Therefore, to uproot the lie sown into your mind and belief you must go to the core not just cut it off at the surface or evil and the false root will regenerate and return possibly worse than your original state. It is hard to change ones dependence on worldly things, routine, weekly cycle or customs; but it must be done. Titus 2:12 "Teaching us that denying ungodliness and worldly lusts we should live soberly, righteously and godly in this present world

After the destruction of Jerusalem and the Temple in A.D.70, bishops of Rome took control of Roman Christian church, began to introduce legislation and other merges to convert believers to "Sun" day worship. Church leaders as Tertullian (A.D.160-220), the father of Latin Christianity, rebuked Christians for worshipping the sun especially on the Day of the Sun. Of course the sun cannot be a god as its movements are predictable i.e. its eclipse, setting and rising. Who or what stops it crashing into other planets, gave it its functions etc. A designer, the true God. Epipharius, an early theologian, confirms Nazarenes persisted in the Sabbath observance until his time in about A.D.350. Meeting in secret on the Sabbath for fear of death by the Romans, for most, came to an end in about 312AD when Emperor Constantine made a compromise between Romans and Jews / early Christians. If Christians stopped worshipping on the Sabbath, the seventh day and changed to the Sunday, the first day, as did the Romans etc who worshipped the sun god, they would no longer be persecuted. History continues to record how the practices and beliefs of the sun worshippers were amalgamated (subtly forced) on the Christians. How their minor gods were given Christian saint names and how the birthday of Tammuz (Ezekiel 8:14) a pagan god, December 25th began to be used as Christ's birthday. The same day another pagan group in ancient Briton, the Celtic Druids celebrated as Yule's day (infant's day). Some of us may remember not so long ago Christmas was (and still is sometimes) referred to as Yuletide. This is also the origin of Easter, Lent and other pagan practices, which had nothing to do with Christ. How ironic and what a masterly deception that the same practices God warned His Old and New Testament followers not to do, they have been tricked into doing (Matt 24:24 "for there shall arise false Christs, and false prophets, and shall show great signs and wonders; insomuch that, if it were possible, deceive the very elect"). Though the bible does not mention the date of Jesus' birth, it is accepted through calculation it was well before December 25. If it was the Romans intention to celebrate His birth, why not set a date in November or 3, 20 or 28 of December. Why specifically the 25th the same date they celebrated a pagan god's birth, the sun god? Think about it. The answer should be obvious. Christians, be careful with what you associate

Some ask, how we can know our present Saturday is God's seventh, Sabbath day. Very easily. Firstly, the Jewish line has been keeping the seventh day practice since it began. Secondly, all accurate historic records showing times of calendar and such changes confirm the same. This evidence is expanded later.

In England, the British Broadcasting Company televised a drama documentary called

The Rise and Fall of Rome. In one of the Episodes a brief mention was made of Emperor Constantine's part and one of the meetings from which these amalgamations were born. The Council of Nicaea on 19th June 325AD.Prior to that on 7th March 321 A.D. the first Sunday law was passed .It read "Let all the judges and town people, and the occupation of all trades rest on the venerable day of the sun" .In that same era the Roman Catholic church was established, the pagan priests made head of Christianity, a pope assumed the right to be God's representative on earth and power to change laws, decree's etc. This could be the fulfilment of the prophesy in Daniel 7:25.

Some of many documented historical facts and quotes from the Catholic church are "The Pope has power to change times, to abrogate (change) laws, and to dispense with all things, even the precepts of Christ". "Saturday is the Sabbath" "by virtue of her (Catholic church) divine mission changed the day from Saturday to Sunday". "We observe Sunday instead of Saturday because the Catholic Church, in the Council of Laodicea (A.D. 364), transferred the solemnity from Saturday to Sunday". "You may read the bible from Genesis to Revelation and you will not find a single line authorising the sanctification of Sunday. The Scriptures enforce the religious observance of Saturday, a day which we never sanctify" (The Faith of our Fathers, 16th Edition, 1880, p111). Sunday is a Catholic Institution, and its claims to observance can be defended only on Catholic principles… From beginning to end of Scripture there is not a single passage that warrants the transfer of weekly public worship from the last day of the week to the first (The Catholic Press, Sydney, Australia, Aug 19900). Protestantism, in discarding the authority of the (Roman Catholic) Church, has no good reason for its Sunday theory, and ought logically to keep Saturday as the Sabbath (John Gilmary Shea, American Catholic Quarterly Review, Jan 1883). It is well to remind the Presbyterians, Baptists, Methodists and all other Christians, that the bible does not support them anywhere in their observance of Sunday. Sunday is an institute of the Roman Catholic Church and those who observe the day observe a commandment of the Catholic Church. (Priest Brady, in an address, reported in the Elizabeth, N.J. "News", March 18, 1903). Reason and common sense demand the acceptance of one or the other of these alternatives: either Protestantism and the keeping holy of Saturday or Catholicity and the keeping holy of Sunday. Compromise is impossible (The Catholic Mirror, Dec 23, 1893). Protestants … accept Sunday rather than Saturday as the day for public worship after the Catholic Church made the change … but the Protestant mind does not seem to realize that … in observing the Sunday, they accepting the authority of the spokesman for the church, the Pope (Our Sunday Visitor, Feb 5, 1950). Not the Creator of the Universe, in Genesis 2:1-3 but the Catholic Church "can claim the honor of having granted man a pause to his work every seven days" (S.D. Mosna, storia della Domenica, 1969, pgs 366-7). If Protestants would follow the bible, they should worship God on the Sabbath Day. In keeping Sunday the are following a law of the Catholic Church (Albert Smith, Chancellor of the Archdiocese of Baltimore, replying for the Cardinal, in a letter, Feb 10, 1920). "We are commanded to keep the seventh; but we are nowhere commanded to keep the first day … The reason why we keep the first day of the week holy instead of the seventh is for the same reason that we observe many other things, not because the Bible, but the Church has enjoined it". "People who think that the scriptures should be the sole authority; should logically become 7th Day Adventist and keep Saturday holy" " (Sentinel, pastor's pge May 21 1995). Maybe the pastor only knew of the 7th D.A. denomination but others also keep the Sabbath.

Some blasphemous claims of the Pope. To blaspheme is to make oneself equal to God either by claiming a power reserved only to Him i.e. forgiving sins or being the son of God. It was for these reasons the Jews sought to kill Jesus and eventually convicted Him. "We hold upon this earth the place of God Almighty" (Pope Leo XIII, in an Encyclinal Letter, June 20 1894). "The Pope is not only the representative of Jesus Christ, but he is Jesus Christ Himself, hidden under veil of flesh" (The Catholic National, July 1895). I wonder when Jesus is suppose to have taken over the fleshly body of the human man titled Pope. Before his appointment as Pope, after and how it was done. On death of one Pope and prior to appointment of the next, where does Jesus go? See Appendixes for some other historical facts.

Thus history neither supports the adherence of Sunday as God's day .Otherwise it would be as saying Moses and the Israelites crossed the Red Sea in an aeroplane when history proves aeroplanes did not exist at the time! So no matter what part of the bible one quotes, it obviously was not talking about observing Sunday and one needs to seek to what it was really referring. An encyclopaedia says "Sunday was a name given by the heathen to the first day of the week, because it was the day on which they worshiped the sun, ... the seventh day was blessed and hallowed by God Himself, and ... He requires His creatures to keep it holy to Him. This commandment is of universal and perpetual obligation." -*Eadie's Biblical Cyclopedia,* 1872 cd., p. 561.

Some quotes from other Christian denomination leaders are: "Is there any commandment in the New Testament to change the day of weekly Sabbath from Saturday to Sunday?

Congregationalist: "None. It is quite clear that however rigidly or devotedly we may spend Sunday, we are not keeping the Sabbath ... The Sabbath was founded on specific, divine command. We can plead no such command for the observance of Sunday ... There is not a single line in the New Testament to suggest that we incur any penalty by violating the supposed sanctity of Sunday." -Dr. R. W. Dale, *The Ten Commandments,* pages 106-107 Congregationalist. "The Christian Sabbath [Sunday) is not in the Scriptures, and was not by the primitive church called the Sabbath." -*Dwig/It's Theology,* Vo!. 4, p. 401.
Anglican: "And where are we told in the Scriptures that we are to keep the first day at all? We are commanded to keep the seventh; but we are nowhere commanded to keep the first day." - Isaac Williams, *Plain Sermons on the Catechism,* pg 334, 336

Methodist: "It is true that there is no positive command for infant baptism. Nor is there any for keeping holy the first day of the week. Many believe that Christ changed the Sabbath. But, from His own words, we see that He came for no such purpose. Those who believe that Jesus changed the Sabbath base it only on a supposition." -Amos Binney, *Theological Compendium,* pages 180-181.

"Take the matter of Sunday. There are indications in the New Testament as to how the church came to keep the first day of the week as its day of worship, but there is no passage telling Christians to keep that day, or to transfer the Jewish Sabbath to that day." -HalTis Franklin Rail, *Christian Adoocare,* July 2, 1942

Pentecostal " 'Why do we worship on Sunday? Doesn't the Bible teach us that Saturday should be the Lord's Day?' ... Apparently we will have to seek the answer from some other source than the New Testament." -David A. Womack, "Is Sunday the Lord's Day!" The Pentecostal" *Evangel,* Aug. 9, 1959, No. 2361, p. 3.

Baptist: "To me it seems unaccountable that Jesus, during three years' discussion with His disciples, often conversing with them upon the Sabbath question, discussing it in some of its various aspects, freeing it from its false (Jewish traditional) glosses, never alluded to any transference of the day; also, that during the forty days of His resurrection life, no such thing was intimated . Nor, so far as we know, did the Spirit, which was given to bring to their remembrance all things whatsoever that He had said unto them, deal with this question. Nor yet did the inspired apostles, in preaching the gospel, founding churches, counselling and instructing those founded, discuss or approach the subject. "Of course I quite well know that Sunday did come into use in early Christian history as a religious day, as we learn from the Christian Fathers and other sources. But what a pity that it comes branded with the mark of Paganism, and christened with the name of the sun-god, then adopted and sanctified by the Papal apostasy, and bequeathed as a sacred legacy to Protestantism." -Dr. E.T. Hiscox, report of his sermon at the Baptist Minister's Convention, *in New York Examiner,* November 16, 1893.

Baptist: "There was and is a command to keep holy the Sabbath day, but that Sabbath day was not Sunday. It will however be readily said, and with some show of triumph, that the Sabbath was transferred from the seventh to the first day of the week, with all its duties, privileges and sanctions. Earnestly desiring information on this subject, which I have studied for many years, I ask, where can the record of such a transaction be found? Not in the New Testament-absolutely not. There is no scriptural evidence of the change of the Sabbath institution from the seventh to the first day of the week." -Dr. E.T. Hiscox. author of the *Baptist Manual* "The Scriptures nowhere call the first day of the week the Sabbath .. . There is no Scriptural authority for so doing, nor of course. any Scriptural obligation." -*The Watchman.*

Southern Baptist: "The sacred name of the Seventh day is Sabbath. This fact is too clear to require argument (Exodus 20:10 quoted) On this point the plain teaching of the Word has been admitted in all ages Not once did the disciples apply the Sabbath law to the first day of the week-that folly was left for a later age, nor did they pretend that the first day supplanted the seventh." -Joseph Judson Taylor, *The Sabbath Question,* pages 14-17, 41.

Lutheran Free Church: "For when there could not be produced one solitary place in the Holy Scriptures which testified that either the Lord Himself or the apostles had ordered such a transfer of the Sabbath to Sunday, then it was not easy to answer the question: Who has transferred the Sabbath, and who has had the right to do it?" -George Sverdrup, A New Day"

Lutheran: "The observance of the Lord's day [Sunday] is founded not on any command of God, but on the authority of the church." -Augsburg Confession of Faith, quoted in Catholic Sabbath Manual, Part 2, Chapter I, Section 10.

Protestant Episcopal: "The day is now changed from the seventh to the first day ... but as we meet with no Scriptural direction for the change, we may conclude it was done by the authority of the church." -*Explanation of Catechism.*

Episcopalian: "We have made the change from the seventh day to the first day, from Saturday to Sunday, on the authority of the one holy, catholic, apostolic church of Christ." -Bishop Symour, *Why We keep Sunday.*

Episcopal "Sunday *(Dies Solis,* of the Roman calendar, 'day of the sun,' because dedicated to the sun), the first day of the week, was adopted by the early Christians as a day of worship .... No regulations for its observance are laid down in the New Testament, nor, indeed, is its observance even enjoined." - "Sunday," A *Religious E7U:Jclopdia,* Vo!. 3, (New York, Funk and Wagnalls, 1883) p.2259.

Presbyterian: "There is no word, no hint in the New Testament about abstaining from work on Sunday. The observance of Ash Wednesday, or Lent. stands exactly on the same footing as the observance of Sunday. Into the rest of Sunday no Divine Law enters." -Canon Eyton, in *The Ten Commandments.*

Presbyterian "Until, therefore, it can be shown that the whole moral law has been repealed, the Sabbath will stand .... The teaching of Christ confirms the perpetuity of the Sabbath." - T. C. Blake, *D.D., Theology Candensed,* pp. 474,475.

Disciples of Christ: "There is no direct Scriptural authority for designating the first day 'the Lord's Day.' "-Dr. D.H. Lucas, *Christian Oracle,* January, 1890

Church of Christ. "Finally, we have the testimony of Christ on this subject. In Mark 2:27, he says: 'The Sabbath was made for man, and not man for the Sabbath.' From this passage it is evident that the Sabbath was made not merely for the *Israelites,* as Paley and Hengstenberg would have us believe, but for *man* ... that is, for *the race.* Hence we conclude that the Sabbath was sanctified from the beginning, and that it was given to Adam, even in Eden, as one of those primeval institutions that God ordained for the happiness of all men." -Robert Milligan, ~ of . *Redemption,* (St. Louis, The Bethany Press, 1962), p. 165.

Moody Bible Institute "The Sabbath was binding in Eden, and it has been in force ever since. This fourth commandment begins with the word 'remember,' showing that the Sabbath already existed when God wrote the law on the tables of stone at Sinai. How can men claim that this one commandment has been done away with when they will admit that the other nine are still binding?" –*D*. L. Moody, Weighed and *\Vaming,* p.47.

American Congregationalist: "The current notion that Christ and His apostles authoritatively substituted the first day for the seventh, is absolutely without any authority in the New Testament." -Dr. Layman Abbot, in the *Christian Union,* June 26, 1890.

Christian Church: "Now there is no testimony in all the oracles of heaven that the Sabbath is changed, or that the Lord's Day came in the room of it." -Alexander Campbell, in *The Reporter,* October 8, 1921.

Lastly from a bishop who changed his congregation from Sunday to Saturday "I have spoken to many church leaders who appear on television and have huge followings. They tell me they know Saturday is the Sabbath; but if they were to preach that it would divide the church, especially after adhering to Sunday for so long". For quotes of other denomination leaders who accept Sabbath as being Saturday, was for mankind at creation not the Jews and was changed by the Catholic church not the bible go to www.sabbathtruth.com

The following letter is taken from page 105 of a book titled Ten Commandments Twice Removed. Its authors are Danny Shelton and Shelley Quinn who both work for the 3ABN (3 Angels Broadcasting Company). Their television programmes may be available for viewing free via the internet. This is What Shelly Quinn says about her and Danny. "Danny grew up in these bible teachings. My Christian experience was just the opposite. Although I was a serious student of the scripture and worked in part time ministry, I had accepted several popular doctrines without thoroughly researching them. I was oblivious even resistant ... until at the dawning of my fifties the Lord taught me a new manner of in-depth Word study".

A letter from, J.L. Day of Thomaston, Georgia, May 22, 1954 to Pope Pius XII, Rome Italy.

Dear Sir,

Is the accusation true, that Protestants accuse you of? They say you changed the Seventh Day Sabbath to the, so-called Christian Sunday: Identical with the first day of the week.

If so when did you make the change and by what authority?

The Reply form Peter R. Tramer, Editor. THE CATHOLIC EXTENSION MAGAZINE 180 Wabash Ave, Chicago, Illinois

(Under the Blessing of Pope Pius XII)

Dear Sir,

Regarding the change from the observance of the Jewish Sabbath to the Christian Sunday, I wish to draw your attention to the facts:

1.   The Protestants who accept the Bible as the only rule of faith and religion, should by all means go back to the observance of the Sabbath. The fact that they do not, but on the contrary observe Sunday, stultifies them in the eyes of every thinking man.

2.   We Catholics do not accept the Bible as the only rule of faith. Besides the Bible we have the living church, as a rule to guide us. We say, this Church instituted by Christ, to teach and guide men through life, has the right to change the ceremonial laws of the Old Testament and hence, we accept her change of the Sabbath to Sunday. We frankly say, "yes", the Church made this change, made this law, as she made many other laws, for instance, the Friday abstinence, the unmarried priesthood, the laws concerning mixed marriages, the regulations of Catholic marriages and a thousand other laws.

3.   We also say that of all Protestants, the Seventh Day Adventists are the only group that reason correctly and are consistent with their teachings. **It is always somewhat laughable to see the Protestant Churches, in pulpit and legislature, demand the observance of Sunday of which there is nothing in the Bible.**

So are you a "thinking man" or following blind sheep? Are you to be laughed at or taken seriously? A Protestant, is a person or group of Christian believers who protested against the Catholic's claim they had the right to represent God on earth, change His commandments and insisted all religions bow to their authority. Protestants profess the Bible only as their source of God's way yet fight to adhere to a Sunday observance instituted by the Church of Rome and unsupported by the Bible. As a former Catholic I was taught, the Pope and Church gets its authority from when Jesus said to Peter "on this rock I build my church". They claim to be that church, descendant of Peter. How they account for the 300 or so year gap I do not know. The same ones who crucified Peter upside-down, tortured, killed and persecuted the early Christians. Maybe you can claim to be a descendant of Peter, albeit almost 2000 year later. 300 or 2000 years gap what is the difference, the principle is the same. Shelly Quinn caps the letter with this sentence: Many protestants say, "what difference does it make?" At least I am taking a day to worship the Lord. Others say I keep every day holy". The component missing from their reasoning is that God blessed and sanctified the day-not the rest. God's definition of keeping a day holy is to cease all secular work (Ex 20:8-11), refrain from buying and selling (Neh 10:31, 13:15-22) and to focus on Him as our delight rather than worldly pleasures (Is 58:13-14). None can keep everyday holy in the eyes of the Lord! Only God can bless and sanctify a day, declaring it to be sacred to Him – as He did with the Sabbath, calling it "My holy day". God's ways are higher than our ways, they do not always make sense. No organisation or claimed representative of God speaks for God when they tell you to go against His biblical written words. Aaron was chosen as

God as His priest, yet when Moses went up to Mount Sinai, he went against God making idols etc. God was displeased.

Since all present day Christians came from breakaway groups of the original Roman Catholic Church that explains conclusively why they break the fourth commandment; as a custom. It should be said that some have put custom and financial benefits aside and returned to holding services and keeping the Sabbath on Saturdays. These are mainly 7th Day Adventist churches; but also Baptist, Pentecostal and independent groups. I have known individuals to keep Sabbath on their own at home or start their own small group at home or a hall. They made the change gradually by holding both Saturday and Sunday ones. Some Sunday congregations, including the Catholics, hold a Saturday evening service as a convenience for those unable to make Sunday. They do not know the Sabbath is not in the one hour service; but the whole sanctified and separated day, commencing sunset Friday evening. This is not acceptable to God, it is still disobedience.

How We Know Which Day Is the Sabbath

Firstly, the same way we know the world is round and not flat. It is accepted knowledge from all academics; encyclopaedias etc which trace recorded history. Secondly, from the cycle of seven days kept by the Jewish nation. Thirdly by our own Christian practice. We celebrate Jesus' resurrection on today's Sunday, which the bible calls the 1st day   Also we are told the Sabbath was the day before the 1st day Mat 28:1 In the end of the Sabbath, as it began to dawn toward the first day of the week, came Mary Magdalene and the other Mary to see the sepulchre. Mar 16:1 And when the Sabbath was past, Mary Magdalene, and Mary the *mother* of James, and Salome, had bought sweet spices, that they might come and anoint him. Mar 16:2 And very early in the morning the first *day* of the week, they came unto the sepulchre at the rising of the sun.   Traditionally Christians keep Good Friday and Easter Sunday as a continuation of the day Jesus died and rose.

Fourthly, as seen below astronomers confirm the stars and our solar system have kept track of time. Lastly, as is now discovered in Chrono-biology, the human body has an inbuilt 7 day cycle timing mechanism. The heart has been detected to beat slightly slower on the seventh day. Working seven or more days has been tried in the past i.e. during 2nd World War when productivity of more planes was urgently needed. It was quickly found that there were more mistakes and fewer good planes than when they were working six days. For the purpose of this book, there is too much to go into on medical discoveries of the body cycle whether for healing, working or so. One can look up "Circadian rhythms" if the y care to learn more. In short, the human and animal body is designed to work six days and rest the seventh.

There is therefore no getting away from it, all evidence points to today's Saturday being the seventh Sabbath as mentioned in the Bible and commanded by God to be kept holy on to Him.

It takes the earth exactly 365 days, 5 hrs, 48 minutes and 47.8 seconds to go around the sun; but there is no way to put that into any calendar so our calendar is constantly being updated. Hence the "leap year". In 1562 they discovered that the year was a little longer than 365 days and so the astronomer s added 10 days to bring the month up to date; **but the week cycle was not altered**. Thursday the 4th was followed by Friday 15th. The calendar was updated without altering the weekly cycle in any way. Although we have had leap years down through the centuries, **the days of the week have never been changed** and not even a minute of time has been lost track of.

There have been many ancient calendars. The first modern calendar as we have today was put into use by Julius Caesar in 45 B.C. The names of the days as used today were also used then. Since the Babylonians worshipped the planets the days of the week were derived from the names of the planets. The Hebrews and the bible writers never did this. Though the names, Sunday, Monday etc existed in Christ's time they were of pagan origin and not followed. The Roman soldiers, who followed the Mithra religion of Babylon and Persia (goes back to before 630 B.C.) spread these names around the world. The Teutonic tribe substituted a few of their own god's names instead of planets for some days (before Christ). The Sun became Sunday, Moon – Monday, Mars/Tiu – Tuesday, Mercury/Woden – Wednesday, Jupiter/Thor – Thursday, Venus/Frigg – Friday, Saturn – Saturday. Historians writings before and around the time of Christ have referred to "the day of the sun" and "the day of Saturn".

Sun worship did not originate in Rome; but came into Christianity via their post apostle merger. Sun worship derived from a belief that the Sun is the source of life (food growth, light, heat, etc) and prosperity rather than Jehovah God who created it. As such it was adored, worship and sacrifices offered to it to bring good fortune. A day was designated to and named after it by the people. Though today the word "Sun" has been deleted from the spoken or sung words of worship and actions handed down by the followers of the belief, the same day is maintained. And despite adding the words as Jesus etc to the service and having "Christians" joining in, the praises are NOT going to or being received by Jehovah God, creator of heaven, earth and all. The praises did not and were not intended to go to God originally so likewise He would not be receiving them now.

It may be of interest to know that from the position of the stars every moment of time has been kept track of since before 500B.C. (quote from the Pentagon in Washington D.C, Dept of Astronomy). Is God the creator, not the only awesome being? Consistent to the moment, nothing irregular or without design. Hence, when He gave a particular slice of that time cycle a name, the "Sabbath" it would not be confused for another slice of time: is not another word for rest; but for a period of time, sunset the sixth day

(Friday evening) to sunset the seventh day (Saturday evening) (Genesis 1:8).Thus one cannot keep the Sabbath at any other time or day. As that would mean one can move the name around to refer to any time. One cannot move a specific time set by the sun and moon around.

Dr W.W. Campbell, director of the Lick Observatory in Mount Hamilton, California assures us "the week of seven days has been in use ever since the days of Moses and we have no reason to suppose that any irregularities have existed to present" (quote from 1972). Dr J.B. Dimbleby, premier chronologist to the British Chronological and Astronomical Association, after years of careful calculations asserts "if men refused to observe weeks and the line of time was forgotten, the day of the week could be recovered by observing when the transits of the planets or eclipse of the Sun and Moon occurred. These great sentinels of the sky keep seven days with scientific accuracy, thundering out the seven days inscribed on the inspired page" ("inspired page" being the bible). Dr G.E. Hale, noted astronomer for whom the great "Palomar telescope" has been named, concurred by stating "No time has been lost". What does the bible say? Gen 1:14 "and God said, let there be light in the firmament of the heaven to divide the day from the night and let them be for signs and for seasons and for days and years". Is that not creation by intellectual design rather than by chance!

It does not matter where you go in the world everyone knows the seven day week, Sunday - Saturday. It is common to all people both developed and developing although the names are those of the local languages. Sunday by dictionary definition is the day of the sun, the name of the first day of the seek In Germany the first day of the week Sunday is called Sontag, and Wednesday is called Mittwoch or midweek. This recognises there are 3 days either side of Wednesday to complete the week which starts Sunday and ends Saturday. Rev William Meade Jones, a Baptist minister and antiquarian of London, made extensive research of this fact and compiled a chart which was over seven feet long with many languages and dialects from around the world showing how the week is named and the fact that all people recognise a seven day week. Again this is too much information for the purpose of this book but for example in Wandala, a language of Central Africa the names of the week translate into The One, The Two, The Three etc. with the seven called Sibda or Sabbath. Many languages call the seventh day Sabbath i.e. Spanish = Sabado, Italian Sabbato, Arabic Assabt, Norman French Sabbedi. The Jews traditionally call their days the first of the Sabbath, the second of the Sabbath etc.

It was probably this change to Sunday observance that led Muhammad, the founder of the Muslim religion, to accuse Christians (the people of the Book / Bible) of distorting the Bible. In the Qur'an (Quran) it states "There is among them a section who distort the Book with their tongues *: (as they read) you would think it is a part of the Book , but it is no part of the Book; and they say, 'That is from Allah; but it is not from Allah: it is they who tell a lie against Allah, and they know it. It is not that a man, to whom is given the Book and Wisdom and the Prophetic Office should say to people: 'Be ye my worshippers rather than Allah's ..." Ali Imran 3:78-79.

"And there are among them illiterates, who know not the Book, but (see therein their own) desires and they do nothing but conjecture. Then woe to those who write the Book with their own hands, and then say 'This is from Allah, to traffic with it for a miserable price!" Al Baqarah 2:78-79 (* note this was written in about 600 A.D. when the word "tongue" was used to mean human speech or language understood by other humans)

I ought to state here that a study of Muhammad, the compilation of the Quran, its accepted numerous contradictions even from Muslims would show it is a flawed derivative of the Bible and based more on the directives of man that God. As a Christian one is closer to understanding God, yet both should heed Jer 17:5 Thus saith the LORD; Cursed *be* the man that trusteth in man, and maketh flesh his arm, and whose heart departeth from the LORD.

Deu 13:1 If there arise among you a prophet, or a dreamer of dreams, and giveth thee a sign or a wonder, Deu 13:2 And the sign or the wonder come to pass, whereof he spake unto thee, saying, Let us go after other gods, which thou hast not known, and let us serve them; Deu 13:3 Thou shalt not hearken unto the words of that prophet, or that dreamer of dreams: for the LORD your God **proveth (test)** you, to know whether ye love the LORD your God with all your heart and with all your soul.
Deu 13:4 Ye shall walk after the LORD your God, and fear him, and keep his commandments, and obey his voice, and ye shall serve him, and cleave unto him. Deu 13:5 And that prophet, or that dreamer of dreams, shall be put to death; because he hath spoken to turn *you* away from the LORD your God, which brought you out of the land of Egypt, and redeemed you out of the house of bondage, to thrust thee out of the way which the LORD thy God commanded thee to walk in. So shalt thou put the evil away from the midst of thee.
Gal 1:8 But though we, or an angel from heaven, preach any other gospel unto you than that which we have preached unto you, let him be accursed.

Remember the story of the man of god in 1 Kings 13:1-26.
We are not to depart from the Bible and the word of God given in His commandments regardless who tells us; angel one claiming to be God's representative or other. Even if that person in the past spoke for God, does miracles or spoke prophesies which came true. God is "proving you" (having you prove your understanding and obedience to His word via a test). Never ever under any circumstance allow yourself to be deceived that god's commandments as in His Bible has been changed or it could be to your eternal detriment! The roaring lion succeeded in devouring you (1Peter 5:8) !

WARNING

You are about to read copies of some historic documents; all of which are available on the internet for confirmation. They are things the (Roman) Catholic Church believes of itself i.e. the Pope is Jesus Christ himself, the son of God, God's representative on earth, having power to change God's laws, commandments and God is bound to obey them etc. Of course these claims are untrue. Some web sites run by Catholics would claim the apostle Peter was the first pope and the present one is a direct successor of Peter with h is authority over God's church etc. Again, of course this is untrue. They have no linage to Peter or authority over God's church. The Pope's linage is traced back to the pagan Church of Rome as under Emperor Constantine. This warning is for those susceptible to believe their claims and who may come across internet web sites propagating these false claims and believe them to be true. This is how the Catholic Church is setting the world up to be the appointed representative of God directing earthly governments and fulfilling the beast prophesies of the Bible books of Daniel and Revelations.

Würdigung dieser Schwierigkeit, was sie bewog, die Scholastiker in jener Reihe von Zeugen der Tradition nicht mit zu nennen. Noch mehr aber mußten sich die Väter bei ihrem sonst so zuversichtlichen Bekenntniße zum Traditionsprincipe davor hüten, einen Satz zu verdammen, der etwa in irgend einem bisher übersehenen Dictum eines beliebigen Kirchenvaters eine nachträgliche Autorität hätte finden können. Das Concil war ganz der Ansicht des Ambrosius Pelargus, daß man um keinen Preis den Protestanten den Triumph bereiten dürfe, sagen zu können, die Synode habe die Lehre der alten Kirche verdammt. Aber diese Praxis verursachte unendliche Mühsal, ohne je Sicherheit gewähren zu können. Es bedurfte zu diesem Geschäfte allerdings jener „fast göttlichen Klugheit", die der Synode am 16. März 1562 von den spanischen Gesandten zuerkannt wurde. In der That aber hatte man sich bisher in den sich wechselseitig durchkreuzenden und labyrinthisch verschlungenen Irrgängen eines älteren und eines neueren Traditionsbegriffes nicht völlig orientiren können. Aber auch dies sollte noch geschehen. — Endlich bei der letzten Eröffnung am 18. Januar 1563 entledigte man sich aller Bedenken; der Erzbischof von Reggio hielt eine Rede, in der er offen aussprach, die Tradition sei über die Schrift erhaben. Die Autorität der Kirche könne schon deßhalb nicht gebunden sein an die Autorität der Schrift, weil jene nicht nach der Anordnung Christi, sondern aus eigener Autorität die Beschneidung in die Taufe, den Sabbat in den Sonntag verwandelt habe. Hiermit war allerdings die letzte Illusion zerstört und erklärt, daß Tradition nicht Alterthum, sondern fortdauernde Inspiration bedeute. Et potuissent paucis verbis totam rem absolvere — so bezeichnet der scharfe Examinator der tridentinischen Rathsherren ihre eigentliche Tendenz — si tantum in ipso synodi ingressu professi essent, se simpliciter praesentem ecclesiae suae statum, qualis ille cunque est, velle retinére et pertinaciter defendere, nec admissuros se, ut ex norma scripturae canonicae aliquid, quidquid illud sit, corrigatur vel emendetur [1]). Nach dieser stillschweigenden Voraussetzung verfuhr man dann auch in der späteren Zeit der Synode. Offen erkannte man an, die communio sub utraque sei von Christo eingesetzt und von den Aposteln den Gemeinden tradirt, aber die Macht, Veränderung in der Verwaltung der Sacramente vorzunehmen, stehe nun einmal der Kirche zu [2]). Jetzt fürchtete man sich nicht mehr vor den männiglich bekannten Stellen Augustin's, sondern setzte einfach das Anathema auf die Kindercommunion und erklärte, die alten Kirchenlehrer hätten dieselbe nicht für nothwendig erachtet [3]).

[1]) Chemnitz, S. 5.
[2]) Sess. XXI. cp. 1. 2.
[3]) Sess. XXI. cp. 4.

Kanon und Tradition.

Ein Beitrag

zur

neueren Dogmengeschichte und Symbolik

von

Lic. **Heinrich Julius Holtzmann,**
Privatdocent in Heidelberg.

Ludwigsburg.
Druck und Verlag von Ferd. Riehm.
1859.

The Council of Trent on the Change to Sunday Worship

Source: Gaspare [Ricciulli] de Fosso (Archbishop of Reggio), Address in the 17th session of the Council of Trent, Jan. 18, 1562, in Mansi *SC*, Vol. 33, cols. 529, 530. Latin.[Gian Domenico Mansi, "Sacrorum Conciliorum nova et amplissima collectio"]

[col. 529] Such is the condition of the heretics of this age that on nothing do they rely more than that, under the pretence of the word of God, they overthrow the authority of the church; as though the church, His body, could be opposed to the word of Christ, or the head to the body. On the contrary, the authority of the church, then, is illustrated most clearly by the Scriptures; for while on the one hand she recommends them, declares them to be divine, [col. 530] offers them to us to be read, in doubtful matters explains them faithfully, and condemns whatever is contrary to them; on the other hand, the legal precepts in the Scriptures taught by the Lord have ceased by virtue of the same authority. The Sabbath, the most glorious day in the law, has been changed into the Lord's day. Circumcision, enjoined upon Abraham and his seed under such threatening that he who had not been circumcised would be destroyed from among his people, has been so abrogated that the apostle asserts: "If ye be circumcised, ye have fallen from grace, and Christ shall profit you nothing." These and other similar matters have not ceased by virtue of Christ's teaching (for He says He has come to fulfil the law, not to destroy it), but they have been changed by the authority of the church. Indeed, if she should be removed (since there must be heresies), who would set forth truth, and confound the obstinacy of heretics? All things will be confused, and soon heresies condemned by her authority will spring up again. [See No. 1444.]

1444. Sabbath, Change of—Cited in Council of Trent as Proof that Tradition Is Above Scripture

Source: Heinrich Julius Holtzmann, *Kanon und Tradition* ("Canon and Tradition") (Ludwigsburg: Druck and Verlag von Ferd. Riehm, 1859), p. 263. German. [FRS No. 72.] [Facsimile (in the original German) below.]

The Council [of Trent] agreed fully with Ambrosius Pelargus, that under no condition should the Protestants be allowed to triumph by saying that the council had condemned the doctrine of the ancient church. But this practice caused untold difficulty without being able to guarantee certainty. For this business, indeed, 'well-nigh divine prudence' was requisite—which the Spanish ambassador acknowledged as belonging to the council on the sixteenth of March, 1562. Indeed, thus far they had not been able to orient themselves to the interchanging, crisscrossing, labyrinthine, twisting passages of an older and newer concept of tradition. But even in this they were to succeed. Finally, at the last opening [see editors' note] on the eighteenth of January, 1562, all hesitation was set aside: [Gaspar de Fosso] the Archbishop of Reggio made a speech [see No. 1443] in which he openly declared that **tradition stood above Scripture. The authority of the church could therefore not be bound to the authority of the Scriptures, because the church had changed circumcision into baptism, Sabbath into Sunday, not by the command of Christ, but by its own authority.** With this, to be sure, the last illusion was destroyed, and it was declared that tradition does not signify antiquity, but continual inspiration.

[Editors' note: This "last opening" of the Council of Trent was not the last day, but the opening of the 17th session, the first meeting of the last series of sessions that was opened, after a lapse of time, under a new pope. The council was in session for longer or shorter periods over a series of years.]

Source: Neufeld, Don F., *Seventh-day Adventist Bible Student's Source Book,* Don F. Neufeld and Julia Neuffer.—Washington, D.C., Review and Herald Publishing Association, 1962, pgs. 887-888

An event at the Tridentine Council... **The Sabbath and the Council of Trent**

It was upon this very point that the Reformation was condemned by the Council of Trent. The Reformers had constantly charged, as here stated, that the Catholic Church had "apostatized from the truth *as contained in the written word.*" The written word," "The Bible and the Bible only," "Thus saith the Lord," these were their constant watchwords; and "the Scripture, as in the written word, the sole standard of appeal," this was the proclaimed platform of the Reformation and of Protestantism. "The Scripture *and tradition.*" The Bible as interpreted by the Church and according to the unanimous consent of the Fathers," this was the position and claim of the Catholic Church. This was the main issue in the Council of Trent, which was called especially to consider the questions that had been raised and forced upon the attention of Europe by the Reformers. The very first question concerning faith that was considered by the council was the question involved in this issue. There was a strong party even of the Catholics within the council who were in favour of abandoning tradition and adopting *the Scriptures only,* as the standard of authority. This view was so decidedly held in the debates in the council that the Pope's legates actually wrote to him that there was "a strong tendency to set aside tradition altogether and to make Scripture the sole standard of appeal." But to do this would manifestly be to go a long way toward justifying the claims of the Protestants. By this crisis there was developed upon the ultra-Catholic portion of the council the task of convincing the others that "Scripture *and tradition"* were the only sure ground to stand upon. If this could be done, the Council could be carried to issue a decree condemning the Reformation, otherwise not. The question was debated day after day, until the Council was fairly brought to a standstill. Finally, after a long and intensive mental strain, the Archbishop of Reggie came into the Council with substantially the following argument to the party who held for Scripture alone:

"The Protestants claim to stand upon the written word only. They profess to hold the Scripture alone as the standard of faith. They justify their revolt by the plea that the Church has apostatized from the written word and follows tradition. Now the Protestants claim that they stand upon the written word only, is not true. Their profession of holding the Scripture alone as the standard of faith is false. PROOF: The written word explicitly enjoins the observance of the seventh day as the Sabbath. They do not observe the seventh day, but reject it. **If they do truly hold the scripture alone** as their standard, they would be observing the seventh day as is enjoined in the Scripture throughout. Yet they not only reject the observance of the Sabbath enjoined in the written word, but they have adopted and do practice the observance of Sunday, for which they have only the tradition of the Church. Consequently the claim of 'Scripture alone as the standard,' *fails;* and the doctrine of 'Scripture *and tradition'* as essential, is fully established, ***the Protestants themselves being judges.***"

Archbishop Reggio of Calabra made his speech at the last opening session of Trent, on the 18th of January, 1562. -- Heinrich Julius Holzmann, *Kanon und Tradition (Canon and Tradition)*, published in Ludwigsburg, Germany, in 1859, page 263.

There was no getting around this, for the Protestants' own statement of faith -- the Augsburg Confession, 1530 -- had clearly admitted that "the observation of the Lord's day" had been appointed by "the Church" only.

The argument was hailed in the Council as of Inspiration only; the party for "Scripture alone," surrendered; and the council at once unanimously condemned Protestantism and the whole Reformation as only an unwarranted revolt from the communion and authority of the Catholic Church; and proceeded, April 8, 1546, "to the promulgation of two decrees, the first of which, enacts under anathema, that Scripture *and tradition* are to be received and venerated equally, and that the deutero-canonical [the apocryphal] books are part of the canon of Scripture. The second decree declares the Vulgate to be the sole authentic and standard Latin version, and gives it such authority as to supersede the original texts; forbids the interpretation of Scripture contrary to the sense received by the Church, 'or even contrary to the unanimous consent of the Fathers,'" etc.

This was the inconsistency of the Protestant practice with the Protestant profession that gave to the Catholic Church her long-sought and anxiously desired ground upon which to condemn Protestantism and the whole Reformation movement as only a selfishly ambitious rebellion against the Church authority. And in this vital controversy the key, the chiefest and culminative expression, of the Protestant inconsistency was in the rejection of the Sabbath of the Lord, the seventh day, enjoined in the Scriptures, and the adoption and observance of the Sunday as enjoined by the Catholic Church.

And this is today the position of the respective parties to this controversy. Today, as this document shows, this is the vital issue upon which the Catholic Church arraigns Protestantism, and upon which she condemns the course of popular Protestantism as being "indefensible", self-contradictory, and suicidal." What will these Protestants, what will this Protestantism, do?

The Dignity of the Priesthood

These are some of the things the Catholics establishment say about themselves.

Priests are more important than humans. **Priests are chosen by God to manage on earth all his concerns and interests. As has been already said, all the lives of men and Angels are not capable of giving to God an infinite honor like that which a**

priest offers to Him by a single Mass. The dignity of the priest is also estimated from the power that he has over the real and the mystic body of Jesus Christ. With regard to the power of priests over the real body of Jesus Christ, it is of faith that when they pronounce the words of consecration the **Incarnate Word has obliged Himself to obey and to come into their hands under the Sacramental Species. (In other words they can make Jesus do what they want as He is under their control!). God Himself descends on the altar, that He comes wherever they call Him, and as often as they call Him, and places Himself in their hands, even though they should be His enemies. And after having come, He remains, entirely at their disposal; they move Him as they please, from one place to another; they may, if they wish, shut Him up in the tabernacle, or expose Him on the altar, or carry Him outside the church; they may, if they choose, eat His flesh and give Him for the food of others. "Oh, how very great is their power,"** says St. Laurence Justinian, speaking of priests. "A word falls from their lips and the body of Christ is there substantially formed from the matter of bread, and the Incarnate Word descended from Heaven, is found really present on the table of the altar! Never did Divine goodness give such power to the Angels. **The Angels abide by the order of God, but the priests take Him in their hands, distribute Him to the faithful, and partake of Him as food for themselves."**

God Himself descends on the altar, that He comes wherever they call Him, and as often as they call Him, and places Himself in their hands, even though they should be His enemies. And after having come, He remains, entirely at their disposal; they move Him as they please, from one place to another; they may, if they wish, shut Him up in the tabernacle, or expose Him on the altar, or carry Him outside the church; they may, if they choose, eat His flesh and give Him for the food of others. "Oh, how very great is their power," says St. Laurence Justinian, speaking of priests. "A word falls from their lips and the body of Christ is there substantially formed from the matter of bread, and the Incarnate Word descended from Heaven, is found really present on the table of the altar! Never did Divine goodness give such power to the Angels. The Angels abide by the order of God, but the priests take Him in their hands, distribute Him to the faithful, and partake of Him as food for themselves." Again meaning God Himself is subject to their directives. If they tell God to forgive someone He is obliged to obey. If they tell God to send someone to hell, similarly their claim He is to obey. This is not the case as the story of Balaam shows. Earthly acts must be in line with God's commands (Num 22:6 - 24:13 especially 23:8, 11, 20, <u>26, 24:13</u>). **The sentence of the priest precedes, and God subscribes to it, writes St. Peter Damian. Hence, St John Chrysostom thus concludes: The sovereign Master of the universe only follows the servant by confirming in Heaven all that the latter decides upon earth." Priests are the dispensers of the Divine graces. Were the Redeemer to descend into a church, and sit in a confessional to administer the Sacrament of Penance, and a priest to sit in another confessional, Jesus would say over each penitent, "Ego te absolvo," the priest would likewise say over each of his penitents, "Ego te absolvo," and the**

penitents of each would be equally absolved. **How great the honour that a king would confer on a subject whom he should empower to rescue from prison as many as he pleased! But far greater is the power that the eternal Father has given to Jesus Christ, and that Jesus Christ has given to his priests, to rescue from Hell not only the bodies but also the souls of the faithful**: "The Son," says St. John Chrysostom, All **the Angels in Heaven cannot absolve from a single sin.** So if the bible through the word of God says the soul that sinneth shall die, go to hell, the priests can supposedly take them out of hell where God sent them! Of the many biblical texts contradicting this Catholic view I shall quote two: Rev 3:7 And to the angel of the church in Philadelphia write; These things saith he that is holy, he that is true, he that hath the key of David, he that openeth, and no man shutteth; and shutteth, and no man openeth; Rev 22:11 He that is unjust, let him be unjust still: and he which is filthy, let him be filthy still: and he that is righteous, let him be righteous still: and he that is holy, let him be holy still.

Lev 26:1 Ye shall make you no idols nor graven image, neither rear you up a standing image, neither shall ye set up *any* image of stone in your land, to bow down unto it: for I *am* the LORD your God.

I saw this warning to those allergic to nuts on a packet of artificial nuts made from Soya beans "RECIPE: No nuts. Ingredients cannot guarantee nut free because in the factory before being prepared for the manufacture of this product, the equipment was previously used to make products containing nuts". If Christians knew of the pagan origins of Valentines, Christmas and such popularly celebrations, true ones would not keep them. This book is limited; but a search and study on the following words should assist in discovering the history of Valentines. Not the false cover up stories.

"Lupercalia" or "day of the wolf." This was a day that was sacred to the sexual frenzy of the goddess Juno. This day also honored the Roman gods, Lupercus and Faunus, as well as the legendary twin brothers, who supposedly founded Rome, Remus and Romulus. These two are said to have been suckled by wolves in a cave on Palatine Hill in Rome. The cave was called Lupercal and was the center of the celebrating on the eve of Lupercalia or February 14th. On this day, Lupercalia, which was later named Valentine's Day, the Luperci or priests of Lupercus dressed in goatskins for a bloody ceremony… (hence red colour!).

If you practice anything with pagan and ungodly origins, sticking a Christian, love or other label on it does not change it!

CELEBRATING THE 1ST DAY OF THE WEEK

There is no instruction given or precedent set by either Jesus, His apostles or any early bible Christian to celebrate the first day of the week to Jesus or God. You will read confirmation of this by many other denomination heads and bible scholars. However, let us take an independent look again. The reason generally given is to celebrate Jesus' resurrection on the first day of the week, today's Sunday. The only commandment Jesus gave for a remembrance of Him is found in Luke 22:19, the breaking of bread at the last supper. It is not for us to create reasons; especially false ones. He also said 'if thou will enter into life, keep the commandments' (Matt 19:17).From Genesis 2:3 the Old Testament refers to keeping the Seventh day and commandments hundreds of times and God killed those who did not, such as the man collecting sticks on the Sabbath (Numbers 15:35) and provided for those who did (Exodus 16:5). From Matthew 5:19 to Revelation 22:14 the New Testament does the same. The Old Testament narrates God's commands to His people, how they dealt with the challenge and the results. New Testament followers are to learn from the Old's blue print and not make the same mistakes. Nothing significantly changed. The character of God is such that He is very specific, total truth and righteousness. He operates on everlasting principles. Lev 27:10 He shall not alter it, nor change it, a good for a bad, or a bad for a good: and if he shall at all change beast for beast, then it and the exchange thereof shall be holy. He will I not break, nor alter the thing that is gone out of His lips. (Psa 89:4) nor accepts an unholy substitute of His day. He and no one else can make a day or period of time holy. An authority that changes its word cannot be trusted and is not respected. No different to a parent setting boundaries to a child and does not stick to them. Esther 8:8 …for the writing which is written in the king's name, and sealed with the king's ring, may no man reverse. Dan 6:12 … The thing *is* true, according to the law of the Medes and Persians, which altereth not. Mar 6:24 And she went forth, and said unto her mother, What shall I ask? And she said, The head of John the Baptist.

Matthew 24:20 'but pray that your flight be not in the winter, neither on the Sabbath day'. Jesus advises his followers to pray to His Father to arrange circumstances for the early church that Sabbath observance would be made easier for them at the time of Jerusalem's capture; an event which took place some 40 years after the crucifixion (in A.D. 70). Ask yourself this question – if the Sabbath commandment was scheduled for cancellation at the cross, then why did Jesus give His disciples this instruction about keeping the Sabbath? The answer is obvious – the Sabbath commandment was not scheduled for cancellation at the cross, it was to continue. The Saviour knew this, and that is why He advised his followers to pray to God to arrange a weekday flight from Jerusalem. They would not be exposed to the temptation of breaking the Sabbath commandment in their haste to get away from the besieged city.

Matthew 5:17-18 "Think not that I am come to destroy the law, or the prophets; I am not come to destroy but to fulfil. For verily I say unto you, till heaven and earth pass, one jot or one tittle shall in no way pass from the law". The Jews then referred to the first five books of the bible as the Torah or the Law. In these books God Himself speaks. Thereafter it is via His prophets. Jesus was clearly saying He had not come to destroy those five books or what followed by the prophets. The meaning of the word fulfil is to establish or confirm (Matt 2:17; 12:17) . From this sentence three points can be seen supporting the Sabbath. Fulfil, means whatever the law and prophets predicted has happened. They predicted the coming of a Messiah. Jesus was that Messiah. Thus He fulfilled their prediction as in Mat 3:15 And Jesus answering said unto him, Suffer *it to be so* now: for thus it becometh us to fulfil all righteousness. Then he suffered him. Did righteousness then end?. (Deu 6:25 and it shall be our righteousness, if we observe to do all these commandments before the LORD our God, as he hath commanded us.) .Zec 9:9 predicted the event of Matt 21:5 … Behold, thy King cometh unto thee, meek, and sitting upon an ass, and a colt the foal of an ass. (see also Isa 53:6; John 5:46; In Luke 4:21 Jesus quoted Isa 61:1. Paul in Acts 17:2 -3 used the scriptures to prove Jesus was the prophesised Messiah. Philip in Acts 8:32 -35 used Isaiah to preach to the Eunuch about the coming of Jesus. Jesus Himself used the scriptures to explain He was the Messiah. Nowhere in the scriptures does any text or prophet say the Commandments will end or be changed by Jesus.

If something is changed, the old form no longer exists. It has been replaced by a new form. Thus the old has been destroyed. Jesus clearly says he has not come to destroy the old. Has heaven and earth passed away yet? Or will it pass away after the day of judgement as in 2 Peter 3:10"But the day of the Lord will come as a thief in the night; in the which the heavens shall pass away with a great noise, and the elements shall melt with fervent heat, the earth also and the works that are therein shall be burned up" Jesus talked about many things being fulfilled. Destruction of the temple, persecution of His followers, etc. When these happened, it did not change anything only that they happened. The Old Testament predicted the coming of a Messiah, i.e. Jesus. John 5:39 Search the scriptures; for in them ye think ye have eternal life: and they are they which testify of me: not that law will be changed.   Nowhere is it predicted God's laws and commandments will change, only that some may think to change them (Daniel 7:25). Thus "fulfil" does not mean to change or cancel. Fulfilling a task does not mean changing it. If I have a blueprint to build a house and fulfil the task, all it means is that I have completed building the house according to plan. But, if it got damaged, I go back to the blueprint and fix it (repair it) accordingly. We were told verbally, in writing and by Jesus' example. There is no more ways to tell us. If we choose to disobey, admit it. Some other scripture uses of fulfil (see also Interpreting the Bible, Choice of Commentary") John 19:28 after this, Jesus knowing that all things were now accomplished, that the scripture might be fulfilled, saith, I thirst. Joh 19:36 for these things were done, that the scripture should be fulfilled, A bone of him shall not be broken. Jesus being the Passover lamb Exo 12:46 in one house shall it be eaten; thou shalt not carry forth ought of the flesh abroad out of the house; neither shall ye break a bone thereof. Luk 4:18 – 21 and he began to say unto them, this day is this scripture fulfilled in your ears. Rom 8:4

In the sixty plus years of the New Testament, reference is made numerous times to Jesus and his apostles keeping the Sabbath (Saturday). It is the nine uses of the words "first day" later termed "Lord's day" by Rome, that has been put forward for a change to Sunday (by those ignorant of the historic documented change that took place hundreds of years after Christ's death). Nine, which are misinterpreted, compared to the numerous that are clear .I will deal with these separately later; but briefly, the "Lord's Day" or generally called "the day of the Lord" in the bible, does not refer to the first day of the week, any particularly numbered or named day. It refers to a time, the day of judgement as in 2 Peter 3:10, Zephaniah 1:7. and Amo 5:20 *Shall* not the day of the LORD *be* darkness, and not light? even very dark, and no brightness in it?

Revelation 1:10 speaks of "the Lord's day". The phase is a typical term used for the Sunday day of worship observed by post Rome's merger with early Christians because, they claim, that was the day of the Lord's resurrection. The term could just as well be referring to the seventh Sabbath Day. However, the "Lord's day" was a Roman term for the day the emperor (the lord) collected taxes (his pay day). In addition to the status and title of "lord", some other claims of Caesar, the Roman emperor, are the son of the gods, the saviour of the world. This is one reason why they were so against the early Christians who claimed there was a real Lord, son of God and saviour of the world; Jesus. Polycarp, the bishop of the church in Smyrna (Rev 2:8), was martyred there in A.D. 156 for refusing to call Caesar "Lord". The Christians there also suffered greatly for refusing to worship Caesar(see Appendixes for the successors to this claim). From here stemmed the age of the state church, which Constantine continued until the first pope was recognised to have authority over the Roman Catholic Church (A.D. 313-590). Acts 12:22-23 "And upon a set day Herod, arrayed in royal apparel, sat upon his throne, and made an oration unto them. And the people gave a shout, saying, It is the voice of a god, and not of a man. immediately the angel of the Lord smote him, because he gave not God the glory: and he was eaten of worms, and gave up the ghost"

Like other mergers between pagan Rome and persecuted Christians, this "Lord's day" reference was imposed on Christians (post apostle period) as a reference to Jesus and pagan gods were made saints. According to how deep your research goes you may uncover that the same images of pagan god's were substituted for those of saints. For example, in St Peter's Church in Rome, the statute of St Peter with the apparent halo was that of Jupiter. The only difference was the apparent halo (sun disc) placed around their heads. We now see this same sun disc placed around the head of Jesus, Mary and other appointed saints and called a halo. The sun was thought to chase away darkness and evil. These images of sun disc are built into the Catholic's worship system with the priest offering the sun shaped communion bread up to the air (sun) and, at least in the churches I once attended, the circular image appears around the chalice etc. The excuse of celebrating Jesus' resurrection came later. Where in the bible does Jesus say to remember his resurrection? NOWHERE. Or his birth? NOWHERE. We are not to remember nor celebrate the day of his resurrection only the fact that He did.1 Corin 15:14 and if Christ be not risen, then is our preaching vain, and your faith is also vain. He had to rise on one day or another. Would we be celebrating Tuesday or Wednesday if that was the day he rose? How was He to stop us celebrating a day, by not rising from the dead?

Another misconception is that when Paul is saying the gentiles did not need to keep the "law" saved by "grace", he was referring to the one of circumcision not the commandments (See Circumcision section below)."Grace" is covered in a separate section below. Need for gentile circumcision was a bone of contention Paul had with the other apostles. I John 3:4 says "Whosoever committeth sin transgresseth also the law: for sin is the transgression of the law". Would Paul really be saying we are no longer under the law, there is no more sin, one can now come and take / steal your property? If one carefully reads the whole of Paul's writings on this subject, he is trying to win the gentiles over and believe that putting a yolk on them that the Jews themselves found hard to keep would be detrimental to his efforts. Should we not follow God's commandments because we find it hard, grievous or inconvenient? "He that saith, I know Him and keep not his commandments, is a liar, and the truth is not in him" (1 John 2:4)."For this is the love of God, that we keep His commandments: and His commandments are not grievous" (1 John 5:3).There are numerous scripture records of God's and Jesus' divine decree to keep and maintain the Sabbath as a perpetual sign as belonging to Him to the end. No such similar decree cancelling or appointing a new day.

Some cite Acts 2:1, the Day of Pentecost as evidence of a Sunday gathering. This Sunday gathering did not start with Acts 2:1. It was one of the prescribed feasts days mentioned in (the O.T.) Leviticus 23:16, Ex 23:14, Deut 16:9-12. Initially called the Feast of Harvest or First Fruits (many churches keep a Harvest Sunday, though at slightly the wrong time), later called the Feast of Weeks and in the N.T. Pentecost. The apostles were celebrating an old feasts knowing that all Jewish men would be coming to Jerusalem for the annual pilgrimage. Note Luke 24:49 and Acts 8:27-28. This day being fifty days (the day after seven Sabbaths) after the beginning of the Feast of Weeks. So of course it would always fall on the first day of the week.

Regarding the nine times when the bible refers to the first day of the week, the reasons are as follows Gen 1:3-5 deals with the light God made on the first day of the week. It says nothing about the Sabbath one way or the other. In the early century A.D. an excuse for the worship of the Sun was taken from Genesis 1:3 "let there be light". This is not a biblical doctrine for Sun-day observance are, God commanded and in Gen 1:14 –16 shows the sun was created on the fourth day. "… to give light upon the earth... two great lights … the greater (sun) to rule the day and the lesser to rule the night (moon).

The following five verses quote the "first day of the week" (Sunday after Christ's crucifixion) and refer to the same event (Matt 28:1, Mark 16:1-2, Mark 16:9, Luke 24:1, John 20:1).Using Matt 28:1 as an example "In the end of the Sabbath, as it began to dawn on the first day of the week, came Mary Magdalene and the other Mary to see the sepulchre." These five texts concern events that took place on the morning when Mary Magdalene and some others brought spices to anoint the body of the Master. The morning of the first day of the week, that is Sunday morning. Note they kept the Sabbath. Rushing to get Jesus into the tomb and preparing spices before sunset Friday. Then in their eagerness, as soon as the Sabbath had passed they, early in the morning of the first day, rushed to the tomb. No change in Sabbath observance.

John 20:19 'then the same day at evening, being the first day of the week, when the doors were shut where the disciples were assembled for fear of the Jews, came Jesus and stood in the midst and saith unto them "Peace be unto you"'. This meeting took place on the Sunday evening after the resurrection. The meeting was not to celebrate Jesus rising as some did not believe (Mark 16:11-14, Luke 24:36-38) it was for 'fear of the Jews'. No mention of the Sabbath or a change. They had kept the Sabbath the previous day.

Acts 20:7 'and upon the first day of the week, the disciples came together to break bread, Paul preached unto them, ready to depart on the morrow, and continued his speech until midnight'. This text is also put forward as 'proof' of Sunday sacredness; but examination of the whole chapter shows:

a)   The meeting was held on the evening of the 1st day (probably because all were at work during the day) and continued till midnight or later. According to which sunset one calculates the 1st day started, the meeting either began Saturday evening till early Sunday morning or Sunday evening till Monday morning. see Gen 1 and John 20:19). The breaking of bread took place after midnight (verse 11).Paul and friends, after bidding farewell walked from Traos to Assos (verse 13), a distance of about 18 miles. So either Paul was walking 18 miles through rough terrain on the Sunday, which is no way for Paul a life long Sabbath keeper to do, or the breaking of bread took place on the Monday. It should be clear that this was simply a farewell meal after a meeting the day before Paul's departure. The term breaking bread was the common way of saying having a meal. See Ruth 1:6 "giving them bread" meaning God gave them food and prosperity. Job 22:7, Prov 9:17, Isaiah 33:16, 55:10, Matt 6:11 "our daily bread" = meal, Matt 15:26 "to take children bread" = food.2 Thes 3:8 "neither did we eat any man's bread" = take his food. Acts 2:46 shows they broke bread everyday as they ate everyday. Nothing special. Even today we use the word BREAD to mean MONEY (ability to feed ourselves). We say, got to work to make some bread, got bring home the bread or dough.

Corin. 16:1-3 'now concerning the collection for the saints, as I have given order to the churches of Galatia, even do ye.Upon the first day of the week let every one of you lay by him in store as God hath prospered him, that there be no gatherings when I come. And when I come, whomsoever ye shall approve by your letters, them will I send to bring your liberality unto Jerusalem.' Here Paul is instructing believers in Corinth to privately set aside some money for the famine stricken brethren in Jerusalem. The Greek word thesaurion means 'treasuring or storing up', meaning lay by him in store, which is translated 'with one's self' i.e. at home. Hence there was no church meeting and this was not a collection in church. This was so when Paul came time would be saved in going around for a collection. already privately saved sums could be totalled and taken by trustworthy brethren to Jerusalem. The collaboration is in Acts 11:29 "then the disciples, every man according to his ability, determined to send relief onto the brethren which lived in Judea. Which also they did and sent to the elders with

Barnabas and Paul". Trophimus, mentioned in 2 Tim 4:20, was an Ephesian Christian who accompanied Paul to Jerusalem as one of the delegates of the Asian churches bringing the collection for church leaders there (Acts 20:1-5). Sabbath or a change is not mentioned. The Corinthian use of the words first day therefore does not say the day was holy.

Acts 17:2 Paul went in unto them and three Sabbaths reasoned (taught) with them out of the scriptures. Acts 13:42 "and when the Jews had gone out of the synagogue, the Gentiles besought that these words might be preached to them the next Sabbath". This was 30 or so years after Jesus' death. If there was a Sunday observance, why would the Gentiles not request teaching the next or any other Sunday? Why specifically the next Sabbath? Because, clearly all Christians and those wishing to follow Jesus kept the Sabbath. God changes not, his commandments change not. The criteria of salvation must be same for all humans. No distinction for race or when born, before or after Jesus. Otherwise God would be accused of being unfair. One who didn't make it into heaven because they were born before Jesus', or on a piece of land making them Jew or Gentile, would say "I could have done that. If you had made it as easy for me born in B.C. as those born in A.D. or into that family rather than this Jewish one, I would be in heaven. It is therefore your fault God why I am in hell". Unless the criterion is the same, no matter how minute the difference, one would pick on it to accuse God.

Rev 6:11 speaks of the righteous dead being at 'rest', Jesus said 'I will give you rest', In Palm 95:11 and Heb 3:11 God says the disobedient shall 'not enter into my rest'. 's 'rest' is on the Sabbath day, (Saturday). To enter into His rest we must do like Him when he did not on a separate day (Sunday) as we shall be in our rest not His. Heb 4:3 "For we which have believed do enter into rest, as he said, as I have sworn in my wrath, if they shall enter into my rest: although the works were finished from the FOUNDATION of the world. he spake in a certain place of the seventh day on this wise, And God did rest the seventh day from all his works." This day was from creation, before any Jew or Gentile or given to Moses in set of Ten Commandments. Therefore is for all mankind. Heb 4:10-11 "There remaineth therefore a rest to the people of God. For he that is entered into his rest, he also hath ceased from his own works, as God did from his. Let us labour therefore to enter into THAT rest, lest any man fall after the same example of unbelief". one's priority were to seek to serve God no matter what the sacrifice and not follow custom they would see that the whole bible supports Sabbath maintenance. Where is God, what is His will that we should be carrying out? Our father who are in heaven. Thy will be done on earth AS IT IS IN Heaven .Is God resting or keeping a Sunday Sabbath in Heaven? If we are to enter into His rest, we are to do as He does! Rest is not to look at television; but cease from work so ones brain and body is free to worship God as ones mind and body cannot do the two simultaneously .Worship with "mind, body and soul" or "all might".35:2 "Six days shall work be done, but on the seventh day there shall be to you a **holy day**, a Sabbath of rest **to the LORD**: whosoever doeth work therein shall be put to death". Not a mere rest as one does under other circumstances. Resting does not make a day or period holy. It is holy because God designated the seventh day as such. Then it is to be given

to the Lord by living in it His word, dedicating your time to Him.

Then ask how did Jesus and God's people keep it in the past and do likewise.

Did the apostles keep the Sabbath? Some say Jesus only kept the Sabbath because he was a Jew and that His apostles changed to Sunday. This was an answer given to me by my former priest under the Catholic religion. I considered whether it is likely that these dedicated apostles, following Jesus around for three and a half years, attending the synagogue weekly on the Sabbath, would, the day after He dies or rise change an almost 200 weekly practice to observing Sunday. Especially when that was the day kept by sun worshippers and taught by God not to do (worship stars, planets etc). I decided it was illogical and uncharacteristic, especially since they had no commandment to do so. The bible, Acts 13:14, and 42 for example, supports my decision. ("the next Sabbath"). Why the next Sabbath? Why not the next day, Sunday, or any other weekly day? Then verse 44 reads "and the next Sabbath day came almost the whole city together to hear the word of God." Same questions, why specifically on the Sabbath if they were not observing it? Clearly the Sabbath was a special day kept by the apostles and the whole city of those wanting to be God's people.

There are other texts like Acts 16:13, 17:2 which reads "And Paul, as his manner was, went in unto them, and three Sabbath days reasoned with them out of the scriptures," Why not three consecutive days, or other days? Acts18:4 "And he reasoned in the synagogue every Sabbath, and persuaded the Jews and the Greeks". Now we have not only the Jews; but non Jews, i.e. Greeks. Acts 13:44 and the next Sabbath day came almost the whole city to hear the word of God. V46 Then Paul and Barnabas waxed bold, and said, it was necessary that the word of God should first have been spoken to you: but seeing ye put it from you, and judge yourselves unworthy of everlasting life, lo, we turn to the Gentiles. Act 18:6when they opposed themselves, and blasphemed, he shook his raiment, and said unto them, your blood be upon your own heads; I am clean: from henceforth I will go unto the Gentiles. Acts 14:1 And it came to pass in Iconium, that they went both together into the synagogue of the Jews, and so spake, that a great multitude both of the Jews and also of the Greeks believed.

The Book of Acts was written by Luke to Theophilus as a supplement to the Gospel of Luke. The Gospels relay "all that Jesus began both to do and teach" (Acts 1:1). Luke's gospel was written thirty years after Jesus' death, yet there is no mention of Sunday observance for Christians. . Now we know that Jesus came to the "house of Israel" to teach and correct improper scripture interpretation. This correction at times contradicted that of the religious leaders of the time. The "house" being God's people, inclusive of strangers that is born in the house, or bought with money of any stranger, which is not of thy seed" (Gen 17:12).Acts continues Jesus' teaching through the apostles fulfilling His commandment to go and teach all nations (the whole world). Part of this teaching was their ability, through the holy spirit, to communicate (be heard) in different languages (tongues) by those travellers congregating from around the world in Jerusalem for the Feast of Harvest or First fruits called in New Testament Pentecost. They had already been taught the scriptures, given power to heal, forgive or bind sins.

What was missing was the final ability, that of spreading the gospel through communication with person of other languages. Today we have the gospel translated into any language necessary. At the time of each of these feasts all males were to make a pilgrimage to the sanctuary, which was at this time the tabernacle and later became the temple after its construction. So you see the apostles kept the Old Testament festivals and Sabbaths after Jesus' death. These hearers would then return to their country of residence and take the gospel with them to propagate to others of the area (i.e. see Acts 8:27-28).

So what have we so far? Jesus born a Jew, doing as they did, raised in adherence to the festivals, Sabbaths and scripture. Continuing in the same manner as adult and teaching mainly Jewish apostles, (who like Him followed the same festivals, Sabbaths, scriptures). Then after His death continue doing what He did, keeping the feasts to which they were accustom, spread these same teaching to other Jews and the world. Acts 18:21 "Bade them farewell, saying I must by all means keep this feasts that cometh in Jerusalem" see also Acts 21:24.How this was done is recorded in Acts and prophesised by Jesus in Acts 1:8 "… and ye shall be witnesses onto me both in Jerusalem and in all Judea and in Samaria and unto the uttermost part of the earth". The bad news to almost all Christians is that the early teachings have been hijacked by the devil's agents (false teachers state and law makers) so that what they are practicing 2000 years later is not what God wants of them and, unless they research, are unlikely to get on that straight road to the true God "which "many seek but few find". Let us examine where it went wrong.

Colossians 2:16-17 "Let no man therefore judge you in meat, or in drink, or in respect of a holyday, or of the new moon, or of the Sabbath days". People misinterpret this text as authority to worship on any day. This is one example where persons have to know their bible. They do not know the difference between "The" seventh day Sabbath and other Sabbath days. These are covered in Leviticus 23.It starts with the seventh day Sabbath in 23:3, then lists other feast days. Verse 32 reads "It shall be unto you a Sabbath of rest. Verse 39 reads "Also in the fifteenth day of the seventh month, when ye have gathered in the fruit of the land, ye shall keep a feast unto the LORD seven days: on the first day shall be a Sabbath, and on the eighth day shall be a Sabbath." So you see there are many sabbaths. Apart from the point that Paul could be saying no "man" (human) should be the judge; but God (Rom 14:4) . I doubt Paul was advocating the eating of meats offered to idols as this was clearly forbidden; i.e. in Acts 15:29. The meaning of this verse is similar to that of Romans 14:5"one man esteemth (considers) one day more sacred than another; another man considers every day alike. Each one should be fully convinced in his own mind". Paul was addressing new comers to Christianity from pagan Roman gods worship. Their former religion had gods for every day of the week. Each person worshiped the god they thought was more powerful or relevant to them. Each to his own choice. The concern that gave rise to Paul's advise was that new converts were concerned about eating meat offered to their former idol gods. The pagan temple was the market place to buy ones meat for food consumption. These sold meats were offered to the pagan gods before going on sale. There was two schools of thought as to whether it was permitted to eat such meat and those who did not were accusing those who did (1Cor 8). One example of how the pagan systems were a religion is seen in the underlined words of Acts 14:13 "Then the priest of Jupiter, which was before their city, brought oxen and garlands unto the gates, and would have done sacrifice with the people". 1Co 10:21 "Ye cannot drink the cup of the Lord, and the cup of devils: ye cannot be partakers of the Lord's table, and of the table of devils". One cannot mix things historically offered to devils (Sun day, the day of the Sun god) to God. Many flock to churches on Sunday for worship as the pagan Sun worshippers of old.

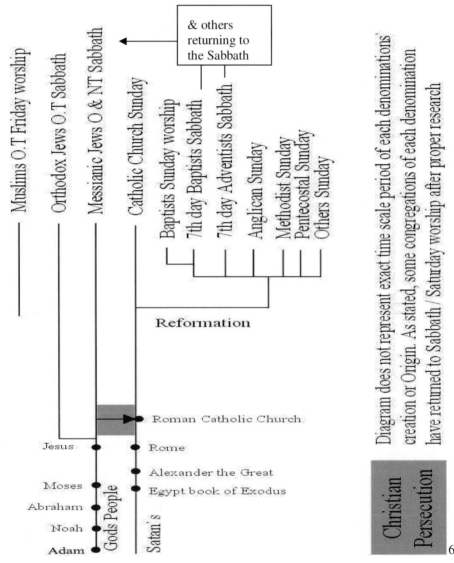

A famous plaque found in carved into stone walls in Egyptian temples. It is of Heleos a human emperor apparently becoming a god and ascending to the father of gods in heaven, the sun god. A similar one exists for Alexandra the Great. Notice the suns rays around his head. This plaque is centuries before the birth of Jesus. St Peter's Cathedral in Rome, the mother church of the Roman Catholic has a similar pictoral of Jesus ascending to heaven in a chariot with a halo / sun disc around His head. Today the same sun rays, or the "halo" version is seen around the head and heart of portraits of Jesus, Mary and made up saints of the Catholic Church. Similarly, statutes of Mary holding the apparent baby Jesus and the statute of St. Peter are centuries old pagan gods transferred into Christianity by the Rome Catholic Church and attributed Christian names. With the following photos of their gods, notice the sun disc on each.

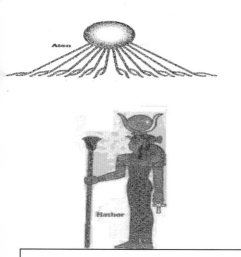

ATEN: The sun as the sole divinity and vital force, embracing the whole world and manifested everywhere in nature. The worship of the Aten – the first monotheistic religion doctrine – was made the state religion by Akhenaten, a fanatical opponent of the polytheism which hitherto prevailed in Egypt. Though first referred to around 1900 **B.C.** This briefly became the chief deity during the Armarna Period (c 1360 –1335 B.C.) the doctrine of the Aten contains some astonishingly modern conceptions. Represented as a solar disk with rays ending in hands. Note how sun and its rays depicted on many things including the Statute of Liberty,

HATHOR: some Gods had different roles in different parts of Egypt. Hathor, known as goddess of love, music, dance, pleasure, lady of drunkenness was shown as a woman or cow. In the Delta she associated with the sky and held the sun between her horns. In Thebes she was a goddess of death.

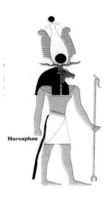

RA HARAKHTY: Sun-disk on head, hawk-headed SUN god identified with Harakhty and primeval creator god Atum as Ra Harakhty-Atum. Often linked with other gods (Amonre etc.) Heliopolis, as, a state god of the new kingdom worshiped at many other places.

Osiris: Mummiform, scepter and flagellum white crown with plumes and horns dying god of vegetation ruler of netherworld. At first he was fertility god, responsible for the floods that brought new life to Egypt every year. As the first king to survive death, he became a god of rebirth.

Harsaphes: Ram-headed or ram / gained importance during the 1st intermediate period when Herakleopohs was Egypt's northern capital. Closely connected with Ra, Osiris and Amun / ihnasya el-Medina.

MONTU: Often hawk-headed, sun-disk and two plumes/was god, connected with the Buchis bull of Armant, but also Karnak, Tod, Nag el-Madamud

SOBEK: Crocodile or crocodile-headed / the Faiyum, but also el-Qibly near el-Rizeiqat (Sumenu), Gebeleil, Esna and Kom Ombo.

APIS: Bull with markings on hide and sun disk between horns or bull-headed / connected with Ptah burial place at Saqqara.

Apis

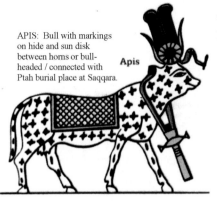

BELOW: SOME ANCIENT EGYPTIAN HEAD DRESS, WITH MODERN DAY CATHOLIC POPE'S

Khnum

Khons

Hathor, Isis

Ra- Horakhty, Sekhmet

Third / Wadjet Eye of Horus who set out to avenge his father's death, eventually

Sobek

vanquishing Seth and took the throne; but in the many fights, lost an eye.

(Left) The plaque of the cornerstone doesnt lie. (Top right) Statute of Liberty (Top left) statute of goddess Ishtar.

You probably didn't realize it but America is steeped in I dols! Yes and the Statue of Liberty is actually a replica of the Babylonian goddess Ishtar the Mother of Harlots and the goddess of Freedom /Liberty. This "artwork" was created by a Freemason who wanted to honor a Masonic doctrine that dates back to before Nimrod!

The Statue of Liberty is another Brotherhood symbol highlighting the lighted torch. The Statue of Liberty is actually the Statue of Liberties – the liberties perpetrated on the American people by the Brotherhood. There she stands on her island in New York Harbour holding her torch of freedom and Americans believe she is the symbol of their liberty in the Land of the Free. Nothing could be further from the truth. The Statue of Liberty was given to New York by French Freemasons and her mirror image stands on an island in the River Seine in Paris. These statues of liberty are representations of Ishtar and Isis et al, with the rays of the Sun around her head. The ancients symbolized the Sun in this way. And they are not holding the torch of liberty, but the torch of the illuminated ones, the reptilian Elite. The Statue of Liberty is a Brotherhood symbol which says: We control this country and we are telling you so, but you are too blind to see it!

The Freemasonry Connection

The Statue of Liberty in New York harbour was presented in 1884 as a gift from the French Grand Orient Temple Masons to the Masons of America in celebration of the centenary of the first Masonic Republic. The maker of the statue was Freemason Frederic-Auguste Bartholdi. He had already made a statue of the Freemason Marquis de Lafayette for the city of New York, for the occasion of the centenary of the signing of the Declaration of Independence. Bartholdi sailed to America, at the suggestion of other Freemasons and kindred spirits in France, for the purpose of proposing the project. Although he had no

70

drawings as he set sail, his Masonic biographer writes, as he entered New York harbor, *"he caught a vision of a magnificent goddess (Nimrod's Semiramis — Isis or Astarte), holding aloft a torch (of Illuminism) in one hand and welcoming all visitors to the land of freedom and opportunity"* (signifying Brotherhood control of the American people by the *"liberties"* perpetrated against them).Returning to France, he managed to raise, through the help of a great deal of Masonic propaganda, the sum of 3,500,000 French francs, a very large sum for the 1870's. For the face of his *"Goddess of Liberty"* he chose his own mother.

Structural framework was provided by Freemason Gustave Eiffel, later to be famous for the 984-feet (300-meter) high Eiffel Tower. Although financial support for the statue was forthcoming in France, America was not willing to put up the money for the pedestal. It was Joseph Pulitzer, the owner and editor of the *New York World,* who managed to raise over $100,000 for the project.

On Washington's Birthday in 1877, Congress accepted the statue as a gift from the French people. Bedloe's Island, now Liberty Island, was chosen by General Sherman, the well-known Atlanta-burner. Meanwhile in Paris the work gradually progressed. Levi P. Morton, the then Ambassador to France, drove the first rivet. The statue was finished on May 21, 1884, and presented to Ambassador Levi Morton on July 4th of the same year by Ferdinand de Lesseps, builder of the Suez canal.

On the American side, the chairman of the American committee to receive the statue contacted the Grand Lodge of the Free and Accepted Masons of the State of New York. It had been a tradition in America to have the cornerstone of major public and private buildings and monuments *"consecrated"* with full Masonic rites, ever since Freemason George Washington, in 1793, had personally laid the cornerstone of the Capitol, with the assistance of the Grand Lodge of Maryland.

The decorated vessel *'Bay Ridge'* carried about a hundred Freemasons, along with some civil officials, to Bedloe's Island. Freemason Richard M. Hunt, the principal architect of the pedestal, handed the working tools to the Masonic officers.

Then Freemason Edward M.,L. Ehlers, Grand Secretary and a member of the Continental Lodge 287, read the list of items to be included in the copper box within the cornerstone: a copy of the United States Constitution; George Washington's Farewell Address; twenty bronze medals of Presidents up through Chester A. Arthur [including Washington, Monroe, Jackson, Polk, Buchanan, Johnson and Garfield, who were all Freemasons]; copies of New York City newspapers; a portrait of Bartholdi; a copy of 'Poem on Liberty' by E. R. Johnes; and a list on parchment of the Grand Lodge officers.

The traditional Masonic ceremony was observed. The cornerstone being found square, level and plumb, the Grand Master applied the mortar and had the stone lowered into place. He then struck the stone three times, and declared it duly laid. Then the elements of *"consecration"* were presented, corn, wine, and oil.

The *"Most Worshipful"* Grand Master then spoke a few words. He posed the question: *"Why call upon the Masonic Fraternity to lay the cornerstone of such a structure as is here to be erected?"*

His answer was: *"No institution has done more to promote liberty and to free men from the trammels and chains of ignorance and tyranny than has Freemasonry."*

The principal address was given by the Deputy Grand Master: *"Massive as this statue is, its physical proportions sink into comparative obscurity when contrasted with the nobility of its concept. Liberty Enlightening the World! How lofty the thought! To be free, is the first, the noblest aspiration of the human breast. And it is now a univally admitted truth that only in proportion as men become possessed of liberty, do they become civilized, enlightened and useful."*

The statue arrived in dismantled pieces in June of 1885. The statue was dedicated on October 28, 1886. President Grover Cleveland [who although sympathetically disposed toward the craft was not a Freemason] presided over the ceremony and Freemason Henry Potter, Episcopal Bishop of New York gave the invocation. Freemason Bartholdi pulled the tricolor French flag off the statue's face. The main address was given by Freemason Chauncey M. Depew, a United States Senator.

She is holding the Masonic "Torch of Enlightenment". Also referred to back in the 1700's by the Illuminati Masons as the "Flaming Torch of Reason". The Torch represents the "Sun" in the sky.

The Statue of Liberty's official title is, "Liberty Enlightening the World".

The cornerstone of the statue records how it was laid in a Masonic ceremony

THE TORCH SYMBOL

Illuminati means to "bare light" one way to symbolize this is by carrying a torch. A torch sits on top of the Statue of Liberty, on top of JFK's grave, and on top of the tunnel where Princess Diana was killed.

Best selling author, Robert Bauval:

"The cornerstone for the Statue of Liberty was placed in a solemn ceremony in 1884 organised by the Masonic lodges of New York.

The Statue of Liberty, which was designed by the French sculptor Bartholdi and actually built by the French Engineer, Gustave Eiffel (both well-known Freemasons), was not originally a 'Statue of Liberty' at all, but first planned by Bartholdi for the opening of the Suez Canal in Egypt in 1867.

Bartholdi, like many French Freemasons of his time, was deeply steeped in 'Egyptian' rituals, and it has often been said that he conceived the original statue as an effigy of the goddess Isis, and only later converted it to a 'Statue of Liberty' for New York harbour when it was rejected for the Suez Canal."

The goddess Isis is known by many names, including Juno

From another article by Bauval:

"The 'torch' analogy is very interesting. The original statue of Bartholdi destined first for Port Said at the mouth of the Suez Canal, was also to bear a torch intended to symbolise 'the Orient showing the way'. The 'Grand Orient', of course, is the name of the French Masonic mother lodge, and to which Bartholdi belonged. There is another similar 'torch' that played a strange role in the French Revolution, but of which I will reveal later in my forthcoming book "Talisman". It still is to be seen in the skyline of Paris today.

People today do not realise the power of such symbolism, and how they can be used with devastating effect on the minds of the unsuspecting masses. And this is worrying. The SS Nazi movement made prolific use of all these 'symbol games', and wreeked havoc in the world.

TEST TWO WHAT DOES THE BIBLE SAY.

For the purist, I have only put "What Does the Bible Say" as the second test in an effort to aid the reader in following how the false teachings and mis-interpretation came into Christianity. Originally it was, as it should always be, the first test.

Difference between the Commandments, the Law and Statutes.

The laws and commandments were present before the Jews, Moses or Mount Sinai. Which should indicate they were for the human race from the start; For example in Gen 4:4 1st fruits and firstling were offered before Leviticus laws given to Moses. Ex 22:29 Thou shalt not delay to offer the first of thy ripe fruits, and of thy liquors: the firstborn of thy sons shalt thou give unto me. In Gen 4:9 Cain lied or tried to deceive God by not being honest, admitting his wrong doing. He knew he had done wrong when God asked him where his brother, who he had killed, was. In Genesis 7:2 Noah knew of clean and unclean animals repeated in Lev 11:4 and Deu 14:7

Though the bible does not list every sin that occurred before Noah, from the examples it gives, we can deduce ALL were present before Sinai. Both Sins against the Commandments and Law. Ham saw the nakedness of his father Noah Gen 9:22 (violation of Lev 18:6-7, 22 and others), Sodom and Gomorrah destroyed for violation of man laying with man / same kind (Lev 8:7,22).From the beginning were offerings made to God before Levitical laws (i.e. Genesis 4:3, 8:20, 22:3, 35:14), man worshiped other gods (violation commandment 1, and bowed to idols (Commandment 2).Gen 20:6 God said from sinning against me, Gen 39:9 Joseph said sinning against God. narrated account of Job 11:5-6 occurred before the law was given to Moses (see Spiros Zodhiates Hebrew-Greek study bible). Yet Job's friends worked on the premise he had sinned against God and thus was being punished. Yet these same laws were not given to Moses and the Jews for generations later. Adhering to these same commandments continued throughout the New Testament with both Jesus and the apostles instructing they should be kept (Matt 15:3,6, Mark 12:30, Luke 18:20, John 15:10, 1 Corin 7:19, 1 John 5:2, James 2:10, Rev 22:14).Proof neither they nor any were cancelled. If any was, Christians should be able to pick out a plain unambiguous divine statement by God or Jesus to that effect.

God gave Moses and the Jews three separate things commandments, laws and statutes or judgements. Numerous places in Old and New Testaments are the distinction made (Gen 26:5, 2 Chron 19:10, Exodus 16:28, Deut 5:31, Neh 9:13, 29; Mat 22:40, Rom 7:12).We should all know what the Commandments are, if not see Exodus 20:1-17. They relate to moral laws. Our moral duty to God and fellow man. Knowledge of the Laws may be scarcer. These are comprehensive regulations by God for various things. For some examples see Leviticus 6:9,14,25; 7:1,11,37; 11:46; 12:7,13:59; 14:2,32,54,57; 15:32 (no mention of commandments or morality). Note they end with "this is the law of ....". You would also note these laws were for all of God's people not only the so-called Jews (**Lev 24:22 "Ye shall have one manner of law, as well for the stranger, as for one of your own country: for I am the LORD your God"**. Then Lev 24:46 states "These are the statutes and judgments and laws, which the LORD made between him and the children of Israel in Mount Sinai by the hand of Moses". No mention of "the Commandments". For an example of statutes see Numbers 27:11, also Psalm 81:1-4 showing holy days as statutes. These were God's laws at the hand of Moses not Law of Moses as later termed in the New Testament. Lastly, read all or the following sections of psalm 119:6-11, 66, 145 and see how the author used and knew the difference between commandments, laws and judgements. Same for Psalm 89:30-31, 34 as spoken by God. So even if for argument sake one accepts the misinformed view that the "law" was done away with, obviously this still leaves two of the three things. You will not find any text in the bible saying the Commandments were cancelled etc. Collaboration of this by various church leaders follows later.

The fact is, the only law that was cancelled by Jesus is that of the Leviticus animal sacrifices as Jesus' death, "the lamb slain" replaced them .John 1:29 "The next day John seeth Jesus coming unto him, and saith, Behold the lamb of God, which taketh away the sin of the world." am sure if Jesus intended to change anything He would have done so during his life not leave it to chance after His death. He would have done it by clear command or example as He did everything else (washing of feet, breaking of bread, healing, teaching, etc. Note the commandments do not mention sacrifices nor the laws mention mans' moral duty to another or God. Sacrifices were covered by some of the laws in the group of laws, so the commandments remain binding. Heb 7:11-12 "If therefore perfection were by the Levitical priesthood, (for under it the people received the law…for the priesthood being changed, there is made of necessity a change also of the law". Jesus was the new priest, through whom one gets forgiveness of sins. He replaced Aaron and priests who offered annual sacrifices. This is where grace and faith comes in (mentioned later); but not in the way you probably think.

As for only being for the Jews. As already said, commandments and laws existed before the Jews. The so titled "Jews" were in Egypt for so long, they practically became Egyptians. Forgot their heritage, how to worship their God etc. Once out of Egypt and in the wilderness, as soon as Moses went away up the mount, they practiced the worship method inherited from the Egyptians. To golden idols and with dancing as under the pagan goddess Hathor (Ex 32:19). God simply had to remind them of His ways and put it in stone with the word remember for His Sabbath so they did not forget it again. Nevertheless, even when it is argued they were given to the "Jews", this can be seen to be wrong. They were given to God's people and not the non God's people. In other words, anyone could have been God's people by choosing to follow the same commandments and laws as they were given to "**he that is born in the house, or bought with money of any stranger, which is not of thy seed" (Gen 17:12).**

Isa 56:6-8 Also the sons of the stranger, that join themselves to the LORD, to serve him, and to love the name of the LORD, to be his servants, every one that keepeth the Sabbath from polluting it, and taketh hold of my covenant; Even them will I bring to my holy mountain, and make them joyful in my house of prayer: their burnt offerings and their sacrifices shall be accepted upon mine altar; for mine house shall be called an house of prayer for all people. The Lord GOD, which gathereth the outcasts of Israel saith, yet will I gather others to him, beside those that are gathered unto him. See also Lev 19:34

The Hebrew word   רֵג   רֵיֵגge^r ge^yr *gare, gare* From H1481; properly a *guest*; by implication a *foreigner:* - alien, sojourner, stranger. They, for the most part, enjoyed same rights as the Israelites and were required to be circumcised. Eze 47:22 And it shall come to pass, *that* ye shall divide it by lot for an inheritance unto you, and to the strangers that sojourn among you, which shall beget children among you: and they shall be unto you as born in the country among the children of Israel; they shall have inheritance with you among the tribes of Israel.

Some other important references to the "stranger" are Gen 17:12, Ex 12:19,49, 20:12, Deut 1:16; Lev19:34, 24:22, Jos 8:33, 20:9; Isa 56:3; Eze 47:22. The stranger that jointed themselves to God's people became one of them. Not only sharing in the blessings and inheritance but also punishment (Lev 20:2). Isaiah 56:6-8. In addition the bible (old and new Testaments) always only segregates people into two groups, i.e. Gen 41:40, Ex 3:7, Lev 26:12, 1 Chron 17:6, 2Chron 7:14, Zec 2:11, Rom 9:25, 2Cor 6:16, Rev 18:4".Obviously others were not His people. Matt 13:29 "wheat and tares", Matt 25:31-33 "sheep and goats". The "my people", "wheat" and "sheep" do His will whether they be born in Israel, Samaria or stranger from other land and the others follow mans' customs regardless of what they call themselves, Jew, Christian, gentile or pagan. So who is really the group we call Jews and how did they come about? I would say a Jew is simply the latest name given to God's separated people., Gen 18:19 For I know him , that he will command his children and his household after him, and they shall keep the way of the LORD, to do justice and judgment; that the LORD may bring upon Abraham that which he hath spoken of him (Abraham's father served false gods Jos 24:2). Deu 7:6 for thou *art* a holy people unto the LORD thy God: the LORD thy God hath chosen thee to be a special people unto himself, above all people that *are* upon the face of the earth. Deu 7:7 The LORD did not set his love upon you, nor choose you, because ye were more in number than any people; for ye *were* the fewest of all people: Amos 3:2 You only have I known of all the families of the earth: 2Sa 7:10 Moreover I will appoint a place for my people Israel, and will plant them, that they may dwell in a place of their own, and move no more; neither shall the .. 2Sa 7:23 and what one nation in the earth *is* like thy people, *even* like Israel, whom God went to redeem for a people to himself, and to make him a name, and to do for you great things and terrible, for thy land, before thy people, which thou redeemedst to thee from Egypt, *from* the nations and their gods? See 1 Chron 17:21-2. 2Ch 6:32 Moreover concerning the stranger, which is not of thy people Israel, but is come from a far country for thy great name's sake, and thy mighty hand, and thy stretched out arm; if they come and pray in this house; 1Ki 8:43 Hear thou in heaven thy dwelling place, and do according to all that the stranger calleth to thee for: that all people of the earth may know thy name, to fear thee, as *do* thy people Israel; and that they may know that this house, which I have builded, is called by thy name. Exo 19:5-6 and ye shall be unto me a kingdom of priests, and a holy nation. (see also Isa 44:8; 43:21, 66:19, Deu 29:13-15) . They are to be a light to gentiles (non God's people) and a Jewel of God. When it comes to keeping God's commandments and laws, some preachers say, they were for the Jews, we are not under the Old Testament; but the New. Yet when quoting prosperity or other good fortune texts, these same pastors get them from the Old Testament and use ones given to a specific Jew or Jews. They patronise congregations by telling them what they want to hear. For their reward they can sell sand to the Arabs, ice to Eskimos, a false god to the lost, mixing truth and lies as did satan. What would Jesus call such people, hypocrites?

As Psalm 4:3 says "know that the Lord has set apart him that is godly for himself". The first separation was Noah and his family as they were the only ones "to find grace in the eyes of the Lord" (Gen 6:8).Others were "evil continually." Gen 6:5.Later came Abraham; whose name God changed from Abram (Gen 17:5).Changing of name for identification purpose was not unique. God and other nations did it i.e. Gen 35:10, (and Saul became Paul of the New Testament). So Jacob renamed Israel, was just another separation and identification of God's people from the rest of the world not doing His will. Jacob's twelve offspring (and others explained above as "strangers") simply continued that separation and identification (Gen 35:22-26).It is interesting to note satan's alternative religion as practiced by Egypt also changes names i.e. Daniel 1:7, Like many offspring, not all the children are good or good all the time. The tribe of Judah, though strayed away from God's ways, were probably the best of the group/sons in God's eyes. It is from them that the name Jew sprung. So to reiterate, it is simply a name to identify God's separated people from the rest of the world. Actual descendants of Jacob, stranger or Gentile who chooses to live by God's commandments, not the world's. See Ex 12:37-8 "And the children of Israel journeyed from Rameses to Succoth, about six hundred thousand on foot that were men, beside children. **And a mixed multitude** went up also with them;" Esther 3:8 "And Haman said unto king Ahasuerus, There is a certain people scattered abroad and dispersed among the people in all the provinces of thy kingdom; and their laws are diverse from all people; neither keep they the king's laws: therefore it is not for the king's profit to suffer them." As God said to Moses in Lev 18:2-4 "I am the LORD your God. After the doings of the land of Egypt, wherein ye dwelt, shall ye not do: and after the doings of the land of Canaan, whither I bring you, shall ye not do: neither shall ye walk in their ordinances. Ye shall do my judgments, and keep mine ordinances, to walk therein: I am the LORD your God."

Esther 8:17"And in every province, and in every city, whithersoever the king's commandment and his decree came, the Jews had joy and gladness, a feast and a good day. **And many of the people of the land became Jews**; for the fear of the Jews fell upon them." v9:27 "The Jews ordained, and took upon them, and upon their seed, and upon **all such as joined themselves unto them**, so as it should not fail, that they would keep these two days according to their writing, and according to their appointed time every year;"

As one of the things Paul says, circumcision counts for nothing if do not do God's will. Jew can be non Jew and Gentile can be Jew. Salvation through Jesus is for all nations. Matthew 12:18 "Behold my servant whom I have chosen; my beloved in whom my soul is well pleased: I shall put my spirit upon him and he shall show judgement to the Gentiles" Mat 12:21 In his name shall the Gentiles trust". " Mat 24:14 and this gospel of the kingdom will be preached in the whole world as a testimony to all nations, and then the end will come. Mat 28:19go and make disciples of all nations, baptizing them in the name of the Father and of the Son and of the Holy Spirit. Mark 11:17 and as he taught them, he said, "Is it not written, my house will be called a house of prayer for all nations? But you have made it a den of robbers". Mark 13:10 and the gospel must first be preached to all nations. Luk 24:47 and repentance and forgiveness of sins will be preached in his name to all nations, beginning at Jerusalem. Romans 15:12 and again, Isaiah says, "The Root of Jesse will spring up, one who will arise to rule over the nations; the Gentiles will hope in him." Rom 16:26 but now revealed and made known through the prophetic writings by the command of the eternal God, so that all nations might believe and obey him. Rom 3:29 he the God of the Jews only? is he not also of the Gentiles? Yes, of the Gentiles also:

These persons are to separate themselves from the non God's (or other god's) persons the same way God in Genesis 2:3 separated and sanctified the seventh day from the others. The same way the number seven is special in God's mind and His plans. The colours of the rainbow are seven, music scale have seven notes (some will say eight; but the 8th is a deviation of one of the seven), 7 seals, churches, trumpets, angels, vials, plagues, candle sticks, time prophesies, spirits of God (Rev 4:5) and of course days of the week.

LORD OF THE SABBATH

Mar 2:27 and he said unto them, The Sabbath was made for man, and not man for the Sabbath: Let us substitute the word house for Sabbath so that the sentence states, "The house was made for the man not man for the house". In other words man came first, then the house to serve his needs of shelter, place to rest, cook etc. Similarly God gave man the Sabbath to serve him. To give him shelter and rest from his six days toils and labour. Time to reflect on, remember and praise God, his creator. Time to remember his origins, the beauty of his surroundings, the world. How it has everything he needs for survival and pleasure. From the colourful birds, flowers, clouds, stars and more. Thus how wise his creator was to fashion him in such a wise way. What a loving God like who there is no other. Made the universe well balance, self sustaining on a cycle where nothing is naturally wasted. No creature is in need; from the unseen micro cell to the largest mammal. To even think of making part of the day dark so that sunlight does not disturb man's sleep. Time to rejuvenate his mind and body, to put life and material things in perspective. Unlike the other six days on which God made things with which Adam could identify each day, God made nothing on day seven. That was time for man to commune with God. To be a desired blessing not a grievous curse as those wanting to do their own thing all the time. If you love someone, you put time aside to spend with them.

Mar 2:28 Therefore the Son of man is Lord also of the Sabbath. Again let us substitute a word like king for son of man and castle for Sabbath so that the sentence reads, "therefore the king is Lord (master) of the castle". Does this in anyway suggest the castle is destroyed, changed or similar? No. merely states a fact that the king has control or ownership of the castle. Do not read or add a man made custom or excuse into the bible text that the Sabbath was ended and no longer to be kept. History confirms it was an excuse added hundreds of years later after Christ. Col 1:16 For by him were all things created, that are in heaven, and that are in earth, visible and invisible, whether *they be* thrones, or dominions, or principalities, or powers: all things were created by him, and for him:" Heb 1:2-3 by whom also he made the worlds; Who being the brightness of *his* glory, and the express image of his person, and upholding all things by the word of his power, when he had by himself purged our sins, sat down on the right hand of the Majesty on high; Ecc 3:14 I know that, whatsoever God doeth, it shall be for ever: nothing can be put to it, nor any thing taken from it: and God doeth *it*, that *men* should fear before him. Ecc 3:15 that which hath been is now; and that which is to be hath already been; and God requireth that which is past.

Jesus created and upheld the Sabbath so is Lord over it as over everything else. and it is to stand forever not to be added to or anything taken away from it.

NEW TESTAMENT (COVENANT / COMMAND)

The title is taken from Matt 26:28 (repeated in Mark 14:24 and Luke 22:20; 1cor 11:25).At the last supper, after Jesus had given the disciples bread to break and eat, He took wine and give them to drink saying "drink ye all of it; for this is my blood of the new testament, which is shed for many for the remission of sins". Note He nor any apostle raised it in offering to the sun god as some denomination priests do. Be careful with what you partake out of ignorance of its history]. Some bible versions have changed the word testament to covenant, then go on to link it with the Ten Commandments, Laws and, possibly everything God ordained in the Old Testament (see bible interpretation section above). I was shown this text in the past from someone else's non KJV bible, which used the word covenant. At the time I was unaware the word should be testament. As a result I was confused. Now I see how satan has deceived many with the popularisation of easy to read bibles containing subtle change of words and hence meaning. Using the tactic, if you can not beat them join them and change from within. is a good reason why the Bible is divided into Old and New "Testaments" and NOT Covenant!

The Greek word used for "new" is reference G2537new in freshness or qualitatively not age or numerically as with G3510.Jesus saying he gives a new "testament". Something for them to use in their witnessing and spreading the gospel. Heb 9:16-17 "For where a testament is, there must also of necessity be the death of the testator. For a testament is of force after men are dead: otherwise it is of no strength at all while the testator liveth". Though some bibles use the word "covenant" in Matt 26:28, in Matt 24:14 they write "And this gospel of the kingdom shall be preached in all the world as a testimony to all…"

Thus the last supper was a prelude to something that had not happened prior. Something that could not be testified to before. The death of Jesus, the son of God, sent by God. How would they be able to testify to this? Act 1:3To whom also he shewed himself alive after his passion by many infallible proofs, being seen of them forty days, and speaking of the things pertaining to the kingdom of God: Act 4:20 For we cannot but speak the things which we have seen and heard. Act 13:31he was seen many days of them, which came up with him from Galilee to Jerusalem, who are his witnesses unto the people. 1 Cor 15:6that, he was seen of above five hundred brethren at once; of whom the greater part remain unto this present, but some are fallen asleep. 1 John 1:1That which was from the beginning, which we have heard, which we have seen with our eyes, which we have looked upon, and our hands have handled, of the Word of life; 1 John 1:2(For the life was manifested, and we have seen it, and bear witness, and shew unto you that eternal life, which was with the Father, and was manifested unto us;)1John 1:3 That which we have seen and heard declare we unto you, that ye also may have fellowship with us: and truly our fellowship is with the Father, and with his Son Jesus Christ.1John 4:14 and we have seen and do testify that the Father sent the Son to be the Saviour of the world.

The apostles were able to testify to what they had seen and experienced firsthand. That was the "new" testimony not cancellation of the Law or commandments. To whom were they to take this testimony and the reason they were given the power to speak in tongues (mans various languages)? Act 1:8 but ye shall receive power, after that the Holy Ghost is come upon you: and ye shall be witnesses unto me both in Jerusalem, and in all Judea, and in Samaria, and unto the uttermost part of the earth. said "Elijah verily cometh first and Restoreth all things" 9:12 (and Matt 11:14, 17:11). To restore means to put as it was in past i.e. adherence to keeping commandments, Sabbath etc so those who argue the "law" was changed can be seen to have mis-interpreted the text. If man or satan changed it, God will restore it to show the change was not from Him. See also feast days restoration.

1Tim 2:6 "Who gave himself a ransom for all, to be testified in due time". When was this time to be? Have you noticed the dots in the line from the old tabernacle and annual sacrifice of Aaron and the priests, to the destroying of the temple and exile of God's people due to their constant sinning, to the rebuilding of the temple and repatriation of the people. They returned to their sinful ways, the coming of Jesus the Messiah, the spreading of His gospel around the world for approximately thirty seven years then the destroying of the temple in A.D.70. God allowed sufficient time for the gospel to spread around the world through the apostles being given the ability to speak in many languages to every nation, kindred and tongue (Rev 14:6). Then came the change. End of the animal sacrifices. Daily, annually and all as explained in the Shadow of Things to Come section. Now the new method of keeping the Passover, with bread and wine rather than slain animal. Thus, the "forever" ordinance as in Ex 12:14 can continue.

The worst sin of God's people is to worship other god's, Baal and his image. What are Baal's images? Deu 4:19 "and lest though lift up thine eyes unto heaven and when thou see the sun and moon and the stars, even all the host of heaven, shouldest be driven to worship them and serve them". The Jewish ancestors succumbed to worshipping these images, our ancestors, through the Church of Rome led Christians to doing the same via SUN day worship. Do not let others make merchandise of you whether deliberately or through ignorance (2Pet 2:3). Is it not time you returned to God, His day and His ways?

The other place where Jesus says to have given a "new command" is John 13:34 "A new commandment I give unto you, that ye love one another; as I have loved you, that ye also love one another" One should note, this commandment is not mentioned in any of the other gospels. Do you not think were it to have the effect some place on it of cancelling the Ten Commandments or the Law, that the Holy Spirit would have guided others to record it? For an indication to what Jesus meant we can refer to 1 John 4:12,24 "No man hath seen God at any time. If we love one another, God dwelleth in us, and his love is perfected in us. If a man say, I love God, and hateth his brother, he is a liar: for he that loveth not his brother whom he hath seen, how can he love God whom he hath not seen?" To me this is the last six of the Ten Commandments which Jesus previously summarized "love your neighbour as your self". Because by following the same, one would not covet or take anything belonging to their neighbour. Love cancels out the devil. If you show love to God and each other, it manifests into, no false god worship, no envy, jealousy, stealing or doing ill to neighbour. The devil then has no way into your heart. This is no difference to the text in 1 Cor 13:13 (charity / love) or 1 Peter 4:8, the sum of the commandments towards fellow humans is love for another.. Ofcourse this is not the physical love as used by some same sex genders to justify their actions against for example, Lev 18:22 and 20:13 "though shall not lie with mankind as with womankind: it is abomination". If you are still not convinced this was not a new commandment see 19:18 "Thou shalt love thy neighbour as thy self". Thus Jesus always reiterates the Old Testament. Nothing was changed in the New. See also and compare Lev 23:10 and 1 Cor 15:20. Remind yourself of the texts in the What is Love section above.

Jer 31:31, Heb 8:8-10, 10:16 "for finding fault with them He saith the days come ..when I will make a new covenant with house of Israel... Not according to one with their fathers. because they continued not in it ... This is the new covenant, I will **put** my **Laws** into their minds and hearts. And their sins and iniquities I will remember no more. .. Now where remission of these is, there is no more **offering** for sin". Note new and old covenants to do with laws not commandments, laws relating to (animal) offerings for forgiveness of sin (see 9:1). Change was place put not nature or wording of Laws which was not defective. Reason, people broke it. Child may brake ornament because of place it stood. A new one exactly same as old could be purchased and placed elsewhere. New or second one does not necessarily mean different.

How many items of clothing have you? Whether shoes, trousers, skirt or other, kitchen items as pots or glasses? Did you always throw away the former ones so that you now only have one of everything? I doubt it. Thus "new" does not necessarily mean replace old. It could mean addition: add to the former. A woman may buy a new dress or shoes for each new special occasion. Jesus was simply adding a new sign to the new occasion. As He said, He did not come to destroy the old. Just like when a new situation arises the government adds a new law or tax to the statutory books. The old, generally, still stand. Jesus was keeping the Passover of old and adding a new one of breaking of bread and the drink of the wine.

People who want to maintain Sunday worship says Jesus died to set them free. (From what, the Law? See 1Tim 1:7-10 explained later under 'Book of Galatians'). Yet they accept that Jesus and God are one and the same. Using their logic it would make no sense that this 'same' person would do one thing in Old Testament and another, totally different thing, in the New. That what they assume is said about the character in the New wipes out what the same person said in the Old. A meticulous character who pays attention to every detail, remains the same in Old and New Testaments. Read at least the first five books of the Old, in which God Himself speaks and note his meticulous and consistent character of, i.e. Lev 19:23 new planted land uncircumcised for 3 years just as new born boy. Be led by the actual word of God not man's custom or your pastor. Jam 2:8 if ye fulfil the royal law according to the scripture, Thou shalt love thy neighbour as thyself, ye do well: Jam 2:9 but if ye have respect to persons, ye commit sin, and are convinced of the law as transgressors. The Israelites made a similar mistake in wanting a king like other nations to lead them when they had God Himself. God said to Samuel "…for they have not rejected thee, but they have rejected me, that I should not reign over them" 1 Sam 8:7.

It was no accident that Jesus chose to use two elements of the Passover meal to institute the Lord's Supper. In Exodus 12:5, 8 they were to "eat a lamb without blemish, a male… eat the flesh and unleavened bread". Jesus was the lamb, His flesh. Similar to the Old. The wine was a "new" addition to the Old Testament habit. Both observances symbolize death and deliverance. Both reflect mankind's plight and God's mighty deed of grace and redemption. Jesus was the lamb slain at Passover and when we eat and drink we are reacting the old Passover and commandments etc but through grafting Gentiles (strangers) can be grafted in to the one "true vine" being nourished by God the husbandman.

Hebrew 8:7 and Jer 31:31 due to people's inability to adhere to written covenant God decided to write it in each person's heart so knowledge of it would not rely on one teaching the other. Satan, the master deceiver and counterfeiter seized on this as a good idea and also decided to make people follow and adhere to his day of worship (Sunday) willingly rather than by adherence to Sunday laws passed in the past. Now 99% unaware of history, fight from the heart to maintain their Sunday keeping worship. What is in the books of the New Testament is not a different message than in the Old. Save for the difference already mentioned, the New is mere repetition of Old. This is seen time and time again. Solomon said in 2Chron 6:36 "for there is no man which sinneth not" In Rom 3:23 "For all have sinned, and come short of the glory of God;"1Kings 11:2-8 Solomon allowed 1,000 foreign wives etc to lead him away from God when he was "old" (verse 4). That is one against 1,000.A king specifically chosen, favoured and blessed by God gradually unawares was led away to worship other gods, not immediately; but as time went by, through following custom of wives. Similarly, early Christians allowed Romans in (though maybe had no choice due to the persecution) who became the majority and changed the Christian customs till now in the 21st century 99% worship other gods and do not know it

WHO IS A GENTILE

God says He has one flock one shepherd not Jew and Gentile (Joh 10:16 And other sheep I have, which are not of this fold: them also I must bring, and they shall hear my voice; and there shall be one fold, *and one shepherd.* That there is only way route to salvation Joh 14:6 Jesus saith unto him, I am the way, the truth, and the life: no man cometh unto the Father, but by me.. One method for all Eph 4:5 One Lord, one faith, one baptism. Isa 42:7 To open the blind eyes, to bring out the prisoners from the prison, *and* them that sit in darkness out of the prison house. Isa 43:7 Even every one that is called by my name: for I have created him for my glory, I have formed him; yea, I have made him. So let us see if the Gentiles have a different legitimate way.

Despite the facts, some argue that they are Gentiles and are given special dispensation from keeping all the commandments and seventh day Sabbath. The Jews are to keep them; but not Gentiles. From what time period or event do they get this notion? Jesus' death and some ambiguous words used by Paul in the New Testament relating to circumcision? We know Jesus gave no indication to that effect. That for at least the next hundred years the apostles and early Christians continued adherence to the Sabbath until Rome's persecution and subsequent amalgamation .of paganism with early apostolic faith It should be unnecessary to go any further. However, let us examine this hypothesis and see if it is not in contradiction to scripture i.e. Rom 1:18 For the wrath of God is revealed from heaven against all ungodliness and unrighteousness of men, who hold the truth in unrighteousness. When Adam and Eve sinned, they lost their salvation being neither Jew nor Gentile. The same for subsequent sinners; Cain who killed Abel, those of Noah's time who "were evil continually", etc. Those who were saved were saved neither as Jew nor Gentile; but for doing God's will and keeping His commandments. The word Gentile is first used in Genesis 10:5 after Noah and family came from the ark, began to multiply and separate; "by these were the isles of the Gentiles divided in their lands; everyone after his tongue, families, in their nation". The Hebrew word being pronounced goy or goee is used 559 times (nation 109, nations 266, heathen 143, gentile 30, people 11). Just like Gen 10:5 elaborates, it describes a foreign nation, heathen, people. (Figuratively also used for a troop of animals, flight of locusts). Thus there were always only two types of people, God's, who followed His commandments and the rest, heathens, who did not. Enoch, Abram, Joseph, etc. were God's. No Jewish nation or tribe had yet been formed. The rest disobeyed God, as did Nimrod building the Tower of Babel and became the ancestors of the Egyptians into whose hands God cast His people for their disobedience. After the allotted punishment period, He called Moses to bring His people out of the corrupt heathen Egypt, gave them a testimony by which they would know He is God and His power. Yet as soon as they lost sight of Moses for a few days, they reverted to the corrupt worship practice of Egypt, "host of heaven" (Sun etc) (Acts 7:42).

This two tier worship system of God and satan continued from the Old Testament to the New. There the Greek word translated Gentile is pronounced "hellen / hel-lane" used 27 times to mean Greeks (13), Greek (7), Gentiles (5), Gentile (2). It comes from; a

Hellen (*Grecian*) or inhabitant of Hellas; by extension a *Greek speaking* person, especially a *non-Jew:* - Gentile, Greek. The Greeks were the first group of heathens to receive the Christian message and embrace it. They joined the Jews in their synagogues for worship on their seventh day Sabbath. Then the message went further a field to the rest of the heathen nations as Jesus commanded. Reading the book of Acts you should note chapters 1-7 records the Christian growth among the converted Jews in Jerusalem and Judea, 8-12 persecution taking movement beyond Samaria, Ethiopia, Syria and other Gentile territories (see 8:1), 13-18 to the wider circles and Rome. The prophesies of Isaiah 49:6, 60:3 and 61:9 being fulfilled. God's people will be a light to bring the heathen (non believing Gentiles in the one true God of creation, Jehovah), non God's people, back to Him (see Pro 6:23). As Paul says in Romans 15:18 to make the Gentiles obedient to God's commandments by word and deed.

The original small Christian followers took in the masses from the heathen until the mass, their legislation and death threats changed the rules, times and days of their worship. The heathen should have been graffed into Christianity (Rom 11:19). Feeding from the same trunk of substance, including their seventh day Sabbath that fed them. Eph 2:19 Now therefore ye are no more strangers and foreigners, but fellow citizens with the saints, and of the household of God; Eph 2:20 And are built upon the foundation of the apostles and <u>prophets</u>, Jesus Christ himself being the chief corner *stone*; (see also Eph 3:6). Eph 3:9 And to make <u>all</u> *men* see what *is* the fellowship of the mystery, which from the beginning of the world hath been hid in God, who created all things by Jesus Rom 9:25 As he saith also in Osee, I will call them <u>my people,</u> which were not my people; and her beloved, which was not beloved. Tit 2:14 who gave himself for us, that he might redeem us from all iniquity, and <u>purify unto himself a peculiar people, zealous of good works.</u> 1Pe 2:9 But ye *are* a chosen generation, a royal priesthood, an holy nation, a peculiar people; that ye should shew forth the praises of him who hath called you out of darkness into his marvellous light: 1Pe 2:10 Which in time past *were* not a people, but *are* now the people of God: which had not obtained mercy, but now have obtained mercy. Act 15:14 Simeon hath declared how God at the first did visit the Gentiles, to take out of them a people for his name. Act 15:17 that the residue of men might seek after the Lord, and all the Gentiles, upon whom my name is called, saith the Lord, who doeth all these things. See also Acts 26:20-23, Paul taught nothing different to the Gentiles than he did to the Jews save for circumcision.

Instead Christians ended up through Constantine and others, gaffed into Sun worship and their Sunday. Today most are fooled by the mix instituted in Rome. Do you really think God would excuse this mix of which he condemned i.e. in Deut 4:19 and 17:3? That changes his day of worship to that of the Sun, Moon or other? The group of heathens whose ways were abominable to Him? There is one way of salvation for all Jew or Gentile (see 1Cor 12:13, Rom 2:9-10, Pro 7:2, 19:16, 28:9).

Some would have you believe the commandments were nailed to the cross, at 3pm when Jesus died. So are we really to believe that one minute (2:59 p.m), non Jewish people (Gentiles) have access to God's salvation (as a stranger) through adherence to the commandments including the Sabbath and the next minute, those same people have to keep only nine of the ten; but the Jews, God's chosen, continue having to keep all ten! That Gentiles who died before 3pm on the day of preparation (Jesus' death) were lost; but had they survived one, thirty or sixty minutes more they would have been excused!! What a fair and just God that depicts. The Jews in Jer 42:6 said they would do all that God instructed. However by 43:12 when the instructions were not to their liking, they said it was not god's instructions and that what they wanted to do, was His instructions. That is the same mind set many Christians have today. Do not make the same mistakes as Psa 95:10, Psa 53:2 God looked down from heaven upon the children of men, to see if there were *any* that did understand, that did seek God. Heb 3:10 I grieved with *this* generation, and said, It *is* a people that do err in their heart, and they have not known my ways: "Psa 14:3 they are all gone aside, they are *all* together become filthy: *there is* none that doeth good, no, not one". See also Rom 3:23.

Neither can you count on the righteous of Abraham or relatives "Eze 14:20 Though Noah, Daniel, and Job, *were* in it, *as* I live, saith the Lord GOD, they shall deliver neither son nor daughter; they shall *but* deliver their own souls by their righteousness". The soul that sinneth shall die (Eze 18:20), including the one deceived.

I have already covered the commandments existed before they were given to Moses. Especially the Sabbath as God said "remember the Sabbath". They were in existence before Abram got the covenant of circumcision. Circumcision merely separated those who were not keeping the commandments i.e. Old Testament Gentiles, from those identified and directed to keep them as an identification of being God's people. Psa 103:7 He made known his ways unto Moses, his acts unto the children of Israel. Psa 103:18 to such as keep his covenant and to those that remember his commandments to do them. Abraham proved his willingness to be obedient to God's command when tested to sacrifice his only son in Gen 22. Once he passed the test, God provided the lamb for the sacrifice. God only provides salvation for His people, those doing His commandments irrespective of their nation. Jew, stranger or heathen (Gentile). Prior to Jesus it was through the animal sacrifice (see Lev 16). The law part of the three things given to Moses, commandments, statutes and laws. Jesus came to be the provided lamb for those in the New Testament that pass His test of keeping His commandments, again Jew or heathen. Remember Jesus' death merely replaced the sacrificial animal system given to Moses as Laws and detailed in Leviticus. Not even the Jews of today keep them. The Commandments and Sabbath keeping are separate to animal sacrifices.

Jesus and God are of one with the same wish and commands for us. John 14:9-15 "He that hath seen me hath seen the father... Believest thou not that I am in the Father, and the Father in me? the words that I speak unto you I speak not of myself: but the Father that dwelleth in me, he doeth the works. Believe me that I *am* in the Father, and the Father in me: or else believe me for the very works' sake. Verily, verily, I say unto you, He that believeth on me, the works that I do shall he do also; and greater *works* than these shall he do; because I go unto my Father. And whatsoever ye shall ask in my name, that will I do, that the Father may be glorified in the Son. If ye shall ask any thing in my name, I will do *it*. If ye love me, keep my commandments". See also John 15:10 "if ye keep my commandments ye shall abide in my love even as I have kept my father's commandments and abide (live) in his love".

CIRCUMCISION

Some pastors use Galatians as a justification not to keep the Sabbath. They fail to note 1:14 "being more exceedingly zealous of the traditions of my fathers" of which adhering to the Sabbath was one. Read the next topic "Book of Galatians in conjunction with this topic to avoid duplication. The letter to the Galatians was in response to influences by Judaizers who had visited them in Paul's absence. The Judaizers insisted these gentile believers had to be circumcised to be true saved (Act 15:1-4, 24).Act 15:1And certain men which came down from Judea taught the brethren, and said, Except ye be circumcised after the manner of Moses, ye cannot be saved. Act 15:2 When therefore Paul and Barnabas had no small dissension and disputation with them, they determined that Paul and Barnabas, and certain other of them, should go up to Jerusalem unto the apostles and elders about this question. Act 15:10 Now therefore why tempt ye God, to put a yoke upon the neck of the disciples, which neither our fathers nor we were able to bear? Act 15:19my sentence is, that we trouble not them, which from among the Gentiles are turned to God:16:1-3 Timothy, the son of a certain woman, which was a Jewess, and believed; but his father was a Greek: Him would Paul have to go forth with him; and took and circumcised him because of the Jews which were in those quarters: for they knew all that his father was a Greek. Could this mean, as a Jew or part Jew you had no excuse not to be circumcised according to the Law; but as a gentile you were given leave?). Act 21:21 And they are informed of thee, that thou teachest all the Jews which are among the Gentiles to forsake Moses, saying that they ought not to circumcise their children, neither to walk after the customs. V24 and all may know that those things, whereof they were informed concerning thee, are nothing; but that thou thyself also walkest orderly, and keepest the law. But as touching the gentiles which believe, they do not have to (be circumcised).

Acts 24:5 confirms that first generation Christians were considered to be a sect, a new branch of Judaism. Necessity of circumcision divided them into two groups Acts 11:2"And when Peter was come up to Jerusalem, they that were of the circumcision contended with him".

There are so many in the Law, so which one are we no longer under as referred to by Paul? The law of Nazarite in Num 6:21, or the one in Lev 11:46 or that of 12:7?If he meant all would he not have used the plural i.e. "the laws"? Paul generally speaks of circumcision; the covenant given to Abraham. Other times, i.e. in Hebrews and 10, it is of animals' blood for the remission of sins as that was replaced by Jesus (see Shadow of Things to come section). Remember, the numerous laws and commandments are different things. In Deut 10:11, Moses explains how they were chosen and set apart from others. Physical circumcision was a sign of their descendacy from Abraham. It did not guarantee them salvation as they were still stiff-necked and continually rebellious. He summarised "circumcise therefore the foreskin of your heart, and be no more stiff-necked (i.e. Deut 10:16)." When gentiles were grafted into these people's (Abraham's descendant's) promise. They could not or need not adopt the physical sign of direct descendacy, circumcision of foreskin; but could in circumcised heart. Not being stiff-necked and rebellious; but following commandments of God. Not seeing them as a curse; but a blessing. Rom 2:25-7 "For circumcision verily profiteth, if thou keep the law: but if thou be a breaker of the law, thy circumcision is made uncircumcision. Therefore if the uncircumcision keep the righteousness of the law, shall not his uncircumcision be counted for circumcision? And shall not uncircumcision which is by nature, if it fulfil the law, judge thee, who by the letter and circumcision dost transgress the law?" Rom 4:10-12"How it was then reckoned? when he was in circumcision, or in uncircumcision? Not in circumcision, but in uncircumcision and he received the sign of circumcision, a seal of the righteousness of the faith which he had yet being uncircumcised: that he might be the father of all them that believe, though they be not circumcised; that righteousness might be imputed unto them also: And the father of circumcision to them who are not of the circumcision only, but who also walk in the steps of that faith of our father Abraham, which he had being yet uncircumcised."

1Cor 7:19 "Circumcision is nothing and uncircumcision is nothing, but the keeping of the commandments of God". So the Commandments still stand and are binding. Eze 44:9 (Thus saith the Lord God, no stranger uncircumcised in heart or flesh shall enter my sanctuary, of any stranger that is among the children of Israel). Was Paul right to conclude gentiles did not need to be circumcised because it was circumcision of the heart that counted? Is Eze 44:9 solely referring to those entering His sanctuary? Were all (including the "stranger") not called to enter the sanctuary albeit not the inner part? Maybe Paul knew if he taught circumcision was mandatory many would not become Christians. He was trying to be all things to all people to win and save some (1Cor 9:22) John 7:22 states circumcision was of God not Moses. Bill of divorce was Moses' not God's (Matt 19:18). Many like pork. Their Mc Donald and other burgers, sausages, bacon etc and if they thought Leviticus 11:7 was mandatory, many would prefer the pork to being a Christian. Hence those use the text of "it is what comes out of the mouth not what goes in that defies a man" to be both Christian and eat pork.

I think Romans 2:13-15 and James 2 explain it well (for James see "Faith" section). First Romans. "For not the hearers of the law are just before God, but the doers of the law shall be justified. For when the Gentiles, which have not the law, do by nature the things contained in the law, these, having not the law, are a law unto themselves: Which shew the work of the law written in their hearts, their conscience also bearing witness, and their thoughts the mean while accusing or else excusing one another;". The commandments and laws are for those who need it not those with the right heart who would do the correct thing whether there is a law or not. An easier to understand comparison is one akin to drugs, drinking or smoking which we know are bad for our bodies. Some people abstain from these acts for the right reasons; because it is harmful. Others do them because the law permits. But if the law was to be changed and abolish the acts, some who use to do them would stop due to their illegal nature and legal consequences. They need a law to make them do what the others were doing from the heart. After a period of time the ex drinkers, smokers, etc may see the benefit to their bodies, health etc so that even if the law later re-permits them to smoke or drink, they now choose not to for the right reason just like the others who abstained from the outset. The law was a schoolmaster to bring the abusers to the benefit and knowledge of the sin; but once the knowledge acquired and understood they can perform the same act through believe rather than the written law. Both groups of people now perform the same act of abstention or obedience. Just that the weaker needed the law and the stronger acted from the heart Galatians 3:24-25). However, whether the law exist or not, wrong doing is wrong doing.

Matt19:8 the same way Moses due to the "hardness of heart" "suffered" (introduced) divorce but Jesus said "from the beginning it was not so", same way Paul because of hardness of people ("yoke we could not bear") suffered (introduced) no need for circumcision.. Purely for the benefit of getting people to accept Christ. At first the governing apostles disagreed. I suppose based on Gen 17:12 and Ex 12:48 which instructed "strangers" joining themselves to God's people were to be circumcised and live the same lives.

A summary of Paul's writings to the gentiles, which must concur with that of the other bible texts of Jesus and the other apostles are; Come to God through Christ by believing in his deity and resurrection. Yes keep the commandments and the laws of God; but do not get disheartened by the claims of the Jews that you have to be physically circumcised. As many get circumcised, keep the Sabbath, abstain from food with blood etc and yet may not be saved because they do it in response to an order rather than from the heart. They believe adhering externally will excuse any internal ill will to others etc. Keeping the commandments and laws is the basics, the external actions (works) that show the internal intent (faith). One needs both. One cannot be saved solely by belief or externally keeping commandments.

I suppose on a strict note, in one sense, Paul was right. God gave every human a chance to be His people by keeping the Commandments, Laws and Statutes explained above. These came after and were not part of the circumcision covenant given specifically to Abraham and his seed. No mention of "stranger", "mixed multitude" or others. An admission of the Catholic Church taken from the Council of Trent: **"...The authority of the church could therefore not be bound to the authority of the Scriptures, because the church had changed circumcision into baptism"**.

It is interesting to note that men in many countries practice circumcision whether they be Jew, Gentiles of other religions or pagan. From where and did they copy this custom?

BOOK OF GALATIANS

Non seventh day Sabbath keepers use the book of Galatians as an excuse not to keep the "Law". I have referred to which law was being discussed in Galatians in several places throughout this book, one of which is "Grace and Relationship with God". However, I am inspired to put some notes under the title "Galatians" for those who may not read the whole book. Nothing in the entire bible is against the law. God had His laws written or spoken from creation. Even Jesus' birth was under the law Gal 4:4 But when the fullness of the time was come, God sent forth his Son, made of a woman, made under the law,.

For clarification as to whether we Christians and the human race are under the Law or whether the New Testament teaches it was cancelled by Jesus see 1Tim 1:7-10 "Desiring to be teachers of the law; understanding neither what they say, nor whereof they affirm. But we know that the law *is* good, if a man use it lawfully; Knowing this, that the law is **not made for a righteous man, but for the lawless and disobedient, for the ungodly and for sinners**, for unholy and profane, for murderers of fathers and murderers of mothers, for manslayers, For whoremongers, for them that defile themselves with mankind, for mensteelers, for liars, for perjured persons, and **if there be any other thing that is contrary to sound doctrine**; Rev 22:14 Blessed *are* they that **do his commandments**, that they may have right to the tree of life, and **may enter** in through the gates into the city. Rev 22:15 **For without *are*** dogs, and sorcerers, and whoremongers, and murderers, and idolaters, and whosoever loveth and maketh a lie.

Self titled pastors "desiring to be teachers" teaching Christians that they are nolonger under the Law, frankly neither understand about the Law nor what they are saying. If they did they would know they are contradicting themselves in their believes (i.e calling on promises given to Law keepers or keeping some i.e tithes). The Law is not for the righteous, they do not need it, they do not commit sin which is breaking the Law. Neither would Jesus need to die to them (Rom 5:7). The Law is for the lawless, disobedient, ungodly and sinner to bring them back into line, keeping God's commandments and laws, being righteous. To tell people to ignore the law, they are nolonger under it, is simply telling them to return to being ungodly, unrighteous, a law breaker. When these "pastors" should be feeding followers hard food, they are giving them worse than milk; poison. Either by ignorance, choice to prevent whole truth of God, financial gain of numbers attending church or other reason. I heard a pastor advocating not keeping God's laws stating laws can be overcome. He used an airborne plane overcoming the laws of gravity. He is wrong, the law was still there. If in doubt, he ought to wait until the plane runs out of fuel, has engine failure or other event cancelling its forward thrust motion.

It should be clear, that In Galatians Paul is referring to the law or promise of circumcision given to Abraham. He goes on to tell the Galatian Gentiles they are heirs to the promise given to Abraham through his seed, Jesus Christ. The reason Paul wrote

Galatians is to counteract the argument of the strict Jews (Judaizers) that, Gentiles (non Jews) could not be true Christians until they submitted to the Jewish ordinance of circumcision. At first the Galatians accepted this teaching as enthusiastically as they did Paul's. In Gal 1:6 Paul is says he "marvelled ye are so soon removed from him that called you through grace (rather than circumcision)". 1:7 These other teachers teach the same gospel of Christ albeit a perverted version which trouble you to be circumcised. From Gal 2:1 Paul refers to the same separating argument of circumcision as narrated in Acts 15:1 "and certain men which came down from Judea taught the brethren and said Except you be circumcised after the manner of Moses you cannot be saved. As a result (15:2) Paul and Barnabas decided to go to the elder apostles in Jerusalem on this matter. Gal 2:3 confirms the topic is still on circumcision. 2:7 "when they saw that the gospel of **uncircumcision** was committed onto me as the gospel of circumcision was to Peter" (see also 2:8). Paul saw himself as the apostle for the Gentiles, to bring them to salvation through Christ and, maybe if he conceded here in Galatia, that Gentiles had to be circumcised, it would deter other gentiles from the road to salvation and end if not severely hinder his ministry.

An explanation to 2:12, why Peter did not want the circumcised Jews to see him eating with the Gentiles is said to be one of fear. Could it be fear of putting a stumbling block before the Jews or his ministry? Christians are told not to go into drinking or such establishments. Suppose we wish to minister to the sinners therein and enter for that purpose? Would fear of what others would say or think of us prevent us? Especially if unknown to us, a weak believer or newly converted sees us entering or exiting. It could put a stumbling block in their way not being privy to our reasoning. Romans 14:13 13 "Let us not therefore judge one another any more: but judge this rather, that no man put a stumbling block or an occasion to fall in his brother's way".

From 3:6 Paul parallels Abraham's faith in God's promise before he was given the ordinance of circumcision to that needed from the Gentiles. Abraham had faith God would provide the lamb for the sacrifice, which he did. The promise came with a curse (3:10 For as many as are of the works of the law are under the curse. It is written, Cursed is everyone that continueth **NOT** in all things which are written in the book of the law to **DO** them). Live in the law and escape the curse (v12 and the law is not of faith; but the man that **doeth** them shall **live** in them. One can do something because they are instructed to i.e. under a law, or by moral believe, faith. Either way you escape punishment or repercussions. Such as parking on yellow lines by a traffic light, prohibited under the law. Or because you know it would cause traffic jams and disturbance to others. V14 "That the blessings of Abraham might come on the Gentiles". The benefits of a traffic free road will come to those who keep the written law and those who through faith. V18 confirms again, it is circumcision as given to Abraham that is being discussed. 4:1-2 talks of the Gentiles as heirs to the promise made to Abraham, under tutors and governors or schoolmasters as stated in 3:24. But once grown from "child" to mature "son" they move from being equal to a servant to an heir. Abraham had two sons, Isaac promised to him through his wife (a freewoman) and Ishmael through his wife's bondmaid, "born after the flesh". Yet through Abraham all "nations are to be blessed" (v21). 5:2 "Behold, I Paul say unto you **if ye be circumcised**, Christ shall profit you nothing." Gal 5:6 For in Jesus Christ neither circumcision availeth any thing, nor uncircumcision; but faith which worketh by love. V11 "..brethren if I yet preach circumcision, why do I yet suffer persecution? Verses 6:12-end has too many references to circumcision to mention. By now it should be clear the book of Galatians referring to the "law" is to do with circumcision not the commandments or breaking the 7th day Sabbath.

As stated earlier some say Galatians calls keeping the law "bondage". However, Gal 4:9 refers to the bondage of serving false gods as the new converts used to. Gal 4:8 Howbeit then, when ye knew not God, ye did service unto them which by nature are no gods. Gal 4:9 But now, after that ye have known God, or rather are known of God, how turn ye again to the weak and beggarly elements, whereunto ye desire again to be in bondage? Gal 4:10 Ye observe days, and months, and times, and years. I hope the underlined texts shows the before, after and return to bondage state.

BOOK OF ROMANS

Similar to his letter to the Galatians, Paul is writing the new Christian church in Rome combating the same teachings of the Judaziers in Acts 15:1 that Gentile converts to Christ had to be circumcised to be saved (Act 15:24 Forasmuch as we have heard, that certain which went out from us have troubled you with words, subverting your souls, saying, *Ye must* be circumcised, and keep the law). These were new Gentile converts (1:13) who needed to know the **basic** doctrines related to salvation (chapters 1 -8) and to help them understand the unbelief of the Jews and how they benefited from it (chaps 9 – 11). He also explained general principles of Christian life for them to understand and practice (chaps 12 – 15:13). However, for this book, I am focusing only on the topic as to whether the commandments and in particular the Sabbath, was abolished.

To appreciate the books of Romans and Galatians the reader has to keep in mind Paul is referring to one of the laws out of all the laws. The one concerning circumcision. Another helpful thought to bear in mind is Rom 2:12 whether one sins under or not under the law, both groups perish. Sin is sin by both definitions, under or not under the law. One cannot expect to get away with sinning because they think they are not under the law and those who are get punished! God and sin(ners) cannot co-exist in heaven. The brightness and righteousness of God would kill them. Hence no one has seen His face and lived and why Moses had to be shielded in the cleft of the rock. Sin is transgression of the Law. I knew not sin except by its description in the Law. Thus sinners do not get into heaven (by then Jesus has cleansed those allowed in so that they are no longer sinners).

Paul states both Jew and Gentile come under the same directives (save for circumcision). He uses the phase "to the Jew first and also the Gentile (2:9, 10). God is no respector of person; all are under sin and there is one way back for all (Rom 3:9 What then? are we better *than they*? No, in no wise: for we have before proved both Jews and Gentiles, that they are all under sin;). Paul said to the Jews circumcision is only of benefit if they keep "the" Law not "a" law. The Law being in total including the commandments. If they do not it is pointless. The Gentiles on the other hand may keep the righteousness of "the Law" yet not be circumcised and counted better.   Rom 2:25 For circumcision verily profiteth, if thou keep the law: but if thou be a breaker of the law, thy circumcision is made uncircumcision. Rom 2:26 Therefore if the uncircumcision keep the righteousness of the law, shall not his uncircumcision be counted for circumcision? Rom 2:27 And shall not uncircumcision which is by nature, if it fulfil the law, judge thee, who by the letter and circumcision dost transgress the law? Rom 2:28 For he is not a Jew, which is one outwardly; neither *is that* circumcision, which is outward in the flesh: Rom 2:29 But he *is* a Jew, which is one inwardly; and circumcision *is that* of the heart, in the spirit, *and* not in the letter; whose praise *is* not of men, but of God. Then Paul states that the Jews were given the "Oracles of God" keepers of His way (Rom 3:2). Rom 11:13 For I speak to you Gentiles, inasmuch as I am the apostle of the Gentiles, I magnify mine office:

Paul was a strict Jew; raised, taught, knowledgeable and living in the Law. Act 24:12 And they neither found me in the temple disputing with any man, neither raising up the people, neither in the synagogues, nor in the city: Act 24:14 But this I confess unto thee, that after the way which they call heresy, so worship I the God of my fathers, believing all things which are written in the law and in the prophets: Act 24:21 Except it be for this one voice, that I cried standing among them, Touching the resurrection of the dead I am called in question by you this day. Act 25:8 While he answered for himself, Neither against the law of the Jews, neither against the temple, nor yet against Caesar, have I offended any thing at all. Act 25:19 But had certain questions against him of their own superstition, and of one Jesus, which was dead, whom Paul affirmed to be alive. Act 26:6 "And now I stand and am judged for the hope of the promise made of God unto our fathers:" Rom 3:10 As it is written, There is none righteous, no, not one: Rom 3:11 There is none that understandeth, there is none that seeketh after God.

The Law is there to bring us to Christ in this and the next life. I am aware the law itself cannot save us; that is not its purpose; but it is by what we measure our actions. It defines and gives knowledge of sin (Rom 7:7). Where there is no law there is no transgression (Rom 4:15). Transgressing the law is therefore sinning, being unrighteous (Rom 4:15). Those who call keeping the law legalistic would change their mind if all they owned was taken. Or cars smashed in to theirs going through a red light. No law, no transgression, no wrong doing! Laws keep order for all. Similar to the motorist driving code which we have to learn, pass and abide by to get a driving license. At first learning to drive is a mental struggle with hand and eye coordination to control the dangerous car and drive in safety for all. Once we have mastered the act, we no longer find it a struggle to keep within the law. We automatically drive the car and coordinate our hands and feet. However, if on occasion you break one of the rules, you may see a police car pull you over and remind you of the law which you broke. (Gal 3:24-5). Faith is the same, yet higher than the law in the sense the law are the regulations which once you know how they work you have faith in them. Thousand of people risk their lives in aeroplanes, bungy jumping and other pursuits. They have faith in the laws of physics etc. They may not be mathematicians; but take faith in calculations of those who are. The law gave them the faith to risk their lives. Others who do not have faith in the laws are afraid to fly in aeroplanes or jump off a bridge with elastic tied to their feet..

WHAT IS FAITH

What one does in the belief something will happen immediately or in the future.

Heb 11:1 Now faith is the substance of things hoped for, the evidence of things not seen. 2Cor 5:7 (For we walk by faith, not by sight: Heb 11:6 But without faith it is impossible to please him: for he that cometh to God must believe that he is, and that he is a rewarder of them that diligently seek him. Rom 3:25 Whom God hath set forth to be a propitiation through faith in his blood, to declare his righteousness for the remission of sins that are past, through the forbearance of God. Christians are told to quote the last part of Rom 1:17 why they are not under "the Law". Rom 1:17 For therein is the righteousness of God revealed from faith to faith: as it is written,

The just shall live by faith. Let us see how the bible explains faith i.e. Jam 2:22

Jam 2:14 "What doth it profit, my brethren, though a man say he hath faith, and have not works? can faith save him? Jam 2:17 Even so faith, if it hath not works, is dead, being alone. Jam 2:18 Yea, a man may say, Thou hast faith, and I have works: shew me thy faith without thy works, and I will shew thee my faith by my works. Jam 2:20 But wilt thou know, oh vain man, that faith without works is dead? Jam 2:21 Was not Abraham our father justified by works, when he had offered Isaac his son upon the altar? Jam 2:22 Seest thou how faith wrought with his works, and by works was faith made perfect. Jam 2:24 Ye see then how that by works a man is justified, and not by faith only. Jam 2:26 For as the body without the spirit is dead, so faith without works is dead also." So the conclusion of Rom 1:17 is Rom 3:31 Do we then make void the law through faith? God forbid: yea, we establish the law. And failing to adhere results in Rom 1:18. The law reveals what is unrighteousness. Jesus Himself said in Matt 16:27 "For the Son of man shall come in the glory of his Father with his angels; and then he shall reward every man according to his works". remembrance of Hezekiah's good deeds is what benefited him. 2Ki 20:3 I beseech thee, O LORD, remember now how I have walked before thee in truth and with a perfect heart, and have done *that which is* good in thy sight. And Hezekiah wept sore. Neh 13:14. Rev 14:13 And I heard a voice from heaven saying unto me, Write, Blessed *are* the dead which die in the Lord from henceforth: Yea, saith the Spirit, that they may rest from their labours; and their works do follow them. Some Christians quote Scriptures about being saved by faith alone; but

93

then require people to have some outward self-righteousness to validate their faith. Clearly they are confusing the ROOT of a believer's faith, which Paul speaks of in Romans; in contrast to the FRUIT of a believer's faith, which is spoken of by James

Anyone can say they believe something until it comes time to prove it and show their faith. In today's society those with real faith that God would provide for them if forsake all and keep the Sabbath is shown in their actions and belief. "To obey is better than sacrifice". If you had faith to say to the mountain move, it would move; but your lack of or level of faith is proved when the mountain moves or not (though not necessarily as explained later). Therefore your faith that God would keep his promise and reward you for honouring His Sabbath and other commandments is shown by whether you keep it or hide behind one of the many excuses. Numerous testimonies are told by those who really wholeheartedly believed in and honoured the Sabbath down to their last morsel of food for self and family. When they placed all their trust in God and proved it to Him by their willingness to die rather than break His Commandment.

One can believe something; but not do it. The believe is then vain. One does not believe what they know to be a lie, though one can believe a lie through being deceived. The devil has more belief in God and Jesus than most Christians following custom. Unlike them, he knows his deceits are lies, thus also the truth that Jesus is "the way, the truth, and the life: no man cometh unto the Father, but by me." John 14:6 Jam 2:19 Thou believest that there is one God; thou doest well: the devils also believe, and tremble." Luk 4:33-4 "in the synagogue there was a man, which had a spirit of an unclean devil, and cried…Jesus of Nazareth…I know thee who thou art; the Holy One of God" Yet the devil nor those who side with him definitely will not be saved in the new heaven and earth. They know and some believe the real understanding of scripture; but choose not to follow it and mislead you with false interpretations. So one has to do more than believe as in the book of Daniel where they did not bow down to the image rather than rely on god knowing their belief in Him. One must also act properly in line with that belief.

Anything we do that is expected to bring a reward or result in the future (immediate or far) we do in the "faith" (believe) it would happen. The strength of our faith is measure on the amount of dependence we place on the outcome. One goes to work in the belief they will get paid, if not, they do not go. Some risks are safeguarded by law or other method so that ones faith has a guarantee of sort. Other risks are assessed on knowledge through personal experience or that of others, so that, again, ones faith is supported. You would not jump out of a twenty storey window and have the faith to walk away from an impact on solid pavement. Peter would never have believed he could walk on water until Jesus bid him and gave him the faith; but almost immediately this was overcome by his previous knowledge and he began to sink.2 Cor 5:7 (For we walk by faith, not by sight:) Who would believe that walking round a fortified enemy's camp blowing a trumpet would collapse its exterior wall? Yet in Heb 11:30 by faith the walls of Jericho fell down, after they were compassed about seven days. We also have the story of Naaman in 2 Kings 5:9-11

In the Old Testament people had the faith their sins would be forgiven by the blood rituals of the priests. Why? Because they believed God's promise just as we exchange bits of printed paper for valuable goods because the banking and government systems says so. If confidence was ever lost in either the system or "promise to pay" our faith in it would crumble or the printed paper loose its value. Num 21:8 the LORD said unto Moses, Make thee a fiery serpent, and set it upon a pole: and it shall come to pass, that every one that is bitten, when he looketh upon it, shall live. John 3:14 "And as Moses lifted up the serpent in the wilderness, even so must the Son of man be lifted up:" In other words, just as the people believed looking on the pole with an image of a serpent would cure them, believers of today are to look on Jesus. The pole onlookers and the people of the animal sacrifice sin forgiveness system still had to keep the commandments, other laws, feasts and holy days etc of God.

I am sure if God had told them to run three miles to get forgiveness for their sins they would. The forgiveness is therefore through "faith" not the actual act. After the death of Jesus, God tells us the "faith" remains but the "act" has changed from that of the blood of animals offered by earthly priests, to that of the blood of Jesus. Not much difference. Blood for blood, earthly priests to heavenly High Priest. No difference, no proof, just take God's word or not. This act in no way nullifies the Commandments: a list of sins. They remain separate from the route, "act" prescribed for forgiveness. At all times, Old and New Testament periods, the sinner needs to believe in the forgiveness process. Rev 7:14 These are they which came out of great tribulation, and have washed their robes, and made them white in the blood of the Lamb.

Gal 5:6in Jesus Christ neither circumcision availeth any thing, nor uncircumcision; but faith which worketh by love. Heb 11:13 Through faith we understand that the worlds were framed by the word of God, so that things which are seen were not made of things which do appear. Heb 11:4faith Abel offered unto God a more excellent sacrifice than Cain, by which he obtained witness that he was righteous, God testifying of his gifts: and by it he being dead yet speaketh. Heb 11:5 by faith Enoch was translated that he should not see death; and was not found, because God had translated him: for before his translation he had this testimony, that he pleased God. Heb 11:7 By faith Noah, being warned of God of things not seen as yet, moved with fear, prepared an ark to the saving of his house; by the which he condemned the world, and became heir of the righteousness which is by faith. Heb 11:8 by faith Abraham, when he was called to go out into a place which he should after receive for an inheritance, obeyed; and he went out, not knowing whither he went.

Faith is what is believed in the heart from whence cometh our works. In Daniel 3:17 the three men had faith that God is able and would save them if it was His will .If God chose not to save them it would not diminish their faith of His ability. They showed their faith in this belief by not bowing to the image and relying on their belief, i.e. they showed their faith by their actions. Faith is not a New Testament concept. Rom 1:17 The just shall live by faith. Hab 2:4 "… the just shall live by his faith" Act 26:20 and do works meet for repentance. Persuading them concerning Jesus, both out of the law of

Moses, and out of the prophets, from morning till evening. Act 28:24 some believed the things, which were spoken, and some believed not. Rev 12:17, 14:12 and 20:4 mention keeping of the commandments of GOD & faith of JESUS. Both Old and New Testament persons are not just saved by "faith" in Jesus. Rev 20:12-13 judged according to works i.e. action of keeping commandment not mere belief in Jesus (22:12).

Another aspect of ones faith I wish to clarify is that it is not the believer's faith that so much saves them; but in what or whom they believe. You can have faith in anyone else but Christ to save you and that faith will be groundless. If Peter had stepped onto that water believing in anyone else but Jesus he would have sank immediately. One can have all the faith in the world that a cow will save them or that they will grow fins and gills like a fish if they stayed in water long enough. Christians know this is not the case. Jesus remains true and the only saviour whether one believes it or not. A false method remains false no matter how much faith one puts in it (Rom 3:3-4 For what if some did not believe? shall their unbelief make the faith of God without effect? God forbid: yea, let God be true, but every man a liar; as it is written, That thou mightest be justified in thy sayings, and mightest overcome when thou art judged). One can also believe in the right person, Jesus; but the wrong things of Him or His character, i.e He will come dressed in black as a thief in the night, put wings on your back and you both fly to heaven where you are placed in Abraham's bosom. Again, Christian's ought to know this is untrue. Thus we have to belief in the right person, the right things about His teachings, ability and prescribed way to be saved by Him. If the Jews in Num 21:8 had touched the staff with the serpent's head rather than look on it as prescribed, all the faith in the world may not have saved them. Again in 1king 13:26 the man of God have faith and believe he was doing the right thing; but his faith was wrong and God killed him. So it is more by grace, God's favour, that we are saved not our faith.

The sum of the misunderstanding that faith in Jesus Christ abolishes the law is in Rev 14:12 here is the patience of the saints: here are they that (one) keep the commandments of God and (two) the faith of Jesus (believing that His blood is the necessary act for forgiveness of the sins listed in the Commandments). Rom 3:31 we then make void the law through faith? God forbid: yea, we establish the law.

WHAT IS LOVE

Some, generally non Christians, ask how can a loving God punish sinners? Our worldly laws follow the same principles. Punish those who break the law. Those who love their neighbour (fellow humans) would not take their assets or life. The punishment is meant to reform them and protect the innocent.. I will not claim to know all the answers, to fully understand nor am qualified to speak on behalf of God. His ways are not our ways. However, some points could be our freewill to eat as we wish harmful processed food slowly contaminating our body, take risks, making wrong decisions could have detriment effects not just for us but our off spring. Then there are those working for the enemy or their own gain whether governments, organisations or individuals (Job 1:15 And the Sabeans fell *upon them*, and took them away; yea, they have slain the servants with the edge of the sword; and I only am escaped alone to tell thee). Also most may think it is their right to be protected by God when they do not obey His commandments nor raise their children to follow Him yet want Him to protect them with His love (Neh ... O LORD God of heaven, the great and terrible God, that keepeth covenant and mercy for them that love him and observe his commandments). Though God maketh his sun to rise on the evil and on the good, and sendeth rain on the just and unjust (Matt 5:45), I doubt we are to show love to the devil and his followers. This does not mean we are to abstain from showing them the way to God through His love. Pro 29:27 An unjust man *is* an abomination to the just: and *he that is* upright in the way *is* abomination to the wicked. We have to balance Jesus' teachings to love our enemies. Our enemies and those who dislike us may be within our own fold not of the world. They "sue thee at the law" Matt 5:40 (of God as repeated to Moses). Mat 7:12 therefore all things whatsoever ye would that men should do to you, do ye even so to them: for this is the law and the prophets.

As God's children we are to follow the same child raising examples as in Ex 20:12 Honour thy father and mother that thy days be long which God giveth thee, Pro 1:7-8 (the fear of the Lord..), 2:1, 3:11-12 "for who the Lord loveth He correcteth", 13:24 (he that loveth son corrects and punish him quickly), 23:13-14, 29:15. So firm direction and correction is a sign of love. Children and humans need guidelines for their own and others protection.

Some Christians use Joh 13:34 "A new commandment I give unto you, that ye love one another; as I have loved you, that ye also love one another" as their excuse not to keep God's forth seventh day Sabbath. The commandment of loving one another is an Old Testament one Lev 19:18, 34 Thou shalt not avenge, nor bear any grudge against the children of thy people, but thou shalt love thy neighbour as thyself: I *am* the LORD". "A new" does not necessarily mean replacement. It could be additional. Joh 14:21 He that hath my commandments, and keepeth them, he it is that loveth me: and he that loveth me shall be loved of my Father, and I will love him, and will manifest myself to him. John's letters affirms this new commandment is one of old 1Jo 2:1-7 my little children, these things write I unto you, that ye <u>sin not</u>. And if any man sin, we have an advocate with the Father, Jesus Christ the righteous: And he is the propitiation for our sins: and not for ours only, but also for *the sins of* the whole world. And hereby we do know that <u>we know him, if we keep his commandments</u>. He that saith, I know him, and <u>keepeth not his commandments, is a liar, and the truth is not in him</u>. But whoso keepeth his word, in him verily is the love of God perfected: hereby know we that we are <u>in him</u>. He that saith he <u>abideth in him</u> ought himself also so to walk, even as he walked. Brethren, I write no new commandment unto you, but an old commandment which ye had <u>from the beginning</u>. The old commandment is <u>the word</u> which ye have heard from the beginning. For "the word" see John 1:1-3, for abide see Jesus' words Joh 15:10 If ye keep my commandments, ye shall abide in my love; even as I have kept my Father's commandments, and abide in his love.. Those who do not abide, (keep all the commandments), are "cast forth as a branch, and is withered; and men gather them, and cast *them* into the fire, and they are burned" (John 15:6). Remember James 2:8-10.

Hopefully the following texts are clear and do not need any further explanation. As Deuteronomy 5:10 shows, it is not a New Testament concept. Simply do His will as it was in the beginning, keep His Commandments whether adhering to the written version or the original moral version followed by Noah, Enoch etc 2John 1:6 And this is love, that we walk after his commandments. This is the commandment, that, as ye have heard from the **beginning,** ye should walk in it.

John 14:23 Jesus answered and said unto him, if a man love me, he will keep my words: and my Father will love him, and we will come unto him, and make our abode with him. John 14:24 He that loveth me not keepeth not my sayings: and the word, which ye hear, is not mine, but the Father's which sent me. Joh 14:21 He that hath my commandments, and keepeth them, he it is that loveth: and he that loveth me shall be loved of my Father, and I will love him, and will manifest myself to him. 1Joh 5:2 by this we know that we love the children of God, when we love God, and keep his commandments. 1Joh 5:3 for this is the love of God, that we keep his commandments: and his commandments are not grievous. Deu 5:10; 7:9; Ex 20:6shewing mercy unto thousands of them that love me and keep my commandments. Joh 14:15ye love me, keep my commandments. Joh 15:10 If ye keep my commandments, ye shall abide in my love; even as I have kept my Father's commandments, and abide in his love. Micah 7:18 Who is a God like you, who pardons sin and forgives the transgression of the remnant of his inheritance? You do not stay angry forever but delight to show mercy. Clearly "love" does not cancel ones obligation to keep the commandments. See also "Grace" section and the explanation of Mat 22:37 -40 Jesus said unto him, Thou shalt love the Lord thy God with all thy heart, and with all thy soul, and with all thy mind. This is the first and great commandment. ... On these two commandments <u>hang</u> all the law and the prophets. It is repeat of Deut 6:5.

GRACE AND RELATIONSHIP WITH GOD

1Joh 1:9 If we confess our sins, he is faithful and just to forgive us *our* sins, and to cleanse us from all unrighteousness.

Saved by grace. What exactly does this mean, not under the commandments? Keep in mind Paul's words in Rom 15:18 For I will not dare to speak of any of those things which Christ hath not wrought by me, to make the Gentiles **obedient,** by word and **deed,**

Like the trial bundle of a large court case, if you read any of the documents in the vast number of files for either the prosecution or defence, you will get a one sided answer of either guilty or innocent. Some Sunday advocates show scriptures stating all Christians have to do to be saved is confess their sins to Jesus, that He is Lord, believe in Him, saved by faith or grace not works. They avoid ones stating without works one's faith is dead, we are judged by our works and deeds, performing a commandment to do an action, doing His Father's will, commandments etc, I and Father are one. Unless both sides of the argue are merged to get all the facts a wrong conclusion may be reached. Hence Christians must be aware of all scriptures. Then they should realise the only way to adhere to both sets is to "keep the commandments of God and the faith of Jesus Christ". (Rev 14:12).

To understand Grace it may be helpful to imagine it as a discount given by God to His followers as we all fall short of the price needed to get to heaven. One must meet the minimum requirement of keeping His commandments and trying to live as He desires. Because we will all sin in thought or action. God therefore needs to give a discount (pay the balance of the price of which we fall short). Discount /Grace alone cannot save; it is God's goodwill (grace). In the O.T. a Hebrew word "chesed" (numerical reference H2617) is translated mercy (Micah 8:8 and Hosea 6:6). The N.T. equivalent is "grace". Remember Jesus said if one does not forgive others they neither will be forgiven. Just like in Eze 33:13 (The righteousness of the righteous will not save them in the day of their transgression) an act of "works" is necessary. It is not once saved always saved. The wicked that turns from their wickedness and do that which is lawful and right, will live (v19). Proof that grace alone cannot save. Not even Bill Gates' billions can get him into heaven without God's grace. The ticket is neither purchased with money nor given away free simply on belief. It is not a New Testament concept. In Gen 6:8 it was God's grace that saved Noah "but Noah found grace in the eyes of the Lord." Also Lot in Gen 19:19. God's benefits have always been a two party covenant, you and Him. The terms were "if" you keep ALL my commandments, I will (i.e. Neh 1:5) Have you kept up your end as God is faithful to keep up His?

A respected brother in Christ did not like my analogy and explained Grace this way. It is a free gift offered to all; but those who accept it, come to God through Jesus, must thereafter live in obedience to His commandments as an act of love to the one who gave the grace. If they do not, they will loose their salvation. I suppose an analogy of my brother's explanation would be, a store owner offers a free gift to all. Of those hearers of the offer who step into the store, they are obligated to abide by his rules; not to steal or damage anything in the store, harm him or other customers. . If they do they will be thrown out without the free gift. Which ever explanation aids your understanding, the bottom line is we are bound to show love and obedience by keeping the all commandments.

Pastors are leading persons away from God, keeping His commandments (4th in particular) using what they term as the "free gift of grace" as the route to heaven Eph 2:8 "For by grace are ye saved through faith; and that not of yourselves: *it is* the gift of God". For one to understand the proper concept of grace they ought to ask themselves what it is, from where did it come, did it exist before Jesus, does it change or abolish the commandments, what does the bible say it does compared to man's common explanations? Separate God's words (in full) from man's, truth from custom, God from satan the deceiver. Note 1Peter 4:18 the righteous are scarcely saved. In other words, just about make it into heaven. So if being righteous just about saves you, how can grace be a free gift to save almost all without them doing the works of keeping all God's commandments? It is because the verse following (Eph 2:9 "Not of works, lest any man should boast") is generally left out or miss used. Paul is talking about boasting. That no one is without sin, is "good", and has not fallen short of the mark. Thus none can boast they got into heaven on their own merit, without the grace of God. Eph 2:10 For we are his workmanship, created in Christ Jesus <u>unto good works</u>, which God hath before ordained that <u>we should walk in them</u>. Rom 6:1 what shall we say then? Shall we continue in sin, that grace may abound? Rom 6:2 God forbid. How shall we, that are dead to sin, live any longer therein? Rom 6:15 What then? shall we sin, because we are not under the law, but under grace? God forbid. Rom 6:16 Know ye not, that to whom ye yield yourselves servants to obey, his servants ye are to whom ye obey; whether of sin unto death, or of obedience unto righteousness? Rom 7:25 I thank God through Jesus Christ our Lord. So then with the mind I myself serve the law of God; but with the flesh the law of sin. Rom 8:3 For what the law could not do, in that it was weak through the flesh, God sending his own Son in the likeness of sinful flesh, and for sin, condemned sin in the flesh: Rom 8:4 That the righteousness of the law might be fulfilled in us, who walk not after the flesh, but after the Spirit. Rom 8:5 for they that are after the flesh do mind the things of the flesh; but they that are after the Spirit the things of the Spirit. Sin is transgression of the Law. I knew not sin except by its description in the Law. Sinners do not get into heaven (by then Jesus has cleansed those allowed in sop that they are no longer sinners). Rom 2:12 whether one sins under or not under the law, both groups perish.

Joh 3:15-16 For God so loved the world, that he gave his only begotten Son, that whosoever believeth in him should not perish, but have everlasting life. Does belief in Jesus Christ save us? In Other words are we forgiven from our sins? Yes and no .One may say belief is like or same as faith. But believing something will happen does not necessarily make it happen, i.e. that you will be saved, that you have done enough. God gave us The Commandments, laws and statutes by which to live. Within these are the identification and description of sin. In times of old, for the forgiveness of sin we had the intercession of priests, i.e. Aaron. He did the rituals as prescribed by God and by that we were and believed our sins were forgiven (explained in other sections). However, on several occasions the people believed God was with them, only to find out the hard way He was not. In Deut 1:41-45 when they went to fight against the Amorites believing God was with them and would give them victory, only to be chased like bees and multitudes killed. In 1 Sam 4:5they put the Ark of the Covenant before them in battle believing God would go before them and give them victory. Again they lost and the Ark was taken. Even when we think our prayers are being noticed, God may be shutting His eyes and ears to them due to our state of mind or actions (Isa 1:15). The deceiver may then intervene to deceive you. It is only by doing what God requires, obedience, that we know God's will is being done in & through us.

For the belief system to work one must do to their best ability the works of God's commandments. From the heart involving one's mind (mental part), body (works and physical part) and soul. Hence why God instructed His commandments be kept in His people's hearts. Deu 6:6 And these words, which I command thee this day, shall be in thine heart Deu 11:18 Therefore shall ye lay up these my words in your heart and in your soul, and bind them for a sign upon your hand, that they may be as frontlets between your eyes and Deut 10:16. Isaiah 58 narrates God saying our actions and sacrifices to Him i.e. fasting are to be enjoyed. They are to be kept; but not as a grievous act. If so they will not be acceptable to Him. Verse 13 shows the state in which your heart is expected to be for God to accept your sacrifice. This is repeated in the N.T. 2 Cor 9:7 "God loves a cheerful giver".

Imagine you own a business and are looking for a new employee. You take up references on three applicants. The previous bosses respond as follows:

Applicant A: did some of his duties, some of his own choosing at his own time.
Applicant B: did all his duties, at the required times; but no more. He left as soon as his daily contracted time ended.
Applicant C: did all his duties, made some errors on occasion but corrected them. Enjoyed his work and did whatever was needed   or stayed behind if required.

Who do you think would get the job, or reward if in heavenly terms? So for clarification, the answer is not, NOT to do the sacrifice; but do it with a joyous heart. Only then if one slips up can we go through Jesus' blood on Calvary in the belief that if we confess and earnestly seek repentance our sin would be forgiven. The grace discount received. We cannot simply do as we will, with little or our standard of effort and have God confirm our belief that our sins are forgiven. If that is your belief, that it is a free gift, you may find out the hard way, on judgement day that you were wrong.

If humans were all righteous like Enoch, Jesus would not have had to die for us. We would get to heaven on our own merit. At best, some may qualify as good. Good being our definition as small sinners not murderers etc. But, even for those "good small sinners", Jesus would have had to die. Rom 5:7-8scarcely for a righteous man will one die: yet peradventure for a good man some would even dare to die. But God commendeth his love toward us, in that, while we were yet sinners, Christ died for us.

In Jesus' definition as he said in Mat 19:17,are good save his father in heaven. The truth is we all fall short, and needed Jesus to die to save us. It is for this reason the justification by faith in Jesus' blood has merit. However, as explained above, that faith cannot be workless. James: "Show me your faith without works and I will show you my faith by my works". God's grace pays the part of the price for which we fall short.

Imagine you own a store in which you buy and sell at a profit commodities. Most people would not sell an item from their store to a loved family or friend at the same price they would to a stranger. If you bought the item for £50.00 and normally sell for £80.00, you may give the family or friend as much as £30.00 discount. They still have to meet your minimum standard of £50.00.That, to me, is the analogy of God's grace. We have to meet the minimum price of trying our best to obey His commandments. Unlike Enoch, we will not succeed in reaching our death sinless; but due to our efforts God will pay the discount. it is not free to everyone, etc. (unless they truly repent and make amends). Neither does pure belief without any works (actions) entitles us to the reward. One may say, it is not the works; but the obedience. That therefore leaves the way as, try to keep God's commandments etc to the best of your ability. If you fail, repent from the heart, confess and believe Jesus' blood will cleanse you and make every attempt not to do the act again. If you truly try with all heartfelt intention of not doing the act again God may forgive you "seventy times seven times".

Many people say it is all about their relationship with Jesus. A saying received via false teachers. Allow me to explain before discounting the thought. First, allow me to give a biblical example of how mis-understanding arises, even when one hears Jesus' words directly. Then think about subsequent preachers who add their own interpretations, translations or mis quotes. John 21:22-23 "Peter seeing him saith to Jesus, Lord, and what *shall* this man *do*? Jesus saith unto him, if I will that he tarry till I come, what *is that* to thee? follow thou me. Then went this saying abroad among the brethren, that that disciple should not die: yet Jesus said not unto him, he shall not die; but, If I will that he tarry till I come, what *is that* to thee?" It would appear that many thought Jesus said that the disciple should not die. John, however, apparently disagrees with this conclusion. If the disciples after years of direct teaching from Jesus could get it wrong, could not you? Is it therefore not better to obey and follow God's words rather than draw your own interpretation this or that is no longer required when there is no clear unambiguous words of God to that effect. Paul the apostle of the Gentiles states we have to do works for repentance Act 26:5 Which knew me from the beginning, if they would testify that after the straitest sect of our religion I lived a Pharisee. Act 26:20 but shewed first unto them of Damascus, and at Jerusalem, and throughout all the coasts of Judea, and *then* to the Gentiles, that they should repent and turn to God, and do works meet for repentance. He also delighted in the law Rom 7:22 For I delight in the law of God after the inward man:

Some pastors, as an excuse not to keep the 4th commandment, say the "Law" has been done away with; it is now about one's relationship with God. Does that mean God did not have a relationship with man before, during the time they kept the commandments and laws? Believers of this concept do not understand what true relationship is. I doubt they will be able to find anyone in the bible who had favour with God (Abraham, Moses, Joseph, David, man of God in 1King 13:1-26 and all prophets) who did not have a relationship with Him. They all had a relationship with God to the extent He favoured their requests. Yet Moses and Aaron did not reach the Promised Land due to their disobedience. The man of God was also punished for his disobedience although he had a heart intent on serving God. God is not a respecter of persons, only if they keep His commands or not. They are there to "prove" you. Thus the relationship criterion is not a New Testament one. They had even more of a relationship with God than most, if not anyone, of today. He walked with and talked to them in person; almost face to face. Visibly, not abstract by a questionable spirit. To have a relationship with someone, one needs to have certain things or purpose in common. The stronger the relationship, the greater the common element, respect, desire to please the other i.e. a shared will. One shows their love and respect to God by "doing His will... "keeping His commandments". So if you are **not** keeping all God's commandments, yet think you have a good enough relationship with Him to get to heaven, ask why should you get preferential treatment above His biblical prophets and others who had a closer relationship yet had to and kept them? In my view, if you do come up with an excuse, it is just that, a hypothetical, optimistic excuse.

One may think they have a relationship with God because they go to church, read His word, say prayers; but if they are your reasoning rather than His commands He may have, as the bible states, closed His eyes and ears to you. "To obey is ....." If you wanted £10.00 ($20.00) at noon on Monday, would you necessarily be happy if the person arrived Tuesday with £50.00 ($100.00)?Remember God is our creator. We are little specks of His vast universal creation. We are not to dictate to Him; but follow His will and all commandments. You may say you know God; but does He know you Matt 7:23? He knows those who observe all things he taught not some, as may be your view of good, love your neighbour, etc (Matt 28:20). Neither are you to add or take anything away from His word (Rev 22:19). Not those calling His name; but only those doing His fathers will, contained in the commandments will enter heaven (Matt 7:21). He does not want you enquiring after customs of others, copying them nor bringing them into His system Deut 12:30, 3John 1:7 3Jo 1:7 Because that for his name's sake they went forth, taking nothing of the Gentiles. (including their day of worship. Rev 22:14 blessed *are* they that do his commandments that they may have right to the tree of life, and may enter in through the gates into the city.

A friend and Sunday school teacher began to read the bible from the Old Testament following a programme of completing it within 365 days. After three months she saw more of God's character and His desire for us to keep the Sabbath. In response to her decision to consider joining a Sabbath keeping church, her pastor gave her an 11 page article. The central title was Understanding Law & Grace with the initial sub-heading of "The Relationship purpose of the Ten Commandments". The extract concluded Christians are no longer under the "Law"; but grace. However, the author's case seems flawed by his own arguments. I shall only comment using the author's own reasoning and his obviously flawed conclusion by his own rational. The points he makes are as follows, with the article commencing with: When the Pharisees learned that the Sadducees could not argue with Jesus' answers to them, the Pharisees met together. One Pharisee, who was an expert on the Law of Moses, asked Jesus this question to test him: *"Teacher, which command in the law, is the most important?"* Jesus answered, "Love the Lord your God with **all** your heart, **all** your soul, and **all** your mind.' This is the first and most important command. And the second command is like the first: 'Love your neighbor as you love yourself.' All the law and the writings of the prophets depend on these two commands." (Matthew 22:34-40) NCV (New Century Version)

The Authors Comments: It is interesting and yet not surprising that Jesus did not answer this Pharisee's question with one specific commandment. Instead, Jesus went deeper in stating the heart commandments from which all the commandments originated. Loving God and our neighbor puts all the other commandments in context. The commandments are encased in **RELATIONSHIP**. A proper understanding of the law will not be achieved outside of this context.

The KJV of Mat 22:34-40 reads "But when the Pharisees had heard that he had put the Sadducees to silence, they were gathered together. Then one of them, which was a lawyer, asked him a question, tempting him, and saying, Master, which is the great commandment in the law? Jesus said unto him, Thou shalt love the Lord thy God with all thy heart, and with all thy soul, and with all thy mind. This is the first and great commandment. And the second is like unto it, Thou shalt love thy neighbour as thyself. On these two commandments hang all the law and the prophets."

Luke 10:25-28 reads "And, behold, a certain lawyer stood up, and tempted him, saying, Master, what shall I do to inherit eternal life? He said unto him, what is written in the law, how readest thou? And he answering said, thou shalt love the Lord thy God with all thy heart, and with all thy soul, and with all thy strength, and with all thy mind; and thy neighbour as thyself. And he said unto him, Thou hast answered right: this do, and thou shalt live."

I will not comment exhaustively on these initial 3 paragraphs but to say: The NCV version from which the quote comes uses the wrong words as in command instead of the obvious commandment, depend instead of hang, etc. Paragraph one shows the intention of the Pharisee was not to seek enlightenment; but trick or test Jesus. In His answer, Jesus could have corrected the Matthew version by clarifying the difference between the commandments and the rest of the laws commonly together titled the Law. Instead, through His perception and wisdom, Jesus went directly to answering the intended question "which one"? .Jesus simply categorised the ten into their two main headings of love God, Love neighbour and confirmed the whole teachings of God and the prophets "hang", depend, on these principles, foundation etc. In fact, later in the article, the author says the same in a sentence "The Ten Commandments are divided accordingly" then has two sub-headings, commandments addressing relationship with God, under which he lists the first four and commandments addressing relationship with others, under which he lists the other six.

The third paragraph says "Jesus went deeper in …"I can see Jesus gave two answers (commandments) instead of the one requested (these two being summaries of the ten); but not that He told the "expert" lawyer anything new that he did not already know. This is confirmed by the answer Jesus gave in Luke 10:25-28 when a different lawyer asked a similar question. Note Jesus qualified his use of the words heart, soul and mind with "all". Yes, many Christians may love God with there heart; but few with their whole heart. There is a limit to what they are willing to give up or for how long. Note "whole heart" in .the following and other scriptures. Psa 119:10 With my **whole** heart have I sought thee: O let me not wander from thy commandments. Psa 119:34 Give me understanding, and I shall keep thy law; yea, I shall observe it with *my* ***whole heart.*** Psa 119:58 I intreated thy favour with *my* **whole** heart: be merciful unto me according to thy word. Psa 119:145 KOPH. I cried with *my* ***whole heart;*** hear me, O LORD: I will keep thy statutes.. Later, I shall comment on how the bible advocates "all" truth, not partial following.

 I am not sure if the author is advocating the law being abolished and replaced by a relationship with God through Jesus because almost everything he states does not say that though one can see that is his intention. He writes "in the New Testament the Ten Commandments serve as a guide to lead us to a personal relationship with God through Jesus Christ in the new covenant". "The first thing we must understand…". I have already covered this new "covenant" in another section. Jesus states in Matt 22:40 the message ("hang") is the same as has been professed by the Law and the prophets. Obviously not a change as supported by Mat 7:12 Therefore all things whatsoever ye would that men should do to you, do ye even so to them: for this is the law and prophets. No individual commandment is more important than the others. They are a group. Break one, you break all. Matt 22:37 is simply Jesus restating the O.T verse of Deut 6:5 love God with all thy heart, soul and might. Matt 7:12, whatever you wish men to do to you, do also to them for this is the law and prophets. See also Mark 12:29-30 the first "is" …. And the second is "like" it…).

I have a wardrobe .It has a rail on which hang all my jackets, jumpers, shirts trousers, shorts, jogging bottoms. I am asked what is the most important purpose of that rail. I reply, it stores all my upper body cloths and equally my lower body. This does not change the purpose of the rail, omit or diminish the service it provides to my shirts or shorts .I have simply condensed the things it supports into two main categories. The relationship, support it gives to the cloths, remains unchanged. This is the same with the "Law" and relationship". The parallel was there before the law and remains after. As the author states, the purpose of the law was to "restore" the lost relationship between God and sinful man. Luk 19:10 "For the Son of man is come to seek and to save that which was lost". Note James 2:8-10 (see diagram on next page).

Rom 13:8 –10 Owe no man any thing, but to love one another: for he that loveth another hath fulfilled the law. For this, Thou shalt not commit adultery, Thou shalt not kill, Thou shalt not steal, Thou shalt not bear false witness, Thou shalt not covet; and if *there be* any other commandment, it is briefly comprehended in this saying, namely, Thou shalt love thy neighbour as thyself. Love worketh <u>no ill to his neighbour</u>: therefore love *is* the fulfilling of the law. This confirms that all commandments are and have always been based on love. And were any others to come, they too would be based on love. Love is not a new commandment, amending or canceling of the old.

LOVE

Commandments showing love to GOD (Exodus 20:3-11)

(see Glossary at rear for text)

1 ... have no other gods ...

2 … not make unto thee any graven image...

3 ...not take the name of the LORD thy God in vain...

4   Remember the sabbath day, to keep it holy....

(One should note it is the keeping of the fourth commandment that distinguishes true Christians and it is one of the essential criteria to get into heaven according to Rev 14:7 & others mentioned in this book. It identifies the God of the Bible from other so called god's. Those who contradict Gen 2:3 and worship on another day or part day will show their allegiance to the beast of the books of Daniel and Revelation. A topic too big for this book to also cover. Donot accept distracting theories!)

Commandments showing love to ones Neighbour (Exodus 20:12-17 see Glossary)

5 Honour thy father and thy mother...

6 Thou shalt not kill.

7 … not commit adultery...

8 Thou shalt not steal.

9 ... not bear false witness…

10 .. not covet thy neighbour's house, thou shalt not covet thy neighbour's wife, nor his manservant,..

(One should note that the Roman Catholic church that brought pagan images into the Christian religion as it was the custom of the pagan church of Rome prior to amalgamation by Emperor Constantine and others., has deleted the second commandment pertaining to images and instead divided No. ten relating to coveting into two. They number coveting the house as (9) and wife as (10).

[Blaspheming against the Holy Spirit is a sin not forgiven by God. (Rom 6:16; Matt 12:31 and Mark 3:29). To blaspheme is to take the position of God and claim to be able to do things solely reserved for Him, i.e forgive sins. It was for this claim and accusation of blaspheme that the Jews wanted to stone Jesus. Of course Jesus was the only one able to make that claim. This is why Martin Luther and other protestors broke away from the Catholic church and spurned the denominations of today. The second blasphemeous claim of the Pope, with which almost all Christianity follow, is the right as "god" to change God's commandment and day of worship.]

The list of the rest of the author's comments is:

1. Author states the Commandments are "encased in RELATIONSHIP.A proper understanding of the law will not be achieved outside this context. In the O.T the Commandments was a covenant of love given by God to Israel".

I have already covered the distinction between the Ten Commandments (TC), the laws and that they were not limited Israel so all arguments on that basis are null and void. Remember a "mixed multitude" left Egypt, not only Jews. When Moses came down from the mount, did he separate them into Jews and non-Jews and only gave the commandments and laws to one group? No, he addressed all as one, God's people. The author later accepts they were for all mankind by stating "The law was in the driver's seat .It was in control for the purpose of leading Israel **and all mankind** to Jesus". On that basis the author should ask were they taken away from any of God's people, why, how and when?

2. Author then partially quotes Neh 9:32 (Now therefore, O God, the great, mighty and awesome God, who keeps His covenant of love) for the purpose of using the word "love". Then adds "In the OT the TC were a covenant of love given by a personal God for the people of Israel". However the sentence in KJV reads "who keepest covenant AND mercy". Mercy; which unlike love, has a specific meaning as does the words "of" and "AND". Is the author saying in the NT or to new believers, God is now void of showing love, or His directives are not based on it? When some writers are trying to convince readers of a point based on flimsy arguments, they miss or partially quote texts as well as out of context. For a proper understanding of Neh 9:32 one has to read the rest of the verse and maybe verses 14 and 29. In Dan 9:4-5 you would read Daniel praying "O Lord the great and dreadful God, keeping the covenant and mercy to them that love Him and to them that keep His commandments". The reason for Daniel's pray is seen in verses 5-12. Some preachers say Jesus, in one place or another in the NT quoted the other nine commandments when answering questions on how to be saved; but not the fourth. Firstly, Jesus should not have to list each commandment individually, simply say, as He did many times, keep the "commandments". One does not list the chapters when saying to another, read the book. Secondly, those asking the questions were Jews, it was unnecessary for Jesus to tell them to keep the Sabbath, as that were a basic one all Jews kept.

3. Author: "We do not keep the Ten Commandments (old covenant) for the same purpose that Israel was commanded to keep them. They kept it as a demonstration of faith in the promise of a Saviour who would institute a new covenant. Once the old covenant was fulfilled there was not reason to still keep it. Now instead we keep the new covenant by grace".

The TC (and other laws) is not a covenant; but a list of commandments just like today's statute books. There is not in the list words stating if you do this God will do that. As Paul said, he knew not sin except for the law (Rom 7:7). Neither does the TC speak of a saviour. That is mentioned elsewhere in the O.T for other reasons (see Shadow of Things to Come and Of a Type sections). In any case, the Jews perceived the saviour as a fighting king wielding a sword against their oppressors. If they kept the TC, they would not sin and hence there would be no need for a saviour. By the author's logic, the only way Jews would have got to plan B (a saviour), was to break plan A by NOT keeping the T.C.I have previously dealt with the term "fulfil" in the section Celebrating the First Day of The Week.

4.   Author: "Jesus did not destroy the TC; He moulded them into a new covenant. Law and grace work together as a team in bringing salvation in Jesus Christ .Law brings conviction of sin and shows our need for a saviour through whom we receive forgiveness of sins and eternal life". Is this not what I have stated in this booklet? In brief, Commandments and laws are actions we ought to do. Should we fail, we go to Jesus who is held up like Moses held up the rod with a serpent's head.

5. Author: "Even in the old covenant it was not keeping of the law that saved Israel – it was grace through faith in God's promise. Nevertheless, in keeping covenant with God, Israel demonstrated faith by living "under" the law. Israel's devotion to God was seen in external works of the law". The author accepts faith and grace existed under his so-called "old covenant" Though I know he is speaking against keeping the law, in favour of grace, his actual words state the opposite. He later states "Under the old covenant people were still saved by faith. Those who kept the covenant by faith were those who looked ahead and believed in God's word for those things which were not seen. He then quotes the covenant with Abraham (circumcision). Similar to today, as hard as we may try; we all fall short and need the grace / discount of God. Similarly in the Old Testament, people were not perfect, the law did not make them perfect, they were human, made similar mistakes and needed God's grace. The belief in God's words that their sin offering would suffice as today we believe in Jesus' offering.

6. Author: Grace gives us the freedom and power to obey Jesus; we are not under the law. If keeping the law was enough to make us acceptable to God, there would have been no need for Jesus to come" .The author already confirmed grace existed before Jesus. Grace does not give us freedom to choose, we had that since Adam and Eve chose to disobey God. Did God not say "to obey is better than sacrifice… to prove you"; showing we already had the choice? Keeping the law was sufficient for the prophets and others. Jesus said in Mat 19:17 (if thou will enter life keep the commandments) it was sufficient. Jesus only came because humans broke plan A. If it

were not enough, why would God institute it? Why is the list of the "new covenant" commandments given later by the author, the same as the TC except for the fourth? People use Gal 3:21 (Is the law then against the promises of God? God forbid: for if there had been a law given which could have given life, verily righteousness should have been by the law") as an interpretation Christians are not under the law. A law cannot give life. It is merely words stating what is wrong .For a law to give life, freewill and choice of whether to obey or not would need to be removed. Just like when God said "let there be light" etc, the light had no freewill or ability to disobey. God did not make robots void of choice. What give life is humans choosing to obey the laws, follow God's will, which has not changed. Though the law or commandments cannot give they can give (lead to) death. Breaking them, as in today's society, could yield the death penalty. In many places Jesus said keeping the commandments gives life. Two examples already quoted were Mat 19:17 and Luke 10:28. The penalty for breaking them was death (i.e. see Lev 24:16, Num 15:32-5, Num 35:17, Deut 17:3-5, 21:18-22)

7. Author: The TC was the "rules" that would govern the covenant relationship. Their purpose was to maintain a right relationship with God and one another as an example to the world of the existence and character of Jehovah God .Israel's commitment to God brought His blessing and God's sole purpose with them was to bring forth a light that would bring salvation to the world". Author quotes Isa 51:4.Israel represents God's people who are to show the rest of the world the way back to Him. By keeping His commandments in full. As for the TC being rules to govern the relationship with God, even the Egyptians and pagans who do not have a relationship with God have the same "rules". Not to murder, commit adultery etc. As seen in Gen 12:19 and 26:10 when Abraham and Isaac called their wife, their sister. It is possible to have rules and follow the same without a relationship, i.e. need for a passport to enter a country on holiday (no relationship). The author says the rules were to "maintain" the right relationship with God. Thus the relationship was there before the rules in order for them to be "maintain" as before .I therefore, cannot see how the author can state Jesus created a new concept of relationship when he repeats all were there before Jesus. Author adds, "Jesus was not an after thought (of God). His coming and purpose was prophesied to the first people ever created - Adam and Eve. His coming was intentional from the fall of mankind". So if the promise was almost from man's creation, a promise to them, how can the author say the Jews only kept the laws as a promise to them of a saviour?

8. Author: "God's covenant was with Israel specifically, but this fact did not exclude non-Jews from making the God of Israel their God too (i.e. Rahab the harlot, Nineveh, Nebuchadnezzar, Ruth)." Again the author affirms what I have said, God's rules are for His people and anyone can choose to be His by following His commandments. He later adds "God desired Israel's obedience to His laws so they could continue to be God's light" Obedience is the key. If God requires anything less now, He would be seen as being unfair to those punished in the past (an. ageist).

9. Author: "Jesus was not an after thought (of God). His coming and purpose was prophesied to the first people ever created – Adam and Eve. His coming was

intentional from the fall of mankind". So if the promise was almost from mans creation, a promise to them, how can the author say the Jews only kept the laws as a promise to them of a saviour?

10. States new covenant was instituted at the last supper. (This has been covered in the New Testament section above). He adds, "the new covenant was also sealed with the blood of a sacrifice. Jesus was the Lamb slain and His blood was poured out for the sins of mankind. This was the end of the old covenant and the beginning of a new one. The TC was part of the old covenant. Jesus was not in conflict with the old covenant as the priests, scribes and Pharisees of the day suggested. And less the people think that Jesus came to bash the law and prophets of the Old Testament, Jesus himself stated that He did not come to destroy the law or prophets Mat 5:17).Jesus became our High Priest, Our sacrifice, our temple." "His power over sin and our welcome into His kingdom is what we call GRACE".

So what were they calling grace in the Old Testament before Jesus' arrival and death?

Since the author agrees the law and commandments still stand, what exactly is the change in human behaviour he is saying took place? The author refers to Mat 27:51 where the separating veil of the Temple was torn. He agrees it signified the end of the animal sacrifice system and access through Jesus the high Priest. The author refers to 1 Cor 6:19 (your body being the temple of God). Could that mean we are to do with our bodies as should have been done with the temple? Place God's commandments and Laws in our hearts like they were placed in the Ark of the Covenant (Deu 31:26). Abstain from meats with blood as was done in the temple? Use our temple to keep the Sabbaths, holy days, etc of God? The author continues "So what is the TC place in an era of grace through the new covenant? The scriptures are very clear where they went". He then quotes Jer 31:31-34 and Heb 8:8-13 (commented on above). He, therefore agrees they were not changed simply moved to ones heart. The place where God has set to meet with us as He did with the Ark of the Covenant and temple. It was a new place not new laws (Rom 2:14).The author quotes Eze 36:26-27 (see also Eze 11:19) "A new heart also will I give you, and a new spirit will I put within you: and I will take away the stony heart out of your flesh, and I will give you a heart of flesh. And I will put my spirit within you, and cause you to walk in my statutes, and ye shall keep my judgements, and do them". He states the change is that now the Holy Spirit would make people keep the laws etc which they could not do on their own. I think there are equally, if not more, people today not keeping the laws of God than before. So is his theory working? I doubt it. It amazes me, persons who claim the Commandments, Laws etc were for the Jews always quote and claim promises to the Jews for their own justifications (see Eze 36:1-4). God has one way and He changes not Jer 32:39 and I will give them one heart, and one way that they may fear me for ever, for the good of them, and of their children after them:

11. Like others I have met in the past, the author uses Jesus' sermon on the Mount, whereby He *clarifies* the Commandments, as a justification for new similar ones; based not on the written law but peoples heart's. the author picks Mat 5:21-2 (Ye have heard

that it was said by them of old time, Thou shalt not kill; and whosoever shall kill shall be in danger of the judgement: But I say unto you, That whosoever is angry with his brother without a cause shall be in danger of the judgement). I do not see any change from that stated under the Old Testament law stated in Lev 19:17 (Thou shalt not hate thy brother in thine heart: thou shalt in any wise rebuke thy neighbour, and not suffer sin upon him). The author concurs with, was Jesus changing the law? No, only explaining what the new covenant would look like.

The author adds that the commandments can be kept literally as well as with a deeper meaning of from the heart. He states many feel they can keep the 4th Sabbath commandment from the heart. Setting aside one day a week for God. The specific day could be Sunday. He states this is wrong as that way, unlike the other nine; the Sabbath would not be kept literally. God clearly stated a specific day (Sabbath, seventh, Saturday), last day of the week. No where in the New Testament (new covenant) was the Sabbath day changed to Sunday or any other day of the week. This type of thinking neglects or disregards the obligation to keep the literal meaning of the commandment. This is an inconsistency and a dangerous method of interpreting scripture. It is a subtle twisting of the Scripture to fit a particular theological viewpoint however traditional the viewpoint may be. This would mean that the larger percentage of the Christian church is in grave error by observing Sunday rather than the Sabbath (Saturday). Rather than quote the whole of the author's assertion; it is similar to mine that the Sabbath ought to be kept literally.

Where he breaks away to find justification for not keeping the Sabbath is as follows. Remember he states it ought to be kept **literally and from the heart** as the other nine. Thus he has come up with a different literal meaning.

a) Day does not equal going to church on Saturday or Sunday. It was never the purpose of the Sabbath to gather together for worship .It was a command to rest from our labour as God did from his.

b) The Sabbath day is not about giving God our time.

For my reply to these points see the section titled Celebrating the First Day of the Week. Even under the authors criteria, Christians should not be keeping Sunday but the (seventh day) Sabbath. What they do with it is discussed elsewhere. However, here I shall quote Lev 23:3 "Six days shall work be done: but the seventh day *is* the Sabbath of rest, a <u>holy convocation</u>; ye shall do no work *therein*: it *is* the Sabbath of the LORD in all your dwellings". Exo 16:23 "…To morrow *is* the rest of the holy Sabbath unto the LORD…" Exo 16:25 And Moses said, for to day *is* a Sabbath <u>unto the LORD</u>:…"

I wonder how the author feels resting, as done any other time, day and usual manner, differs from that necessary to make the Sabbath rest a "holy convocation". The original Hebrew word, miqra, from which "convocation" is translated, means something which has been called out i.e. a public meeting a calling together, a convocation, an assembly, a congregation; a place of meeting, a reading, a recital. In the Old Testament, there are two basic meanings (I) a convocation of Israel i.e. God summons them (ii) the result of reading aloud (Neh 8:8) an appointed time or appointed gathering. Miqra, designated the weekly Sabbath (Lev 23:2). It was also used for the seven special convocation Sabbaths. Such times included a formal call of the people to worship by means of the blast of the trumpets (Num 10:2,10).Thus a "convocation" is about a gathering of God's people to worship Him and give Him their time at His prescribed time. On a visit to Turkey I, on numerous occasions, heard the blowing of the trumpet sounding horn at their prescribed times calling persons to worship. It is a pity; they too changed their day of worship from Sabbath to Friday due to trying to separate themselves from the Jews. Is not the safest thing to do simply obey God's words? As when one uses their own reasoning they may, like the author being discussed, get it wrong.

The author states, through keeping the Sabbath day, God wanted Israel to remember that they served the creator of the universe who Himself rested on the seventh day and sanctified it as holy .It was a reminder to Israel of God's sovereignty and rule in their lives. Sometimes the author says the commandments and laws were for Israel and other times that it was for everyone. He needs to look at texts as Gen 9:2-17. 17:12.God always makes provision for all to come to Him.

God rested on the seventh day so He could spend it with you. Will you be coming to meet Him or miss the meeting by arriving on a different day? This life is a try out for the next, where you will spend eternity. You will spend more time there than on this earth. Your total obedience, reasoning etc will determine your destiny. The bible constantly talks about tests to ones character, faith, obedience, love, integrity, loyalty, trials, temptations, refining etc. Do not succumb to the influences of i.e. Egypt as did God's early people. Though you may be "in the world", resist becoming "of it". Aim to get it 100% right (entering at the narrow gate), by man's standards, doing all God commanded. By God's you will fall short and His grace will do the rest.

SHADOW OF THINGS TO COME

The New Testament has two original Hebrew words translated as "shadow". One, skia (G4639) used seven times in the bible, meaning something permanent (or also used to mean a shade as in cooling place out of the heat of the sun) and the other aposkiasma (G644), a derivative of G4639 used only once in the bible in James 1:17, meaning shading off or gradual reduction (Strong's Hebrew / Greek dictionary). However, James only uses it to state God has not variableness, shading off or gradual reduction.

Whether the Sabbath or the feast days, some people think they are not to be kept, have passed away, because were a "shadow of things to come". This phrase is mentioned twice in the bible, 2:17 and Hebrews 10:1; dealt with in a moment. When told they ought to, they reply "so are we still to kill animals as sacrifices then?" They confuse the old animal blood sacrifices of Aaron and the priests with everything pertaining to, all the various laws or even law and commandments (distinction already given earlier). If you have been told to state that as a justification you are wrong. The answer is No; Christians are not to kill the former animal sacrifice of old. In line with God's prediction, He destroyed the temple in which these sacrifices were to be made and scattered the people because they constantly polluted His house with Baal worshipping (i.e. 2 Kings 21:3-5). Even the Jews of today no longer do the annual or daily animal sacrifices for lack of the temple (daily sacrifice mentioned in Exodus 29:36).God replaced the animal for the annual sacrifice with His own pure sacrifice similar to what He did with Abraham and his son. As for the "red heifer without spot, wherein is no blemish and upon which never came yoke" mentioned in Numbers 19:2, none can be found today. So apart from the animal sacrifices, everything else stands. One way for all human race. No discrimination for age (old or new testament birth date), nationality (piece of land or family in which born), or other variances.

Others may quote the man made instituted habits of the Scribes and Pharisees, i.e. only walking a certain number of steps on the Sabbath (covered under Sabbaths day journey section Acts 1:12).). I doubt you would find any law or command of God or Jesus in the bible stating the number of steps one is to walk on the Sabbath. Thus these are man's interpretations of God's way and cannot be used as an excuse.

Exo 24:7-8 "And he took the book of the covenant, and read in the audience of the people: and they said, All that the LORD hath said will we do, and be obedient. And Moses took the blood, and sprinkled *it* on the people, and said, Behold the blood of the covenant, which the LORD hath made with you concerning all these words". I think similarly Jesus' blood is the way to the remission for our sins (Heb 9:22 And almost all things are by the law purged with blood; and without shedding of blood is no remission.) However, we must also be like those under the above covenant. Go to God and state "ALL that He says we will do and be obedient" then can Jesus' blood be sprinkled on us too.

Now to the two times where "Shadow of things to come" is mentioned and used as an excuse. I suggest users of this reasoning note this warning given in Colossians 2:8 "Beware lest any man spoil you through philosophy and vain deceit, after the tradition of men, after the rudiments of the world, and not after Christ." For centuries the ways of God has been replaced by customs of men, of the world. Some call it changing with the times, being modern etc. Is that a justification for going against the God you claim to be your Lord and master? Following the ways of the ungodly, the mass, because the world operates on a system, weekly cycle and customs instituted by the deceiver, Christians are to do the same? I say no. We are to stand alone, like Jeremiah if necessary, as a light to the ignorant, those who have forgotten the way of God the creator, have been taught or inherited the ungodly ways excuses or false justifications of the deceiver.

Col 2:11 "In whom also ye are circumcised with the circumcision made without hands, in putting off the body of the sins of the flesh by the circumcision of Christ." Here we read, as usual, Paul talking about the demands of the Jews that gentile believers be circumcised and according to their custom handed down via Abraham. Paul states the sacrifice of Jesus was their salvation not circumcision. Col 2:14"Blotting out the handwriting of ordinances that was against us, which was contrary to us, and took it out of the way, nailing it to his cross". Commandments were written by the finger of God, do not contain ordinances and was placed in the Ark of the Covenant Exo 31:18; Deut 9:10. Moses did the "handwriting" of the laws some of which contained ordinances Ex 24:4 and placed them in the side of the ark (Deut 31:26) Num 19:2 This *is* the ordinance of the law which the LORD hath commanded, saying, Speak unto the children of Israel, that they bring thee a red heifer without spot, wherein *is* no blemish, *and* upon which never came yoke: Num 19:3 And ye shall give her unto Eleazar the priest, that he may bring her forth without the camp, and *one* shall slay her before his face: Num 19:4 And Eleazar the priest shall take of her blood with his finger, and sprinkle of her blood directly before the tabernacle of the congregation seven times: (some bibles, i.e. NKJV, change "ordinances" to "requirements". Thus lumping the commandments, laws, statutes, judgements and ordinances together to distort God's instructions by implying none have to be kept rather than limiting the instruction to ordinances. The Hebrew word translated as "ordinance" can be traced back to other places in the bible where it is also used. This cannot be done with requirements.) Another example of an ordinance is Ex 12:24. So to which "ordinance" is Paul referring? today's society, when people do not want to do something, they commonly use the term "it is against the law", meaning law of the land rather than a specific one. When pressed, they think of one i.e. "Freedom of Information Act". When told that law does not contain they restriction they claim; they end with "well that is the way our company operates". What they may be going by is a company suggestion, recommendation, instruction which they call law. Unfortunately, similarly bible readers confuse and lump together commandments, laws, statutes and ordinances of God. Maybe due to limitations of the English language and understanding gained from similar word all of which give instruction. God knew what He meant when he used different words. An ordinance is an instruction; but not limited or exclusive to animal sacrifices or holy days. Neither to God, as the following examples show: 1 Sam 30:25, Num 31:21, Ex 15:25, Lev 18:30 (abominable sexual practices), Lev 22:9 (to do with holy items), Num 10:8 (blowing of trumpet, Eze 45:14 (oil).

Which ordinance did people find contrary? Acts 15:10 Now therefore why tempt ye God, to put a yoke upon the neck of the disciples, which neither our fathers nor we were able to bear?" The yoke of circumcision as mentioned in Acts 15:1-2 "And certain men which came down from Judea taught the brethren, and said, Except ye be circumcised after the manner of Moses, ye cannot be saved. therefore Paul and Barnabas had no small dissension and disputation with them (on circumcision), they determined that Paul and Barnabas, and certain other of them, should go up to Jerusalem unto the apostles and elders about this question." Which resulted in the text of 15:10. So is it not circumcision to which Paul was referring and not the Sabbath or God's holy days? The holy days did not cause division and were forever inclusive of strangers (Ex 12:14, Ex 12:17, Num 9:14). I doubt Paul would be saying we were not to keep any ordinances as this is contrary to Rom 13:2.

Another aspect of the book of Colossians is seen in 2:8 "beware lest any man spoil you through philosophy... rudiments of the world". V20 "if ye be dead with Christ from the rudiment of the world, why as though living in the world, are ye subject to ordinances, touch not, taste not, handle not after the commandments and doctrines of **men**". Note Paul speaks of the world not Jews, Israel or anything particularly limited to them as the law. He speaks of commandments of the men not God or contained in the Old Testament. Remember also on numerous occasions Paul states he is a jealous follower of the Law, has never spoken or taught anything against the Law and so on. Paul's letter was to warn against Judaist tendencies and customs similar to Jesus' correction of the Pharisees who accused Him of breaking the Law by healing on the Sabbath. Amongst other things, Paul was concerned about the new teachings of worshipping angels as intermediaries between God and man (v2:18).

Hebrews 10:1 "For the law having a shadow of good things to come, and not the very image of the things, can never with those sacrifices which they offered year by year continually make the comers thereunto perfect". The key words in this sentence are "law" (which one), "sacrifices" "annually". If one knew the route to forgiveness of sins via the annual animal sacrifices of Aaron and subsequent priests (one of the laws in Leviticus, Lev 16:34), they would understand the sentence is talking about the replacement of this annual system by the once and for all sacrifice of Jesus. The sacrifice system is expanded on in Hebrews 9 (especially verse 9 and 22) [v9was a figure for the time then present, in which were offered both gifts and sacrifices, that could not make him that did the service perfect, as pertaining to the conscience; v22"And almost all things are by the law purged with blood; and without shedding of blood is no remission".] Hebrews 9 narrates the sacrifice system. Some other sections of which are verses 1, then verily the first covenant had also ordinances of divine service, and a worldly sanctuary. V7 "But into the second went the high priest alone once every year, not without blood, which he offered for himself, and for the errors of the people:" In the Old Testament, Aaron offered a lamb (shed blood for forgiveness of sins Lev 17:11 "for it is the blood that maketh atonement for the soul"). A blood sacrifice is needed for the remission of sins. Thus the temple had to be destroyed due to constant polluting; God was forced to institute a replacement.

These make it clear that Hebrews 10 is on that system. That one issue contained within the Law which consists of numerous individual issues or laws. Obviously not the Sabbath or feast days. Verse 23, 25 [Heb 9:23 It was therefore necessary that the patterns of things in the heavens should be purified with these; but the heavenly things themselves with better sacrifices than these. Heb 9:25 Nor yet that he should offer himself often, as the high priest entereth into the holy place every year with blood of others;] refers to the patterns of things in heaven (as regards the sanctuary and sacrifice system). A pattern must follow or match the actual thing. Heb 8:5 "Who serve unto the example and shadow (4639) of heavenly things, as Moses was admonished of God when he was about to make the tabernacle: for, See, saith he, that thou make all things according to the pattern shewed to thee in the mount." Thus one can see that a shadow is a copy of the real thing just like a pattern copies the real thing. Neither changes nor does away with the real thing. They both co-exist. Shadow and real object. Just like in Act 5:15"Insomuch that they brought forth the sick into the streets, and laid them on beds and couches, that at the least the shadow of Peter passing by might overshadow some of them." Peter's shadow cannot exist without him. Similarly we are to do on earth as it is in heaven. In heaven is the real thing on which a light shines to cast its shadow onto earth. We are to follow that shadow to arrive at the real thing, just as if one follows any shadow, sooner or later they both meet at a certain point. Before Jesus, there was the sacrifice system administered by Aaron and the priests on our behalf. On Jesus' death, the veil separating the two sanctuaries (inner and outer, public and priests) was torn.

Now compare this to the word shadow used in James 1:17"Every good gift and every perfect gift is from above, and cometh down from the Father of lights, with whom is no variableness, neither shadow (G644) of turning." Here James says God has no variableness, i.e. one rule for one group or individual and a different rule for others. It is the only place in the bible this meaning is used. It means there is no shading off or gradual reduction. In other words, there is permanence. God does not institute Sabbaths then take them away.

If the two things, shadow and its object, were not meant to be connected in its strict sense, Paul could have used an analogy or parable as did Jesus. In Matt 13:44-7 and other places. [v44 Again, the kingdom of heaven is like unto treasure hid in a field; the which when a man hath found, he hideth, and for joy thereof goeth and selleth all that he hath, and buyeth that field.] Or words as "example", maybe "sample", or say "similar to". A choice of words would have told us like but not the same as, temporary, not permanent. Instead he chose the permanent meaning of the word shadow.

The cleaning system took two elements; the priests and the saving sacrifice of the lamb. Most Christians may see Jesus solely as the saviour. His death as the lamb alone forgiving all their sins and they have to do nothing more but believe in Him. They omit his Priestly roll and the thought He simply replaced one element of the Law not the Law in its entirety. Some try to justify this by claiming Jesus changes us from the inside rather than from outside as did the Law. There are probably equal amount of humans in the world whose heart has not been changed by Jesus similar to the number before Jesus. Let us be real, as Rom 2:14-15 says "For when the Gentiles, which have not the law, do by nature the things contained in the law, these, having not the law, are a law unto themselves: Which shew the work of the law written in their hearts, their conscience also bearing witness, and their thoughts the mean while accusing or else excusing one another;." Those wishing to serve and obey God will do so from the heart without the need for it being written in stone. Others who find obedience grievous will use the law to either accuse others or excuse themselves. In other words, justify doing what they want or validating an inherited false belief. Do not add nor take away from the written word of God with your own or others interpretations (church leaders or authors) (Deut 5:22 and 5:29-31 ye shall not turn aside to the right hand or to the left, Deut 4:2, 6:2, 12:32, 28:14).As said elsewhere, the Holy Spirit would not guide an obedient person to go against the written word of God; though the deceiver does. It is interesting to note that Moses sealed the covenant of God's Commandments and Laws with the people using a ceremony and blood, as Jesus' blood allowed all nations in to partake of God's salvation. Ex 24:7 and he took the book of the covenant, and read in the audience of the people: and they said, all that the LORD hath said will we do, and be obedient. Exo 24:8 And Moses took the blood, and sprinkled *it* on the people, and said, Behold the blood of the covenant, which the LORD hath made with you concerning all these words.

OF A TYPE

The titled phase is being used by some to separate what God said we should do and what was done in the Old Testament (follow the commandments and Laws), to changes people want to now do (not keep the Commandments and Laws). This excuse is growing in use.

In the O.T. the daily sacrifice was done in the morning and evening (Exo 29:39). In the N.T. these times are recorded as the third and ninth hour; 6.00 a.m being zero hour. Without a place to implement the animal sacrifices, the Jews continued the custom with gathering and prayers at these times. Could Jesus' death at the "ninth hour" be more than coincidence? (Mark 15:34-37)? Acts 2:15 and 3:1 shows the apostles continued these set time meeting and prayers; Now Peter and John went up together into the temple at the hour of prayer, being the ninth hour. You would notice from Appendix "I" how satan has also changed these times.

"For the law having a shadow of good things to come" is taken from Heb 10:1.I have dealt in part with this in the section titled "Shadow of Things to Come". Here, I wish to briefly focus on the word "type". I read a lesson study on Hebrews 9 and 10, the justification given for the "type" concept. The Author stated there were several ways to read chapter 9.One is to take a linguistic or literal approach to it. The other "essentially bypasses all that". Then why did God use words to convey His messages? Why not drawings in abstract modern art, where each viewer visualises what impresses them? What does God have to do beyond put it into words to make people follow and not change His meanings to their own? When God or Jesus used unclear images, were they not clarified with words soon after or elsewhere in the bible? Denominations have a habit of starting with what their denomination does then interpreting God's words to fit. Should we not start with God's words and compare what we do against His wishes? Your denomination ancestors may have had good intentions; but may not necessarily have got it all right. You may need to take a fresh appraisal of all or some of what you do against the bible as it states, not what you are told it does. I accept in many cases the bible cannot be taken literally, i.e. Jonah was not in the whale's belly forever only three days. However, the context of a "type" was not to signify the doing away or changing of God's commandments. Simply the replacement of the animal lamb by Jesus. Exo 26:33 and thou shalt hang up the vail under the taches, that thou mayest bring in thither within the vail the ark of the testimony: and the vail shall divide unto you between the holy *place* and the most holy. Mat 27:51 And, behold, the veil of the temple was rent in twain from the top to the bottom; and the earth did quake, and the rocks rent; see Lev 16:1-19 for purpose of the veil. Man was separated fro God through sin and could not approach Him except through the purified priest and the blood sacrifice. On Jesus' death and the tearing of the veil, He went beyond that veil (Heb9:12, 24) as our high priest (Heb 9:11; 7:23-28) taking His own blood (Heb 9:12) and making full atonement (Heb 10:10, 12). See also Heb 10:11, 12, 16, 18-21 However, we cannot call on Jesus' sacrifice for nought works.

God is the real thing. His words are the real thing that withstands the test of time for all generations. He does not deal in the artificial, forgeries or types. That is the deceiver's method. Just like the replica of things in real life. They are not the real thing but a "type of" to fool, and convince you or others it is, or almost like, the real thing. They would claim the difference is minimal, insignificant and not worth the extra cost or effort. Do not be fooled. When Jesus preached, He may have used analogies; but not types. For example in the one on wheat, tares and planting seeds. We know He simply replaced the word people and gospel. As one is, so is the other. As it is in heaven, so should it be on earth." Psalms "The Lord looked down from heaven upon the children of men, to see if there were any that did understand and seek God."

Note: See "The Sanctuary" Section for elaboration.

Keeping the Commandments is not mitigating in any way the power of Jesus or His death; but showing you understand and, more importantly, are deserving of it. Throughout the Bible it has always been those keeping the Commandments, confessing their sins and sincerely seeking forgiveness through God's prescribed method that were forgiven. Sincerely being having no intention to recommit that sin and attempting to live up to that intention.

TEST THREE, COMMON SENSE OR LOGIC.

I do not really recommend using common sense as criteria because "Common" "sense" is not God's creation or equal to His intelligence. "Common" and "sense" = what" most" humans do. Most humans do things UNcommon to God. Nevertheless, for those to whom it would help, here are some common sense thoughts.

Does God not know His own mind?

Would God, whose character and words are consistent, who refers to Himself as "never changing" give a verbal command to the first man on earth, Adam; to Moses in stone, all prophets on paper and by Jesus' example and all subsequent generations whereby for over 4,000 years the Jewish race have kept the Sabbath, suddenly change it? Especially to a day which he detest and warned about because it was kept and worshiped by his adversary (satan) and his followers; Sun day?

Is God Racist,

having strict rules for the Jews (His chosen) and leniency for Gentiles? 2Ch 16:9 For the eyes of the LORD run to and fro throughout the whole earth, to shew himself strong in the behalf of *them* whose heart *is* perfect toward him You have a best friend, favourite person or child, would you sell them something at a higher price than to others? God chose the Jews (and strangers) to be His chosen people, would He make them have to obey laws and commandments but not his un-chosen who get it free (through mere believe, grace or faith)? Or they have to keep ten rules and others nine or less? Would that not be unfair? Would He, being a fair God, not have the same saving rules for all if not leniency for His chosen? If one can not understand earthly things how can they decipher heavenly ones? This point alone should be sufficient to cancel the argument that we are now saved by mere faith, belief or other excuses God has one rule for all as God's people Jew or Gentile are of one body. Gal 3:28 There is neither Jew nor Greek, there is neither bond nor free, there is neither male nor female: for ye are all one in Christ Jesus. Psa 100:3 Know ye that the LORD he *is* God: *it is* he *that* hath made us, and not we ourselves; *we are* his people, and the sheep of his pasture.

Is God is an Ageist?

(Against older people). In Numbers 15:33 God killed the man for collecting sticks on the Sabbath as it was classed as work. He could not have been the first man to work on the Sabbath. Surely, the Egyptians and other pagans did so why were they not killed. Because they did not belong to the group He had set aside to be His people. His people were bound by the commandments and others were not. Can that man or any other accuse God of being an ageist because persons wanting to be His people today working on the Sabbath are not killed? Are the younger persons born after Christ exempted from death for doing same things for which those born before Christ lost their salvation? If you read Deut, Numbers etc you will see the whole group of God's people were punished as a group when an individual broke His commands. In Joshua 6 God gives Israel victory over Jericho. However, being their first battle after crossing the Jordan, the first fruits belonged to God (Ex 23:19).He commanded nothing of the city was to be taken. One man secretly stole and hid some of the bounty and the whole nation was punished by loosing the next battle. When they found out the reason, identified and killed the man, God's favour was restored Joshua 6:17-19, 7:12, 15, 21, 25).For another example of one man sinning and the whole nation being punished see Num 25:6-9. In 2 Sam 24:17 David pleads for the people who God is punishing for his sole sin of taking a census.

Would the apostles be with Jesus and keep the Sabbath with Him over 170 times, every week and the day his back is turned or He dies change to the Sunday? 4) Would Jesus who taught by parables i.e. analogies and example, not lead by example and have kept Sunday or tell His disciples to change after His death and resurrection?5) Any law abiding reasonable non believing person could keep the other nine commandments. I have non believing, law abiding friends who do. Other religions similarly keep the other nine, but worship on a different day or time to Christians. Thus the only way to distinguish a believer in the God we call Jehovah, who created heaven, earth and all things seen and unseen is them keeping His Sabbath as He did. A testament to His creative status. Take away that "mark" and one is the same as the rest of non-believers.

These are some of the other circulated excuses .I will be saved by my works (excluding Sabbath keeping), if God wants me to change He will tell me, it doesn't matter what day I praise God, we should praise God every day, God knows my heart, I am saved by grace and faith and many more.

The controversy started with satan wanting Adam to disobey God and rely on him, then calling all subsequent people away from God to worship him. Making promises to Jesus of wealth etc if He would worship him (Matthew 4:9).When those tactics failed, next was to exterminate true followers of Christ both from within and without. From within meant infiltration and change Christian beliefs through majority rule, false leaders and custom. Some references to false prophets and shepherds are Prob 16:25, Isaiah 29:13-14, 2Corin 11:14-15.From without by persecution and death. Under state laws, bibles were taken away from everyone (early leaders and believers) except the chosen and burnt. This being so future generations would forget and not know about the Sabbath or contents of the Bible. Possessing one or meeting on the seventh day meant death. Services were spoken in Latin, a language the congregation did not understand. They were told what the bible said or meant. The Walden's, who later translated the bible into common language, paid with their lives. So today not only does ignorance prevail; but supported by false reasons. The history of wars, monarchies and emigration is partly religious. Saved by your works mean doing the work and will of God, i.e. keeping all 10 commandments. Not ones own in ones own manner (Matthew 19:17, John 14:15).

Would you keep your job unless you did the "works" as required and turned up for work at the stipulated times? Do not expect God to give you a personal message. Why should He? He has given you the bible, a brain and taught you to read. Would you put a Notice on a board and still think it reasonable to be expected to visit all 5 million people who wanted a personal visit and explanation? If it did not matter what day one worships God or keeps as the Sabbath why take away their bibles, why have so many been hunted, tortured and killed for keeping the Sabbath and not the same for any other day, i.e. Sunday?

Yes, one should worship God everyday; but really with the pressures of life, who does? Who takes a whole 24 hours to worship God or would if He had not commanded it? We could do anything at any time (our time); but that would not show dependence, obedience or love to our God. Can one go to work when they want or do the work contrary to how the owner says? Can one turn up for a plane flight when they want? If those earthly things are tied to time why should God get less? Doing it at His prescribed time shows respect and puts Him above self. God did not say once a year you will keep this or that feast. He set a day, time and manner of how it was to be done. He did not say you will offer up an animal. He set the gender, age, type and other factors of the animal. With God everything has to meet His stipulations and those substituting one factor for another according to their own understanding suffer the consequences.

Daniel was a man after God's own heart; yet he did not rely on God knowing his heart when asked to copy everyone else and kneel down to a statute in Daniel 3:18.Neither did Mordecai in the book of Esther 3:2-4.2 Sam 6:6 Uzzah had good intentions when he put his hand out to stop the Ark falling off the cart. Yet God killed him for breaking the commandment given years before to others that it should not be touched (1 Chron 13:9 and Ex 25:14).We can always find a reason to follow the crowd and pretend little things do not matter. Daniel did not drink the wine offered him in Dan 1:8.He did not say, it is only wine which is alright to drink. It was not the wine he refused; but its meaning and association. In 10:3 one sees Daniel does drink wine as a norm. Christians too should be careful with what they associate.

Imagine holding your hands up saying or praying "Lord God…" To whom would you be praying? Does it not depend on who is present and where it is taking place? If it was in the open when the moon was out, it could be said to be to the moon god. If it was at high noon when the sun is out, to the sun god. Similarly if one sings "happy birthday to you…" It would be to who is present and whose birthday it is. Obviously not someone who is not present or whose birthday had gone. If you are still not convinced, imagine a football pitch is used to host a match between Arsenal and Chelsea on Saturday and Tottenham against Ipswich on Sunday. You like football, support Arsenal; but can not make it on Saturday so decide to go on Sunday to the same pitch. You pay your money and cheer just as if you were there the previous day. Who does your money and cheering go to? Not Arsenal, they were there yesterday! Do not be naïve. One cannot outwardly participate in something yet think their internal personal reason excuses them. Remember Daniel? In that sense God is not everywhere all the time. He is present to receive an earthly choir of praises on His day, not part of the choir on various days. That is why He condemned worship in high places, groves and under trees as those were pagan practices. Jesus said one is either for Him or against Him by choice or default. Hot or cold. No middle ground.

Three examples of persons who did things their way and what God did to them are, King Uzziah who offered incense to God. "Though (otherwise) did right in sight of God", struck with leprosy till death because he was wrong person. It was priests' job (2Chron 26:4 & 18).Aaron's sons offered strange incense to God. Killed because, though were priests, was wrong incense (Lev 10:1).The bible has numerous examples of God's disgust to abominable things (pagan adopted practices) done in His house in worship to Him (2Kings 21:3-6). So much so that in Rev 3:9 He terms them "churches of satan".

JESUS IS OUR REST

REST = rely on God for our food etc. Rest in His assurance and promises. Exodus 35:2 "Six days shall work be done, but on the seventh day there shall be to you a **holy day**, a Sabbath of rest **to the LORD**: whosoever doeth work therein shall be put to death". Not a mere rest as one does under other circumstances. Resting does not make a day or period holy or every night you sleep would be holy. It is holy because God designated the seventh day as such. Then it is to be given **to the Lord** by living it in His word, dedicating your time to Him. Then ask how did Jesus and God's people keep it in the past and do likewise.

Some say the need to keep the fourth Commandment (the 7th day Sabbath / Saturday) has been replaced by Jesus because; the Sabbath was only about resting which Christians can now do in Jesus. They rely on Matt 11:28 "Come unto me, all *ye* that labour and are heavy laden and I will give you rest". I have referred to "rest" in the Celebrating the 1st Day of the Week section. In addition, we are to ask ourselves, how do we get rest in Jesus, how do we "come" onto Him, where is He heading and how do we follow Him? In Matt 19:17 Jesus directs if we are to enter into life (get rest), we are to keep His fathers commandments. Joh 10:27 "My sheep hear my voice, and I know them, and they follow me: Joh 12:26 If any man serve me, let him follow me; and where I am, there shall also my servant be: if any man serve me, him will *my* Father honour". Psa 40:7-8 "Then said I, Lo, I come: in the volume of the book *it is* written of me, I delight to do thy will, O my God: yea, thy law *is* within my heart". Jesus was heading to His father in heaven by doing His will, using the laws and commandments as His guide. Jesus confirmed He had not come to destroy or change the "Law". In fact, He came to magnify it. Show how it is to be kept. Shine a light on it and make it clear through clarification and examples. Isa 42:21 "The LORD is well pleased for his righteousness' sake; he will magnify the law, and make *it* honourable". Jesus was the living Law. Scripture speaks of their attributes in the same way. **Truth** (Joh 14:6, Psalm 119:142), **holy** (Acts 4:27, **Rom 7:12**), **perfect** (Heb 5:9, **Psalm 19:7**) **righteous** (1 Cor 1:30, Psa119:172), **light** (Joh 8:12, Pro 6:23), **just** (Acts 22:14, Rom 7:12), **abide in forever** (Joh 8:35, Psa 111:7-8), **should be in the heart** (Eph 3:17, Psa 40:8), **gives freedom, no condemnation and liberty** (Rom 8:1, James 2:12). Rejecting the Law is rejecting Jesus (and visa versa), which brings wrath (Joh 3:36, Neh 13:18). Jesus was pure; in Him was no sin. 1 Joh 3:4 defines sin as transgression of the Law, going against Jesus; "whosoever committeth sin transgresseth also the law: for sin is the transgression of the law". Therefore, how can any Christian professing to follow Christ think they are no longer under the law; under Jesus' directive? That they are now free to commit sin against God and man (Rom 7:7)? Psa 19:7 The law of the LORD *is* perfect, converting the soul: Psa 19:8 The statutes of the LORD *are* right, rejoicing the heart: the commandment of the LORD *is* pure, enlightening the eyes. Psa 19:11 Moreover by them is thy servant warned: *and* in keeping of them *there is* great reward. (See Psa 119:18, 97-8, 115, 165) Psa 89:34 My covenant will I not break, nor alter the thing that is gone out of my lips.

What is the reward or wages of sin, breaking the Law, going against God or Jesus? Death not rest (Rom 6:23)! Separation from God. So if you wish to "rest" in Jesus, keep ALL His and His father's commandments. Whether you get to heaven in obedience to the Law or faith in Jesus; following for what he stands, do as he did.

Some are taught they are free from the bondage of the law. A negative spin is put on the law to turn people against it. This is not a new trick, it happened during the historic merger between Rome's pagan religion and Christians. There is a positive side to this binding concept. When the Jews in Exodus marked their door posts, they were bound under God's promise and protection. Similarly a person is protected by the legal system under which they are bound. Thus being bound by the law has its positive benefits of protection. However, the bondage spoken of by Paul in Gal 4:9 is not of the Law. See Book of Galatians topic.

Thus if there is any of the commandments you are not keeping, even one, it means you do not yet know Christ, only possibly, part of Him. 1 Joh 2:3-4 "And hereby we do know that we know him, if we keep his commandments. He that saith, I know him, and keepeth not his commandments, is a liar, and the truth is not in him". As I said in the Introduction, Jesus said some hard things. We are not to take offence at hard, plain talking. Truth should not be concealed or compromised for fear of offending. Proverbs 27:17 "iron sharpens iron…"

HEALING AND PLUCKING CORN ON THE SABBATH DAY

Healing is not working Luk 13:16.As Jesus asked, is it unlawful to do good on Sabbath? And His accusers had to keep quiet Mark 3:4.Jesus also said the priests who perform their religious duties on the Sabbath or one circumcising a baby because the 3rd day of its birth happened to fall on the Sabbath, is not breaking the law under their own understanding so how can healing be .John 7:22-3"Moses therefore gave unto you circumcision; (not because it is of Moses, but of the fathers ;) and ye on the Sabbath day circumcise a man. If a man on the Sabbath day receive circumcision, that the law of Moses should not be broken; are ye angry at me, because I have made a man every whit whole on the Sabbath day?"

As for the other accusation of the Pharisees and used as an excuse today, the plucking of corn on the Sabbath by the disciples. Eating is not violation of the Sabbath; but working is (Deut 23:24-5).Were the disciples plucking the corn for storage or resale? Did they have to work to prepare the food like others who may cook, butter bread or add an ingredient of any sort? No, it was simply pick and eat, just like picking an apple from a tree and biting it. From its natural place to your mouth, no preparation or work. Less than it would take someone else to go to a storage place of food, cupboard, jar, bread bin etc, retrieve and eat it. In Exodus 16:4-5 God rained a daily portion of manna from heaven, save for the sixth day when two days supply fell "that I may prove them whether they will walk in my law or not". Did they not have to store and retrieve the manna for use the next Sabbath day? More effort than the apostles picking and eating.

This seventh day observance being a test of obedience before being given to Moses on mount Sinai in Exodus 24:12.Remember the so titled religious leaders of the time were seeking any reason to discredit Jesus. They were jealous of loosing their power and standing. John 11:48 "If we let him thus alone, all men will believe on him: and the Romans will come and take away both our place and nation".

The best and only two things they could come up with then and used, as justification today to abstain from the Sabbath is disciples plucking the corn and Jesus healing on the Sabbath. Neither of which if looked into constitute work. Jesus was simply clarifying what the Sabbath is.

A lawyer can know the law, but not how to practice it. Hence they loose cases. A lawyer could practice law; but only have blinkered view, i.e. prosecutor or defender; hence the need for a judge to clarify the position .Lawyers can also be corrupt as many are thought to be today. Hence when Jesus accused the Pharisees of knowing the law but not understanding it; this is not a precedent for us to disobey the numerous times Jesus said we are to keep the commandments and the law. Whose words should carry more importance Jesus' or Paul's? Well in Luke 10:25 a lawyer asks Jesus "what shall I do to inherit eternal life"? Jesus replies "What is written in the law, how readest thou" is saying the answer is written in the law; but how do you understand it .Lawyer replies "Love God, with all heart, soul, strength and mind and neighbour as self". Jesus, "you read and understand it right. Do this and live". A similar example is in Matt 19:17 "Good master, what shall I do to inherit eternal life?" reply, "keep the commandments". Clearly Jesus is saying the way to eternal life is written in the law which we are to keep. If this was not so He would have said. Thus when reading Paul's words either Paul is wrong or we are misunderstanding Paul. It is ironic the leaders were accusing Jesus of breaking the law for healing within the temple and having a healed man carry his bed on the Sabbath yet they were allowing on a weekly basis breaking of the same law, within the temple by allowing trading and carrying of vessels on the Sabbath day (Mark 11:15-16).

Is saving a life on the Sabbath really work? Suppose you are a plumber on holiday and there is an incident on the plane and the question is asked "is there a doctor on board? There is no doctor but you having watched a programme or TV a few nights before or maybe having some 1st aid training at work decide to come fwd and help the person. Are you classed as working? I think not. Now suppose you did a good job; but there is a doctor on board then steps up and says good job; but you also need to do a, b, c. When asked why he didn't come forward before he says "I'm on hols and didn't really want to get involved, I was hoping there would be another doctor to help out". Would he be working for helping out? I think not.

MIRACLE PERFORMING "CHURCH", IS GOD IS THERE?

Remember there have always been the satan's miracle workers. The magicians of Moses' and Daniel's times, to today's devil worshippers, witch doctors etc. Acts 8:9-10 states "But there was a certain man, called Simon, which beforetime in the same city used sorcery, and bewitched the people of Samaria, giving out that himself was some great one: To whom they all gave heed, from the least to the greatest, saying, This man is the great power of God. Act 13:6, 8 …they found a certain sorcerer, a false prophet, a Jew, whose name *was* Barjesus: …But Elymas the sorcerer …seeking to turn away the deputy from the faith. Act 19:19 Many of them also which used curious arts brought their books together, and burned them before all men: and they counted the price of them, and found it fifty thousand pieces of silver.7:21-24 "in thy name" have we not done this and that, yet Jesus replied "I never knew you, depart from me you workers of iniquity". See also Acts 19:15. Such is the parallel between real and fake. John 7:24 "not according to the appearance; but judge righteous judgement". Miracle workers have never been afraid to masquerade as and call themselves persons of God and use Jesus' name. It is a lucrative business. Yet none of these miracle workers were of Jesus.

God can use anyone for His purpose. A heathen, non-believer etc to heal or punish a believer. It happened many times in the Old Testament with Israel, Judah and even Jonah. the healing of an individual could be either the Holy Spirit working through the healer, who could be good or bad, to bring healing to a deserving person. Maybe so that person can then witness to and convert a neighbour who God has called and that neighbour ends up keeping the Sabbath. God works in mysterious ways and His ways are not ours. Job 1:16 "fire of God falls from heaven". With the catastrophes of Job we know it was the work of satan. Yet this miracle of the falling fire from heaven was attributed to God by the servant who saw it. Satan can do a miracle to deceive and cause us to attribute it to God. Maybe to make you stay in or join his false parallel system for what you hope to get out of it rather than what you should give to God regardless of your desires or illness .In Job 4:12-21 and chapter 5 Eliphaz rebukes Job according to a vision and voice speaking to him. In the end of Job we read God punishing and rebuking Eliphaz for getting it wrong. Obviously the visions and voices received by Eliphaz were not from God. So, remember, test the spirits guiding you with the written word of God and actions of His former prophets.

Why did Jesus / does God heal people? To show that He is God or confirm a person as His prophet, from Him. In Num 12:13 Moses proved he was from God when his authority was challenged, 1 Kings 17:24After Elijah had raised the widows son, "And the woman said to Elijah, Now by this I know that thou art a man of God, and that the word of the LORD in thy mouth is truth".2 Kings 20:5 Hezekiah is cured through God. Luke 10:9 "heal the sick and say unto them, the kingdom of God is come nigh unto thee". John 12:38, 42, 44 "Lord who have believed our report and to whom has the arm of the Lord been revealed" "Nevertheless, among the chief rulers also many believed on him..." "Jesus cried and said he that believe on me, believieth not on me, but on him that sent me". John 9:3Jesus answered, Neither hath this man sinned, nor his parents: but that the works of God should be made manifest in him".

Healing, fabricated or otherwise, is not to bring fame, glory, riches or a following to a human; but believers to God solely, nothing else. An example of such purpose is this testimony of a lay preacher who got no material reward on this earth for his efforts.

Sanjay's Testimony:

Sanjay was a musician and played in a band in India. He was a Christian and did not join his fellow musicians when they went drinking or dancing. But something was missing from his life. Sanjay felt bad when his fellow musicians made fun of his Christian faith.

One day he prayed that God would show His power to his friends so they would know that He was the only true God. That evening the band loaded their equipment into a small bus to drive across a mountain pass to their next appointment. They passed the summit and began their descent when the driver suddenly realized that he had no brakes. The bus veered off the road and rolled into the valley far below. No one was killed, but everyone was injured except Sanjay.

Some of the musicians confessed that Sanjay's God had saved him from harm and began calling him "God's man." Sanjay met a Sabbath keeping church (SKC) pastor who urged him to surrender his life totally to God. Sanjay agreed, but even though he felt God wanted him to use his talents to bring people to Christ, still he hesitated to give up the band. Then something happened that changed the course of his life.

One day he climbed an old coconut tree to pick fresh coconuts. He grasped a palm frond to balance himself while he reached for a coconut. However, the palm frond broke loose, throwing Sanjay off balance. He fell from the tall tree into a field of cut sugar cane. The stalks that remained in the field had been cut at an angle and were as sharp as needles. "Lord, save me!" Sanjay cried as he fell.

His brother heard Sanjay's cry and watched in horror as his brother fell into the sharp stalks. He raced to his side, expecting to find his brother dead, but Sanjay was unhurt. He picked himself up and dusted himself off. Sanjay realized that God had saved his life a second time. "OK, Lord," he said, "I'm Yours. Give me something to do for you."

He asked the SKC pastor for work, and the pastor invited him to come and train to become a lay evangelist. Sanjay agreed. But how could he lead others to Christ? He had no experience with any work but music.

Sanjay realized that God had miraculously saved his life twice, and now he dedicated himself to work for God. He became a lay evangelist with the church and was sent to a village where no one had even heard of that church denomination before.

Sanjay found a family who let him stay in the room in which the family kept their idols.

Sanjay prayed that his host family would be blessed by his presence and would not force him to leave when they learned that he was Christian.

Sanjay learned that his host had a health problem. He asked to pray to his God for the man's healing. The man agreed, and the homeowner was healed. Sanjay told the man that he was a Christian and invited him to study the Bible. The man invited his family to study with him, and within a few months the entire family gave their hearts to Jesus and offered their home for small group meetings.

Sanjay visited people, prayed for their needs, and urged them to trust in the living God, who hears and answers prayer. When one family mocked him, saying that their god protected and blessed them, Sanjay left feeling that he had failed. The next day the homeowner told Sanjay that after the family had gone to bed the night before, a rat had entered their home and knocked over the oil lamp, which caught the straw walls on fire. The family barely got out alive. "We were wrong about your God. Please, may we attend your prayer meetings?"

Another woman, Ompatti, was troubled by evil spirits. Her husband abandoned her and their three children. Doctors couldn't cure the woman, and trips to religious shrines brought her no relief. Then someone asked Sanjay to pray for her. As he prayed, Sanjay touched the woman, and she fell to the ground screaming. The devils left her. She told everyone of her healing. When her husband learned that she was no longer possessed, he returned. But he objected to Christianity and refused to have anything to do with them. Soon after, he became possessed by demons. Church members continue to pray for him.

In the years that Sanjay has worked as a lay evangelist, some 200 people in seven villages have given their lives to Christ and been baptized.

TIME ZONES

It was argued by one pastor that the Sabbath could not be kept by every nation especially those in certain parts of Norway, where the sun never sets. Therefore others around the world can be exempted also. Firstly, he did not understand the concept of sunset. It is basically when the sun appears to stop drifting (or the earth's rotation around it) so that it does not pass the equator and does not sink below the horizon. Daylight, albeit a lesser level, continues for certain number of days during part of the year. However, once the sun has reached its lowest point on the horizon, it has actually set though not disappeared out of sight past the horizon. It will later appear to rise again (as the world turns) and daylight will be brighter. If one noted the sunset times of their local area, they would note there is still sunlight past sunset times; possibly for thirty minutes before the sun disappears below the horizon and darkness sets in. Thus, the Sabbath is capable of being measured and kept by every one; sunset to sunset NOT darkness to darkness or any other formulae.

PLANET WORSHIP AND PAGAN ROME

From early on in the Bible God warned against adoration and worshipping of the Sun and planets. Deut 4:19 "And lest thou lift up thine eyes unto heaven, and when thou seest the sun, and the moon, and the stars, *even* all the host of heaven, shouldest be driven to worship them, and serve them, which the LORD thy God hath divided unto all nations under the whole heaven. Deut17:3 And hath gone and served other gods, and worshipped them, either the sun, or moon, or any of the host of heaven, which I have not commanded;" It was an abomination to God punished by death via stoning. Would God subsequently forgive such a practice in the New Testament, even if done under the banner and in belief is to serve Him; albeit on a Sun day rather than His sanctified Sabbath? 1 Cor 10:21, Christians cannot serve Jehovah God in a Sunday denomination just like Moses and God's chosen were called out of the pagan land to remember and keep His commandments. Only God made and can make a day holy and it was not the Sun's day. So as He calls His people out of Babylon (Rev 18:4) you are called. Neither is their necessarily security in the fact it is a "church of God" as many subtle pagan practices occur in "church". Eze 8:16 And he brought me into the inner court of the LORD'S house, and, behold, at the door of the temple of the LORD, between the porch and the altar, *were* about five and twenty men, with their backs toward the temple of the LORD, and their faces toward the east; and they worshipped the sun toward the east. Eze 9:6 states god's punishment will start with those in churches.

Act 14:12 And they called Barnabas, Jupiter; and Paul, Mercurius, because he was the chief Speaker. Act 14:13the priest of Jupiter, which was before their city, brought oxen and garlands unto the gates, and would have done sacrifice with the people." Sacrifice to whom? satan's false system. Act 19:35And when the town clerk had appeased the people, he said, ye men of Ephesus, what man is there that knoweth not how that the city of the Ephesians is a worshipper of the great goddess Diana, and of the image which fell down from Jupiter?

Sun worship did not originate in Rome; but came into Christianity via their post apostle merger. (See section How We Know Which Day is the Sabbath). Sun worship derived from a belief that the Sun is the source of life (food growth, light, heat, etc) and prosperity rather than Jehovah God who created it. As such it was adored, worship and sacrifices offered to it to bring good fortune. A day was designated to and named after it by the people. Though today the word "Sun" has been deleted from the spoken or sung words of worship and actions handed down by the followers of the belief, the same day is maintained. And despite adding the words as Jesus etc to the service and having "Christians" joining in, the praises are NOT going to or being received by Jehovah God, creator of heaven, earth and all. The praises did not and were not intended to go to God originally so likewise He would not be receiving them now. Christians have been joined to the false parallel system praising the "Sun" in ignorance. Adding the word Jesus to a cigarette or other ungodly thing does not make it holy. Because Jesus said it is lawful to do good on the Sabbath, some persons try justifying going to church on Sunday as "doing good". I refer them to Amos 5:21-23 where God despised the wrong church service, offerings and ended with "take away from me the noise of your songs, for I will not hear the melody of thy viols". This is just one of many biblical texts supporting that worshipping God in the wrong way is unacceptable to Him. He does not accept unholy or blemished items offered as holy.

Another example of how the world follows planetary times rather than God's is it's celebration of New Year on the 31st December commencing at mid night, the start of the day. Mid night is the peak of the moon as mid day is the peak of the sun. Whereas God's day begins with the evening and is followed by the morning (Genesis 1:5, 8, 13) man's start with the planets. Whereas God's new year starts in spring (Exodus 12:2) or September (Ex 23:16) according to whether you follow the harvest or feast day calendar, the Christian world uses the pagan Dec 31.

IS HISTORY RELEVANT

1Jo 2:6 "He that saith he abideth in him ought himself also so to walk, even as he walked".

One cannot understand or reconcile the message of the bible without history or you will end up off track or false teachers will lead you astray, probably to hell. Not all professed Christian leaders speak for God i.e. Aaron and Miriam Num 12:2, Korah numbers 16:32-35. The Old. T. instructions are the same as the New T. New T. writers quoted from Deut nearly 200 times. Christ quoted in Matt 4:1-11, Deut 6:13, 16; 8:3; 10:20; Deut 12:8, Judge 17:6, 21:25.

Some say they do not care about history. Then how do you know which God to serve, why and how? Is it because they do not care to get it right; but do it their way? The bible is the oldest history book. It tells of creation, sets out the origin of sin, plan of salvation, the promises and their conditions made by God to us. In that history book is a record of the exodus, individuals and nation's methods and mistakes in serving God, punishment, repentance, deliverance etc. God continually reminded receivers of His promises and conditions to pass them onto all future generations. Those receivers knew of the importance of future generations remembering and the consequences if they failed. So much so that they thought of ways to assist memory i.e. putting information into a song (Exodus 15:1, Deut 31:19-21). Then we know the content of that history book is correct through our own human historical records of wars, reigning kings etc. Fortunately for us, our predecessors knew the importance of recording history. The Egyptians, Romans and others kept records that were later discovered and collaborated by our archaeologists. Records of subsequent empires confirm previous prophecies i.e. in Daniel. On that basis we can rely on foretold but yet unfulfilled prophesies in that history book and take steps to ensure we, as an individual, do not fall with those to be punished.

Today we use metric measurements, before that we used imperial feet and inches, in years to come we may move onto another system. If history was not relevant, we would not know the size of a cubit, the measurement quoted in the bible. Thus an appreciation on the size of the temple and other constructions would be lost. History is clearly relevant and those ignoring it wish to remain in ignorance". Christians also need to know how the enemy fights. Methods of deception, his powers, musical status, how he gets thoughts into your mind, through which he affects your actions and following of your heart. Being forewarned enables preparation to protect yourself and others. As I have said many bible readers focus on the New Testament, spend their time on guided daily reading and never end up reading the whole bible. Try solving these two sequences 1) **60, 62, __, __** 2) **gh, gj, __, __.** You should find the solution later in the booklet.

If God was to forget about history how could we go to Him and say you promised this or that? Would you be happy if He said, I do not care about history or my promises. Would you be happy if He used that excuse to get out of promises to you the same way you are using it to get out of your obligations, yet expect the reward? It was history that played a part in the saving of Mordacai in Esther 6:1, the rebuilding of Jerusalem Ezra 4:15, 6:2, and other events based on history being recorded (see Exodus 17:14, 24:7, Num 21:14, Deu 17:18, 28:58, 29:20, 31:24 and especially Deu 31:26, 2Kings 22:8, 11-17, Isaiah 8:2).Through those and similar records we know of the wonders of God such as the standing still of the sun, the falling of the wall of Jericho and others.

The history book foretells the coming of the Messiah, from where He came, His destiny etc. How would the world know to recognise Him in His first and second comings if our predecessors, future generations or we ignore history? Carrying out the commission of spreading the gospel given to us by Jesus would be pointless as future hears would not know or care about history. By ignoring history you are likely to be unaware of previous errors of others and do the same or similar whether your action is religious or worldly. You may be friends and trade with the same people or their descendants who killed, conspired against, deceived or did other atrocities to your grandparents or previous generation. What you would be saying is I do not care or want to know that beliefs I hold were imposed by an act of government way after the period or for different reasons to what I am told. That the customs I follow and the ways I worship were started by an individual starting a religion one hundred years ago. It is how I like and want to do it and God should accept it.

Matt 8:27 the disciples say "what kind of man is this? Even the winds and waves obey him!" In Isaiah 1:3 God says, "The ox knows its master, the donkey his owner's manger, but Israel does not know, my people do not understand". Many Christians profess the kingdom of heaven; but do not and will not possess it. They follow the crowd rather than word of God. Is what you are doing or the preacher preaching coming out of the bible or reading into the bible? Out of their head into the bible? Their interpretation, custom etc.? Choosing to follow unbiblical reasoning? True Christians must be part of the remnant. The small group within the bigger group, genuine within the fake, nucleus within the cell.

NOT UNDER THE LAW; But The HOLY SPIRIT.

The title is taken from another reason some persons give. What is the Holy Spirit? If you read about John the Baptist (Luke 1:15 "He shall be filled with the Holy Ghost/Spirit even from his mother's womb"), Jesus (Matt 3:16, 4:1, 12:18, Luke 4:14) and some persons of the Old and New Testaments (Ex 28:3, 35:30-35; 2 Chron 15:1, 24:20, Num 11:17, 25; Jdg 14:19 Luke 1:41-2, 67), you would see they were either filled with the Holy Spirit or the spirit of God came upon them and as a result they spoke the word of God, was given wisdom or the skill to perform task. Note in Ex 28:3 those chosen were "wise hearted". So it could be said the Holy Spirit is God imparting His wisdom or words to you by inspiration. Some people excuse their wrong doing or do as they want by claiming to be guided by or under the Holy Spirit of the New Testament rather than the law or written word of the Old without realising they are one and the same. They claim the Holy Spirit told them either through pray or other message form knowing it can't necessarily be disproved (See 1Ti 4:1). They may pick New Testament texts which refer to the Holy Spirit guiding us etc. The same people accept the holy trinity: yet somehow think God the father, His son and Holy Spirit could be working against each other. With one saying one thing and another something different. It is like one hand of your body stirring a pot with a spoon while the other hand is trying to take away the spoon or move the pot. This is not the unison of the Trinity. Joh 10:30 I and *my* Father are one 1Jo 5:7 For there are three that bear record in heaven, the Father, the Word, and the Holy Ghost: and these three are one. Joh 12:44 Jesus cried and said, He that believeth on me, believeth not on me, but on him that sent me. (see also John 1:2-3; 8:58; Heb 1:2). They all take us to the same place, say and do the same thing without contradiction. You can take away one or two of the three and be left with the same instructions otherwise they will be opposing each other. God the father, Emmanuel (God with us), Holy Spirit (our teacher, etc in the absence of Jesus) Joh 16:7 "Nevertheless I tell you the truth; It is expedient for you that I go away: for if I go not away, the Comforter will not come unto you; but if I depart, I will send him unto you" (see also Joh 7:39 Joh 14:16, 26, 15:26 that the Holy Spirit is from and speaks as God). Joh 16:13 Howbeit when he, the Spirit of truth, is come, he will guide you into all truth: for he shall not speak of himself; but whatsoever he shall hear, *that* shall he speak:

The texts people choose to quote are, of course correct; but it is their interpretation that is wrong. They need to test the "spirit" they claim is guiding them to their interpretation1Jo 4:1 Beloved, believe not every spirit, but try the spirits whether they are of God: because many false prophets are gone out into the world. .1Jo 3:24 and he that keepeth his commandments dwelleth in him, and he in him. And hereby we know that he abided in us, by the Spirit which he hath given us. 1Jo 5:3 for this is the love of God, that we keep his commandments: and his commandments are not grievous. 2Jo 1:9 whosoever transgresseth, and abideth not in the doctrine of Christ, hath not God. He that abideth in the doctrine of Christ, he hath both the Father and the Son. Joh 14:17 Even the Spirit of truth; whom the world cannot receive, because it seeth him not, neither knoweth him: but ye know him; for he dwelleth with you, and shall be in you.

Test it against the other two of the trinity. What God the father said in the past and what Jesus His son did. If your interpretation is out of line, it is more than likely wrong. Joh 14:22 Judas saith unto him, not Iscariot, Lord, how is it that thou wilt manifest thyself unto us, and not unto the world? Joh 14:23 Jesus answered and said unto him, "if a man love me, he will keep my words: and my Father will love him, and we will come unto him, and make our abode with him". Jesus, God and the Holy Spirit manifest themselves to those, like the apostles, keeping all God's commandments or sincerely wishing to above following custom. They may bring those who do not keep them a message (as this book or other method Ezra 1:1 God use people for His will) to keep them. Then leave your freewill to obey or excuse; but He does not continue to bless those transgressing His commandments 2Ch 24:20 In John 10:30 Jesus proclaims Himself and God as one. In Malachi 3:6 it states God changes not. Matt 28:20 Jesus instructs his disciples to "teach them to observe all things I have commanded you". Meaning things which He and His father who are one, have commanded. James 2:10 who keeps the whole law, yet offend in one point of it is guilty of all. If Christians were no longer under the law after Christ, James would not be writing this text; but say we are no longer under the law. God requires Deu 10:12 And now, Israel, what doth the LORD thy God require of thee, but to fear the LORD thy God, to walk in all his ways, and to love him, and to serve the LORD thy God with all thy heart and with all thy soul. Hos 6:6 for I desired mercy, and not sacrifice; and the knowledge of God more than burnt offerings. Especially when those offerings are polluted as in Mal 1:7-8.

It could not be any simpler. He created us; but from the beginning were beguiled and disobey (Gen 3:6), sinning continually (Gen 6:5). He started again with Noah making a covenant not to bring another earth destroying flood. Instead identified and separated a genealogy of humans unto Himself through Abraham and Isaac. They were also beguiled by surrounding pagans and disobeyed. He sent prophets and lastly his son Jesus. Yet many still do not want to understand. 2Ti 4:1, 3-4 Now the Spirit speaketh expressly, that in the latter times some shall depart from the faith, giving heed to seducing spirits, and doctrines of devils;   For the time will come when they will not endure sound doctrine; but after their own lusts shall they heap to themselves teachers, having itching ears;

"And they shall turn away *their* ears from the truth, and shall be turned unto fables". One cannot make someone understand something when it is profitable not to understand it. That is how Christians get beguiled by satan showing them profits and pleasures of the world and diminishing that of the after life. Making them think they can offer Him an hour or more of a strange day of worship Sunday, then go about their business. He set apart and sanctified the seventh day Saturday for His service and the whole day not a part.

Jesus would not dishonour His father by changing their commandments; everything He did was to glorify His father "that the Father may be glorified in the Son" (Jesus was present from creation and took part in Genesis 2:3 when the 7th day was made holy etc). Nor would the Holy Spirit go against the written word of God. Nor can any person change the written word of God. If it is not clearly in the bible, it could be your interpretation. People are always blaming the Holy Spirit for their own thoughts, beliefs etc. If it is not categorically backed up by the bible in total (not singular text) then it is not from the Holy Spirit but unholy, spirit of error. Then some say, if God wants me to change, He would tell me. He has a written bible on the subject with clear commandments, history of those who did not follow His ways and those who did. What more do you want? Why should He visit every person individually giving them personal messages all similar in content? You have a manual, follow it. We are to seek God not Him us. Is it because of Isa 30:9 That this *is* a rebellious people, lying children, children *that* will not hear the law of the LORD: Isa 30:10 Which say to the seers, See not; and to the prophets, Prophesy not unto us right things, speak unto us smooth things, prophesy deceits: Jer 5:31 The prophets prophesy falsely, and the priests bear rule by their means; and my people love *to have it so*: and what will ye do in the end thereof? Gentiles should not become the lost sheep as the bible does not say another Messiah is coming to teach them.

I heard the words of a song which said sentiments as "follow me God wherever I go". That is the problem; people have adopted the wrong understanding that God is to follow them rather than they seek and follow God, His way not their own. In Mark 10:50 Jesus asked Bartimaus to come to Him. Jesus could easily have gone to him; but that is not the way it is to be. We need to show our faith by seeking God in a place where He is then accepting His terms and commandments.

Satan can be that spirit guiding you. Cor 11:14-15 "and no marvel; for satan himself is transformed into an angel of light". His purpose is to deceive you by hook or by crook even as an angel or spirit of light to keep you in darkness in the belief you are following God's true way. Only to find out when it is too late and you are his forever. We are to make sure we are not subject to the wrong spirit, which Jesus gave His chosen 70 power to cast out. Imagine you dropped a diamond ring; but as you looked for it, someone emptied a crate of false but similar appearance glass stone rings in its midst. Eventually you may give up looking for the real thing.

In Matt 4:1-12, satan came to Jesus when He was hungry or weak. Satan may come to us when we are in problems and tempt us to let him solve it. We may get hooked on his way like a drug. The devil took Jesus from the desert to two places, even to the holy city and pinnacle of the temple church). How and does it not show his power and methods. The devil asked Jesus to worship him; what he wanted all along via try to get Jesus' trust. Same deceiving method via false day of worship. It took someone as strong and knowledgeable of the word as Jesus to withstand him. Jesus knew His scriptures in total and was able to counter the devil's use of the same. A test of God's prophets or messengers is not only must their prophesies come true (not by guess or being vague) but they must also coincide with all prior revelations and scripture. In the O.T. Eze 13:3 and Deut 13:2-4 guides. In the N.T. Paul and John taught that the content of the message already received was the standard by which to judge any new message even if it came from an angel (Gal 1:8) or a spirit masquerading as God's Spirit (1 Joh 4:1-3). Hence one reason why in Matt 7:22 Jesus denounces those claiming to prophesy in His name.

The written word of God as He instructed through His prophets are the same as Jesus' living example and subsequent Holy Spirit guidance. The Holy Spirit would not say anything contrary to or change the written word of God. How would you feel if you gave specific instructions to someone to do something, which they saw others from you doing in the past? They do not do it, claiming someone told them not to because you had changed your mind. Would you not tell them that person was not from you? So Christians, when a pastor or spirit tells you to do or not to do something, check it against what God told others to do in the old testament. What Jesus did in the New Testament. Then do the same. The chances are, if it was good enough for them, it will be good enough for you. Anything different is a risky gamble.

Joh 14:26 "But the Comforter, *which is* the Holy Ghost, whom the Father will send in my name, he shall teach you all things, and bring all things to your remembrance, whatsoever I have said unto you". The Holy Spirit brings to remembrance what the bible says not something new. If you do not know your bible thoroughly, you may not be equipped to remember. Act 5:32 "And we are his witnesses of these things; and *so is* also the Holy Ghost, whom God hath given to them that obey him." The Holy Spirit is given to those keeping God's commandments. Any other messenger may be an impersonator. Act 7:51 "Ye stiff-necked and uncircumcised in heart and ears, ye do always resist the Holy Ghost: as your fathers *did*, so *do* ye". Are you doing what God commanded or what suits you. Can you make a "U" turn or are you an addict to custom?

The devil asked Jesus to worship him; what he wanted all along via trying to get Jesus' trust. The same deceiving method via a false day of worship. First he took a third of the angels from heaven. Second, tried to take Jesus from God. Third to take humans from God or worshipping God on His sanctified seventh day. I remind you satan targets the head or leaders of the group; Adam and Peter.

DOES IT MATTER WHAT DAY WE REVERENCE

Deu 7:25 the graven images of their gods shall ye burn with fire: thou shalt not desire the silver or gold *that is* on them, nor take *it* unto thee, lest thou be snared therein: for it *is* an abomination to the LORD thy God. Deu 7:26 neither shalt thou bring an abomination into thine house, lest thou be a cursed thing like it: *but* thou shalt utterly detest it, and thou shalt utterly abhor it; for it *is* a cursed thing. Deu 12:32 what thing soever I command you, observe to do it: thou shalt not add thereto, nor diminish from it. Lev 27:10 He shall not alter it, nor change it, a good for a bad, or a bad for a good: and if he shall at all change beast for beast, then it and the exchange thereof shall be holy. Lev 22:15 "And they shall not profane the holy things of the children of Israel, which they offer unto the LORD;". Profane is un-holy. God or His true representatives do not accept unholy things. It is represented in His character. i.e priests cannot marry widowed women (Lev 21:14 or the whole chapter) and why David, a man of war, could not build His temple. He only made one day holy and no one else can make another day holy. God will not break, nor alter the thing that is gone out of His lips. (Psa 89:34). Ex 20:24 in all places where I record my name I will come unto thee, and I will bless thee. God has never recorded His name in any place associated with pagan customs by origin or other. Would you put your name to something of uncertain or dubious origin or intention? He is particular that nothing involved in His worship is to be polluted in any way i.e Ex 20:25 And if thou wilt make me an altar of stone, thou shalt not build it of hewn (cut) stone: for if thou lift up thy tool upon it, thou hast polluted it.

God never said in any way or form to worship on Sunday. That is agreed by all denominations (see quotations in Early Christians are Jews). As mentioned above, God deals in specifics not discretion. One example is Ezekiel 46:9, where people are told to go in one way and come out another. Why? What should it matter if people came out the same way they went in? Another example of God's meticulous nature is where His instructions leave nothing to mans judgement is Eze 5:1 And thou, son of man, take thee a sharp knife, take thee a barber's razor, and cause *it* to pass upon thine head and upon thy beard: then take thee balances to weigh, and divide the *hair*. Can you imagine dividing hair by guesswork not to mention exactly to the individual strand so each exact and weight does not vary. Cain and Able both offered of their first; yet God accepted Abel's and not Cain's. Abel's was as prescribed, Cain's was as he thought.

Some say it is what is in their heart that counts. Treating fellow man as would be treated. However, God says "To obey is better than sacrifice" (1Sam 15:20-23). Jos 24:14 Now therefore fear the LORD, and serve him in sincerity and in truth: The bible is full of occasions when people did according to their own understanding and were punished by God. Even Saul, a king chosen by God (i.e. 1Sam 13:9-11). v23 "for rebellion is as sin of witchcraft and stubbornness is as inequity and idolatry". Read 1 Sam 15:10 to Saul's death. Note Saul believed he was keeping God's commandments. When it was pointed out to him he had misunderstood or used his own judgement, he pleaded for forgiveness, hanging onto Samuel's skirt till it tore. Yet he apparently was not forgiven. God spoke to him no more despite his prayers. . At the day of judgment many Christians may similarly be gnashing their teeth, holding onto Jesus' mantle, pleading for pardon v25, blaming the pastors or false teachers v21. end result 16:14 the spirit of God leaves him. Even if you do not understand the rest of the bible. God's commandments (Ex 20) are simple enough for all to understand. Doubt is a powerful weapon in the world, political and spiritual. There is a saying a man will not understand something if it is profitable not to understand it! We wrestle not against flesh and blood, but principalities, powers, rulers of darkness, spiritual wickedness in high places (Eph 6:12).His ways are not our ways. So the best way to avoid being deceived is to follow God's word to the letter. See Deut 12:8, Judge 17:6, 21:25.

If God set up the Sabbath by commandment (Ex 20:8), the only one with the word "remember" (and the longest explanation) because God knew as in (Deut 31:19-22) His people (not only Jews as shown elsewhere) would forget it. And many, through lack of a bible, did until the Reformation, when some returned to it. 31:19-22"(Now therefore write you this song for you, and teach it the children of Israel: put it in their mouths, that this song may be a witness for me against the children of Israel. For when I shall have brought them into the land which I swore unto their fathers, that flowed with milk and honey; and they shall have eaten and filled themselves, and waxen fat; then will they turn unto other gods, and serve them, and provoke me, and break my covenant. And it shall come to pass, when many evils and troubles are befallen them, that this song shall testify against them as a witness; for it shall not be forgotten out of the mouths of their seed: for I know their imagination which they go about, even now, before I have brought them into the land which I swore."

Symbols are signs of the real thing. Daniel and his friends were renamed by a pagan king as was Joseph; and those in 2King 23:34; 24:17 why? The pagan kings did not say it is only a name, any name would do, the same way some say it is only a day, and any day of worship would do. These names had particular significance to their god(s) just like the Sabbath has a particular significance to the Christian God of Abraham, Isaac and Jacob. Today, in our world, a family name carries prestige or shame. If you accept God deserves a day of your time, why not make it the right day rather than a false one? Would you accept a fake £50.00 note, $100.00 bill etc? So why think God should? Eze 22:26 her priests have violated my law, and have profaned mine holy things: they have put no difference between the holy and profane, neither have they showed *difference* between the unclean and the clean, and have hid their eyes from my Sabbaths, and I am profaned among them. God only accepts things separated and made holy by Him and His appointed agents. It has been shown how He separated and made only the seventh day holy. Read Numbers chapter seven and see how He also separated and made holy things for His service by His hands. The building, priests, vessels etc. People could not choose to make something holy to Him and if they tried to offer such to Him or they themselves were not made holy by Him, He did not accept it (Lev 10:1-2; 2 Chron 26:4, 18, Exo 29:36-7). Neh 7:64 and Ezra 2:62 prohibited men acting as pastors who could not prove they had His appointed linage. Without intentionally offending, it appears to me nothing or preacher in the Sun day system has been sanctified by God and though

He says He has sheep in other folds, He calls them out from being partakers of the sin and suffering His plagues. Especially when this system is the continuation of the pagan Sun worship on Sunday. In Acts 16:13 Paul, in a city without synagogues, would rather go down to the river bank on the Sabbath and do his teaching than enter into a false or pagan place of worship. Pagan worship rituals were similar to those of the God's in some aspects (possibly copied from God's as satan wishes to be god). For example, they offered meat sacrifices slaughtered in the same way except theirs was offered to the sun or other god. Their temples were the market place for meat. Hence converts to the real God, Jehovah, later felt guilty buying and eating meat offered to pagan gods. Act 16:13 And on the Sabbath we went out of the city by a river side, where prayer was wont to be made; and we sat down, and spake unto the women which resorted *thither*.

Many Christians would agree the devil is in the church, some even in theirs; but would deny their preacher is one of the false ones because he speaks the word of God and gives good sermons. I remind you of the satan's parallel system section. satan can fool the preachers the same as a member. Leaders are targeted as he did with Adam in the garden, Jesus in the wilderness and Peter, on whom Jesus said would build His church (Matt 16:18). In Luk 22:31. It was only Jesus' intervention that saved Peter. satan had entered him once before (Mat 16:23 But Jesus turned, and said unto Peter, get thee behind me satan: thou art an offence). Therefore watch where your pastor is taking you; under a Sun day system or God's. People in a building does not equal Christ in people. Calling something Christian does not make it Christian or holy. satan convinced a third of the angels to join his rebellion, speaks the truth just not the whole truth. Even if the pastor constantly quotes from the bible, as satan did from scripture, it would be a true sermon. You may think it was a good uplifting sermon. The fact certain messages are not preached i.e. the whole truth, means the message is a lie by omission if not intent. Act 16:17 the same followed Paul and us, and cried, saying, these men are the servants of the most high God, which shew unto us the way of salvation. This devil followed Paul and spoke the truth for many days. Similarly some false preachers do to get a Christian following. As with Mark 5:5-10 Christians under these leaderships struggle to break free of the hold and serve God in the truthful way. Being held by various ties.

I could go through all the excuses I have heard but they all come down to ego, laziness and wanting to do and go to places of worship that the individual likes rather than where and in the manner God prescribes. Deut 12:13 Offer your praises and sacrifice in the place where God chooses. Ex 20:24 "...all places where I record my name I will come unto thee, and I will bless thee". God may come into that church to call you out; but if you refuse to move… He may not be in every church seeking Him yet openly not keeping or trying to keep all His commandments, Practicing disobedience. They are thus taking the risk that on judgement day when they come before God saying "did I not prophesise and do good works in your name", God may reply "I know you not" you had your reward on earth (Luk 16:25) doing what you liked rather than what I wanted. You were told if you break one commandment you are no different from those who break them all and so end up with them. The prize is the best ever and only "...they that do his commandments enter in..." you chose to gamble with your salvation. Like the person who went up to another on the steet and asked for their inheritance. The other replied, sorry I cannot give it to you. Why not said the first, I am a good person. That may be so said the other; but I do not know you!

A reason why some Christians do not want to keep God's seventh day Sabbath may be because they covet the customs of the world on that day. Either the pleasures or income. Luk 11:23 He that is not with me is against me: and he that gathereth not with me scattereth. Luk 11:28 But he said, Yea rather, blessed *are* they that hear the word of God, and keep it. Luk 11:34 the light of the body is the eye: therefore when thine eye is single, thy whole body also is full of light; but when *thine eye* is evil, thy body also *is* full of darkness. Luk 11:35 Take heed therefore that the light which is in thee be not darkness. Here Jesus is warning those who think they have light, have found the way to Him; but infact are living in darkness. Luk 11:36 If thy whole body therefore *be* full of light, having no part dark, the whole shall be full of light. Have no part of your belief fake or untrue. as the Sunday worship introduced by satan. Deu 8:2 "to humble thee, and to prove thee, to know what was in thine heart, whether thou wouldest keep his commandments, or not." Eze 3:20; 33:12-16 states if a righteous man commits iniquity all his righteousness will not be remembered. And visa versa for the sinner who stops sinning. Jon 3:10 And God saw their works, that they turned from their evil way; and God repented of the evil, that he had said that he would do unto them; and he did *it* not. Have you proved or convicted yourself? Lastly, remember to whom your tithes and offerings are going. If not to God's God's true church then to His adversary's organisation. They may be using it to take persons away from the true God even if they spend some of it on charitable causes to convince you.

WHAT IS THE SABBATH

It is not another word for rest; but for a period of time, sunset the sixth day (Friday evening) to sunset the seventh day (Saturday evening) (Genesis 1:8).Thus one cannot keep the Sabbath at any other time or day. As that would mean one can move the name around to refer to any time. One cannot move a specific time set by the sun and moon around. Reasons to keep Sabbath, Acts 5:29 "to obey God rather than man". Many Churches and individuals around the world are accepting the truth of the Sabbath and change to its observance without changing their denomination, i.e. they remain, Methodist, Baptist, Pentecostal or other only simply change their day of worship. Whether theology professors, authors against the Sabbath or church leaders, once they really discover that the Sabbath is a sign used to distinguish God's people and will be one of the separating factors at the end of the world. Eze 20:12 Moreover also I gave them my Sabbaths, to be a <u>sign between me and them, that they might know that I *am* the LORD that sanctify them</u>. Exo 31:13 Speak thou also unto the children of Israel, saying, Verily **my Sabbaths** ye shall keep: **for it *is* a sign between me and you** throughout your generations; that *ye* may know that I *am* the LORD that doth sanctify you (also Eze 20:20). Remember Israel is His real people, separated from the pagans. Eze 22:26 Her priests have violated my law, and have profaned mine holy things: they have put no difference between the holy and profane, neither have they shewed *difference* between the unclean and the clean, and have hid their eyes from my Sabbaths, and I am profaned among them.   Do not act out Acts 7:51

HOW IS THE SABBATH KEPT

By abstaining from work, ones own pleasures and self indulging conversation. It is the Lord's Day.   Isaiah 58:13 "If thou turn away thy foot from the Sabbath, *from* doing thy pleasure on my holy day; and call the Sabbath a delight, the holy of the LORD, honourable; and shalt honour him, not doing thine own ways, nor finding thine own pleasure, nor speaking *thine own* words".   Not buying, selling or trading (Neh 10:31 And *if* the people of the land bring ware or any victuals on the Sabbath day to sell, *that* we would not buy it of them on the Sabbath, or on the holy day. Also Neh 13:15, 19). Devoting it to God, the creator of heaven and earth. Lev 23:3 "7th day is Sabbath of rest, a holy convocation". Now is this rest purely for our pleasure and benefit or so we can focus on and worship God without distractions? This was answered above with Isaiah 58:13Him or good works free from personal gain, not simply resting .It also benefits us by keeping our perspectives real, not working ourselves into the ground 24, 7, chasing material things. Of course some may be ordered to work on that day; but with effort and prayers, it may be possible to negotiate a change in hours or job. Your obedience and keeping of His Sabbath day as He prescribed is your honourable sacrifice to Him. If you offer Him your time on Sun day as "your" Sabbath it is an insult like Aaron's sons offered strange fire. 1Co 10:21 "Ye cannot drink the cup of the Lord, and the cup of devils: ye cannot be partakers of the Lord's Table and of the table of devils". One cannot mix things historically offered to devils (Sun day, the day of the Sun god) to God.

Sun day worship was a pagan set aside time. Lev 18:3 After the doings of the land of Egypt, wherein ye dwelt, shall ye not do: and after the doings of the land of Canaan, whither I bring you, shall ye not do: neither shall ye walk in their ordinances. Lev 18:4 Ye shall do my judgments, and keep mine ordinances, to walk therein: I *am* the LORD your God Lev 19:26 Ye shall not... observe times. God detests the things of the pagans so much that not even the best or gold He wants or us to keep See 1 Sam 15:21, Deu 7:25 The graven images of their gods shall ye burn with fire: thou shalt not desire the silver or gold *that is* on them, nor take *it* unto thee, lest thou be snared therein: for it *is* an abomination to the LORD thy God. Deu 7:26 neither shalt thou bring an abomination into thine house, lest thou be a cursed thing like it: *but* thou shalt utterly detest it, and thou shalt utterly abhor it; for it *is* a cursed thing. How individuals keep it varies. It could include singing of hymns, church service attendance, Christian and bible discussions, study, board game playing, family meal and relaxing. Principal restraint, no worldly work.

SABBATH DAY'S JOURNEY

Acts 1:12 "Then returned they unto Jerusalem from the mount called Olivet, which is from Jerusalem a Sabbath day's journey." A pastor quoted me this text as a justification not to keep the Sabbath which restricted persons travelling distance on a Sabbath. He could not see that God or Jesus would be so concerned about keeping such laws and regulations. As a result, he changed from holding service on a Sabbath, to Sunday. Whether any other factors as an availability of rental space influenced his decision, I cannot say. I will return to some other comments of this pastor after dealing with Acts 1:12.

I asked two Jewish followers of the law what a "Sabbath's day journey" constituted. Both explained it was staying within one's residential city regardless of the size of the city (i.e. London) and not venturing more than about one hour travel outside its borders. I asked what is the distance between the Mount of Olives and Jerusalem? I was told it is about 2km or within one hour walking journey. The prescribed distance is about 2000 cubits. A cubit being the distance from one's elbow to finger tip. The reasoning being that outside ones living city they would not have sustenance and such necessities. A one hour journey outside their city would enable them to return and get the food, shelter etc they may need. Coincidentally, a few days later I read Jeremiah 17:21, 22, 24, 27, some of which state "Thus saith the LORD; take heed to yourselves, and bear no **burden** on the Sabbath day, nor bring it in by the gates of Jerusalem; Neither carry forth a **burden** out of your houses on the Sabbath day, neither do ye any work, but hallow ye the Sabbath day, as I commanded your fathers. And it shall come to pass, if ye diligently hearken unto me, saith the LORD, to bring in no **burden** through the gates of this city on the Sabbath day, but hallow the Sabbath day, to do no work therein; But if ye will not hearken unto me to hallow the Sabbath day, and not to bear a **burden**, even entering in at the gates of Jerusalem on the Sabbath day; then will I kindle a fire in the gates thereof, and it shall devour the palaces of Jerusalem, and it shall not be quenched." See also Jer 23:28 and Isaiah 58. So unlike the pastor's reasoning, God is concerned about such laws! It was a requirement of God that no burden is carried to or from one's home on the Sabbath. If one went on a long journey, they would be tempted to carry packed meals, shelter etc. The apostles mentioned the "Sabbath day's journey" to show, though they were travelling, it was a distance within the law.

Some Christians accuse others of being judgemental and think it is unbiblical. I disagree. There are two realms of judgement. Spiritually, say, who gets into heaven and who does not. That is reserved for Jesus. The second is earthly and the knowledge of God's requirements to be saved. Indirectly, we are told to teach those we judge to be in error; either sinning or wrong biblical understanding. Not having the knowledge of Jesus, the whole truth about Him or being deceived. To carry out Matt 28:19 and other similar instructions we have to assess (judge) those we think in need. We do not teach those we judge to already have the knowledge or level needed. The judgement is on ones theology not salvation! I believe the accusation is to silence Christians from speaking out against sin or deceitful false teachers. We should not shy away from bringing others to the truth 2 Tim 4:2 to save some. Paul did not become a sinner to save sinners; he kept all the Law and preached the true gospel.

Another accusation levied against Sabbath keepers is of being too legalistic, adhering to the Law. Is it legalistic for all to stop at red traffic lights? If drivers did not there would be chaos and fatalities. Or discard the laws relating to murder and stealing? Yet another accusation is not showing love because some go around trying to convert them. They use similar accusation of Jesus to the Pharisees as i.e. Luke 11:39 KJV "But woe unto you, Pharisees! for ye tithe mint and rue and all manner of herbs, and pass over judgment and the love of God: these ought ye to have done and not to leave the other undone". One may find what their heart is seeking; excuse or understanding. I sought understanding of the passage and how it would tie in with the rest of scripture. The following is what came to me: Jesus never said not to keep the Sabbath. To the contrary. He and apostles kept and taught they were to be kept. So what else could the passage mean? I noted in v39 Jesus refers to inside <u>and</u> outside not <u>or</u> outside. V40 God made outside and <u>also</u> inside. Again both elements not one. V41 You give of your material and think that is enough to get you to heaven (make you clean). V42 Not only are we to give of our material things (even small ones), mint, rue herbs; but <u>also</u> of our love to God and fellow man. Is this not a restating of the Ten Commandments, which Jesus summarised as two, love God and fellow man? I then noted the NIV version read: "Woe to you Pharisees, because you give God a tenth of your mint, rue and all other kinds of garden herbs, but you neglect justice and the love of God. You should have practiced the latter <u>without</u> leaving the former undone." So the interpretation is not that hard.

As for the accusation of not showing love, if you have found something valuable, does love not inspire you to tell others? Is that not what Christians are called to do, go forth and preach the true gospel as each is convicted. Do you, or should you not do the same in your own way. This is love. The intent is to share a gift they have received irrespective of the individuals' methods. Methods which may be driven by the recipients' hostility to information. Any loving person would try and stop someone committing suicide or pull them out of a situation which has numbed their senses.

Not everyone in a church or denomination may get the exact Christian life. Each may be at different points of the journey. We should not look at them; but where they are or should be heading; living God's words. Let us look to the destination, heaven, not the traveller nor their route. How to get to God as He prescribed not excuse ourselves because others may not have both inside and outside actions. I am sure the Sabbath keepers; those who feel they may not quite be showing total love to fellow man, are working on that part. At least they have half right, the outside. You, as a non Sabbath keeper may feel you have the inside. Learn from each other so you both acquire the two elements and get to heaven, rather than neither of you / us. Is it so hard to comprehend God requires both elements from us. Is the comprehension influenced by your reluctance to totally submit?

Imagine a crowd fleeing a besieged city. All attempting to get to another safe city, Heaven. Many are stretched out on various roads, in various directions. Some do not believe there is a city of refuge and are content to live off the plight of others on the journey. Robbing, murdering or selling false maps or information to the city. Some, unsure which way to go, decide to make camp and wait for someone to return from Heaven and show them the way. They do not realise there is a big gulf between Heaven and the route there, from which no one can return. When those who have arrived at the city request permission to return and show others the way, the king replies "it is a straight and narrow entry point to Heaven. Those outside already have the prophets and other directions on how to get here (Luke 16:19-31). Some travellers are hindered in the distance and speed they can travel due to dependants, i.e. children, some are laden with their possessions, and others go where their friends go or the route more comfortable, scenic, etc rather than over the snowy mountain pass. A remnant group have headed out along an overgrown track they read was travelled by their ancestors. They follow the ten signs made up of heaps of stone left by the ancestors to mark the way. The journey is hard, it would be easier to turn back and do as the 99% have. Many reasons present themselves if one was seeking one; yet they continue singing as they go, taking joy in the knowledge one day they will reach the heavenly city of refuge. Heb 11:16 But now they desire a better *country*, that is, a heavenly: wherefore God is not ashamed to be called their God: for he hath prepared for them a city.

Returning to some comments of the former Sabbath keeping pastor I mentioned. He used to attend a Pentecostal Sabbath church (of which there are many), but left because he found it impossible to keep the Sabbath. In addition to Acts 1:12, he stated his tiredness at the end of the day due to working hard holding Sabbath school in the morning, service and other activities. He thought most Sabbath keepers were not keeping the Sabbath as prescribed and gave the example of some Seventh Day Adventist churches who hold congregational meals after worship service at which they serve cooked or warmed food by a "fire" (Exo 35:3 "Ye shall kindle no fire throughout your habitations upon the Sabbath day"). His other interpretations of the Law were one cannot look at television, have mail, groceries or a newspaper delivered to their door. I assume he referred to Jer 17:21, 22, 24, 27 "Thus saith the LORD; Take heed to yourselves, and bear no burden on the Sabbath day, nor bring *it* in by the gates of Jerusalem; Neither carry forth a burden out of your houses on the Sabbath day, neither do ye any work, but hallow ye the Sabbath day, as I commanded your fathers. And it shall come to pass, if ye diligently hearken unto me, saith the LORD, to bring in no burden through the gates of this city on the Sabbath day, but hallow the Sabbath day, to do no work therein; But if ye will not hearken unto me to hallow the Sabbath day, and not to bear a burden, even entering in at the gates of Jerusalem on the Sabbath day; then will I kindle a fire in the gates thereof, and it shall devour the palaces of Jerusalem, and it shall not be quenched".

He said he was aware of Constantine's influence and the Roman Catholic's claim that they have the power to change God's commandments. A power he rejects. His stance came from the apparent difficulty to keep it and not knowing anyone who kept it as biblically prescribed and enjoyed it. He therefore, concluded that our loving God would understand and excuse the human predicament, leading us to be saved by "grace" not keeping the law or commandments. He simply found it a "burden" rather than joy like those of old in Jer 23:33-40. Whereas, the Sunday school teacher mentioned in the Grace and Relationship section was moved to keep the Sabbath after reading the book "Ten Commandments Twice Removed". It showed how keeping it could and should be a joy. My suggestions to him were a result of my approach to the same problem. Starting from a point of wanting to get to heaven and searching God's scripture of how He prescribes is the route. Comparing what I did to the route prescribed and changing what I did to suit, not the other way round. Change the method not the Command!

Distance travelled: Though I later found out the truth behind a Sabbath's day journey (explained above), I suggested he found or started up a closer church, met with persons closer to his home or simply worshipped at home with his family.

Deliveries: The text actually says you should not take in or out a burden through your door. You are responsible for your actions not others bringing things to your home. This does not permit you to have workmen enter your house on the Sabbath because you are not actually doing the carrying. However, if mail comes through your door, simply leave it on the mat, kick it into a corner, close up the letter box preventing mail coming through, ask the postmen not to deliver on Sabbath etc. Where there is a will, there is a way.

Purchases: Save for a daily newspaper, milk and most things can be purchased in advance any other day prior to the Sabbath. Like the double portion of manna that fell from heaven. Missing one day's newspaper will not kill you. Topics tend to run on for days and are repeated on both the radio and television in the night after Sabbath. If there was an earthquake or other catastrophe, which threatened our lives instantly, I am sure you will not be reading about it in a newspaper. At times as these, which are extremely rare, Jesus said "pray that flight not on a Sabbath day".

Busy Church schedule: Cut out part of schedule if too much for one person; especially business meetings. Delegate tasks so each person not over worked and can enjoy the day. Do God's agenda not one's own to bring people into church or keep them there satisfied. Serve God and make sure you the pastor, get to heaven as an individual. Don't save others and loose your own salvation. Do not let others steal your place nor give it away. I know a former Sunday worshipping pastor who gave up his church to become an attendee and keep the Sabbath.

Cooking by Fire: Eat a menu that does not entail cooking or warming food. According to a Jewish Rabbi their custom is to keep food warm from before Sabbath in an oven. A Seventh Day Adventist church pastor told me they have cooked food because one of their pioneers recommended cooked food over cold for health reasons and thus, the "Law" is not so stringent on such matters. Some may appreciate the health reason; but disagree with the solution since it goes against the written word of God. This is a good example of what Paul meant when he said in Rom 14:5 "let every man be fully persuaded in his own mind". Similarly with looking at television. Some Sabbath keepers may look at Christian lectures, worship or other Christian programs on the Sabbath; but not ordinary programs. I once heard a Sabbath keeping pastor preach that Sabbath viewing should not be different to other days' viewing. He stated, if the programme was not fit to be watched on a Sabbath, it should not be watched at all. You make up your own mind. Consider whether God made every day holy to be treated the same. If an action would distraction you from keeping it holy "unto the Lord", maybe it should be cut out for that Sabbath period.

Non Christians enjoying the pleasures and lust of the world, think Christians are silly. Bound by a way of life from a person (Jesus), they think, did / does not exist. Who can make no difference to ones life or death. Of course Christians know better and that the contrary is true. Those outside may never appreciate the rewards of being inside Christianity. Even if they come in and try it for a period, it is as a visitor searching for the selfish benefit to them. When they do not get in abundance, benefits to compensate them for the little sacrifice they make in trying to be "good", they leave. They were never truly converted. Similarly non Sabbath keepers see being in the Sabbath as a bind. Giving up their Saturday is not rewarded as they would like, compared to the things they have to forgo doing on that day. A person is protected by the legal system under which they are bound. Thus being bound by the law has its positive benefits of protection. Until Christians are fully converted to Jesus, they will not appreciate the joy of giving up all to follow Him in total, including keeping His day. In my suggestions I commented I could not see God would create the Ten Commandments for some and then take them away permitting murder, adultery etc. Or that He would leave human ones & abolish any applicable to Him, His godly, worship & creator of the world status.

A Personal story:

I met a fellow Christian, Sabbath keeper; but not a member of any church. Though he visits churches occasionally, I think he keeps it with a fellow Christian reading God's word (like a few others I have met). His story of how he came to God is: as a non believer, not going to church or knowing about God he was socialising with friends when one of them made a comment about God's character. Intrigued, he went home to find a bible he was given years ago whilst decorating a church. He read it from cover to cover and decided to follow what it said. Remember he knew nothing of God or ever went to church. Some time after, his neighbour asked him to give away her daughter at her wedding. Speaking to the other church goers he was amazed to find every church goer did not keep the seventh day Sabbath. One explained they were no longer under that Sabbath keeping system and used one of the reasons discussed above. He disbelieved them, having found nothing in the bible to support what was told to him. Here we have a person, going purely by what is in the bible discovering the Sabbath and adhering to it despite what other Sunday church attendees told him.

In brief another added testimony as book went to print. Couple with wife going to church on Sunday, husband (whose mother elder in a church) not church goer and thinking all hypocrites, wife's uncle Anglican vicar. Husband began to read old bible handed down to wife from 2 generations. in Exodus discovered 4th commandment and historical notes in back of bible, told wife she going on wrong day, discussed with mother who told him it cancelled. He not believed and began to research which confirmed his view got from the bible. Did not want to go Jewish church, one Sabbath keeping religion knew of. Then discovered Adventist, Sabbath keeping Christians. Have been there since for past 15 years. Later uncle's wife died, he became ill and wife stayed there to assist him. Told uncle she going church on Saturdays. He old her to stay right there. When he came to country to study for vicar he discovered the change but his wife would not let them change.

In Luke 1:80 John the Baptist was in the desert isolated from traditions and influences of the Pharisees from his birth until "showing unto Israel". This was about thirty years. If you are a Sunday worshipper, I suggest doing the same. Isolate yourself away from the tradition of Sun day observance and only be guided by the reading of the bible. Pray for God to open your eyes and give you a fresh and true understanding for which you earnestly seek. Then, maybe, you have given Him the right environment to speak to you without distractions of others.

PROSPERITY SERMONS.

I saw an advertisement for an annual conference with the title and slogan "Prosper". It brought together a string of popular, charismatic pastors from around the world. The organisation's previous year's conferences were along the lines of "Gathering of Champions". To me a champion is one who stands above or is better than others at a certain task. Jesus said to be the greatest (champion) one is to serve others. Mat 18:4 "Whosoever therefore shall humble himself as this little child, the same is **greatest** in the kingdom of heaven" Mat 23:11 but he that is **greatest** among you shall be your servant." Yet by this church's criteria it seems to be to serve self, get prosperity in material things as a sign of God's blessings. Christianity is not a product to be marketed to consumers. If it is yours or a pastor's desire to get rich, do so in the labour market and yet live a Godly life, not make riches from religion. Jud 1:4 For there are certain men crept in unawares, who were before of old ordained to this condemnation, ungodly men, turning the grace of our God into lasciviousness, and denying the only Lord God, and our Lord Jesus Christ. Denying the real character of Jesus rather than the one they preach. Jer 12:10 "Many pastors have destroyed my vineyard, they have trodden my portion under foot, they have made my pleasant portion a desolate wilderness". Remember satan targets our leaders as they are the ones that give the false directions to the congregation. Maybe speaking part of the truth from the bible; but not all truth as i.e. John 16:13. As in a testimony in a court room, the truth consists of "the truth, the whole truth and nothing but the truth"; any deviation is a lie aimed to deceive. A pastor can spend a human's life time preaching on the goodness of God and what He can do for you. Maybe get ten sermons out of one verse or story as Jonah. Three on Jonah, three on the whale four on Nineveh etc and never get round to preaching about keeping God's commandments which is probably the most important sermon. Even satan can give a "good" sermon in church once he quotes from the Bible; but as 1Tim 1:8 says "the law is good if used lawfully" bad if used for evil. So it is with the Bible. People want to hear pleasant "truths" rather than the present truth! Pleasant truth is not all truth or necessarily the truth. As one book puts it "And there are among them illiterates, who know not the Book, but (see therein their own) desires and they do nothing but conjecture. Then woe to those who write the Book with their own hands, and then say 'This is from Allah, to traffic with it for a miserable price!". This being similar to 1Tim 1:7 speaking of some pastors: "Desiring to be teachers of the law; understanding neither what they say, nor whereof they affirm" (explained in the topic 'Book of Galatians').

I believe a pastor's salary and benefits should be set by his congregation and accounts of the ministry verified by external accounting or government agencies. If you cannot verify your pastor's income and benefits, I suggest you ask whether your funds are going to God's work or the individual, friends or family coffers. Mic 3:11 "The heads thereof judge for reward, and the priests thereof teach for hire, and the prophets thereof divine for money: yet will they lean upon the LORD, and say, Is not the LORD among us? none evil can come upon us". We should show people how to worship God not conform to societies' shortfalls. Society teaches there are no absolutes; no right or wrong; but matter of choice, opinion, etc. Excuses like homosexuality are not against God, but nature, a psychological sickness etc is used. God has clear lines of right, wrong, acceptable and not if one cares to seek them.

Many of today's preachers are more akin to commercial motivational, personal development speakers. Slightly using the word of God for a platform on how to get this or that. They quote and propagate scripture as Deut 8:18 "But thou shalt remember the LORD thy God: for *it is* he that giveth thee power to get wealth, that he may establish his covenant which he sware unto thy fathers, as *it is* this day". But leave out the condition of the previous verses i.e. Deu 8:1 All the commandments which I command thee this day shall ye observe to do, that ye may live, and multiply, and go in and possess the land which the LORD sware unto your fathers. ..., to humble thee, *and* to prove thee, to know what *was* in thine heart, whether thou wouldest keep his commandments, or no. ...; that he might make thee know that man doth not live by bread only, but by every *word* that proceedeth out of the mouth of the LORD doth man live.

Deu 8:6 Therefore thou shalt keep the commandments of the LORD thy God, to walk in his ways, and to fear him. Deu 8:11 Beware that thou forget not the LORD thy God, in not keeping his commandments, and his judgments, and his statutes, which I command thee this day: See also Lev 26:3 If ye walk in my statutes, and keep my commandments, and do them; Lev 26:4 Then I will give you ... and 26:14-15.... Those calling on these promises of wealth are the same ones who claim the commandments were for the Jews and not them yet not the wealth part! The group given the promises of wealth is the same as led by Moses and the prophets etc.

These pastors speak to the worldly, personally dissatisfied. Not only did Jesus die for them; but now they spoil His body for whatever else He can do for them. They want the benefits but only take the real Jesus and His requirements as an optional side dish. It is all about them getting not giving, finding contentment, seeking and drawing closer to God except, possibly, in lip service. Isaiah 29:13 "Wherefore the Lord said, forasmuch as this people draw near *me* with their mouth, and with their lips do honour me, but have removed their heart far from me, and their fear toward me is taught by the precept of men:" These people should stop their craving, read and learn from Ecc 2:11 written by the wisest man ever lived "Then I looked on all the works that my hands had wrought, and on the labour that I had laboured to do: and, behold, all *was* vanity and vexation of spirit, and *there was* no profit under the sun". We are God's creation made for His purpose Luk 17:9 Doth he thank that servant because he did the things that were commanded him? I trow not. Luk 17:10 so likewise ye, when ye shall have done all those things which are commanded you, say, we are unprofitable servants: we have done that which was our duty to do.

Luk 5:1-11 And it came to pass, that, as the people pressed upon him to hear the word of God, he stood by the lake of Gennesaret, And saw two ships standing by the lake: but the fishermen were gone out of them, and were washing *their* nets. And he entered into one of the ships, which was Simon's, and prayed him that he would thrust out a little from the land. And he sat down, and taught the people out of the ship. Now when he had left speaking, he said unto Simon, Launch out into the deep, and let down your nets for a draught. And Simon answering said unto him, master, we have toiled all the night, and have taken nothing: nevertheless at thy word I will let down the net. And when they had this done, they inclosed a great multitude of fishes: and their net brake. And they beckoned unto *their* partners, which were in the other ship, that they should come and help them. And they came, and filled both the ships, so that they began to sink. When Simon Peter saw *it*, he fell down at Jesus' knees, saying, depart from me; for I am a sinful man, O Lord. For he was astonished, and all that were with him, at the draught of the fishes which they had taken: And so *was* also James, and John, the sons of Zebedee, which were partners with Simon. And Jesus said unto Simon, Fear not; from henceforth thou shalt catch men. And when they had brought their ships to land, they forsook all, and followed him."

You have worked hard, achieved nothing. No riches, yet obey God's commands. Not for self benefit or in anticipation of any reward but solely because He asked. Then your prosperity reward may come, because you obeyed willingly, from the heart not your head. It is seen as from your heart because you are willing to leave it all and follow God, catching people for His kingdom of heaven not furnishing your home or life with riches. Phil 3:7-8 "But what things were gain to me those I counted loss for Christ. Yea doubtless, and I count all things *but* loss for the excellency of the knowledge of Christ Jesus my Lord: for whom I have suffered the loss of all things, and do count them *but* dung, that I may win Christ," John 12:25 "He that loveth his life shall lose it; and he that hateth his life in this world shall keep it unto life eternal". Where is the earthly prosperity motivation speech by Jesus or Paul?

Jesus is the solution to your problems. Not by you bringing them to Him (need of materialism or healing), getting them satisfied and then moving on; but by the renewing of your mind away from earthly concerns onto spiritual ones. A wise person invests for the next life not this one from which many can be taken at any time leaving all assets behind. Your only assurance (insurance) against death is that which gives eternal life. The premium for which is not monetary. (see Matt 6:19-21). Solomon in Proverbs 30:7-9 prays "Two *things* have I required of thee; deny me *them* not before I die: Remove far from me vanity and lies: give me neither poverty nor riches; feed me with food convenient for me: Lest I be full, and deny *thee*, and say, who *the LORD is*? Or lest I be poor, and steal, and take the name of my God *in vain*." What wisdom. God gives blessings which may not be riches but a change in character. One that keeps His commandments, humble, long suffering and endures to the end for the prize of heaven not necessarily on earth. satan cannot give the prize of heaven so he gives his riches of earth as offered to Jesus in the wilderness, also EZE 28:1-5 shows the king of Tyrus is really satan as in verse 13 so when these sun day preachers preach prosperity to you under the banner of come and get your blessing, it is not necessarily from God, though they may be using the word "Lord" "Jehovah or Jesus" there is a way to tell how to get God's blessing which they leave out. Read all the promises of blessings God made and you should see they were conditional on His commandments (EX 20), laws and statutes being kept. Never unconditional and one would be ignorant to think N.T. believers can call on New or Old Testament promises without keeping God's commandments in total or at least attempting and persevering to keep them.

I am constantly hearing from Christians who succumb to the prosperity sermons. A recent one being at a very large gathering the preacher was saying Christians are always saying or preaching how good God is and how He blesses them yet do not attract non believers to God by the cars they drive. In the pub car parks one sees expensive cars yet in the church car park old ones. He then asks, who do you think the non believers would want to be like? Like others, this preacher is obviously missing what God and Jesus is about. He thinks God's blessings are exhibited in the material things you put on show. Offering candy to people is the way to convert them; like a drug dealer giving free tasters. The world and many Christians think at the material level. At the end of these sermons is generally a request to give a big donation as a sign God has blessed you (Eze 22:25). I have discussed this false thinking and preaching elsewhere; but on this example I will add. The type of people the preacher advocates to follow probably do not give their time to Jesus' work. If they did their cars would be in the church car park. They live and work for self. Maybe in debt, having to do ungodly things to earn the extra money (i.e. over pricing), and many other considerations. Compared to the simple content life of a Christian who focuses on what is most important, the things of the next world not this one.

I noticed in the 2008 Paralympics how contented and talented participants were with their disabilities, playing all manner of sports, some in wheel chairs or others who are blind. Some pastors and Christians coming to Jesus for material benefits can learn contentment from these athletes. A principle found in the tenth commandment "thou shall not covet" anything of your neighbour. Your neighbour being a fellow human being as depicted by Jesus in the Good Samaritan story. Some profess to be Christians and say they want to follow God's will. Yet when the choice comes to do God's or the world's they choose the world's or their own way just like in Jer 42:6-7; 43:1-4 and 44:15-18. At the end of those texts the people state that when they went against God and served the "queen of heaven" they were prosperous and the punishment they were now receiving was due to stopping serving her. They could not see it was because God was longsuffering.

Mark 10:24 "and the disciples were astonished at his words. But Jesus answereth again, and saith unto them, Children, how hard is it for them that trust in riches to enter into the kingdom of God" I heard of lady who stopped praying because God did not grant her indefinite stay in a country. Instead, for the past 12 years she has been getting one year extensions. People forget the purpose of praying is to give thanks and praises not for desires. They could be thankful for what they have as it could be worst. I receive emails of African country inhabitants using plastic bottles as shoes, short of food and other basic necessities. God gave her 12 years to thank Him. It took her 12 years to stop praying. Maybe God, in His wisdom of her heart, knew that had He given her the desire of her heart in year one, her prays would have stopped then or continue for another material desire.

A booklet written by an author with initials R.W expresses some similar sentiments to mine on the topic relating to the reasons humans are on the earth or why some attend church. However, I have seen quotes from this author's book which I cannot recommend. He writes and advises churches, many of whom use his book as a type of manual for church growth. RW advocates a "needs" concept rather than God leading people to church. He says he did a survey of his area asking people what they wanted from a church. Then advises pastors how to meet these needs. Supply the rock or jazz music, tone down the dress code and make persons comfortable. He says they are more important than the message! In other words go against God's directives as in Exodus 20:26 where God forbids the exhibition of nakedness. Some may even say this directive is part of the commandments we call the Ten; for was it not for the interruption of the people moving in verses 18-23, God would have continued with His commandments without the pause at the end of verse 17. The concept is preach materialism and many so called pastors, recognising this market "need" preach to satisfy it. This makes people rely on the giver (preacher) not God and raises the giver's prestige, self esteem, ego etc. I heard a sermon and then was told by others it is common, where a pastor said no revelation comes to a church or individual unless comes through the pastor. This is to succumb to their ego and mitigate God's word through His Bible onto reliance on them for interpretation. Do not succumb to those speaking this message of ego and greed exalting themselves. A DVD titled Strange Fire by Prof Walter Veith from Total Onslaught producers elaborates on this type of ministry. I am told he has other video material available from Utube on the internet.

Though I partially agree with Mr W on parts of his booklet, I cannot support unbiblical theories. Thus I am not endorsing the rest of his ministry. The following are extracts from his booklet minced with my own views on the topic.

The purpose of your life is far greater than your own personal fulfilment, your peace of mind or even your happiness. It is far greater than your family, career or your wildest dreams and ambitions. If you want to know why you were placed on this planet, you must begin with God. You were born for and by His purpose. Until you understand that, life will never make sense. It is only in God that we understand our origin, identity, meaning, purpose, significance and destiny. Every other path leads to a dead end. The search for the purpose of live has puzzled people for years. That is because we typically start from the wrong point - ourselves. We ask self-centred questions like, "What do I want to be? What should I do with my life? What are my goals, dreams, ambitions, dreams for my future? But focusing on ourselves will never reveal our life's purpose. The bible says in Job 12:10, it is God who directs the lives of His creatures, everyone's life is in His power. Contrary to what many popular books, movies and seminars tell you, you will not discover your life's meaning by looking within yourself. You did not create yourself, so there is no way you can tell yourself for what you were created. If handed an invention you had never seen before, you would not know its purpose without referring to the inventor or manual. The invention itself would not be able to tell you.

Many people try to use God for their own self-actualization. They try to use God to be a personal "genie" serving their self-centred desires. But that is a reversal of nature and doomed for failure. Life is about letting God use you for His purpose not you using Him. You were made for God and not visa versa (see Romans 8:6).

Non biblical books (some written by "pastors") directing people how to fulfil their lives suggest self help methods starting from the person's needs or desires. They suggest that individuals should identify their dreams, values (etc), identify what you are good at, set goals, aim high, believe you can achieve, be disciplined and never give up. A friend reading from such a book told me of a suggestion of making a pie chart of one's time, then re-slicing the chart to allow more time for this and that. No where in that chart did it mention time for or increasing that given to God. Does this sound like some sermons with a biblical input? (Some pastors who may advocate more time for God is simply to help their church). Of course these recommendations are all good and often lead to great success. One can usually succeed in reaching a goal if they put their mind to it; but being successful and fulfilling your life's purpose is not at all the same issue! One can reach all their goals; become a great success by world's standard and still miss the purpose for which God created them. Worldly success could come with a high price of a busy schedule, stress and ill health. Godly success and following His purpose will allow you to do less, by focusing your time and efforts on what matters most. Jesus said in Matt 11:28 come unto me, all *ye* that labour and are heavy laden, and I will give you rest i.e. from chasing things of no spiritual value.

Your options of knowing your life's purpose is either by speculation, guess work or various other theories. Dr Hugh Moorhead, a philosophy professor at North-eastern Illinois University, wrote to 250 of the world's best known philosophers, scientists, writers and intellectuals in the world asking "What is the meaning of life?" Their replies were their best guess, some admitted having just made up a purpose, some said they were clueless, others asked Dr Moorhead to tell them if he discovered it. The other option is by having a relationship with God your Creator. God, through His word, the Bible, beats speculation any day. He has not left us in the dark to wonder or guess. In the Bible He explains why and how we are alive, how life works, what to avoid and what to expect (see 1 Cor 2:6-8). God is not only the starting point of your life; but also its source. Turn to Him not the world's best guesses. Build your life on eternal unchanging truths not ever changing opinions.

Many people are driven by materialism. Their desire to acquire becomes the whole goal of their lives. This drive to always get more and God to assist, is based on the misconception that having more will make me happy, more important or more secure - all of which are untrue (Pro 13:7). Possessions only provide temporary happiness, soon we get bored with them and want a newer, bigger or better version. Self worth and net worth is not the same. Your value is not determined by your valuables. The most valuable things in life are not things. It does not matter who knows of or respects you now, what legacies you leave: but whether God accepts and remembers you (Rom 14:12). More money does not make one secure as wealth can be lost instantly. Real security can only be found in that which can never be taken from you, your proper relationship with God (Isaiah 26:3). The earth is not meant to be your permanent home so do not look to get total happiness here. Look to the day when you will be going home; to God. Do not seek acceptance by others. Those who follow the crowd get lost in and with it. Do not base your worship to God on how you like it or opinions say. See how God prescribed it and maybe how it was done in the bible. Be one of those who say to God "Thy will be done" rather than have God say to you "all right then, have it your way". Worshipping God is not simply going to church or singing some songs. It is with your very being, lifestyle, keeping all His commandments and enjoying Him. Your life is your "living sacrifice".

Knowing your purpose simplifies your life. Without it you have no foundation on which to base decisions, allocate your time and use your resources. You will tend to make choices based on circumstances, pressure or your mood at that moment. People who do not know their purpose try to do too much and that causes stress, fatigue and conflict. It is impossible to do everything people want you to do. You have just enough time to do God's will. If you cannot get it all done, it means you are trying to do more than God intended you to do or, possibly, wasting your time in some way. Focus on God, prune away even good activities and only do what matters most. Never confuse activity with productivity. Do not look to the world to make you happy, look to God and be content with what He gives you without comparing with what He may or may not have given others (Rom 12:2). The earth is not meant to be your permanent home so do not look to get total happiness here. Look to the day when you will be going home; to God. On judgement day, when God asks you "What did you do with all I gave you, your gifts, talents, opportunities, energy, relationships and resources? Did you spend them on yourself or use them to fulfil my purpose for your life?

It is a fatal mistake to assume that God's goal for your life is material prosperity or popular success, as the world defines it. The abundant life has nothing to do with material abundance and faithfulness to God does not guarantee success. The instant person wants things in an instant and is prone to fall for satan's temptations. God is far more interested in your character than your comfort. He is more interested in what you are becoming than in making this life easy for you. Where did Paul and John the Baptist end up for their faithfulness? In prison. What the world sees and how it judges you is not the same as how God sees or rewards. 1Pet 2:11 "Dearly beloved, I beseech *you* as strangers and pilgrims, abstain from fleshly lusts, which war against the soul". 2Cor 4:18 "While we look not at the things which are seen, but at the things which are not seen: for the things which are seen *are* temporal; but the things which are not seen *are* eternal. "

Do not look to get attached to the earth and its valuables. That maybe why God does not answer some of the prayers you think you deserve. This is a temporary residence. A hotel from which, you will soon be checking out. You only need a suitcase of things and the smaller the more agile and manoeuvrability you will have. Maybe that is why Jesus said in Mark 10:25 it is easier for a camel to go through the eye of a needle, than for a rich man to enter into the kingdom of God.

Who are you going to live for, yourself or God? God calls people who want to follow Him, out of Babylon (Rev 14:4). This could well be your calling, as no one knows when his or her hour comes, in the blink of an eye tomorrow may never come. Do you respond and come or cling to custom? The call comes in your lifetime not after you are dead, in your grave or on the day of judgement when realisation may set in. Then there would be nothing one can do to change their destiny. You may have come to know "of" Christ through a needs concept preacher. Getting non-believers into church via this method is one thing; but only becomes positive if those people move onto knowing God. From milk onto hard food in another proper church that teaches how to serve God as He prescribed; which is the purpose of this book. The problem comes when they have got so comfortable in that artificial church, are indoctrinated with teachings of tradition rather than fact, do not care to listen to reason or proof that they are wrongly taught. If the message of Jesus had to be lowered to meet you where you were, now you see Him, let Him show you the way to His home. It is time for you to raise your standards and aim to meet Him where He is. Like in Matt 22:1-12 many are called from where and in what garment they are in; once they respond and come in, unless they change and put on the wedding gown of doing God's commandments as did Jesus, they will be bounded and cast into outer darkness.

I visited a grand big church with seating for over 2,000 persons. They hold three services on a Sunday, probably for lack of space. Around the walls were very large television screens used to show the service; but also used to advertise various merchandise. I also heard of a visiting pastor to another church starting off his sermon on a bible scripture; but then redirecting it to do with tithes and how much one gives. He had written ten books, sold at about $16 USA (£10.00) each. He come prepared with his credit card machine to take payment. A few days later he was on the God television. channel fixing the sum he wanted the congregation to give that week, $80 USA (£52.00). I have heard these Sunday pastors start preaching about a promise of God, or so; but stop before the verse stating to keep His commandments. Many use the church congregation as a sheep market place to be shear the sheep of their money. Mat 10:8 "heal the sick, cleanse the lepers, raise the dead, cast out devils, **freely ye have received, freely give.**

BAPTISM

The word "baptize" is derived from the Greek word "baptizo" meaning to dip, submerge or immerse. Jesus, the son of God, sinless and blameless chose to get baptized. He is our example as Christians in being Christ like, walking as He walked. His baptism consisted of total body submersion in water Mar 1:9-10 Jesus came from Nazareth of Galilee, and was baptized of John in Jordan. And straightway coming up out of the water, he saw the heavens opened, and the Spirit like a dove descending upon him: John the baptism, the prophet of whom Jesus said there was no other, on whom was the holy Spirit from his birth (Luke 1:15) was also baptized Joh 3:23 And John also was baptizing in Aenon near to Salim, because there was much water there: and they came, and were baptized. If a little water was acceptable no one would come out the church, waste their time and effort going to the river, getting soaking wet (and for the women, messing up their hair), changing their cloths and walking back. Immersion is therefore necessary.

Eph 4:5 One Lord, one faith, one baptism. Joh 3:3 Jesus answered and said unto him, Verily, verily, I say unto thee, except a man be born again, he cannot see the kingdom of God. Joh 3:5 I say unto thee, Except a man be born of water and *of* the Spirit, he cannot enter into the kingdom of God Mar 16:16 He that believeth and is baptized shall be saved; 1Pe 1:23 Being born again, not of corruptible seed, but of incorruptible, by the word of God, which liveth and abideth for ever. (Mat 28:19-20) Go ye therefore, and teach all nations, baptizing them in the name of the Father, and of the Son, and of the Holy Ghost: Teaching them to observe all things whatsoever I have commanded you:

There are over fifteen various ceremonies called baptism today; but only one real biblical one. Unbiblical ones include being sprinkled with water, having water poured on you, or rose petals or salt used, being anointed with oil, the no water dry clean method i.e. only the words spoken, words spoken over the phone or sent by email and some saying the event is only symbolic. Some may say the apostles changed the baptism from total immersion. Paul's answer to this would be, even if an angel tells you something different to what Jesus said and did, do not believe it. The curse of heaven would be on them (Gal 1:8, 9, 11, 12). We see that Phillip who preached after the ascension of Jesus baptized the eunuch of Ethiopia in the river Act 8:38 "And he commanded the chariot to stand still: and they went down both into the water, both Philip and the eunuch; and he baptized him". (in the same way as Jesus and John the Baptist). Thus the change was not by the apostles; but by man. Do you want to follow man or God? Matt 15:9 but in vain they do worship me, teaching *for* doctrines the commandments of men. Again some say it is only the baptism of the Holy Spirit that is needed or of your heart. However Acts 10:44-8 shows this not to be the case Act 10:44 While Peter yet spake these words, the Holy Ghost fell on all them which heard the word. ...on the Gentiles also was poured out the gift of the Holy Ghost. . Then answered Peter, Can any man forbid water, that these should not be baptized, which have received the Holy Ghost as well as we? And he commanded them to be baptized in the name of the Lord.

One must be taught and accept the truth about Jesus and His gospel. Believe the same, repent and ask for forgiveness for their sins. Accept Jesus Christ only as your personal saviour and only one to forgive your sins directly, NOT by an earthly intermediary. Earthly forgiveness, blessings and acts need to be in line with God's commands and principles. One cannot claim a blessing etc yet act contrary to His commandments. See the story of Balaam in Num 22:6 - 24:13; especially 23:8, 11, 20, 26, 24:13. Act 2:38 "Then Peter said unto them, Repent, and be baptized every one of you in the name of Jesus Christ for the remission of sins, and ye shall receive the gift of the Holy Ghost". Baptism is not for children; but adults who can fulfil the requirements (See also

Rev 2:5, 16, 21, 22. 3:3, 19, Rom 6:5, 6, 2Cor 5:17) Gal 3:27 for as many of you as have been baptized into Christ have put on Christ. Gal 3:28 there is neither Jew nor Greek, there is neither bond nor free, there is neither male nor female: for ye are all one in Christ Jesus. 2Co 5:17 Therefore if any man *be* in Christ, *he is* a new creature: old things are passed away; behold all things are become new.

Rom 6:3 Know ye not, that so many of us as were baptized into Jesus Christ were baptized into his death? Rom 6:4 Therefore we are buried with him by baptism into death: that like as Christ was raised up from the dead by the glory of the Father, even so we also should walk in newness of life. Rom 6:5 For if we have been planted together in the likeness of his death, we shall be also *in the likeness* of *his* resurrection: Rom 6:6 Knowing this, that our old man is crucified with *him*, that the body of sin might be destroyed, that henceforth we should not serve sin. 1Co 12:13 For by one Spirit are we all baptized into one body, whether *we be* Jews or Gentiles, whether *we be* bond or free; and have been all made to drink into one Spirit. Act 22:16 and now why tarriest thou? arise, and be baptized, and wash away thy sins, calling on the name of the Lord. Luk 7:30 But the Pharisees and lawyers rejected the counsel of God against themselves, being not baptized of him.

The facts taken from the above texts are that baptism is essential to get into heaven. It must be by full body immersion into water. There is only one baptism and I would say it must be performed by legitimate representatives of Christ's system of keeping all His commandments not by a corruptible seed who do not (1Pet 1:23). 2Ch 13:9 Have ye not cast out the priests of the LORD, the sons of Aaron, and the Levites, and have made you priests after the manner of the nations of *other* lands? so that whosoever cometh to consecrate himself with a young bullock and seven rams, <u>the same may be a priest</u> of *them that are* no gods. 2Ch 13:10 But as for us, the LORD *is* our God, and we have not forsaken him; and the priests, which minister unto the LORD, *are* the sons of Aaron, and the Levites *wait* upon *their* business: 2Ch 11:14 For the Levites left their suburbs and their possession, and came to Judah and Jerusalem: for Jeroboam and his sons <u>had cast them off from executing the priest's office unto the LORD</u>: 2Ch 11:15 and <u>he ordained him priests</u> for the high places, and for the devils, and for the calves which he had made. 2Ch 13:9 Have ye not cast out the priests of the LORD, the sons of Aaron, and the Levites, and have made you priests after the manner of the nations of *other* lands? so that whosoever cometh to consecrate himself with a young bullock and seven rams, *the same* may be a priest of *them that are* no gods. 2Ch 18:6 But Jehoshaphat said, *Is there* not here a prophet of the LORD besides, that we might enquire of him? 2Ch 33:5 And he built altars for all the host of heaven in the two courts of the house of the LORD. Ezra 2:62 and Neh 7:64 These sought their register *among* those that were reckoned by genealogy, but it was not found: therefore were they, as polluted, put from the priesthood.

God's true representatives teach that <u>all things</u> commanded by Jesus are to be kept. Once you believe in and accept Jesus as He is not a false or partial version preached, you come up out of the water a new person, washing away your previous sins and with the earnest conviction to sin no more. Remember, sinning is transgression of the Law, the commandments including the fourth (Exodus 20:8). The old person has been buried in the watery grave, a new person is reborn. Paul re-baptised twelve of John the Baptist's disciples (Acts 19:5). Not everyone saying "Lord Lord" and conducting baptisms are recognised by Jesus. Their baptisms may be invalid. Do you want to take the gamble? Catholic, Zurich, Ana Baptist (Re-Baptisers of the 16th Century defied the Pope and returned to biblical baptism by re-baptising themselves as adults in a river. As a warning the authorities drowned four of them in the same river in January 1525. This is one example of how the Church kept Christians doing unbiblical things.

SPEAKING IN TONGUES

Joh 15:3 now ye are clean through the word which I have spoken unto you. Joh 17:17 sanctify them through thy truth: thy word is truth. It is the true word of God that brings us closer to Him. Rev 16:13 And I saw three unclean spirits like frogs *come* out of the mouth of the dragon, and out of the mouth of the beast, and out of the mouth of the false prophet. Rev 16:14 for they are the spirits of devils, working miracles. 2Co 11:13-15 for such *are* false apostles, deceitful workers, transforming themselves into the apostles of Christ. And no marvel; for Satan himself is transformed into an angel of light. Therefore *it is* no great thing if his ministers also be transformed as the ministers of righteousness; whose end shall be according to their works.

The main topic of this book is the Sabbath. However, many people have succumbed to the Pentecostal speaking in tongues phenomena, in the belief they possess the gift of the Holy Spirit as given to the apostles in Acts 2. I thought I would add this section on speaking in tongues. There is a legitimate gift of the Holy Spirit of speaking in tongues (ST) and like anything else, a false one of satan. Let us see what the bible and history say on the topic. We will have to put all the information together rather than base our conclusion on one or two texts.

Those speaking in tongues claim it is a gift and sign of the Holy Spirit generally received at or shortly after baptism. If we look at those of the Old Testament who had the Holy Spirit or Spirit of God given to them, we would see it was for the purpose of His work. This is the same with the New Testaments (Ex 35:30-35; 2 Chron 15:1, 24:20, Num 11:17, 25; Jdg 14:19, Luke 1:41-2 (see Not Under the Law but guidance of Holy Spirit. Section). The supernatural identity of having the Spirit was prophesy (see Act 2:17 as also a N.T sign. When it came to communication, God used His prophets and they spoke in a human language to other humans. Eze 3:5 for thou *art* not sent to a people of a strange speech and of a hard language, *but* to the house of Israel; Eze 3:6 Not to many people of a strange speech and of an hard language, whose words thou canst not understand. Surely, had I sent thee to them, they would have hearkened unto thee. Eze 3:7 but the house of Israel will not hearken unto thee; for they will not hearken unto me: for all the house of Israel *are* impudent and hardhearted. Even when God used an ass to speak to a human (Num 22:28 And the LORD opened the mouth of the ass, and she said unto Balaam, What have I done unto thee, that thou hast smitten me these three times? Num 22:29 And Balaam said unto the ass, Because thou hast mocked me: I would there were a sword in mine hand for now would I kill thee) It was in human tongue / language; not the human speaking "Eee haaw" donkey language or other sounds he could not under- stand. God has always spoken to humans in clear human language and visa versa.

In the Old Testament time, God spoke to His chosen people, including the strangers who attached themselves to His people and followed His commandments. Communication between humans and God was by prayers in human language either vocally or in thought. Communication between God and man was also in a human language for men to understand though many chose not to listen for fear of being in His awesome presence. Exo 19:19 And when the voice of the trumpet sounded long, and waxed louder and louder, Moses spake, and God answered him by a voice. Exo 19:20 And the LORD came down upon mount Sinai, on the top of the mount: and the LORD called Moses *up* to the top of the mount; and Moses went up. Exo 19:21 And the LORD said unto Moses, Go down, charge the people, lest they break through unto the LORD to gaze, and many of them perish… When God's angels communicated with His people and them with the angels it was by voice (Gen 16:9-11, 21:17, 22:11,32; Jug 2:1; 5:23, 2 King 1:3, Mat 28:5, Luke 1:13, 18, 28, 30, Acts 5:19, 11:13) Luk 1:13 But the angel said unto him, Fear not, Zacharias: for thy prayer is heard; and thy wife Elisabeth shall bear thee a son, and thou shalt call his name John. …Luk 1:18 And Zacharias said unto the angel, Whereby shall I know this? for I am an old man, and my wife well stricken in years. Luk 1:19 "And the angel answering said unto him, I am Gabriel, that stand in the presence of God; and am sent to speak unto thee, and…". Jesus conversing with Paul and Ananias in Act 9:6, 11 did it in human language. No indication it was ever otherwise.

Some tongue speakers claim they speaking to God so the devil cannot understand their prayer. The bible says of the devil Eze 28:3 Behold, thou *art* wiser than Daniel; there is no secret that they can hide from thee: The devil knows each person's weaknesses, desires etc and presents them to the individual for his ultimate plan. We see from scripture once the devil possesses or part possess an individual, their thoughts are (in part) controlled by him. Either to cutting themselves, throwing self around on the floor or a calmer character questioning God as Peter did with Jesus and ofcourse Joh 13:2 "And supper being ended, the devil having now put into the heart of Judas Iscariot, Simon's *son*, to betray him". Thus speaking in tongues cannot prevent the devil understanding (remember Eze 28:3). As for it being a secret language only for God to understand, does God need you to make up a language in order to communicate with Him? Especially one you yourself do not understand? We are told when we pray "enter into thy closet, and when thou hast shut thy door, pray to thy Father which is in secret; and thy Father which seeth in secret shall reward thee openly" Mat 6:6 No mention of another language. In Matt 6:9 Jesus' reply to His disciple's request on how to pray did not mention a special language. Lastly of the numerous times we are told Jesus prayed, none of the gospel or other writers mentioned Him using any non human language. In fact God does not even need our words as all Christians know He reads our hearts (Gen 6:5; 17:17, 18:12-13 Therefore Sarah laughed within herself, saying, After I am waxed old shall I have pleasure, my lord being old also? And the LORD said unto Abraham, Wherefore did Sarah laugh, saying, Shall I of a surety bear a child, which am old? Gen 24:45 And before I had done speaking in mine heart, behold, Rebekah came forth with her pitcher on her shoulder; and she went down unto the well, and drew *water*: and I said unto her, Let me drink, I pray thee. Luke 9:47 And Jesus, perceiving the thought of their heart, took a child, and set him by him... In fact even when we do not know for what to pray the Holy Spirit reads our heart and makes supplication on our behalf to God Rom 8:26 Likewise the Spirit also helpeth our

158

infirmities: for we know not what we should pray for as we ought: but the Spirit itself maketh intercession for us with groanings which cannot be uttered. Note this is "the" Holy Spirit not our spirit as some try to justify. The groanings of "the Spirit" "cannot be uttered" by humans. So far there is no benefit to God for these "unknown tongues" or biblical precedent for their use to God. The precedents we find are with pagan use first at the Tower of Babel. Then Mat 6:7 But when ye pray, use not vain repetitions, as the heathen do: 1Ti 6:20 O Timothy, keep that which is committed to thy trust, avoiding profane and vain babblings, 2Ti 2:16 But shun profane and vain babblings: for they will increase unto more ungodliness. .

Of the 27 books in the NT only 3 mention the gift of tongues. Of the 39 Bible authors, only three - Luke, Paul, and Mark mention the subject of tongues. The users of the unknown tongue claim it from Acts 2; a gift given to the Jewish apostles before the gospel was preached to the Gentiles in Acts 13:46. As usual, they claim the law was for the Jews; but claim the bits they want for themselves! So what was the real and ongoing purpose of the gift of speaking in (known) tongues? Remember the apostles had already been given power over devils; to cast them out etc and the power to heal. Later, Jhn 20:22, also the Holy Spirit. The only un-received gift was that of tongues, why? Because the time for its use was not needed until after Jesus' death and the purpose, like all gifts, was to show unbelievers the wonders of Jesus and God His father, bringing them to Him. Act 1:8 "But ye shall receive power, after that the Holy Ghost is come upon you: and ye shall be witnesses unto me both in Jerusalem, and in all Judaea, and in Samaria, and unto the uttermost part of the earth" (see also Luke 24:47, 49, "beginning at Jerusalem. …tarry ye in the city of Jerusalem, until ye be endued with power from on high)". That is exactly what happened and no room was left for mis- understanding because the Holy Spirit did not come again to give them the power to speak in tongues too early; but on the actual day of Pentecost. Act 2:1 "And when the day of Pentecost was fully come, they were all with one accord in one place". I have explained in the section "Celebrating the First Day of the Week", how the day of Pentecost was initially called the Feast of Harvest or First Fruits later called the Feast of Weeks and in the N.T. Pentecost. The apostles were celebrating an old feast knowing that all Jewish men would be coming to Jerusalem for the annual pilgrimage. The perfect time for the preaching of repentance of sin through Jesus to beginning at Jerusalem, the Jews, and then throughout the world. Is this not very simple and clear? Rather than the apostles having to travel the world converting individuals on a slow basis, the world came to them. When theses visitors to Jerusalem returned to their cities of residence and on their journey they spread the good news of the New Testament of the apostles far quicker than they could. For this clear purpose they needed unique multi lingual skills unlike those claimed by the impersonators of today. The apostles spoke one word in the given new tongue and it was instantly heard by all present in their own native language. They did not have to repeat the same message in numerous languages nor have an interpreter(s). Once that job was done they remained (mostly see Act 8:1) in Jerusalem and we do not hear of them speaking on tongues again, possibly because the need had been satisfied. However, Paul the travelling evangelist claimed to speak in tongues (1Cor 14:18) Today if a politician or preacher who claims to have the power of tongues goes to a foreign country to give a speech, there are many interpreters repeating what is said. An interpreter for each language present.

How was satan able to cause such confusion and deceive so many. One possible answer could be because of the lust of their hearts (all desiring a "gift" though they would not admit it). Similar to the gentile converts of the first century as explained below. satan is responsible for all miracles and supernatural manifestations that occur contrary to God's holy word. Humans want to be more than humans. More special or gifted than others. Able to do magic and be immortal. Have a gift of the super natural. satan knows this and thus appeals to their ego with gifts of the supernatural as speaking in tongues. One was always able to see the practical use of the gift of the Holy Spirit or Spirit of God and know it was of God i.e. the gift of prophecy when the thing came true. But since people cannot prove their prophesies or it will be discovered to be false they opt for speaking in tongues. The benefit or proof of which can neither be seen nor confirmed. God's gifts are for the church or others, satan's is for self.

The new language concept of tongues is a New Testament (NT) one. The promise was given by Jesus in Mark 16:17   And these signs shall follow them that believe; In my name shall they cast out devils; they shall speak with new tongues. "In my name" implies the same can be done in another's otherwise Jesus could have omitted those words.   The Greek word used is "glossa" meaning either the physical tongue with which one speaks or language, one naturally acquired. When the KJV Bible was translated in 1611 the word "tongues" was commonly used for "language". Thus to speak with "new tongues" simply means "new language". Note the Muslim's accusation against early Christians "there is among them a section who distort the Book with their 'tongues' … This was in about 600 A.D. when the word "tongue" was used to mean human speech or language understood by other humans. The 'Book' being the Bible.

The first NT usage is in Act 1:19 " insomuch as that field is called in their proper tongue, Aceldama, that is to say, The field of blood". Acts 2:4 "And they were all filled with the Holy Ghost, and began to speak with other tongues, as the Spirit gave them utterance". When the visitors to Jerusalem heard them, they each recognised the language they were speaking. "in his own language" Acts 2:6 "in our own tongue" Acts 2:8. All three places it is the same Greek word translated as tongue in Acts 1:19; 2:6 and language in Acts 2:8. (see also Acts 21:40; 22:2; 26:14 for other examples of "speak in Hebrew tongue"). The men were "every nation under heaven" Acts 2:5. are not all these which speak Galilaeans? Act 2:8 And how hear we every man in our own tongue, wherein we were born? Parthians, and Medes, and Elamites, and the dwellers in Mesopotamia, and in Judaea, and Cappadocia, in Pontus, and Asia, Act 2:10 Phrygia, and Pamphylia, in Egypt, and in the parts of Libya about Cyrene, and strangers of Rome, Jews and proselytes, Act 2:11 Cretes and Arabians, we do hear them speak in our tongues the wonderful works of God. It is clear that the "other tongues" spoken by the disciples were the languages of these visitors from every nation under heaven, with over a dozen given as examples. The purpose of the gift of tongues, speaking in various languages so all present could understand the gospel of Jesus.

The facts from the event:
* Speaking in tongues is speaking in another human language "in our own tongue, wherein we were born?" 2:8
* Those who heard recognised their own language being spoken.
* Those who heard were able to understand the words being spoken by those who spoke in "tongues".
* No interpretation was necessary.

The next instance of tongue speaking is recorded in Acts 10, the home of Cornelius. We are told Act 10:44 While Peter yet spake these words, the Holy Ghost fell on all them which heard the word. Act 10:45 And they of the circumcision which believed were astonished, as many as came with Peter, because that on the Gentiles also was poured out the gift of the Holy Ghost. Act 10:46 For they heard them speak with tongues, and <u>magnify God.</u> From the previous verses it is clear this experience took place so the Jews who came with Peter could see that Gentiles as well as Jews were accepted by God. We are not told what languages or dialects each of those present understood and could not understand. There were Jews and Gentiles of various levels of expertise in each others language; but the speaking in tongues enabled all to understand. As a result Peter and circumcised Jewish companions were convinced Cornelius and his household should be baptised. Notice the speaking in tongues happened before baptism so is not a sign of receiving the Holy Ghost resulting from the baptism as some teach.. Act 10:47 Can any man forbid water, that these should not be baptized, which have received the Holy Ghost as well as we? Thus Peter recognised it was the same gift to his at Pentecost of speaking in a language all could understand. If it was not; but mere ecstatic utterances, it would not have convinced Peter nor the "circumcised". This is supported by the account Peter relays to his fellow apostles in Act 11:17 Forasmuch then as God gave them the <u>like gift</u> as *he did* unto us, who believed on the Lord Jesus Christ; what was I, that I could withstand God?

So the facts from the event are: Cornelius and his household spoke in tongues, it was recognised to be this by Peter and his companions who had accompanied him and only had one prior event of Pentecost by which to compare, Peter was definite it was the same gift as he received at Pentecost, this would mean that Cornelius spoke foreign languages too. Peter was convinced by the event that God was granting the Gentiles repentance and they should be baptised.

The third instance of the gift of tongues came when Paul was visiting Ephesus Acts 19:6 And when Paul had laid *his* hands upon them, the Holy Ghost came on them; and they spake with tongues, and prophesied. These twelve believers were baptised by John the Baptist and knew nothing of the Holy Spirit. Paul explained John's baptism was a preparation for Jesus the Messiah. He then baptised them in the name of Jesus, laid hands on them and probably prayed they got the gift of the Holy Spirit. We are told "they spake with tongues, and prophesied". Whether all of them received both gifts or some tongues and others prophecy we are not told. This event does not add much more to the first two in understanding the gift of tongues except here Paul laid hands on them. It was not the baptism in Jesus' name that gave them gift of the Holy Spirit as in [Act 8:16 (For as yet he was fallen upon none of them: only they were baptized in the name of the Lord Jesus.)] those baptised had not received it. Even when Peter Act 8:17 Then laid they *their* hands on them, and they received the Holy Ghost. It was not manifested in the speaking of tongues. Those are the only three episodes of Acts whereby the gift of tongues is mentioned. We have no other evidence; but that it was speaking foreign languages so all present could understand without the need of an interpreter. Note none of the three was in a church building or meeting, happened regularly on a Sun day etc. Never again do we see of all the church meetings Paul and the apostles held were anyone or the congregation as a majority speaking in tongues.

In Corinth there was a lot of problems with the church. Members were divided into factions, each supporting a different leader. Some Paul, others Apollos or Peter, etc. There was a case of incest with one member having an affair with his stepmother and the church took no action. Some suing others in the courts, divorce widespread. There were disputes as whether it is a sin to eat food that had been blessed at the pagan temples. There were other examples of blatant sin among the members, including idolatry, some female members coming to church looking like prostitutes. The Lords supper was degenerating into a common feast, a time of eating and drinking. People were taking their own food along with them and not sharing with the poor. These are the chapters (in brackets) dealing with each topic divisions over who to follow (1-4) adultery (5) taking one another to court (6) sexual immorality divorce and remarriage (7) things sacrificed to idols (8-10) suitable hair-lengths (11) keeping the Lord's supper (11) issues over spiritual gifts (12-13); misuse of speaking in tongues (14); rejection of the resurrection (15)

These gentile converts all sort the spiritual gifts of the apostles by whom they were converted 1 Cor 12:1-2, 8-10. 1Co 12:29 *Are* all apostles? *are* all prophets? *are* all teachers? *are* all workers of miracles? 1Co 12:30 Have all the gifts of healing? do all speak with tongues? do all interpret? 1Co 12:31 But covet earnestly the best gifts: and yet shew I unto you a more excellent way.

Perhaps the most divisive was the strive about spiritual gifts. Some gifts were more highly prized than others leading to spiritual snobbery. Pandemonium was being caused in church meeting turning them into a madhouse as people claiming to have this gift were determined to display it to others. In their determination they did not bother to check whether anyone understood them as in Acts 2. A gift originally given to communicate the gospel to foreigners was not communication to anyone (except sarcastically, God 1Cor 14:2). 1Co 13:1 "Though I speak with the tongues of men and of angels".... When did angels speak and man not understand? Whether to Lot or Mary at Jesus' tomb it was always in a humanly understandable language.

Neither were the Corinthians taking turns to speak; but speaking all at once. Paul said in such events any non believer coming into the church would think Christians were mad.1 Cor 14:23. They brought their pagan custom into Christian church Mat 6:7 But when ye pray, use not vain repetitions, <u>as the heathen <i>do</i></u>: for they think that they shall be heard for their much speaking.

1 Corinthians 14 Examination of <i>unknown</i> Tongues

We have seen what tongues is now let us examine why Paul commented as he did. Paul was saying, the tongues you profess to have is not the tongues of which I know. However, I am not going to call it fake as maybe God has given you an "unknown tongue". But this is the test. The word "<i>unknown</i>" preceding the word "tongue" is generally in <i>italics</i> to show it is an insertion by the translators to assist in understanding the sentence. That the tongue being spoken of is not the understood one as exercised in Acts 2:4; 10:44; 19:6; but another, false or unknown one.

Chapter 14 which deals specifically with unknown tongues; but is part of a longer letter reply to a letter Paul received from them 1Co 7:1 Now concerning the things whereof ye wrote unto me. Chapter 12:4-10 deals with spiritual gifts; but does not give a complete list (see Rom 12:6-8, Gal 5:22-3; Eph 4:11). These may have been mentioned because they constituted a portion of their questions. Note in 12:10 and 28, tongues come at the end of the lists. There is a subtle reprimand or warning in verses 29-31, 14:1 Be charitable and desire the spiritual gift of prophesy above others.

14:2 "For he that speaketh in an <i>unknown</i> tongue speaketh not unto men (as in the Acts events), but unto God: for <u>no man understandeth <i>him</i></u>; howbeit in the spirit he speaketh mysteries." In the speakers mind they nor anyone else know what they say so it is a mystery to all. Neither can any man interpret. Only God who knows and can decipher all, would have a clue or know. This is not a confirmation that the person is speaking to God as we shall see later, just that none knows what is going on in the speaker's mind. Jesus said "I spake openly to the world; I ever taught in the synagogue, and in the temple, …in secret have I said nothing" .1Ch 28:9 And thou, Solomon my son, know thou the God of thy father, and serve him with a perfect heart and with a willing mind: for the LORD searcheth all hearts, and understandeth all the imaginations of the thoughts: 14:3 comparatively, prophesying passes the tests of a true gift edifying the church (Eph 4:12 For the perfecting of the saints, for the work of the ministry, for the <u>edifying of the body of Christ</u>) ..14:4-5 speakers of unknown tongues fail the test of being beneficial to the church. They only edify their ego 1Cor 12:7 But the manifestation of the Spirit is given to each one for the profit <i>of all</i> Joel 2:28 And it shall come to pass afterward, <i>that</i> I will pour out my spirit upon all flesh; and your sons and your daughters shall prophesy, your old men shall dream dreams, your young men shall see visions: Phi 2:3 "<i>Let</i> nothing <i>be done</i> through strife or <u>vainglory</u>; but in lowliness of mind <u>let each esteem other better than themselves!"</u>. All these texts confirm the gifts are for others not self.

14:6-11 voices are for communication otherwise what profit is it?. Even lifeless objects as musical instruments are played to make sense or convey a message. If one is not communicating with their listeners they are wasting their time speaking into the air (That every idle word that men shall speak, they shall give account thereof in the day of judgment. Matthew 12:36. Would you be able to give an account of what you do not understand?)

All worldly voices have their significance without which the speakers and hearers become like barbarians to each other. In other words, even dogs and foreigners do not need words to understand; but can go by the tone, pitch etc of the voice. A dog conveys its message by barking, whining, or growling. If no communication is needed they will lie or walk past in silence verse six states any tongue spoken must be word of God i.e. His doctrines. Verse 9 says words uttered should be easy to understand. 1 Cor 14:12 As eager as you are to possess and show a gift seek excellence in character or other to the edifying of the church.. v13 Wherefore let him that speaketh in an *unknown* tongue pray that he may interpret (see also "he" interpret v5). The speaker should know and be able to interpret what they are saying not another person. As in Daniel 5:25 And this *is* the writing that was written, MENE, MENE, TEKEL, UPHARSIN. Dan 5:26 This *is* the interpretation of the thing: MENE; God hath numbered thy kingdom, and finished it..... That way what the person says can be tested as to whether or not it comes true. Remember any revelation must be in line with the word of God (Deut 13:3, 1Cor 14:32)

14:14-15 Praying and singing praises to God must be done in the spirit and understanding of what you are saying or you may be possessed ignorantly cursing God or exalting satan in an unknown language! Young children like to copy sware words heard and think it funny because they do not know better. Paul warns about being ignorant as a child in 1 Cor 14:20. Remember satan put words in Peter's mouth Mat 16:23 But he turned, and said unto Peter, Get thee behind me satan: thou art an offence unto me: for thou savourest not the things that be of God, but those that be of men. I urge you to worship God without speaking in unknown tongues. It was never prescribed by Him for His service. I have previously talked about where things to God must be in spirit and truth (Jhn 4:23-4, 14:17, Eph 5:9, 2 Thes 2:13,).

V18-19 I thank my God, I speak with tongues more than ye all: Yet in the church I had rather speak five words with my understanding, that *by my voice* I might teach others also, than ten thousand words in an *unknown* tongue. Paul, the travelling evangelist, had need of the gift to spread the gospel of Jesus. He indicates his use of it was outside the church "Yet in the church". He then adds its use in the church was for teaching others and again states that the speaker ought to understand what they are saying and be able to explain it to others, be understood. Whatever is done in church services must be understood. See 14:21 Paul confirms other "tongues" (languages) are for communication with men, spoken by men using their lips not mysterious thoughts or sounds. V22 He adds tongues are for a sign not for those inside the church (hence why it is suppose to be used outside church) as they already believe. Unbelievers are generally found outside the church and its meetings. Inside church and among members they are served (edified) by the gift of prophesy. The numerous simultaneous acclaimed tongue speaking members (as in today's congregations) makes God's house and it's members appear to be mad. V25 "God is within you of a truth" meaning the tongues shambles would lead him to think god is not within the church or its individuals. Note the gift of prophesy is not speaking what cannot be proved or some future impersonal event; but one instantly heart felt and known as Jesus with the lady at the well Joh 4:18 For thou hast had five husbands; and he whom thou now hast is not thy husband: in that saidst thou truly. The woman saith unto him, Sir, I perceive that thou art a prophet.

1Cor 14:26 How "when ye come together" all claim to have gifts so as not to be outdone or feel left out, inferior etc as is probably the reason for today's partakers. Cor 14:27 **Give particular attention to this verse.** Paul laid down the one at a time principle "If any man speak in an *unknown* tongue, *let it be* by two, or **at the most** *by* **three,** and *that* by course; and let **one interpret**. 1Co 14:28 But if there be no interpreter, let him **keep silence in the church**; and let him speak to himself, and to God. Note not more than three of the congregation are suppose to speak aloud in a language unknown to others. When a strange tongue is spoken that all present cannot easily and clearly understand as in their own language, an interpreter needs to be present, otherwise silence is required. One interpreter who really has the gift, should be able to interpret any speakers "unknown tongue" not an interpreter for each speaker. Remember in v2 Paul said "no man understandeth" i.e. can interpret. Also note clarification of verse 2 "but unto God". Speaking to God should be done in silence. Just like as advised in Matt 6:6 (in the closet). God does not need your vocal sound to understand you as He reads hearts (1Ch 28:9 for the LORD searcheth all hearts, and understandeth all the imaginations of the thoughts):. V34 In any case, Paul advises that women should not be speaking in tongues within the church (as saith the law). This verse can also be applied in other areas. 1Cor 14:33 God is not author of confusion. Anything unlike the peaceful reverend service as prescribed by God is likely to be confusion, distracting people and putting emphasise in places God does not want.

20th Century usage of glossolalia

In recent years, a practice which is widespread in pagan religions entered some Christian sects. This activity is technically called 'glossolalia' and should be distinguished from the Biblical spiritual gift of tongues which was always genuine languages and, when correctly employed, was for communication of the Gospel. Confusingly, those Christians who adopted this practice call it 'speaking in tongues.'

The sounds produced in this activity do not resemble any known language and exhibit no syntax or sentence structure. Linguists who have studied this phenomenon are unanimous that this is not language. Instead they notice that the sounds produced are nearly always sounds and syllables taken from the normal language of the speaker. Thus American 'tongues speakers' sound American and English 'tongues speakers' sound distinctively English. They notice that the sounds produced are highly repetitious, again markedly different from genuine speech in another language.

When the sounds are translated by those who claim to be interpreters, it is noticed that two interpreters of the same 'speech' will generally give widely differing interpretations. There have been occasional reports of 'tongues speakers' speaking in genuine languages but often in such cases it has been noted by the person whose language was being spoken that the words used were blasphemous or obscene.

Instances of glossolalia were noted in early Methodism, Mormonism, among the Shakers and, most markedly, in the congregation of Edward Irving, the most popular preacher in London in the 1820s. (Irving himself did not practice glossolalia, though he gave it his support, as he also supported the supposed visions of a young Scot called Margaret MacDonald). The glossolalists gradually took over Irving's church and led it into wilder and wilder excesses. In 1832 the elders of his church, alarmed at the goings-on asked Irving to forbid glossolalia in church services, though they were willing to compromise and allow this activity in the early prayer meeting. When he refused, many leading members resigned from his church. The elders ordered Irving to appear before them. On the morning of this meeting, Robert Baxter, a lawyer, who had been the leader of the glossolalists in his church, came to his home to confess that this 'speaking in tongues' was 'a grand delusion.' Even after this confession, Irving sought to defend himself at the meeting and was dismissed from the pulpit. Later he was convicted on a charge of heresy and dismissed from the Presbyterian ministry. He tried to continue his ministry elsewhere but he had no authority; the glossolalists were in total control and he was wanted only for his reputation as London's leading preacher. When he preached, he was frequently interrupted by 'tongues speakers'. Irving accepted this as, by now, he was convinced that this was the voice of God. Within two years, he was dead. In his last two years, men noted how his manner had changed. Where before he was noted for his graciousness, he was now caustic, bitter, intemperate in language. Irving came to believe that 'no Christian ought ever to be overcome by sickness.' A cholera epidemic broke out. Irving was warned about the purification of drinking water. He ignored the advice and lost three of his children. He himself contracted tuberculosis at the age of forty-one and died the following year. His followers survive today as 'the Catholic Apostolic Church.'

Modern 'Speaking in Tongues.'

The modern Pentecostal movement finds its historic roots in the Azusa Street Revival in Los Angeles, California, USA from 1904 to 1906. Several years earlier, in 1901, Bible college students at a school founded by Charles Parham in Topeka, Kansas prayed to be baptised with the Holy Spirit and 'spoke in tongues'. The account of the first event was, Mr Parham a former Methodist preacher, was convinced there was more to receiving the baptism of the Holy Spirit. He was studying the same with his bible study class for some time and ended one week with instructions they go home and read Acts 2 to see what they could learn about the Holy Spirit. This directive turned out to be like asking someone to look to heaven and think of a colour. At the next week's study, one member, Agnes Ozman, asked Mr Parham to pray for her to receive the Holy Spirit. She then went into babbling strange ecstatic words which Parham claimed was evidence of her receiving the Holy Spirit. He was ridiculed by many press and church leaders of the time; but went on to popularise the practice and Pentecostal movement claiming speaking in tongues was Evidence of the Baptism of the Spirit, to be used in public worship for edification of the body, to be used for edification in private prayer. This is the same directives of today's Charismatic Movements. There are professional pastors who hold seminars and write books on how to speak in tongues. These courses and books are attended and read by other pastors. It is like a pyramid business with one concept being widely accepted propagated to the masses. If it was by the Holy spirit why would such teaching seminars be needed and fees charged? Today, this is how the majority of Christians get their beliefs.

Parham moved to Houston, Texas, where in spite of segregation, William Seymore, a one-eyed African-American preacher was allowed to listen in to the Bible classes. Seymore went to Los Angeles, where his preaching helped spark the fires of the Azusa Street revival. Most Pentecostal denominations can trace their roots to the Azusa Street revival or were strongly influenced by it.

Pentecostalism fragmented into various sects, whose common denominator is glossolalia, some believing it to be essential for salvation, others a kind of superior spiritual state (the 'second blessing'). It is widely taught that 'speaking in tongues' is the evidence that one has received 'the baptism of the Spirit', which Pentecostals teach is a distinct and different experience from baptism.

Pentecostals have different views on the idea of what 'speaking in tongues' actually means. Some believe 'tongues' is a prayer language in which they themselves do not understand what they are saying. Others believe 'tongues' is an actual language and the ability to speak the mysteries of God unto the unsaved using their language. In both views the ability to speak and the ability to interpret are separate gifts. One may be able to speak in a certain language but will lack the ability to interpret any other language they have not been gifted with the understanding to speak (contrary to 1Cor 14:5 & 13 "he interprets") . Both generally believe there must be an interpreter present so the listeners will understand when a different language, or tongue, is spoken to them. Many Pentecostals believe the 'tongues speaker' will not understand what he is saying. This conflicts with 1 Corinthians 14:13-19. Today's speaking in tongues in therefore not from Acts 2 of the bible but from about 100 years ago.

The Charismatic Renewal

In the late 1960s and early 1970s Christians from mainline churches in the United States, Europe, and other parts of the world began to accept the Pentecostalism teaching that the baptism of the Holy Spirit is available for Christians today. Charismatic movements began to grow in mainline denominations. There were Charismatic Catholics, Anglicans, Lutherans, Methodists, etc. During that time period, the term 'Charismatic' was used to refer to these movements that existed within mainline denominations. (Pentecostal was used to refer to those who were a part of the churches and denominations that grew out of the earlier Azusa Street revival.)

In recent decades, many independent Charismatic churches and ministries have formed or have developed their own denominations and church associations. There is a great deal of overlap now between the Charismatic and Pentecostal movements. Pentecostals typically believe in water baptism as an outward sign of conversion and that the baptism in the Holy Ghost is a distinct spiritual experience that all who have belief in Jesus should receive. Most classical Pentecostals believe that the baptism in the Holy Ghost is always accompanied initially by the outward evidence of 'speaking in tongues'. It is considered a liberalising tendency to teach contrary to this historic position.

This is a major difference between Pentecostals and Charismatic Christians, who believe that a Christian baptised in the Holy Ghost may exhibit various supernatural signs, including speaking in tongues, being slain in the spirit, (where people fall to the ground as if asleep), hysterical and uncontrollable laughter, rolling on the ground, barking like dogs or making other animal noises, prophecy (i.e. a vision, dream or a word of God, spoken or felt in the spirit), miraculous healings, miraculous signs, etc.

The two most influential movements in the Charismatic Renewal, as it has been called, are 'the Toronto Blessing' and 'the Alpha Course.' The Toronto Blessing describes the revival and resulting phenomena that began in January 1994 at Toronto Airport Vineyard Christian Fellowship, located in Canada. Participants in the conferences and meetings sponsored by TACF have reported healings, incidents of personal transformation and a greater awareness of God's love. It has also been referred to as "The Father's Blessing", "The Anointing", "The Awakening", "The River", "The Fire".

At TACF Revival services, worshippers exhibit unusual behaviour, which they attribute to an encounter with God and the "fire of the Holy Spirit." The most common behaviour includes hysterical laughter (or "holy laughter"), physical spasms or jerks, falling to the floor under the Holy Spirit's power (also known as "slain in the Spirit") and "speaking in tongues." Other less common behaviour includes manifestations that resemble roaring like lions and barking like dogs. The TACF website described it thus: "The Toronto Blessing is a transferable anointing. In its most visible form it overcomes worshippers with outbreaks of laughter, weeping, groaning, shaking, falling, 'drunkenness,' and even behaviour that has been described as a 'cross between a jungle and a farmyard."

Exhibitors of these things claim them as necessary acts to prove God is with them. Some even say that congregations which do not have exhibits of emotionalism, shouting, clapping, lively music or supernatural manifestations are either spiritually "cold" or "dead". But is this true of congregations not, for example, speaking in *unknown* tongues? Or could it be the devil saying, you want a spirit to posses you, well I will! After rising from the dead, how did Jesus make himself known to His disciples Luk 24:32 "And they said one to another, Did not our heart burn within us, while he talked with us by the way, and while he opened to us the scriptures?" By the scriptures. The same as when He was alive. The same example followed by His apostles Act 8:29 Then the Spirit said unto Philip, Go near, and join thyself to this chariot. Act 8:35

Then Philip opened his mouth, and began at the same scripture, and preached unto him Jesus. Act 28:23 , there came many to… whom he expounded and testified the kingdom of God, persuading them concerning Jesus, both out of the law of Moses, and *out of* the prophets. The scripture is Jesus in word form. To show someone Jesus or that He is with you, show them the TRUE and only scripture is within you. Remember the truth, the whole truth and nothing but the truth. Many can do miracles etc to appeal to your emotion Act 8:9 But there was a certain man, called Simon, which beforetime in the same city used sorcery, and bewitched the people of Samaria, giving out that himself was some great one: Act 8:10 To whom they all gave heed, from the least to the greatest, <u>saying, This man is the great power of God</u>. People of the devil claim to be people of God through emotional influences. Compare this sorcerer with John the Baptist who did no miracles (John 10:41) yet is said to have been filled with the spirit and power of Elijah and also Mat 11:11 ..”Among them that are born of women there hath not risen a greater than John the Baptist:.”

It may be difficult for some to accept the fact that satan could be in partial control of notable ministers, preachers, or apparently sincere believers who speak highly of ? Christ, work miracles, speak in unknown tongues and exalt the things of God. But why should anyone doubt this? Is this not what the whole concept of deception entails?

Some church worships are characterised by members of the congregation rocking to and fro, swaying and dancing to the music. When questioned about their party like displays in the house of God, many respond that we are suppose to praise the Lord “in the dance” Ps 149:3) and “make a joyful noise unto Him (Ps 95:1); while others call on “David danced before the Lord” (2Sam 6:14). Others claim cultural differences of having more emotion or rhythm in their bones. Firstly, Jesus is our example not our ancestors, their activities or cultural practices. Jesus did not worship in this way. As a Jew, (separated people unto God to do it His way as He prescribed) temple services were not noisy or excessively emotional. Their actions were characterised by reverence and solemnity and this tradition still exist is most Jewish synagogues today. It is also interesting to note that the three religions based on the Bible that can trace their practice to 500A.D. or before, none have dancing and noisy music. Instead their services are more scriptural reading (Jews, Roman Catholics and Muslims). Though a small number of Catholics are now moving towards the joyful manner in an effort to deter members from leaving. The Psalms of David were not written in the context of a church worship but outside. David knew it was the Levitical priesthood that directed and followed God's prescribed ways and an outsider could not change it. Neither was the episode of him dancing in the sanctuary.

It was the same with the early Christians of the bible. They brought their pagan ways into Gods house blending the two rather than accepting God's prescribed way. Many pagan temple worship rituals included dancing, loose dressing to nakedness and even prostitution (remember Ex 32:29 and). Maybe the apostles, in their limited time with each church plant, taught the love of Jesus, repentance of sin etc and had not the time to go into worship method. Dancing is associated with folly and social revelling. Morals are sacrificed for pleasure. There is no bible record that dancing is acceptable to God in His sanctuary or church. Christ said it is a house of prayer (Matt 21:13). Music has never been used by Jesus or His apostles to promote His message nor has the Holy Spirit revealed itself in an atmosphere of noise. It is better not to have the worship of God blended with music than to use the noise of music to do the work. Though I am aware music draws congregations to the church where the true message could them be preached to them. And hopefully, wean them off the need for the music.

In 1King 18:21 + we see the difference between Elijah's worship and those of the Baal prophets. 1Co 14:33 For God is not *the author* of confusion, but of peace, <u>as in all churches of the saints.</u>   Psa 46:10 Be still, and know that I *am* God: I will be exalted among the heathen, I will be exalted in the earth. Isa 30:15 For thus saith the Lord GOD, the Holy One of Israel; In returning and rest shall ye be saved; in quietness and in confidence shall be your strength: and ye would not. Lam 3:25 The LORD *is* good unto them that wait for him, to the soul *that* seeketh him. Lam 3:26 *It is* good that *a man* should both hope and quietly wait for the salvation of the LORD. 1Pe 3:4 But *let it be* the hidden man of the heart, in that which is not corruptible, *even the ornament* of a meek and quiet spirit, which is in the sight of God of great price. (Joh 4:23) But the hour cometh, and now is, when the true worshippers shall worship the Father in spirit and in truth: for the Father seeketh such to worship him.   The above bible verses show stillness, meekness, quietness, dignity and peace as characteristics of true worship. No shouting or simultaneous talking, dancing or noise as many churches where the music is equal to or louder than the singing. We must keep in mind the awesome truth that God will never condone something that operates opposite to His holy word and that sin or disobedience of any kind does not bring glory to Him. Therefore those who expect God's blessings while knowingly or consciously trampling upon His laws or the truths found in His inspired Word (including His instructions regarding having only two or at the most three persons speaking in tongues at a time and the need for the speaker themselves to interpret what they say when this phenomenon is manifested) are presumptuously asking this god of truth and righteousness to uphold things that are contrary to His divine nature and holy Word. The God of the Universe will not uphold or support anything that is wrong, partial truth or is of the pagans. Christians should live by "every word that proceedeth out of the mouth of God" Matt 4:4.

We must remember that God's truths were promoted after the outpouring of the Holy Ghost on the day of Pentecost, and "they that gladly received the word were baptised and the same day there were added unto them about three thousand souls" Acts 2:41. thus it is evident that God's gifts are imparted to aid the advancement of truth. The gift convinced and previously unconverted i.e. for unbelievers as Paul says in 1 Cor 14:22. Yet what do we generally see today? Those who claim to be filled with the gift of the spirit do not follow in the footsteps of the disciples, going out into all the world proclaiming the gospel. Instead most of the time the manifestations and labours of church members are limited to within their church, among their church brethren and for the benefit of their church. Failing to edify those in the highways and byways. Failing to "Let your light so shine before men, that they may see your good works, and glorify your Father which is in heaven. " Matt 5:16. We should be "stedfast, unmoveable, always abounding in the work of the Lord" 1Cor 15:58 not succumb to pagan influences or desires of our lusts for emotional worship.,

The Alpha Course.

Alpha was started by Rev. Charles Marnham, a curate at Holy Trinity Brompton, a high-profile Charismatic Anglican church in London. In 1990 Rev. Nicky Gumbel, at that time a curate at Holy Trinity, took over the running of the course at the invitation of the Rev. Sandy Millar, the then vicar, and oversaw its revision and expansion.

The course purports to be an introduction to the Christian faith, though Christian teachings are dealt with swiftly and in a cursory manner. The approach is informal and social with much emphasis on food. In university settings, it is by no means uncommon for Alpha Courses to be held in the bar.

The most controversial element of the Alpha Course is its charismatic slant. Three of the fifteen sessions are given to the person and work of the Holy Spirit, and cover the infilling of the Spirit; 'speaking in tongues' and miraculous healing. The heart of the Alpha Course is 'the Weekend Away' where participants attend a residential weekend in which they are taught to practise glossolalia. In 2007, over 33,500 courses were offered in more than 160 countries, and in many Christian denominations. By 2007 it was reported that over 10 million people worldwide had attended an Alpha course.

Summary of Behavioural Science Research Data on Glossolalia

1. Glossolalia is an ancient and widespread phenomenon of most societies, occurring most usually in connection with religion.
2. Glossolalia may occur as part of a larger condition of hysterical, dissociative, or trance states, or it may occur completely alone.
3. Glossolalia is not necessarily related to specific personality types.
4. Glossolalia may be deviant behaviour due to abnormality of the mind, or it may be normal expected behaviour, depending on the social and cultural environment.
5. Glossolalia is a form of partially developed speech in which the thought-speech apparatus of the person is used for a variety of internal mental functions.

(Source: "Behavioural Science Research on the Nature of Glossolalia" which appears in the September, 1968, issue of the *Journal of the American Scientific Affiliation.*)

People are being misled, oftentimes quite earnestly and sincerely, into identifying a purely psychological phenomenon, of which many temperaments are capable, a kind of self-induced hypnosis which results in a repetition of sounds and syllables that have no meaning in themselves . . .

William Samarin, Professor of linguistics, University of Toronto

There are those who will treat as something of great importance these peculiar manifestations, which are not of God, but which are calculated to divert the minds of many away from the teaching of the Word. "However, when He, the Spirit of truth, has come, He will guide you into all truth; for He will not speak on His own *authority,* but whatever He hears He will speak; and He will tell you things to come. 14"He will glorify me, for He will take of what is mine and declare *it* to you. John 16:13-14.

Conclusions of Tongues.

Glossolalia, commonly called 'speaking in tongues', entered mainstream Christianity very recently. Apart from the Irving fiasco on the 1830s, and similar manifestations among early Mormons, Shakers and some Methodist groups, glossolalia only really began to make an impact on Christendom in early 20th century America with the growth of Pentecostalism sects. It was the Charismatic Renewal of the 1960s that saw glossolalia breaking out into Roman Catholicism and mainstream Christian denominations. This gave glossolalia a degree of respectability, which it had lacked in Pentecostalism.

Today practising glossolalia, as well as other charismatic activities (see Toronto Blessing, above) has become accepted in many churches. Indeed charismatic activity has been actively promoted to break down mainstream denominations and to advance the Ecumenical Movement. In particular, the songs and song books associated with the Charismatic Movement have been accepted across denominational boundaries. The prefaces/forewords of such song books clearly set out the agenda of the song writers, to promote ecumenism. This is why such songs have little or no doctrinal content and, like glossolalia itself, are often heavily repetitive, either in content or performance. Glossolalia bears no resemblance to the Biblical gift of tongues and should never be confused with it. Glossolalia has formed an element in pagan worship since pre-Christian times and is still practised in non-Christian religions. It is interesting to note that glossolalia is not a phenomenon confined to Christianity.

Pagan religions throughout the world are frenzied with tongues. This is reflected in an article in the *Journal of the American Scientific Affiliation* entitled "An Ethnological Study of Glossolalia" by George J. Jennings, March 1968. Jennings observes that glossolalia is practised among the following non-Christian religions of the world; the Peyote cult among the North American Indians, the Haida Indians of the Pacific Northwest, Shamans in the Sudan, the Shango cult of the West Coast of Africa, the Shago cult in Trinidad, the Voodoo cult in Haiti, the Aborigines of South America and Australia, the aboriginal peoples of the sub-Arctic regions of North America and Asia, the Shamans in Greenland, the Dyaks of Borneo, the Zor cult of Ethiopia, the Siberian shamans, the Chaco Indians of South America, the Curanderos of the Andes, the Kinka in the African Sudan, the Thonga shamans of Africa, and the Tibetan monks. Surely we wouldn't attribute glossolalia in these heathen religions to the work of the Holy Spirit. Behavioural Scientists have conducted extensive research on glossolalia and for the most part concur that supernatural forces are not necessary to explain its existence.

But glossolalia is not the work of the Holy Spirit. It is not the Biblical gift of speaking in tongues. If you speak in tongues, I recommend abstaining from

172

practicing it for a few months; be strong not follow others or feel you are missing out. You will see you will not loose anything. The rest of the world, Christians and Jews have got along without it from creation. God can hear your prayers purely by your thoughts. You may even get closer to God by getting one step further from satan.

One copies the environment in which they are; hence why Christians should abstain from secular non Christ like entertainment otherwise, eventually you are dragged along with the current even thinking it was your decision. Throughout the bible God warned His people "that thou enquire not after their gods, saying, How did these nations serve their gods? even so will I do likewise" (Deut 12:30). When in Egypt, eventually you practice as the Egyptian. Though God led Israel out of Egypt, Aaron still made idols and wrongly credited them with being the God who delivered them. To these false gods they made sacrifice and worshipped (Ex 32:4, 8). Even when Moses, the leader they knew stood for God, gave them the chance to choose between Jehovah and idols, 3,000 chose the idols. Egypt was too much in their blood from association for so long that they willingly chose the fake. That is the danger of mixing with the fake (Ex 32:26) Pro 13:20 He that walketh with wise *men* shall be wise: but a companion of fools shall be destroyed. Pro 14:7 Go from the presence of a foolish man, when thou perceivest not *in him* the lips of knowledge. Pro 14:25 A true witness delivereth souls: but a deceitful *witness* speaketh lies. Pro 15:2 The tongue of the wise useth knowledge aright: but the mouth of fools poureth out foolishness. Pro 15:28 The heart of the righteous studieth to answer: but the mouth of the wicked poureth out evil things.

Especially when the snare is camouflaged with joyful music as in the Pentecostal and Charismatic worship methods. Music is so powerful in changing a person's perception, desensitising them to receive information being propagated. That is a big psychological topic; but see 1Sa 16:23 And it came to pass, when the *evil* spirit from God was upon Saul, that David took a harp, and played with his hand: so Saul was refreshed, and was well, and the evil spirit departed from him. Music can invoke certain desired behaviour and accompanies most movie scenes to take your sense along with the picture images on the screen.

One cannot make what they want holy and dedicate it to God. Whether it is a day of worship, language or music to liven up his worship or other. Some of our customs are adopted from our pagan ancestry who sometimes went away from Gods way. God does not need His service livened up by our reasoning. Yes his worship should be in song and praises but none of these should be putting anyone in a hyped up emotional state. Worship should always be by Jesus' example of reading the truth of His word which is still practiced today in Jewish services as it was then. One may find it a big difference going from say a vibrant Pentecostal manner to a solemn Catholic method and visa versa. Transformation may not be to your liking. The Catholic may find the Pentecostal noisy and some confusing whereas the Pentecostal may find theirs dead and cold. It is to what one is accustom and the devil knows by getting us accustom to vibrant praise and worship we would not be comfortable when we come to God's right way and will not stay there. Christians are to fight this deceit and do God's will not theirs. As Jeremiah says as for me and my household I will do Gods will and not because I like it so but because He has stated it so. And it is from that I will get my pleasure knowing I am doing His will rather than giving myself satisfaction by external inducements and influences.

This is the sum of the matter. God is not the author of confusion, the devil is as part of deceiving God's teachings are complete, plain simple and open the devil's copies God and gives incomplete information. God's speech is easy to hear, to know what is said, speaks forward, satan is opposite and speaks backwards. In ancient times for a witch or similar to put a spell on you it was spoken backwards, or sent to you written in reverse. The receiver would hold it up to a mirror so the words are seen legible to read aloud. Or the spell to be said would be said backwards or sent to you written backs so that for example the cat becomes eht tac. The reader of the message received would pronounce the message unknown they are speaking backwards. To the ear it sounds like a different language being spoken. People copying these satanic sounds or making up their own is the origin on ST. Christians today are simply trying to react a satanic ritual without knowing how the sounds are made (reading backwards) and brought it into Christianity under the guise of ST from Acts 2 in the bible. Paul and John (1Jhn 4:1-3) states any message even if from him or an angel must correspond with previous revelations and if it does not it is a false spirit in disguise. There are no similar types of tongues in the bible as those commonly practiced today. 1Ti 4:1 Now the Spirit speaketh expressly, that in the latter times some shall depart from the faith, giving heed to seducing spirits, and doctrines of devils;

A phone tex message read "Hos 4:6, lack of knowledge destroys. Devil come to destroy by keeping u away from knowledge. So lack of knowledge ungodly. The truth will set u free. Devil keep U in bondage with untruth. U servant of whom U follow truth or lie. God or devil Don't belive or mis interpret not under The Law/Commandments. Check again and see 1Tim 1:7-10 Law to make U godly. Not under mean back to being ungodly. Only law (of the many) not under is circumcision Gal 5:2, 3, 6 & muh more too many to mention. Fwd to all deceived following tradition of man rather than Commandments of God.

Humans always catching up to wisdom of God. Today medical profession practice sterialisation as if it is their discovery when God directed it 3000 or so years ago Num 31:23 Every thing that may abide the fire, ye shall make *it* go through the fire, and it shall be clean: nevertheless it shall be purified with the water of separation: and all that abideth not the fire ye shall make go through the water.

And quarantine Lev 13:4 "..then the priest shall shut up *him that has* the plague 7 days. The only discovery humans need is to follow the Bible to the letter without question, amendment or own ideas from flashy preachers. Thus Gods people must likewise quarantine themselves from world Deut 12:30 don't even enquire how they live!

174

WHAT HAPPENS AFTER DEATH

Are the dead living in another world? Can the dead see, hear and know what is going on in this world? When a good man dies, does his soul go immediately to heaven? When a bad man dies, does his soul go immediately to hell? Do the dead go first to a stopping-off place called purgatory? When a man dies, does he go off to a spirit world d where he is able to send messages to his loved ones? At death, is that the end of him forever? Are "outer body" experiences to do with death? Or could it be that when a man dies, he peacefully sleeps until the resurrection day? Let us see what God, the Author of life, has to say on the subject.

The deceiver stops at nothing to get us to miss out on heaven and burn with him in hell. The more deceits one falls for the better his hold. I have talked about the false day of worship, the false baptisms, false communication, and the fourth common one is our belief on what happens after death. At the core of this deceit is the second coming of Jesus, the need for His death, resurrection and reward for following His commandments. If satan can make us believe in life after death whether immediately or later; but before Jesus' second coming, we are actually doubting the need for His second coming. It amazes me how many Christians believe that when a person dies they immediately go to heaven or hell. Does that not mean they have already been judged? Then what would be the point of Revelation 20:12 and numerous similar texts? "And I saw the dead, small and great, stand before God; and the books were opened: and another book was opened, which is *the book* of life: and the dead were judged out of those things which were written in the books, according to their works." I have heard people say things like "she looked so peaceful that I know she is with God in heaven". "God came and told me he / she is with me". Such beliefs cancels out the whole bible. Such beliefs cancels out the whole bible, the concept of faith without sight or knowledge from messages from the dead. Do not believe dreams, visions or imaginations of the dead. We dream of the living, conversations with them and present existence so why not of the dead?

The life immediately after death concept is an Egyptian belief. Most should know at least a little about the pharaohs who believe in life after death and buried their possessions with them. This belief continued into Greek mythology and roman paganism whereby it was thought kings could become gods. Martin Luther the protestant reformer said the theory of immortality of the soul was one of those false doctrines that Rome took from paganism and incorporated into Christendom *"monstrous fables that form part of the Roman dunghill of decretals"* (E. Petavel, The Problem of Immortality, p255). Luther commented on the words of Solomon in Ecclesiastes, that the dead know not anything *"another place proving that the dead have no ... feeling. There is, saith he, no duty, no science, no knowledge, no wisdom there. Solomon judged that the dead are asleep and feel nothing at all. For the dead lie there, accounting neither days nor years but when they are awaked, they shall seem to have slept scarce one minute"* (Martin Luther, Exposition of Solomon's Booke Called Ecclesiastes, p152)

William Tyndale, the martyr who translated the bible into English said *"I confess openly, that I am not persuaded that they be already in the full glory that Christ is in, or the elect angels of God are in. Neither is it any article of my faith; for if it were so, I see not but then the preaching of the resurrection of the flesh were a thing in vain"* [William Tynsdale, preface to New Testament (ed 1534) reprinted in British Reformers – Tindal, Frith, Barnes, p349]

Dr Adam Clarke in his Commentary, remarks on 1 Corinthians 15, para 3 said the doctrine of the resurrection was given serious consequence and preaching by the apostles and early Christians. They insisted on it. There was not a doctrine in the gospel on which more stress was laid Today it is seldom mentioned. There is not a doctrine which is treated with more neglect (save for the Sabbath, I would add).

I saw carved into the ceiling of an old "Catholik" church an old version of their creed. I found part of it curious as it referred to Jesus descending into hell. An extract read "…Suffered under Pontius Pilate. Was crucified dead and buried. He descended into hell. The third day he rose again from the dead…." To my knowledge the descending into hell is no longer part of today's Creed.

Before I go onto quote scripture, let me give a summary of the bible and what happens after death so you follow the quoted scriptures. Note when leaving His disciples Jesus did not say in John 14:2, 3 that they would soon come to Him; but that He would come again and receive them to himself.

God made Adam and Eve in His image to inhabit and fill the earth with other humans. Gen 2:7 "And the LORD God formed man of the dust of the ground, and breathed into his nostrils the breath of life; and man became a living soul". Body + breath = soul. We are souls not we have souls. Act 27:37 And we were in all in the ship two hundred threescore and sixteen souls. (See Gen 12:5). When we die the separation of dust and breath is made with "the dust return to the earth as it was: and the spirit shall return unto God who gave it" Ecc 12:7. Jesus said Mar 8:36 For what shall it profit a man, if he shall gain the whole world, and lose his own **soul**? Luk 9:25 ... "if he gain the whole world, and lose **himself**, ...?" He is the soul. That is it, no ghosts, need to be afraid of ghosts in graveyards, talking to images of dead people etc.

satan is jealous of God, wanted the praises for himself and went about recruiting Adam and Eve by getting them to doubt God and obey him. When God said Gen 2:17 But of the tree of the knowledge of good and evil, thou shalt not eat of it: for in the day that thou eatest thereof thou shalt surely die, satan said they would not die (Gen 3:4). Then he appealed to their lusts via their senses Gen 3:6 And when the woman saw that the tree *was* good for food, and that it *was* pleasant to the eyes, and a tree to be desired to make *one* wise, she took of the fruit thereof, and did eat… From then they put satan above God and that is the method satan has continued to use. Mis quoting God's instructions and causing confusion and doubt in God's instructions. Creating a desire that was not there then showing how it could be satisfied. Appealing to our senses, feel in stomach or experiences of an unholy spirit pretending to be holy. God says in Rom

6:23 "the wages of sin is death". Satan is saying it is not, there is life after death.

Some who do not know their bible may think satan was right; they did not die that day. This is wrong on two counts of the meaning to die in the sentence. One, death is separation from God which happened that day when they were put out of the garden. Secondly, a day to God is a thousand years to man. Adam and all men died before reaching a thousand years (2 Pet 3:8). There after, satan has gone to and fro throughout the earth like a roaring lion tying to enlist through temptation or deceit each individual or group of individuals. God has constantly told humans not to have anything to do with those speaking or claiming to speak to spirits, the supposedly dead. Because God knew it was not the dead; but satan's agents posing as the dead. All manner of mediums are used by satan to control the world. By making people believe they can get advice from the dead they seek such advice. Television, music, Hollywood and more constantly portrait contact with those of the spiritual world to the extent leaders of companies and governments who write laws, call on the dead for advice. The astrologer giving Nancy Reagan, (wife to former president Ronald Reagan of USA) advice during the presidency said her star gazing advice influenced the course of history in big and small ways. She set the times some presidential events would occur down to the minute (The Morning News Tribune, Friday March 16, 1990). Laws that go against God's way are passed. Children not punished for not listening to parents, thus cause havoc and great expenditure to judicial system and society. Marriage undermined by equal tax and other benefits to non married and homosexuals.

The dead is really satan giving advice. Do not believe in any thing depicting life after death, even if it is good winning against evil. Whether children cartoons as Pokemon or adult ones as the Matrix, zombies and so. Years ago people were afraid of witches, Dracula and such. Now they have been desensitised through events like Halloween. I saw a two year old toddler being taken out by a parent trick or treating dressed as a witch. The child has no idea of the significance of the occasion; yet is being raised to embrace evil for a reward.

The bible speaks of a saviour / Messiah coming to reunite mankind back to God. This uniting to be with those identified under Rev 14:12 Here is the patience of the saints: here *are* they that <u>keep the commandments of God, and the faith of Jesus.</u> satan's task is to separate us by breaking either or both criteria; commandments, faith in Jesus. The faith in Jesus is believing in the reward of a resurrection. If the reward is not believed then all to do with Jesus crumbles. 1Co 15:12 Now if Christ be preached that he rose from the dead, how say some among you that there is no resurrection of the dead? 1Co 15:13 But if there be no resurrection of the dead, then is Christ not risen: 1Co 15:14 And if Christ be not risen, then is our preaching vain, and your faith is also vain.

As already said, satan would like us to think that we go to our destiny after death some time soon after. The bible says all, good and bad from all generations, sleep in the ground until a special day at the end of the earth (the day of judgement 2 Pet 3:10) apart from some who will still be alive when Jesus comes like a thief in the night (Matt 24:40). Thereafter, the dead will be raised and all mankind judged individually by their actions (works). The death of humans when they leave this earth is called the first death or sleep. After judgement the righteous will inhabit a new heaven and earth with Jesus. The place He said He is going to prepare and mentioned in several places in both the Old and New Testaments (Rev 21:3 And I heard a great voice out of heaven saying, Behold, the tabernacle of God is with men, and he will dwell with them, and they shall be his people, and God himself shall be with them, and be their God. Rev 21:4 And God shall wipe away all tears from their eyes; and there shall be no more death, neither sorrow, nor crying, neither shall there be any more pain: for the former things are passed away). Those who sided with satan for whatever reason would receive the second and final death burning in fire. The reason why satan wishes as many to be deceived as possible is so they burn for their own disobedience (sins). He would have to burn for the sins of the saints which was put on him just like Aaron put the sins of the people on the scrape goat under the annual earthly atonement system. A clarification for those who say God is unjust because they think they will burn forever or other reasons, when they only lived so many years (i.e 40 yrs) or other reason. They will not burn for ever. Their length of time is set by the sum of their wickedness. Luk 12:48 "But he that knew not, and did commit things worthy of stripes, shall be beaten with few stripes. For unto whomsoever much is given, of him shall be much required: and to whom men have committed much, of him they will ask the more." They will be burned to ashes. Malachi 4:1 and 3 reads: "For, behold, the day cometh, that shall burn as an oven; and all the proud, yea, and all that do wickedly, shall be stubble: and the day that cometh shall burn them up, saith the Lord of hosts, that it shall leave them neither root nor branch." "And ye shall tread down the wicked; for they shall be ashes under the soles of your feet in the day that I shall do this, saith the Lord of hosts."

Another mis conception is that the dead can see and interfere in the operations of the living. Maybe advise them etc. We will see this is false later. However, using their own hypothesis. If good people immediately went to heaven when they are suppose to be at peace and happy yet still see their loved ones etc. Would they be happy seeing their family making mistakes, about to get hurt or so? Will they not be living every day anxious for their safety etc. i.e. unhappy? If they could protect the living, then surely no one would die, as a former friend or family would be protecting them. The living would not have control of the world nor their actions. Thus the dead have no knowledge or part of any world, the living or the grave. satan will try and fool people he is Christ coming again as the bible states. Just like how the world is being set up to believe in magic and miracles as evidence of God, satan would exploit that belief. However, the bible gives a stern warning if you hear Christ is here or there DO NOT GO whether out of curiosity or any other reason. The deceit would be so convincing that even the very elect would be fooled if it was possible to fool them. Mat 24:24 For there shall arise false Christs, and false prophets, and shall shew great signs and wonders; insomuch that, if it were possible, they shall deceive the very elect. Mat 24:25 Behold, I have told you before. Mat 24:26 Wherefore if they shall say unto you, Behold, he is in the desert; go not forth: behold, he is in the secret chambers; believe it not. Mat 24:27 For as the lightning cometh out of the east, and shineth even unto the west; so shall also the coming of the Son of man be. Rev 1:7 Behold, he cometh with clouds; and every eye shall see him, and they also which pierced him: and all kindreds of the earth shall wail because of him. Even so, Amen. Jesus will not be coming at any place on the earth; but be in the air. 1Th 4:17 "Then we which are alive and remain shall be caught up together with them in the clouds, to meet the **Lord in the air**: and so shall we ever be with the Lord." If you are still alive and yet not called up to the clouds to meet Jesus, then you too will be lost.

Now let us look at other scriptural evidence.

The soul (person) does not exist after death: without the breath of God within: Gen 2:7 And the LORD God formed man of the dust of the ground, and breathed into his nostrils the breath of life; and man became a living soul. Soul = body + breath of God. Breath of God =The spark of life given by God only. On death they separate with breath returning to God and body to earth. And soul (living person) ceases to exist.

Jam 2:26 For as the body without the spirit is dead, so faith without works is dead also... Eze 18:4 Behold, all souls are mine; as the soul of the father, so also the soul of the son is mine: the soul that sinneth, it shall die. Eze 18:20 The soul that sinneth, it shall die. The son shall not bear the iniquity of the father; neither shall the father bear the iniquity of the son: the righteousness of the righteous shall be upon him, and the wickedness of the wicked shall be upon him. Psa 104:29 Thou hidest thy face, they are troubled: thou takest away their breath; they die, and return to their dust. Psa 104:30 Thou sendest forth thy spirit, they are created: and thou renewest the face of the earth. Job 21:32 Yet shall he be brought to the grave, and shall remain in the tomb. Job 27:3 All the while my breath is in me, and the spirit of God is in my nostrils Act 2:29 Men and brethren, let me freely speak unto you of the patriarch David, that he is both dead and buried, and his sepulchre is with us unto this day. Act 2:34 For David is not ascended into the heavens: but he saith himself, The LORD said unto my Lord, Sit thou on my right hand, Joh 11:11 These things said he: and after that he saith unto them, Our friend Lazarus sleepeth; but I go, that I may awake him out of sleep. Joh 11:12 Then said his disciples, Lord, if he sleep, he shall do well. Joh 11:13 Howbeit Jesus spake of his death: but they thought that he had spoken of taking of rest in sleep. Joh 11:14 Then said Jesus unto them plainly, Lazarus is dead. ... (and has been for four days v17). Act 7:60 And he kneeled down, and cried with a loud voice, Lord, lay not this sin to their charge. And when he had said this, he fell asleep. Only God is immortal 1Tim 1:17

Man knows nothing after death, while sleeping in the ground and cannot do or think anything either in the living or spiritual world: Psa 146:4 His breath goeth forth, he returneth to his earth; in that very day his thoughts perish. Job 14:12 So man lieth down, and riseth not: till the heavens be no more, they shall not awake, nor be raised out of their sleep. Job 14:21 His sons come to honour, and he knoweth it not; and they are brought low, but he perceiveth it not of them. Job 7:9 As the cloud is consumed and vanisheth away: so he that goeth down to the grave shall come up no more. Job 7:10 He shall return no more to his house, neither shall his place know him any more. Psa 6:5

For in death there is no remembrance of thee: in the grave who shall give thee thanks? Isa 38:18 For the grave cannot praise thee, death can not celebrate thee: they that go down into the pit cannot hope for thy truth. Isa 38:19 The living, the living, he shall praise thee, as I do this day: the father to the children shall make known thy truth. Psa 115:17 The dead praise not the LORD, neither any that go down into silence. Ecc 9:5 For the living know that they shall die: but the dead know not any thing, neither have they any more a reward; for the memory of them is forgotten. Ecc 9:6 Also their love, and their hatred, and their envy, is now perished; neither have they any more a portion for ever in any thing that is done under the sun. Ecc 9:10 Whatsoever thy hand findeth to do, do it with thy might; for there is no work, nor device, nor knowledge, nor wisdom, in the grave, whither thou goest. So anyone claiming they died, had an outer body experience then returned to their body and came back alive is mistaken, deceived or out to deceive you. By chance doctors in England recently discovered the part of the brain responsible for outer body experiences. They connected electrodes to a seated man for medical tests who claimed during those test he had an outer body experience. Of course the doctors and equipment showed he was very much alive in their presence. We may yet to learn the truth about these experiences and possibly not until judgement day; but they are definitely not death.

Resurrection of the Dead Joh 3:13 And no man hath ascended up to heaven, but he that came down from heaven, even the Son of man which is in heaven. 1Co 15:12 Now if Christ be preached that he rose from the dead, how say some among you that there is no resurrection of the dead? 1Cor 15:13 But if there be no resurrection of the dead, then is Christ not risen: 1Cor 15:14 And if Christ be not risen, then is our preaching vain, and your faith is also vain. 1Cor 15:20 But now is Christ risen from the dead, and become the first fruits of them that slept. 1Co 15:21 for since by man came death, by man came also the resurrection of the dead. 1Cor 15:22 for as in Adam all die, even so in Christ shall all be made alive. 1Co 15:23 But every man in his own order: Christ the first fruits; afterward they that are Christ's at his coming. 1Co 15:24 Then cometh the end, when he shall have delivered up the kingdom to God, even the Father; when he shall have put down all rule and all authority and power. 1Cor 15:25 for he must reign, till he hath put all enemies under his feet. 1Cor 15:26 the last enemy that shall be destroyed is death. (See Ecc 12:7). Joh 5:28 Marvel not at this: for the hour is coming, in the which all that are in the graves shall hear his voice, Joh 5:29 And shall come forth; they that have done good, unto the resurrection of life; and they that have done evil, unto the resurrection of damnation. 1Cor 15:51 Behold, I shew you a mystery; We shall not all sleep, but we shall all be changed, 1Cor 15:52 In a moment, in the twinkling of an eye, at the last trump: for the trumpet shall sound, and the dead shall be raised incorruptible, and we shall be changed. 1Cor 15:53 For this corruptible must put on incorruption, and this mortal must put on immortality. 1Co 15:54 So when this corruptible shall have put on incorruption, and this mortal shall have put on immortality, then shall be brought to pass the saying that is written, Death is swallowed up in victory. 1Cor 15:55 O death, where is thy sting? O grave, where is thy victory? 1Cor 15:56 The sting of death is sin; and the strength of sin is the law. 1Cor 15:57 But thanks be to God, which giveth us the victory through our Lord Jesus Christ. Immortality means not subject to death: 1Th 4:13 But I would not have you to be ignorant, brethren, concerning them which are asleep, that ye sorrow not, even as others which have no hope. 1Th 4:14 For if we believe that Jesus died and rose again, even so them also which sleep in Jesus will God bring with him. 1Th 4:15 For this we say unto you by the word of the Lord, that we which are alive and remain unto the coming of the Lord shall not prevent them which are asleep. 1Th 4:16 For the Lord himself shall descend from heaven with a shout, with the voice of the archangel, and with the trump of God: and the dead in Christ shall rise 1Th 4:17 Then we which are alive and remain shall be caught up together with them in the clouds, to **meet the Lord in the air**: and so shall we ever be with the Lord. 1Ti 6:15 Which in his times he shall shew, who is the blessed and only Potentate, the King of kings, and Lord of lords; 1Ti 6:16 Who only hath immortality, dwelling in the light which no man can approach unto; whom no man hath seen, nor can see: to whom be honour and power everlasting. Amen. Luk 20:35 But they which shall be accounted worthy to obtain that world and the resurrection from the dead, neither marry, nor are given in marriage: Luk 20:36 Neither can they die any more: for they are equal unto the angels and are the children of God, being the children of the resurrection. 1Jo 5:12 He that hath the Son hath life; and he that hath not the Son of God hath not life. Joh 6:54 whoso elated my flesh and drinketh my blood, hath eternal life and I will raise him up at the last day. Joh 11:23 Jesus say unto her, Thy brother shall rise again. Joh 11:24 Martha saith unto him, I know that he shall rise again in the resurrection at the last day.

I am sorry to have to tell you plainly what you have just read the bible says. No dead person can help or protect you in this world or the next. Not Mary, the Catholic saints or anyone except Jesus. So it is no point praying to them (Eze 14:14-20). If you do you are disbelieving the bible, God and choosing to believe satan over Him, as did Eve. You will not find any scripture where the dead received prayers or could help the living. Such prayers are really to the pagan queen of heaven (Jer 7:18; 44:17, 25). Neither do any return from the dead after an "outer body experience".

<u>Who or what are these speaking dead?</u> 2Co 11:13 For such are <u>false apostles</u>, deceitful workers, <u>transforming themselves into the apostles of Christ.</u> 2Co 11:14 And no marvel; for <u>Satan himself is transformed into an angel of light</u>. 2Co 11:15 Therefore it is no great thing if his ministers also be transformed as the ministers of righteousness; whose end shall be according to their works. Rev 16:13 And I saw three unclean spirits like frogs come out of the mouth of the dragon, and out of the mouth of the beast, and out of the mouth of the <u>false prophet</u>. Rev 16:14 For they are the spirits of devils, working miracles, which go forth unto the <u>kings of the earth </u>and of the whole world, to gather them to the battle of that great day of God Almighty. Rev 18:23 …for thy merchants were the great men of the earth; for <u>by thy sorceries were all nations deceived</u>. 1Ti 4:1 Now the Spirit speak expressly, that in the latter times some shall depart from the faith, giving heed to seducing spirits, and doctrines of devils; Isa 8:19 And when they shall say unto you, Seek unto them that have familiar spirits, and unto

wizards that peep, and that mutter: should not a people seek unto their God? Isa 8:20 to the law and to the testimony: if they speak not according to this word, it is because there is no light in them.

Heaven; who gets in and who is left out. Heb 5:9 And being made perfect, he became the author of eternal salvation unto all them that <u>obey him</u>; Mat 13:48 Which, when it was full, they drew to shore, and sat down, and gathered the good into vessels, but cast the bad away. Mat 13:49 So shall it be at the end of the world: the angels shall come forth, and sever the wicked from among the just, Matt 13:50 And shall cast them into the furnace of fire: there shall be wailing and gnashing of teeth. Mat 25:31 When the Son of man shall come in his glory, and all the holy angels with him, then shall he sit upon the throne of his glory:

Mat 25:32 And before him shall be gathered all nations: and he shall separate them one from another, as a shepherd divideth *his* sheep from the goats: And he shall set the sheep on his right hand, but the goats on the left. Then shall the King say unto them on his right hand, Come, ye blessed of my Father, inherit the kingdom prepared for you from the foundation of the world: ...Mat 25:41 Then shall he say also unto them on the left hand, Depart from me, ye cursed, into everlasting fire, prepared for the devil and his angels:

The Scriptures teach that fire is the final destiny of all who refuse to follow Jesus, "The Lord knoweth how to deliver the godly out of temptations, and to reserve the unjust unto the day of judgment to be punished" (in the future) (2 Peter 2:9)."The wicked is reserved to the day of destruction" (Job 21:30). "As therefore the tares are gathered and burned in the fire; so shall it be in the end of this world" (Matthew 13:40).Rev 22:14 Blessed are they that <u>do his commandments</u>, that they may have right to the tree of life, and may enter in through the gates into the city. Rev 22:15 <u>For without are </u>dogs, and sorcerers, and whoremongers, and murderers, and idolaters, and **whosoever loveth and maketh a lie.** Lev 20:6 And the soul that turneth after such as have familiar spirits, and after wizards, to go a whoring after them, I will even set my face against that soul, and will cut him off from among his people. Gal 5:19 Now the works of the flesh are manifest, which are these; Adultery, fornication, uncleanness, lasciviousness, Gal 5:20 Idolatry, <u>witchcraft</u>, hatred, variance, emulations, wrath, strife, seditions, <u>heresie</u> Eph 5:11 And have <u>no fellowship </u>with the unfruitful works of darkness, but rather reprove them. Rev 2:11 He that hath an ear, let him hear what the Spirit saith unto the churches; He that overcometh shall not be hurt of the <u>second death</u>. Rev 20:14 And death and hell were cast into the lake of fire. This is the <u>second death</u>. Rev 21:4 And God shall wipe away all tears from their eyes; and there shall be no more death, neither sorrow, nor crying, neither shall there be any more pain: for the former things are passed away. Isa 65:17 For, behold, I create new heavens and a new earth: and the former shall not be remembered, nor come into mind. Read Isaiah 65. The new life would be as it should have been, as you would like. No more pain, crime or misery. You could not be happier nor can fully imagine. Try to make it there by keeping God's commandments.

Two scriptures on the topic that may require some explanation are Luke 23:43 and

Luke 16:22. Luke 23:43 The comma is put in the wrong place. When the Bible was written in Greek, no punctuations was present nor when it was first translated. The punctuation came later around the thirteenth century. The text should actually read "…verily I say unto thee today, shalt thou be with me in paradise" not "… I say to thee, today shalt thou…" The facts support this change of the comma. Jesus did not ascend into heaven that day, the day of His death. Neither on the following Sunday when He rose. Infact He did not ascend for 40 days later. John 21:17 after His resurrection "I am not yet ascended to my Father".

Luke 16:16 – 31 This was a parable like the many spoken by Jesus to make a few points. One being people are set in their ways that nothing or anyone can change them from doing what they want. It was not meant to be taken literally. V22 Persons on death are not "carried" unto "Abraham's bosom". What an odd place to end up and with how many other people, how big is his bosom? Notice the beggar was not buried as was the rich man. V23-4 He saw Abraham "afar off" yet was able to shout and be heard. What distance is between hell and Abraham, apparently in heaven? A person in burning hell's flame would request more than a finger dip of water. That could not even be swallowed, wet his tongue or have any effect. One of the points Jesus was making is in v29 "they have Moses and the prophets" to tell them what to do. The commandments and the law. In fact one did come from the dead, Lazarus (John 11) yet the leaders did not believe.

A man's wife died. He by chance saw an advert for a Christian crusade and attended the meetings. One topic taught was what happens after death and how ghost are satan deceits. One night after the meetings he was home alone in bed when an image of his wife came and talked to him. For a moment he was comforted; but then remembered what he had learnt about the dead. Plucking up the courage he pointed at the image and sternly said with conviction and belief, you are not my wife, get away from me. The image disappeared and never returned.

THE SANCTUARY

The Old and New Testaments are one depiction of the love our creator Jehovah God has for us His creation. The Old narrates His creation in Genesis. How Adam and Eve succumbed to satan's temptation of disobedience for the imposed illusion of gain of eternal life and wisdom (you will not die and your eyes will be open to know …). Things they already possessed satan offered them for a price; but instead of making a gain or acquiring anything they actually lost what they already had and paid a dear price for it. Human nature has not changed from the beginning to now. Willing to give up what is in ones hand for an illusion of something more shiny. It was satan's original sin and characteristic of those who follow him. Jesus showed how to overcome such temptations when satan offered Jesus what was already His. Be satisfied with what you have even if you do not know the scriptures sufficiently to rebut satan. That is why prosperity sermons are so dangerous to the Christian's salvation. They preach dis-satisfaction and create desire for earthly material things rather than focusing on not sinning in all forms not only some. Matt 5:3—12 "Blessed *are* the poor in spirit: for theirs is the kingdom of heaven…."

They had eternal life; but disobedience brought human life span gradually down to an average of "three score and ten". They were wise with the fear of God [Psa 111:10 The fear of the LORD *is* the beginning of wisdom: a good understanding have all they that do *his commandments*: his praise endureth for ever. (also Psa 9:10)]. Now many say there is no God. After Adam humans have strayed far from God's desire for them and choosing to commit sin (Gen 6:5 And GOD saw that the wickedness of man *was* great in the earth, and *that* every imagination of the thoughts of his heart *was* only evil continually). The rest of the bible narrates God's longsuffering efforts to save us from our own demise and bring us back to His wonderful plan for us. How He separated those who followed Him (Noah, Abraham, Jacob) from those who did not. Yet did not destroy the offenders (strangers or gentiles); but gave them a chance to return to Him by following the example of His people. Baptism in Christ is a symbol of that separation. Similar to Noah and Moses coming through the waters of the flood or the Red Sea, we come through the separating waters of baptism. Hopefully leaving our past lives and sins on the other side. However, as we know sin followed the and reappeared on the other side as it does with us after baptism. We have to constantly drink the water fro the Jesus our rock in the wilderness of the world.

In the Old Testament, the example was the way of life followed by the descendants of Abraham / Jacob. The way of life being detailed in His commandments, laws, statutes etc. Part of which was the sanctuary system depicted in Leviticus 16. The annual Day of Atonement ceremony for the forgiveness of sins was conducted in the sanctuary by the High Priest. The layout of the camp enclosing the sanctuary is seen in the later diagram. The Old Testament system is symbolic of the New Testament one in which Jesus becomes the High Priest, the sacrifice etc and satan becomes the scapegoat cast into the lake of fire to perish with those who side with him by disobeying Jehovah God. The whole system symbolises and points to Jesus the Messiah coming to take away our sins, cleanse us and return us to God His father. Completing the restoration. By one man sin entered by one man sin is banished.

The people came in via the East Gate. This symbolises there is only one way to God (Ephesian 4:5) and that way is through Jesus. (Joh 14:6 Jesus saith unto him, I am the way, the truth, and the life: no man cometh unto the Father, but by me). Not everyone claiming to be a follower of Christ (Christian) will be known by Him (Luk 6:46, 13:25; Matt 7:22) Matt7:22 Mat 7:21 Not every one that saith unto me, Lord, Lord, shall enter into the kingdom of heaven; but he that doeth the will of my Father which is in heaven. Joh 14:15 If ye love me, keep my commandments. Thus there are not many ways to God, many denominations, only one. Those keeping the commandments of God **and** faith of Jesus Christ (Revelations). The faith being His truth.

The Brazen Altar represents Calvary. Something innocent has to die for our sins. It was then the goat, later replaced by Jesus' innocence.

The laver is to cleanse us similar to entering the baptism pool and emerging a clean person in Christ. However, the process did not stop there as many Christians do. Thinking that once they are baptized that is them saved. No, that is only the outward sign of your intention. The process does not end until the Most Holy Place has done its part and the scapegoat (satan) is given the punishment for those righteous ones he tormented.

The candlestick represents Jesus, the word (Joh 1:1), as the light of the world. [Joh 8:12 Then spake Jesus again unto them, saying, I am the light of the world: he that followeth me shall not walk in darkness, but shall have the light of life. Psa 119:105 NUN. Thy word is a. lamp unto my feet, and a light unto my path. Pro 6:23 For the commandment is a. lamp; and the law is light; and reproofs of instruction are the way of life:]. Note Psalm 119:105 guides us how to live a Godly life, by adhering the very things some say are no more.

The showbread is Jesus as the bread of life Joh 6:35 And Jesus said unto them, I am the bread of life: he that cometh to me shall never hunger; and he that believeth on me shall never thirst. Mat 4:4 But he answered and said, It is written , Man shall not live by bread alone, but by every word that proceedeth out of the mouth of God. Jesus was quoting Deu 8:3. He quoted the Old Testament numerous times as that was His script. He had not come to change anything.

The Arc of the Covenant represented God's character and contained the Ten Commandments, some of the manna from heaven and Aaron's budding rod. The blood of an innocent goat was offered annually to God as a replacement for our sins. Non corrupt for corrupt. Hence one cannot offer an alternative day of worship in place of His sanctified one. Only Jesus' once and for all blood, offered in accordance with the Law absolves us for breaking it (Heb 9:22). The new High Priest has the unblemished qualities to come before God to plead our case as an intercessor. He brings to the Arc confessed sins and not ones unto death; blaspheme. Choosing to follow the laws of man over God's. One is not saved until the day of judgement when all come before Jesus to be judged and sentenced (Rev 20:12-13). Those to be saved will <u>then</u> be saved and inherit the new heaven and earth (Rev 21- 22). Those who disobeyed God will suffer the <u>second death </u>and exist no more. The restoration process would have been completed. No more crime, tears or hard work for those who understood and made adhering to God's ways a no compromise decision. Psa 9:10 and they that know thy name will put their trust in thee: for thou, LORD, hast not forsaken them that seek thee.

The people and the priests came in through the East gate (Right hand side). Two goats were chosen for the Day of Atonement ceremony. One to be killed on the brazen altar (5), its blood sprinkled in the Most Holy Place and the other let into the wilderness to take / bare the **confessed** sins of the priests and the people. The priests and especially the High Priest would wash themselves in the Brazen laver (6). Only the priests could enter the Holy Place and only the High priest the Most Holy Place once per year wearing special holy garments. If he entered at any other time he would be killed as would anyone else ever entering. The High Priest had a rope tied to his feet so that, should he be killed, he could be pulled out without any one else going in. The seven branch candlestick was never to go out, being kept supplied with oil. The showbread (3) consisted of twelve loaves. The altar of incense (2) was for the prayers as described in Rev 5:8 and 8:3. Inside the Most Holy Place was the Mercy Seat and the Arc of the Covenant (1), inside of which was the Ten Commandments written on the stone tablets, some manna as fell from heaven when they were in the wilderness and Aaron's rod which budded.

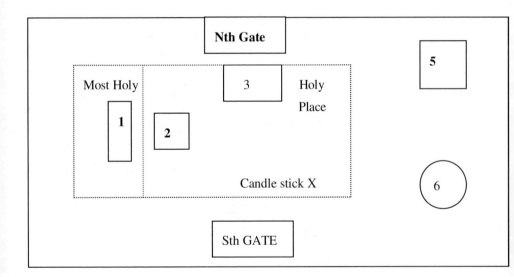

CONCLUSION

To understand exactly what God requires of us, we must grasp the structure of His system. There are three main and totally different components, which I want to emphasise and make clear.

Commandments: Moral framework and recognition of :

(i) God your creator, provider and ruler. I know in today's society of broken families a biological parent can be replaced by a step parent: but, would a parent, without fault, who brought a child into the world, nurtured them to adulthood, really want that child to recognise another human for their efforts? It is the same with God. He would not abolish this section of the Commandments and permit you to recognise any other God, either in worship or image.

(ii) Of others. Would it become right to kill, steal, commit adultery or break any of the other six commandments relating to man? Of course not. So the Ten Commandments are still binding in their entirety forever. Have you noticed how fossils are preserved in stone? The same with cave drawings discovered thousands of years after they were made. Stone is the most permanent record. Pappia (paper) was around in Moses' time. God chose stone for its permanency.

Breaking any of the commandments was punishable by death; i.e. see Lev 24:16, Num 15:32-5, 35:17, Deut 17:3-5, 21:18-21, 22.

Laws: These were numerous. I think some say approximately 636. Within these were ones relating to the annual sacrifice for the forgiveness of human sin. This was not all sins because if an individual sinned, there were other prescribed offerings for that particular type of sin. This was an annual sacrifice for the people as a whole. They could have continued these yearly sacrifices till eternity. Say one lamb for the next million years. However, due to reasons explained above, God gave them a Lamb worth a million plus lambs, for a sacrifice forever. The annual law sacrifice was not replaced, merely paid in advance. This formed the basis of Paul's advice in the New Testament. He was saying, believers had to believe and have faith that Jesus had made the advance payment for them on this issue. It was a payment they could not afford; but through the goodwill, grace of God, they were given a discount. The need for that annual sacrifice ritual has been performed till eternity by Jesus. Today medical practice still operates on biblical principles. Quarantine a disease just as God prescribed for leprosy.

Circumcision: This was a covenant between God and Abraham (Genesis 17:11), not part of the things written on the tables of stone; but still binding on God's people as a bodily sign of separation (save for Paul's concession to the Gentiles).

For this fact, it was grouped under the Laws written by Moses. Note in Exodus 4:25-26 failure to circumcise his son almost led to the death of Moses. If you are not familiar with the bible, this happened before Moses returned to Egypt and contested with Pharaoh. Though God made the circumcision covenant with Abraham and his descendants, it was not adhered to. Joshua 5:2-5 tells how those who went in the wilderness were circumcised but not those newly born and coming out. i.e. in forty years no one was circumcised. Paul, knowing that even the Jews found it hard to keep the circumcision covenant, did not want to deter new believers with the same yoke.

Feast Days/God's Holy Days: These are special remembrance days set by God to be kept "forever". Paul kept the feasts days. Acts 20:6 after celebrating the feast he sailed away "And we sailed away from Philippi after the days of unleavened bread…" Rushed to Jerusalem to keep the feast of Pentecost Act 20:16 "For Paul had determined to sail by Ephesus, because he would not spend the time in Asia: for he hasted, if it were possible for him, to be at Jerusalem the day of Pentecost". See also Acts 1:21; 24:11. The feasts "of the Lord" were commanded to be kept in Lev 23. They were kept before Jesus, by Him and his apostles and will be in the end as many scriptures state: i.e. Isa 66:23 "And it shall come to pass, *that* from one new moon to another, and from one Sabbath to another, shall all flesh come to worship before me, saith the LORD." New moons were feasts celebrating the start of each month similar to the weekly seventh day Sabbath cycle. Zec 8:22 Yea, many people and strong nations shall come to seek the LORD of hosts in Jerusalem, and to pray before the LORD. Zec 8:23 Thus saith the LORD of hosts; In those days *it shall come to pass*, that ten men shall take hold out of all languages of the nations, even shall take hold of the skirt of him that is a Jew, saying, We will go with you: for we have heard *that* God *is* with you. Zec 14:16 And it shall come to pass, *that* every one that is left of all the nations which came against Jerusalem shall even go up from year to year to worship the King, the LORD of hosts, and to keep the feast of tabernacles. Zec 14:17 And it shall be, *that* whoso will not come up of *all* the families of the earth unto Jerusalem to worship the King, the LORD of hosts, even upon them shall be no rain. Zec 14:18 And if the family of Egypt go not up, and come not, that *have* no *rain*; there shall be the plague, wherewith the LORD will smite the heathen that come not up to keep the feast of tabernacles. Zec 14:19 This shall be the punishment of Egypt, and the punishment of all nations that come not up to keep the feast of tabernacles. See Micah 4:2 "the God of Jacob". Jesus is our N.T. Passover lamb to be kept as a significant remembrance to God "forever" (Ex 12:14, 17) even by the "stranger" (v19, 49). The lamb was replaced not the feast or memorial.

Most people keep some special days of remembrance; but pagan ones merged with Christianity by "the church" or state rather than God. God's are (* indicates main ones):

*New Year. **Rosh HaShanah**	9th Sept 2010 two day celebration with church service **and meal. (some follow Ex 12:2).** It is not the pagan's 31st December which is based on the "hosts of heaven".
*Day of Atonement: **Yom Kippur**	**18th Sept 2010 Held ten days after New Year. This is** **the day of the Old Testament annual sacrifice for the** **whole of God's people. Consist of twenty five hours of** **fasting, one hour before sunset to sunset next day**.

*Feast of Tabernacle	**23-30th Sept 2010, 8 days to Shemini Atzeret. No work on first and last days. The Jews build a booth in their garden or use the synagogue's.**
Simhat Torah	Some celebrate this day of rejoicing with the Torah. No work
Chanukah	Some celebrate the miracle of the light that lasted eight days.
Tu Bishvat	Some celebrate New year for the trees.
Purim	Sun 28 Feb 2010 Feast of Esther (not ordained by God but in memory Esther 9:26)
*Pesach/Passover	**30 March 2010 seven days of abstention from work, eating bread and products Containing yeast or rising agents. One can eat vegetables as potatoes etc.** (some only abstain from work 1st, 2nd, 7th and 8th days). Christians celebrate pagan Easter around the same time.
*Shavuot Feast of Weeks	**19 May 2010** Kept similar to New Year. This was the feast being kept by the Jews by 2 days of Pentecost their annual gathering in Jerusalem from around the world and for which the gift of speaking in tongues was given Acts 2:1. Not for vain babbling to God as of today God reads hearts and minds and does not need vocal sounds.

You can find these days in most diaries which show the Jewish holidays or on the internet. Passover became today's Easter. For the pagan origin of Easter, Christmas and other such days try a book titled Christmas, Easter and Halloween, Where did they come from? By Vance Ferrell, published by Harvestime Books, Altamont, TN 37301 (U.S.A).

In simple terms to keep them one has to take the day off work. Just like keeping the Sabbath, it is simply switching the day you cease work, your days off. Not very hard. Many other religions get by without keeping Easter, Christmas etc. With today's working patterns where many businesses operate 365 days per year, just arrange with your employer to switch days. Work the days others do not wish to as Good Friday etc and take your days off at God's time. What are you prepared to do for yourself or other humans? Do you not take the day off work to attend a funeral, wedding, child's sports day or holiday? Do you not keep your wedding anniversary, family member's birthdays? Yet not for God. Of all the days you celebrate per year, how many are what God set not man's custom? I see children as young as 2 dressed up in witches outfits on Halloween being led around the streets by their parents. Not too long ago the country would not want anything to do with witches. Seeing them as evil, ungodly etc. Now gladly they embrace being one. It could be soon the country would willingly turn to and crave to be like satan the deceiver. How should He view your commitment to wanting the invaluable prize of heaven?

When the merger came between Roman paganism and early Christians, the parallel system of satan was entwined with God's. Not only was the weekly day of worship changed from Sabbath to Sunday, but pagan memorial days were substituted for God's holy days. Though some worshippers have now seen through the false justifications for Sunday, they are still embedded in Christmas, Easter and such so called Christian days. Though some know of the real pagan origins of these days, they either do not know where to go instead or have been taken so far from God's days that the journey back seems to much effort. The deceiver knew the nature of man, saying to himself, those I do not get via the Sabbath, I will get via the other days. I will take them so far away from each and give them reasons as "nailed to the cross", etc that they will want to find it convenient to believe the same. Jer 4:22 "for my people is foolish, they have not known me, they are sottish children and have none understanding, they are wise to do evil; but to do good they have no knowledge". Jer 5:31"The prophets prophesy falsely and the priest bear rule by their means and my people love to have it so; and what will you do in the end thereof? Also view Eze 22:26

I am told by a Jewish rabbi, instead of the animal sacrifices they now read about the same and pray. This was instituted when the temple was first destroyed and they exiled to Babylon. On the rebuilding of the temple by Ezra and Nehemiah, God spoke to Ezra and instructed people to learn about and readopt the sacrifice system. When the temple was destroyed for the second time in A.D. 70 they returned to and have continued onto today, the reading and pray practice.

It only takes about ten years of use for a new word to be included in a dictionary. Imagine what a deceiver could accomplish in 2000!

Some congregations fast on the weekly Sabbath, probably because it is a convenient day when most people are in church and off work. However, my understanding is the bible is against fasting on God's Sabbath and other feast days save for the Day of Atonement. It is one of His feast days as in Lev 23:1-3. One does not fast at a feast in the presence of God on His feast day. Just like when Jesus said in Mark 2:19 "Can the children of the bridegroom fast while the bridegroom is with them? As long as they have the bridegroom with them, they cannot fast". The Jews do not fast on a Sabbath and think it an insult to God to do so.

Neither the bible, history nor logic justifies the breaking of God's commandments and the Sabbath. One may believe they know someone and do not. Believe they know God and do not because it is based on what others explain to them.1John 4:1 'Beloved, believe not every spirit but try the spirits whether they are of God, because many false prophets are gone out into the world" i.e. spirits of satan to deceive. Thessalonians 2:4 "the son of perdition (satan) …showing himself that he is God" (satan acting as and fooling humans that he is the true god not Jehovah God). Pastors and teachers should beware of their teachings on this matter as Jesus said it would be worse for those who teach others to break one of the commandments. However, even if you are still in doubt, one should be prudent and do the safe action. We know, as the bible testifies, that those who were loved by God and would be with Him kept the commandments and the Sabbath. No such record exists for those who did not or kept Sunday. Do you want to be ignorant, rely on your own reasoning, wishful thinking and take the chance? To turn up saying "Lord have we not prophesied in thy name" only to hear His reply "I never knew you, depart from me". The word of God, the bible, is a light onto your path to heaven. Satan comes as an angel of light to confuse your choice of route so you do not get there. He will cause you to make wrong choices, in understanding of the bible, cause disbelief. The best way is to obey the bible in full; Old and New Testaments. Follow path others took and avoid errors of ancestors. God's directions must be consistent, the route consistent. Paul and the apostles were Jews first, keepers of God's commandments. To that they added the belief in and testimony of Jesus (Rev 12:17, 14:12) 2Co 11:13 For such *are* false apostles, deceitful workers, transforming themselves into the apostles of Christ. 2Co 11:14 And no marvel; for Satan himself is transformed into an angel of light.

2Cor 11:15 Therefore *it is* no great thing if his ministers also be transformed as the ministers of righteousness; whose end shall be according to their works. Paul had to go through that transition. We are too. We are all human aiming for the same place regardless of the century in which were born. (Matt 7:22).Similarly in Zech 7:3-6 people thought they were fasting for God but He said it was for themselves. It was fear of losing his job why Pilate had Jesus killed. Today leaders may have the same fear or the reduced size of the congregation and collection or because it is the church organisation's building. Such leaders should step out in faith. Make a stand for God and then see His reward. I know of some who have and are not disappointed. What would you give to save your soul? (Mark 8:36).1 Cor 15:30 Corruption cannot inherit incorruption. Sunday worshippers have adopted a corrupted message (as confirmed by the above article with biblical and historic references). I submit they would not be allowed to inherit the uncorrupted reward of God.

Do not be or necessarily want to be like everyone else, be special. In Samuel God warned against wanting a king like other nations because it was not good for them; i.e. would take everything and make them slaves. Yet people still wanted a king like every other nation rather than be led by God being different, His set apart to be holy onto Himself to keep His ways. Sun day worshippers want to be like everyone else, following the false system inherited from ancient Egypt.

John 12:42 many believed in Jesus but did not confess to this for fear of being put out of the synagogue. So today many Sunday church leaders do the same and feed followers false reasons.

I was searching through the Christian satellite channels and noticed a lot of Christmas celebrations, coral singing, etc .Everyone was singing about it, exchanging presents and all in the name of Christ. Even many Sabbath keeping churches or individuals have succumbed to celebrating the pagan festival. Possibly for not wanting or their children to feel excluded from or different to society. One pastor told me he knows and teaches his congregation that it is nothing to do with when Christ was born. Excuses for doing unbiblical things in the name of Christ are taught to Christians; but you are having a party, wedding or other special day celebration; annually. Someone else is also having a celebration a few days later: annually. You and them are wondering whose event would people attend and remember. You give them free choice to come if they wish. The other person's objective is to get everyone to come to theirs and not yours. They promote enjoyment, music, dancing, whatever people want and like to do; no restrictions. They even go as far as to say you have cancelled yours and are having a joint celebration with them on their day. The result, your family and true friends come to yours, the other 99% go to the other. Take a minute to reflect how you would feel? Eventually no one save your family and true friends would know of your annual day. Well everyone seems to be celebrating the pagan days and do not even know of God's feast days. If only they knew what these days originally celebrated and to which are still associated.

1John 2:15-16 "Love not the world, neither the things that are in the world. If any man love the world, the love of the Father is not in him. For that is in the world, the lust of the flesh and the lusts of the eyes and the pride of life is not of the Father but is of the world."

You cannot love the world and love God. The word says you cannot, so it really does not matter what people say. We get so caught up in what people are saying that we often forget to consult the word of God about it. For instance, we listen to these talk radio programs (including Christian ones), talk shows that debate issues and hear all kinds of comments that reflect people's opinions. "I think it's okay" and "I don't see anything wrong with it!" But God's words were never meant to be debated. People get convicted by certain things or people and think they have to move with the times or the world. Not everyone gets convicted by the same thing, by popular belief or teachings. On what authority do these ministers guide you? Is it one above the word of God which you can access for yourself? To be able to discern between the false teachers and the real as prophesied in the bible, is to do your own study of the entire bible. Have questions in your mind, and then set out with a notebook to have them answered as you read it from cover to cover over and over yearly. Each new reading brings new insight.

Rev 17:5 speaks of   And upon her forehead *was* a name written, MYSTERY, BABYLON THE GREAT, THE <u>MOTHER</u> OF HARLOTS AND ABOMINATIONS OF THE EARTH. . Protestant churches are the daughters of the mother from whom they came. As the true God can not tolerate any strange gods, the true church of Christ (that keeps all His father's commandments especially the true Sabbath) cannot tolerate strange churches beside herself. It is in this exclusiveness of "all truth" lies Her unique strength. Many Christians use what the Jews did as an excuse for them not following God's commandments i.e. Jews killed Jesus, Jesus called some of the leaders hypocrites etc. It is not about them or someone else; but you   Two or two thousand wrongs do not make something right or give you reason not to do what is right. Consider your actions and no one else's. They will be judged as individuals as will you. It is about YOU and YOUR ACTIONS.

Matt 7:23 Jesus says depart from me, I NEVER knew you. Why "never" rather than as

Paul said of some believers (Phil 3:18), who in past times walked with Jesus; but succumbed to the lust of their belly and the world. Jesus did not say, I knew you once but you backslid or anything close. He was speaking to pastors, evangelists, claimed healers and those casting out devils, church goers, all believing they were doing good things and calling on the name Jesus. In Matt 18:20 Jesus says where two or three gather in my name, I will be there in your midst. Does this mean when some go to the wrong "Christian" Sun day church; Jesus never knew them and was never there in their midst because it was never His day? He never knew them once. At their baptism, praise and worship, pray meeting or bible study. Was that because they were baptised into a "Sun" day system not His? Think about this very seriously. Satanists go to church, study the bible; and may even call the name Jesus. One preacher recited a visit to a Spiritualist Christian church where took place a séance conjuring up spirits pretending to be Jesus. Could it not be you were deceived by the wolf in sheep clothing and baptised into and followed satan's false parallel Sun day system? Met in a building that architecturally resembled a Christian church; but inside the service was not that as prescribed by God. Have you been to Egypt and seen the pagan altars, temples, animal sacrifices, ancient priests, all similar to the Jew's saved for the worship being directed to the Sun? Heb 10:26 "For if we sin willfully after that we have received the knowledge of the truth, there remaineth no more sacrifice for (your) sin".

Some denominations recognise a post bible modern day prophet. This deters some believers from attending their services. A prophet, modern or old, can only repeat the word of God. Providing you are following the word of God as in the bible, you should automatically be in line with any prophet. If you are not, then it should not matter as God is the sole one to recognise.

It saddens me that breachers of the Sabbath are so sure they are right when even the Apostles who were taught directly by Jesus on a daily basis for three and a half years, saw miracles first hand etc were not sure of themselves. When Jesus at the last supper said one of you would betray me they asked if it was them, NOT confidently say I KNOW, it is not me.

My brothers and sisters, please hear me. The word of God does not change with the times. If you are a lover of the things of this world then the love of God is not in you. I do not care what the talk show says, what the radio personality says or what commercial ministries told you. Being popular, worldly or part of the 99% is not being Christ like. Numerous place sin the bible it mentions the majority being wrong, will not get to heaven. If you still want all the false scripture popular interpretations or customs; sinful things that you desired before you accepted Christ, then the question is, did you accept Him or did you accept a form of Him? If you accepted Him, then you must accept his word and the consequences of not choosing Him over the things of the world. Bottom line: check your desires. They will tell who you serve. Are you serving yourself or God? Worshiping our attending where you get or where you give to God in His way as He laid down? Does God for example like ALL kinds of music as in Daniel 3:7 or specific instruments? Is the dancing that David did in the streets outside the tabernacle on a specific occasion an excuse to do it inside church like the Egyptians did for their goddess Hathor? Did God prescribe we could wear what we want before Him and then go shopping after in the same items? Serve God to the fullest, otherwise maybe you went through the formality of accepting Him, but never really made a place in your heart for Him and His ways.

God is calling His people out of the world, from following worldly customs for so long. Mat 22:14 "For many are called; but few are chosen". Try keeping the Sabbath for a month. Pray to God on the Sabbath not Sunday as answers received may not be from the right spirit. To receive a radio programme, one has to be in the correct reception area, at the right time and on the right frequency otherwise one may get another message. Hope you see time, place and state of heart counts. All three. Have you ever wondered why of all the sick people wanting help and healing from Jesus, He heard the cries of those like Bartimaus Mark 10:50 (through the noise of the crowd)? Could it be like in Acts 14:9, even from a distance, Jesus could "perceive" who really wanted to be saved and did not incur the time on those superficial believers of custom? How would the Holy Spirit view your heart, one tied to custom or earnestly seeking the truth? Many find the truth as they did Jesus; but turn away from it saying it is too hard to follow. Preferring pleasures, comfort or acceptance of the world.

Did you know the Muslims who follow the Old Testament, originally worshipped on the Sabbath, the same as the Jews, rather than on Friday as they do today? We worship the same God and all had the same day of worship. How that came about is another topic. So all who serve the God of creation and use the same bible history, should be doing the same thing, God's way. Would it not be great if all believers in the God of creation and the Bible returned to Him and how it was in the beginning and forever should be? I have a dream that one day Jews, Gentiles, all bible believers whether black, white or in between would worship God, the creator of heaven and earth, on His Sabbath day. Are you sure you have it right?

You have reached the end of this booklet. What are you going to do with this knowledge? If not abide by the commandments in full, including the Sabbath, then Jesus' sacrifice may not cover you. Regardless of whether you got it wrong in the past, Eze 33:14-16 says if you turn now and do it right, you will be saved. It also says that whatever righteousness you may have had will be forgotten if at the end of your life you are found committing iniquity, breaking His Sabbath commandment. Just like in the parable of Matt 20:1-16, it is those who stay to the end will receive their wages. Rev 3:20 Jesus says "Behold, I stand at the door, and knock: if any man hear my voice, and open the door, I will come in to him, and will sup with him, and he with me". Some pretend not to hear, distracting themselves with worldly noise, some call out "what you want" and other questions to take up time, some say come back as I am busy or not ready for you yet. Remember delayed obedience is disobedience. You may have let the deceiver into your life in the belief it was Jesus. Identify Jesus by His and His father's commandments and do likewise. Do not be one of those set in their ways giving excuses not to open the door. You have the facts, throw that impostor out and let the real Jesus in.

The battle has begun for YOUR soul. Satan will try his best to keep you. Keep the frequency clear for God's message to get into YOU. Like weaning off a drug, you have to isolate yourself from it. Stop going to those Sun day churches or listening to such false pastors sermons either on T.V. or radio; at least for a year until God's truth has a chance to take root inside YOU. Weaning you off those false vines onto His one and only "true vine". You cannot do it on your own, friends and loneliness may send you back. Preferably attach yourself to a convicted Sabbath keeper to teach and keep you refreshed daily when doubt knocks.

The facts presented are clear and shown to be undisputed by all denomination. Sunday worship is not of God, Jesus or the bible; but of the Catholic Church who set themselves up as your god to practice pagan customs. They also introduced infant baptism to replace the eight day circumcision custom of the bible. Replaced baptism by immersion into by sprinkling. Propagated the pagan belief taken from Egypt of life after death. Tongues as spoken today is not as spoken in Acts where all present heard and understood without an interpreter. Paul and Jesus said to speak to God in silence or in the closet. Today's tongues started in 1906 and is the successor of speaking backwards as in witchcraft. The books of Daniel and Revelation talks about the final battle between God and satan. Satan's representative sets himself up as god on earth to get humans to disobey Jehovah God. His Sabbath in particular and worship on a false day of sun worship. Those who are saved for the new heaven and earth are those keeping Gods Commandments and the faith of Jesus Christ. Two things not one. You may need to re-read this book as it contained a lot to digest.

Your old friends and pastor may seem concerned with what may appear to be genuine advice like "are you sure you know what you are doing, think about it carefully, etc". All meant to plant a seed of doubt in your mind and keep you attached to the comfort option. Plead with God; maybe through the prayer below, for God to help you. Many new converted Sabbath keepers are the only ones in their family. Sometimes the young teenager who has not the rot of the old customs imbedded in them, like their parents, etc. They make me proud. Join them, put Jehovah first. Jesus established one church based on truth. Delayed obedience is disobedience. Do not say you are serving God, want to get to heaven yet not keep all His commandments including the seventh day (Saturday) Sabbath (remember, break one break them all). It is a well known fact man changed it. If you are still hesitant re-read about two of God's chosen who were killed by Him. Saul in 1Sam 13:5—15:35 and the man of God in 1King 13. One used his own judgement in believing he was doing God's commandment as he understood it. The other listened to one calling himself a prophet claiming to speak on behalf of God. Both wanted, tried and thought they were doing God's will. Saul was willing to die or kill his son Jonathan to maintain his relationship with God, yet he had a total different outcome to Abraham. Also Deut 13:1-26.

What are you really being asked to do?

Blot out the stain on your live inherited by Adam's wrong freewill choice with your right one and reject the present day deceits of satan and his self titled "Christian" agents.

* (Jhn 3:3) One cannot get into heaven unless properly baptised. Remember the Church of Rome replaced circumcision with the false baptism. Be baptised as an adult with full body immersed in water by a pastor of the Sabbath system. (It is better to be safe than sorry and there is no other chance after death). I recently saw some newly re-baptised Christians in   their adulthood. Some former Sunday keeping Pentecostal, a seventy year old Methodist and I am unaware of the others history; but some again were between forty and seventy year olds.

* Change your day of worship from in honour of the Sun god (Sunday) to the Sabbath (Saturday) as God requires. Ex 20:8

* Make your worship more than a few hours of church attendance. If your employer allows, start your Sabbath at the right sunset time on Friday evening. Abstain from work and work conversations, spend time with family or friends, rest, study God's word and attend the right church service.

* Substitute your celebrated days to God's rather than the world's historic pagan ones i.e. Christmas, Easter etc. If you   feel you must keep Christmas for the sake of children or so, try not giving presents etc on 25 December. Send New Year or other message cards rather than Christmas ones.

* I would also recommend abstaining from meat with blood i.e. buy your meat from a kosher supplier not the regular supermarket . Alternatively eat scaled fish. Abstain from religions containing idols or fornication.

* Stop speaking in false tongues where you cannot interpret nor can all present understand you.

* Stop believing in any form of life after death unless via the biblical version of only when Jesus comes again, at the end of the world and judges all, good and bad on judgement day. Stop praying to the dead or believing they can assist you including Mary or saints. It goes against Exodus 20:3 by believing another over Gods word. Deny the deception of satan.

The devil is really after you and me; and will stop at nothing to reason with you not to keep God's words. Do not use your emotions or reasoning like Saul; but only the clear word of God. To obey is better than all sacrifice. I hope we both make it. In any battle certain principles would protect you. These are more vital when dealing with the master deceiver, satan. Know your enemy. do not under estimate him. Believe you cannot over estimate him. Expect any deceit from any direction in any form. Satan knows you better than you know him or yourself. He Could deceive the very elect if it were possible. Sell sand to the Arabs, ice to Eskimos and you to yourself. Do not rationalise but put on the armour of God. As God advises, tie His commandments to your hand, plant them in your head and constantly speak them into your heart. Do not leave any way in. Not malice, envy, jealousy, lust or unholy desire. Have total love for Jesus and His Father. Imagine Jesus' pain, humiliation and crucifixion all for you to prove He loves you. Love like you will never know. Look into His eyes as He hangs on that cross for you. Then see if you can say to Him for all He has done for you, that you cannot keep His commandments; including the Sabbath days. Are you really going to turn your back on Him? Jesus came to restore us back to His father and the keeping of His father's will as reflected in the Old Testament commandments. Matt 6:10, 7:21, Luk 18:19, 22:42 "thy will be done on earth ...not my will but thine be done ... none is good save one and that is God ...he that do my father's will shall enter heaven.

A PRAY FOR YOU.

My Dear God Jehovah in Heaven. The creator of the Universe, all things seen, unseen, known, unknown and especially me. Without whom no one or anything would be in existence. The God of Abraham, Isaac, Jacob, Moses and Jesus Christ our saviour. The only true God who separated His people from the disobedient ones. Gave them the commandments of life and yet, by these same commandments all mankind have access to your forgiveness and salvation.

From the foundation of the world you made provision for our bad choices and disobedience. From Genesis 3:15 we were scheduled to constantly battle with satan the deceiver and his agents. As you said through Abraham all nations can be saved. In Revelations 14:6 all those that dwell on the earth of every nation, kindred and language. You have sheep not in your chosen fold of Israel; but of whatever country or nation, Jew, Samaritan or Gentile, each can have access to you through the same strait narrow gate.

Father I kneel before you in humble adoration knowing nothing is impossible if it is thy will. That you can save anyone who proves they truly want to be saved in preference to the lusts, pleasures or comforts of this temporary world. Father I pray that you would consider me who is trying to find my way off the wide road of destruction followed by most, onto your narrow way which of those even seeking, few find.

Father throughout your bible it is stated adherence and obedience to your Commandments is the way of life. This directive being repeated by your prophets and Jesus, your son, own words. That we are to do His father's will, not contrary ones of family or friends. We wish to be Jesus' brethren, the ones that do your will. Jesus said He came to show us the way to you (that it can be done by those of flesh and blood). Mother will be against daughter, father against son, one family member against another. If one put family before him, they are not worthy of His kingdom. So if family or friends speak against your Sabbath commandment, refusing to go to your house on your day and put obstacles in my way, give me the courage to speak out and choose your will over theirs as whoever denies you and your commandments, you will deny them. Two will be in a field, in a bed, at work, i.e. close companions and family, yet one will be saved and other lost. If it must be so, let I be one of those saved in your kingdom. Let me put your commandments in my heart to lead me to you for I know the seventh day you set apart, sanctified for a holy convocation onto you.

Satan presents his deceptive message to us all in order for us to disobey you. Many are and will be deceived, even the very elect were it possible. Choosing your way would be against the norm. Let me not be deceived as Eve by the partial, misquote or mis-interpretation of your word. Help me, if necessary to stand alone for your commandments as did Elijah against a whole nation; king, queen, appointed prophets and false spiritual leaders. Empower me to isolate myself from false Sunday worship and, should I get weak, at least give equal if not more weigh and access to those who stand for your Sabbath as I may do to those advocating satan's deceptions. The deception originating from Sun and planetary worship of which you warned in Deut 4:19, 17:3 and other places. Which history proves did not come into Christian worship until hundred of years after the death of the apostles and thus your original bible. Thus make it obvious to me that the concept of your grace was not advocating breaking your laws, commandments or worshipping on a Sun day. As Paul said, "God forbid".

Open my understanding of Christian history that I become one who has an ear and hears, understanding and understands. That I would fill my time with looking at, reading and listening to confirmation of your Sabbath and commandments and not leave any gap in my mind or heart into which the deceiver can enter, occupy, cause doubt and make ineffective your true message. Change any selfish ways into selflessness, any desire to please self into conviction to please you. Father many worship they know not what in the hope it is you. Let my worship be not only in spirit, i.e. intention; but also in truth, in your Sabbath system and church not the deceiver's counterfeit. Fill me with a bubbling spring of your knowledge, constantly refreshing my belief in all your commandments. Do not let this spring become stagnant through abstaining from those who preach your commandments, nor get polluted by listening to those who speak for a change.

Lord though I, your child has been barren from the true knowledge of your ways, strengthen me not to be saddened or fret by any provocation of those ignorant to your ways. Give unto me a worthy portion of your Holy Spirit. Move me to be newly converted to your ways. From this new conversion, let me give birth to believers in your pure ways (as that of young Samuel) through the spreading of your word. Lastly, father, I ask you give me peace, contentment joy, your protection and wisdom. I ask these things in Jesus Christ's name.   Amen.

For a broader insight into the historic position, a book titled National Sunday Law by A. Jan Marcussen, which can be read in two hours and cost a mere £1 can be purchase from sabbathstudy@hotmail.com

This Book does not advocate changing from Christianity to any other religion, as they may be more flawed. Simply returning to true and original Christ like practices. Please give it a wide distribution. For an email version send your email to that above.

APPENDIX A

In the Council of Toulouse, the church leaders ruled "We prohibit laymen possessing copies of the Old and New Testament ... We forbid them most severely to have the above books in the popular vernacular." "The lords of the district shall carefully seek out the heretics in dwellings, hovels, and forests and even their underground retreats shall be entirely wiped out." Council Tolosanum, Pope Gregory IX, anno. Chr 1229

APPENDIX B

The second Council of Nicea ... AD. 787, was called to establish image worship in the church. This council is recorded in Ecclesiastical Annals by Baronius, Vol 9, pp. 391-407. (Antwerp, 1612); and Charles J. Hefele, A History of the Councils of the Church from the Original Documents, book 18, chapter 1.

J. Mendham, in The Seventh General Council, the Second of Nicea. Introduction, pgs iii-vi, says "The worship of images ... was one of those corruptions of Christianity which crept into the church stealthily and almost without notice and observation. This corruption did not, like other heresies, develop itself at once, for in that case it would have met with decided censure and rebuke. Images were first introduced into churches, not to be worshipped; but either in place of books to give instruction to those who could not read, or to excite devotion in the minds of... but it was found that images brought into churches darkened rather than enlightened the minds of the ignorant – degraded rather than exalted the devotion of the worshiper."

APPENDIX C

The following extracts are from authoritative works by Catholic dignitaries concerning the title and position of their leader." All the names which are attributed to Christ in Scripture, implying His supremacy over the church, are also attributed to the Pope," Bellamin, "On the Authority of Councils" book 2, chapter 17.

"For though art the shepherd, thou art the physician, thou art the director, thou art the husbandman, finally thou art another god on earth". Labbe and Cossart's "History of the Councils," Vol XIV, col. 109.

For the title "Lord God the Pope," see a gloss on the Extravagantes of Pope John XXII, title 14, Declaramus.

In an Antwerp edition of the Extravagantes, the words "Dominum Deum Nostrum Papam" ("Our Lord god the Pope") occur in column 153.In a Paris edition they occur in column 140.

"Hence the Pope is crowned with a triple crown, as king of heaven, and earth and purgatory." Pompta Bibliotheca, Feraris, Vol. VI, Pg. 26, article "Papa".

In a passage which is included in the Roman Catholic Canon Law, Pope Innocent III declares that the Roman pontiff is "the vicegerent upon earth, not a mere man, but of very god;" and in a gloss on the passage it is explained that this is because he is the vicegerent of Christ, Who is "Very God and very man." See Decretales Domini

Gregorii Papae IX (Decretales of the Lord Pope Gregory IX), liberi, de translatione Episcoporum, (on the transference of Bishops), title 7, chapter 3; Corpus Juris Canonice (2nd Leipzig ed., 1881), col. 99; (Paris, 1612), tom. 2, Decretales, col. 205.

APPENDIX D

"Although the ten commandments are found in the Roman Catholic Versions of the Scriptures, yet the faithful are instructed from the catechisms of the church and not from the bible. As it appears in these, (catechisms) the commandments of God has been changed and virtually re-acted by the papacy. The second commandment which forbids the making of and bowing down to images, is omitted in the Catholic catechisms and the tenth, which forbids coveting, is divided into two". Washington Review 1942.

APPENDIX E

Exodus 23:14 sets out three of the seven annual feasts of God's people. At these times in the year the people were to make appearances before God. See Lev 23:16,17, 33-36.They are the Feast of Unleavened Bread (which was closely associated with the Passover; see Ex 12:1-11, 14-20; Lev 23:4-8; Deut 16: 1-8), the Feast of Harvest or Firstfruits (later called the Feast of Weeks and in N.T times known as Pentecost [see Lev 23:9-14; Deut 16:9-12]), and the Feast of Ingathering (later called the Feast of Tabernacle; see Lev 23:33-36, 39-43, Deut 16:13-15).

APPENDIX F

Suggested reading on this subject.

New versions and Old Heresies by Prof Walter Veith of Total Onslaught producers. See Utube on internet

From Sabbath to Sunday by Dr S. Bacchiocchi also Sabbath Under Crossfire

National Sunday Law by A. Jan Marcussen

Ten Commandments Twice Removed. By Danny Shelton and Shelley Quinn

Internet web sites and television links: ████████████████████████
www.inthebeginningseries.com www.sabbathtruth.com

APPENDIX G

I cannot list all Sabbath keeping churches; but for the denomination with branches worldwide go to www.ssnet.org   For more information on the Sabbath one can try www.seventhdaybaptist.org

Appendix H

Let us not be fooled, like Eve, by Satan's logic which he is so skilfully repeating today, "Yea, hath God said...." How do you know this is the Word of God? ....Come, try this new version and your eyes will be opened...." Rather, my brethren, let the Word of God stand as it is.

Let not human wisdom presume to lessen the force of one statement from the scriptures.

A List of Bible Verses Omitted from Most Recent Bible Versions.

Matthew 17:21 Howbeit this kind goeth not out but by prayer and fasting.
Matthew 18:11 For the Son of man is come to save that which is lost.
Mark 7:16 If any man has ears to hear, let him hear.
Mark 9:44 & 46 Where their worm dieth not, and the fire is not quenched.
Mark 11:26 But if ye do not forgive, neither will your Father which is in heaven forgive your trespasses.
Mark 15:28 And the scripture was fulfilled, which saith, And He was numbered with the transgressors.
Luke 17:36 Two men shall be in the field; the one shall be taken, and the other left.
John 5:4 For an angel went down at a certain season into the pool, and troubled the water: whosoever then first after the troubling of the water stepped in was made whole of whatsoever disease he had.
Acts 8:37 And Philip said, If thou believest with all thine heart, thou mayest. And he answered and said, I believe that Jesus Christ is the Son of God.
Acts 15:34 Notwithstanding it pleased Silas to abide there still.
Acts 24:7 But the chief captain Lysias came upon us, and with great violence took him away out of our hands.
Acts 28:29 And when he had said these words, the Jews departed, and had great reasoning among themselves.
Romans 16:24 The grace of our Lord Jesus Christ be with you all. Amen.
1 John 5:7 For there are three that bear record in heaven, the Father, the Word, and the Holy Ghost: and these three are one.

These are a sample of verses which have portions omitted in most modern versions:

Matthew 5:27, 5:44, 6:13, 15:6, 15:8, 19:9, 19:20, 20:7, 20:16,24;36 20:22, 20:23, 22:13, 23:4, 25:13, 26:3, 26:60, 27:35, 25:2, 28:9, **Mark** 1:14, I:42;2:17 3:5, 3:15, 6:11, 6:33, 6:36, 7:2, 7:8, 8:9, 8:26, 9:8, 9:45, 9:49, 10:7, 10:21, 10:24, 11:8, 11:10, 11:23, 12:23, 12:29, 12:30,12:33, 13:11, 13:14, 14:19, 14:27, 14:68, 14:70, 15:3, **Luke:** 1:28, 1:29, 2:14,42, 4:4, 4:18, 5:38, 7:31, 8:43, 8:45, 8:48, 8:54, 9:10, 9:54,   9:55, 9:56, 11:2, 11:4, 11:11, 11:44, 11:54, 12:39, 17:9, 18:24,19:45, 20:13, 20:23, 20:30, 22:31, 22:64, 22:43-4,68, 23:23, 23:38, 24:1 22:42, 24:46, **John** 1:27, 3:13, 3:15, 5:3, 5:16, 6:11, 6:22, 6:47, 8:9, 8:10, 8:59, 9:6, 10:14,26, 11:41, 12:1, 16:16, 17:12, 19:16, **Acts** 2:30, 3:11, 7:37, 9:5, 9:6, 10:6, 10:12, 10:21, 10:32, 13:42, 15:18, 15:24, 18:21, 20:15, 21:8, 21:22, 21:25, 22:9, 22:20, 23:9, 24:6, 24:8, 24:26, 26:30, 28:16, **Romans** 1:16, 8:1, 9:28, 10.15 11:6, 13:9, 14:6, 14:21, 15:24, 15:29, **1 Corinthians** 6:20, 10:28, 11:24, **Galatians** 3:1, **Ephesians** 3:14, 5:30, **Philippians** 3:16, **Colossians** 1:2, 3:6, **1 Thessalonians** 1:1, **1 Timothy** 3:3, 6:5, 6:7, 6:19, **2 Timothy**: 1:11; 3:16; 4:1,

Hebrews:2:7, 3:6, 7:21, 8:12, 10:30, 10:34, 11:11, 11:13, 12:20, **1Peter** 1:22;4:3;4:14, **2Peter** 3:10, **1John** 4:3, 5:13, **Revelation** 1:8, 1:11, 5:14, 11:1, 11:17, 14:5, 15:2, 21:24. 22:1 4

Hello... yes, this is the Bible book shop ... Well, we have a version for every belief. I'm sure we can find one to prove your doctrine is correct!

Appendix I

FORTY-EIGHT changes by the Roman Catholic Church to take Christian worship away from God and to them, their leader (Pope) and directives. They seek to change God's Laws and times.

1-Prayers for the dead **Begins about**	**A.D.** 300
2-Making the sign of the cross . ,	300
3-Wax candles . . . ." " About	**A.D.** 320
4-Veneration of angels and dead saints . . , , ,	375
5-The use of images . . , . , , , , ,	375
6-The Mass as a daily celebration . . ~ ~ ~ .	394
7-Beginning of the exaltation of Mary: the term "Mother of God" first applied to her by the Council of Ephesus .	431
8-Priests begin to dress differently from laymen.	500
9-Extreme Unction	526
10-The doctrine of Purgatory is established by Gregory I. . .	593
11-Latin language used in prayer and worship is commanded by Gregory I.	600
12-Prayers directed to Mary, dead saints and the angels. . ~	600
13-Title of pope (bishop of the universe) given to Boniface III by the Emperor Phocas , . , , , .	607
14-Kissing the pope's foot, begins with Pope Constantine . 709	
15-Temporal power of the popes is conferred by Pepin, king of the Franks . .	750
16-Worship of the crass, images and relics is now officially authorized .	786
17-Holy water (mixed with a pinch of salt and blessed by a priest) come into use 850	
18-Worship of St. Joseph . . . . " " , " "	890
19-The College of Cardinals is established . ,	927
20-Baptism of bells is instituted by Pope John XlII .	965
21-The canonization of dead saints is first done by Pope John XV	995
22-Fasting on Fridays and during "Lent" begins . .	998
23-The Mass has gradually developed into a "sacrifice"and attendance is now made obligatory . . .	1050
24-The Celibacy of the priesthood is required by Pope Gregory II (Hildebrand) 1079	
25-The Rosary a mechanical praying with beads is invented by Peter the Hermit1090	
26-The Inquisition, in operation for centuries, is now made official by the Council of Verona . . . . , ,	1184
27-The sale of Indulgences (certificate of forgiveness of sins) begins ,	1190

28-The error of Transubstantiation is proclaimed by Pope Innocent III as
the power to bring down God out of heaven into a cup and wafer, .., ., , 1215
29-Auricular Confession of sins to a priest, instead of To God, is instituted
by Pope Innocent III in the Lateran Council. 215
30-The Adoration of ~the wafer ~(Host) is decreed by Pope Honorius III 1220
31-Laymen are officially forbidden to have or read the Bible –
It is placed on the "Index of Forbidden Books" by the Council of Valencia. 1229
32-Protection by a piece of cloth, the Scapular is invented by Simon Stock,
a British monk 1251
33-Laymen are forbidden to drink the Cup at Communion, by order of the
Council of Constance .. . 1414
34-Purgatory is proclaimed as a dogma by the Council of Florence . . 1439
35-The doctrine of Seven Sacraments is affirmed on pain of mortal sin. . 1439
36-The first part of the "Ave~Maria'º saying is made official. .. 1508
37-The Jesuit order is founded by Ignatius Loyola . . 1534
38-Tradition (the sayings of popes and councils) is declared to be equal in
authority with the Bible, by the Council of Trent 1545
39-The Apocryphal books are added to the Bible by the Council of Trent 1546
40-The Creed of Pope Pius IV is imposed as the official creed of the Church . 1560
41 -The last part of the "Ave Maria" has been prepared, and is required of the
faithful by Pope Sixtus V . 1593
42-The Immaculate Conception of the Virgin Mary is proclaimed by
Pope Pius IX . . .. .1854
43-The "Syllabus of Errors" is proclaimed by Pope Pius X, and ratified by the
First Vatican Council, as the truth of God. (!t condemns freedom of religion,
speech, press, and all scientific discoveries that have not been approved by
the church) 1864
44-The temporal Authority of the pope over all rulers is officially reaffirmed. . .1864
45-The absolute Infallibility of the pope in all matters of faith and morals is
proclaimed by Vatican I . . 1870
46-Public schools are condemned by Pope Pius XI . . 1930
47-The Assumption of the Virgin Mary (bodily ascension into heaven
shortly after her death) is proclaimed by Pope Pius XII 1950
48-Mary is proclaimed to be the Mother of God, by Pope Paul VI. 1965
The above is taken from the second printed publication of "The Great Controversy" by
E.G. White. I am not sure if it is in newer publications. At the time of print it stated
"Two additional doctrines are now being discussed, and may soon be adopted: Mary as
the Mediatrix of mankind. This means that God and Christ can only be approached
through her. The second is the dogma of Mary as the Co-redemptrix of the world. The
thought here is that the redemption of our race, from start to finish, is done through
Mary, working together at each step with Christ.". [Note Mary's name was given to the
pagan Queen of Heaven, wife of Nimrod the man against God in Gen 10:9. "Before" =
against)

Solution to sequences: 1) 12, 14, 28, 30, 60, 62, **124, 126**   2) ab, ad, de, dg, gh, gj, **jk, jm**

For number 1) some of you may have put 64, 66. Or maybe 70, 72. Your solution would depend on how you were trained or untrained to solve problems. Taking the obvious answer, giving it more thought or guessing. To assert the future, whether sales targets or an individual's behaviour, knowing the past helps get a better prediction. In short, it is based on identifying the pattern and continuing the same. To fully understand what God requires of us we ought to know what he required of our ancestors since time began. Get a continuous history without gaps and then do the same. Of course this does not mean following their mistakes; but avoiding them.

The Old and New Testaments describe the same person. Imagine a court trial that last three months. The prosecution's bundle of documents may be three feet high and similar for the defence. Taking any number of documents from, say the prosecution's, would make you think the person is guilty. Or innocent if read any of the thousand of pages from the defence pile. Though both piles describe the same event or person, one needs to thoroughly understand both piles as a combination to arrive at the truth.

Glossary of Bible verses *In Alphabetical Order.*

Unfortunately, due to the vast number of scripture quoted and the number of pages needed, some have been omitted where it is thought other bible versions would not change the meaning. However, you are reminded to use the King James where possible.

Try just reading verses from start to end and get the message they depict. One rule of salvation for all humans regardless of generation, kindred, nation or tongue.

Act 1:19 And it was known unto all the dwellers at Jerusalem; so that field is called in their proper tongue, Aceldama, that is to say, The field of blood.

Act 2:1   And when the day of Pentecost was fully come, they were all with one accord in one place.

Act 2:8 And how hear we every man in our own tongue, wherein we were born?

Act 2:15 For these are not drunken, as ye suppose, seeing it is *but* the third hour of the day.

Act 2:31 He seeing this before spake of the resurrection of Christ, that his soul was not left in hell, neither his flesh did see corruption.

Act 7:42 Then God turned, and gave them up to worship the host of heaven; as it is written in the book of the prophets, O ye house of Israel, have ye offered to me slain beasts and sacrifices *by the space of?* forty years in the wilderness?

Act 8:1 And Saul was consenting unto his death. And at that time there was a great persecution against the church which was at Jerusalem; and they were all scattered abroad throughout the regions of Judaea and Samaria, except the apostles.

Act 8:9 But there was a certain man, called Simon, which beforetime in the same city used sorcery, and bewitched the people of Samaria, giving out that himself was some great one:

Act 8:13 Then Simon himself believed also: and when he was baptized, he continued with Philip, and wondered, beholding the   miracles and signs which were done.

Act 8:14 Now when the apostles which were at Jerusalem heard that Samaria had received the word of God, they sent unto them Peter and John:

Act 8:15 Who, when they were come down, prayed for them, that they might receive the Holy Ghost:

Act 8:16 (For as yet he was fallen upon none of them: only they were baptized in the name of the Lord Jesus.)

Act 8:17 Then laid they *their* hands on them, and they received the Holy Ghost.

Act 8:18 And when Simon saw that through laying on of the apostles hands the Holy Ghost was given, he offered them money,

Act 8:19 Saying, Give me also this power, that on whomsoever I lay hands, he may receive the Holy Ghost.

Act 8:20 But Peter said unto him, Thy money perish with thee, because thou hast thought that the gift of God may be purchased with money.

Act 8:27 And he arose and went: and, behold, a man of Ethiopia, an eunuch of great authority under Candace queen of the Ethiopians, who had the charge of all her treasure, and had come to Jerusalem for to worship,

Act 8:28 Was returning, and sitting in his chariot read Esaias the prophet.

Act 8:32 -5 The place of the scripture which he read was this, He was led as a sheep to the slaughter; and like a lamb dumb before his shearer, so opened he not his mouth: In his humiliation his judgment was taken away: and who shall declare his generation? for his life is taken from the earth. And the eunuch answered Philip, and said, I pray thee, of whom speaketh the prophet this? of himself, or of some other man? Then Philip opened his mouth, and began at the same scripture, and preached unto him Jesus

Act 8:37 And Philip said, If thou believest with all thine heart, thou mayest. And he answered and said, I believe that Jesus Christ is the Son of God.

Act 13:14 But when they departed from Perga, they came to Antioch in Pisidia, and went into the synagogue on the Sabbath day, and sat down.

Act 13:42 And when the Jews were gone out of the synagogue, the Gentiles besought that these words might be preached to them the next Sabbath.

Act 14:9 The same heard Paul speak: who stedfastly beholding him, and perceiving that he had faith to be healed,

Act 15:1   And certain men which came down from Judaea taught the brethren, *and said*, Except ye be circumcised after the manner of Moses, ye cannot be saved.

Act 15:2 When therefore Paul and Barnabas had no small dissension & disputation with them, they determined that Paul and Barnabas, and certain other of them, should go up to Jerusalem unto the apostles and elders about this question.

Act 15:24 Forasmuch as we have heard, that certain which went out from us have troubled you with words, subverting your souls, saying, Ye must be circumcised, and keep the law: to whom we gave no such commandment:

Act 17:25 Neither is worshipped with men's hands, as though he needed any thing, seeing he giveth to all life, and breath, and all things;

Act 17:29 Forasmuch then as we are the offspring of God, we ought not to think that the Godhead is like unto gold, or silver, or stone, graven by art and man's device.

Act 18:21 But bade them farewell, saying, I must by all means keep this feast that cometh in Jerusalem: but I will return again unto you, if God will. And he sailed from Ephesus.

Act 19:5 When they heard *this*, they were baptized in the name of the Lord Jesus.

Act 20:16 For Paul had determined to sail by Ephesus, because he would not spend the time in Asia: for he hasted, if it were possible for him, to be at Jerusalem the day of Pentecost.

Act 20:22 And now, behold, I go bound in the spirit unto Jerusalem, not knowing the things that shall befall me there:

Act 21:11 And when he was come unto us, he took Paul's girdle, and bound is own hands and feet, and said, Thus saith the Holy Ghost, So shall the Jews at Jerusalem bind the man that owneth this girdle, and shall deliver *him* into the hands of the Gentiles.

Act 21:24 Them take, and purify thyself with them, and be at charges with them, that they may shave *their* heads: and all may know that those things, whereof they were informed concerning thee, are nothing; but *that* thou thyself also walkest orderly, and keepest the law.

Act 21:40 And when he had given him licence, Paul stood on the stairs, and beckoned with the hand unto the people. And when there was made a great silence, he spake unto *them* in the Hebrew tongue, saying,

Act 23:12 And when it was day, certain of the Jews banded together, and bound themselves under a curse, saying that they would neither eat nor drink till they had killed Paul.

Act 24:5 For we have found this man *a* pestilent *fellow*, and a mover of sedition among all the Jews throughout the world, and a ring leader of the sect of the Nazarenes:

Act 24:11 Because that thou mayest understand, that there are yet but twelve days since I went up to Jerusalem for to worship.

Act 25:9 But Festus, willing to do the Jews a pleasure, answered Paul, and said, Wilt thou go up to Jerusalem, and there be judged of these things before me

Act 25:10 Then said Paul, I stand at Caesar's judgment seat, where I ought to be judged: to the Jews have I done no wrong, as thou very well knowest.

Act 25:11 I be an offender, or have committed any thing worthy of death, I refuse not to die: but if there be none of these things whereof these accuse me, no man may deliver me unto them. I appeal unto Caesar.

Act 25:12 Then Festus, when he had conferred with the council, answered, Hast thou appealed unto Caesar? unto Caesar shalt thou go.

Act 26:20 But shewed first unto them of Damascus, and at Jerusalem, and throughout all the coasts of Judaea, and *then* to the Gentiles, that they should repent and turn to God, and do works meet for repentance.

Act 26:21 For these causes the Jews caught me in the temple and went to kill *me*.

Act 26:22 Having therefore obtained help of God, I continue unto this day, witnessing both to small and great, saying none other things than those which the prophets and Moses did say should come:

Act 26:23 That Christ should suffer, *and* that he should be the first that should rise from the dead, and should shew light unto the people, and to the Gentiles.

Act 28:17 And it came to pass, that after three days Paul called the chief of the Jews together: and when they were come together, he said unto them, Men *and* brethren, though I have committed nothing against the people, or customs of our fathers, yet was I delivered prisoner from Jerusalem into the hands of the Romans.

Amo 5:21 I hate, I despise your feast days, and I will not smell in your solemn assemblies.

Amo 5:22 Though ye offer me burnt offerings and your meat offerings, I will not accept *them*: neither will I regard the peace offerings of your fat beasts.

Amo 5:23 Take thou away from me the noise of thy songs; for I will not hear the melody of thy viols.

1Ch 13:9 And when they came unto the threshingfloor of Chidon, Uzza put forth his hand to hold the ark; for the oxen stumbled

1Ch 17:6 Wheresoever I have walked with all Israel, spake I a word to any of the judges of Israel, whom I commanded to feed my people, saying, Why have ye not built me an house of cedars?

1Ch 17:21 And what one nation in the earth *is* like thy people Israel, whom God went to redeem *to be* his own people, to make thee a name of greatness and terribleness, by driving out nations from before thy people, whom thou hast redeemed out of Egypt?

1Ch 17:22 For thy people Israel didst thou make thine own people for ever; and thou, LORD, becamest their God.

2Ch 15:1 And the Spirit of God came upon Azariah the son of Oded:

2Ch 7:14 If my people, which are called by my name, shall humble them selves, and pray, and seek my face, and turn from their wicked ways; then will I hear from heaven, and will forgive their sin, and will heal their land.

2Ch 19:10 And what cause soever shall come to you of your brethren that dwell in their cities, between blood and blood, between law and commandment, statutes and judgments, ye shall even warn them that they trespass not against the LORD, and *so* wrath come upon you, and upon your brethren: this do, and ye shall not trespass.

2Ch 24:20 And the Spirit of God came upon Zechariah the son of Jehoiada the priest, which stood above the people, and said unto them, Thus say God, Why transgress ye the commandments of the LORD, that ye cannot prosper? because ye have forsaken the LORD, he hath also forsaken you.

2Ch 26:4 And he did *that which was* right in the sight of the LORD, according to all that his father Amaziah did.

2Ch 26:18 And they withstood Uzziah the king, and said unto him, *It appertaineth* not unto thee, Uzziah, to burn incense unto the LORD, but to the priests the sons of Aaron, that are consecrated to burn incense: go out of the sanctuary; for thou hast trespassed; neither *shall it be* for thine honour from the LORD God.

2Ch 26:19 Then Uzziah was wroth, and *had* a censer in his hand to burn incense: and while he was wroth with the priests, the leprosy even rose up in his forehead before the priests in the house of the LORD, from beside the incense altar.

Col 1:16 For by him were all things created, that are in heaven, and that are in earth, visible and invisible, whether *they be* thrones, or dominions, or principalities, or powers: all things were created by him, and for him:

Col 2:18 Let no man beguile you of your reward in a voluntary humility and worshipping of angels, intruding into those things which he hath not seen, vainly puffed up by his fleshly mind,

Col 2:19 And not holding the Head, from which all the body by joints and bands having nourishment ministered, and knit together, increaseth with the increase of God.

Col 2:20 Wherefore if ye be dead with Christ from the rudiments of the world, why, as though living in the world, are ye subject to ordinances,

Col 2:21 (Touch not; taste not; handle not;

Col 2:22 Which all are to perish with the using;) after the commandments and doctrines of men?

Col 3:9 Lie not one to another, seeing that ye have put off the old man with his deeds;

1Co 1:30 But of him are ye in Christ Jesus, who of God is made unto us wisdom, and righteousness, and sanctification, and redemption: 1Cor 2:6 Howbeit we speak wisdom among them that are perfect: yet not the wisdom of this world, nor of the princes of this world, that come to nought:

1Co 2:7 But we speak the wisdom of God in a mystery, *even* the hidden *wisdom*, which God ordained before the world unto our glory:

1Cor 2:8 Which none of the princes of this world knew: for had they known *it*, they would not have crucified the Lord of glory.

1Co 7:19 Circumcision is nothing, and uncircumcision is nothing, but the keeping of the commandments of God.

1Co 9:21 To them that are without law, as without law, (being not without law to God, but under the law to Christ,) that I might gain them that are without law.

1Cor 9:22 To the weak became I as weak, that I might gain the weak: I am made all things to all *men*, that I might by all means save some.

1Cor 12:13 For by one Spirit are we all baptized into one body, whether *we be* Jews or Gentiles, whether *we be* bond or free; and have been all made to drink into one Spirit.

1Co 13:3 And though I bestow all my goods to feed *the poor*, and though I give my body to be burned, and have not charity, it profiteth me nothing.

1Co 14:22 Wherefore tongues are for a sign, not to them that believe, but to them that believe not: but prophesying *serveth* not for them that believe not, but for them which believe.

1Co 14:23 If therefore the whole church be come together into one place, and all speak with tongues, and there come in *those that are* unlearned, or unbelievers, will they not say that ye are mad?

1Co 15:20 But now is Christ risen from the dead, *and* become the firstfruits of them that slept.

1Co 15:30 And why stand we in jeopardy every hour?

2Co 5:7 (For we walk by faith, not by sight:)

2Co 6:16 And what agreement hath the temple of God with idols? for ye are the temple of the living God; as God hath said, I will dwell in them, and walk in *them*; and I will be their God, and they shall be my people.

2Co 11:14 And no marvel; for Satan himself is transformed into an angel of light.

2Co 11:15 Therefore *it is* no great thing if his ministers also be transformed as the ministers of righteousness; whose end shall be according to their works.

Dan 1:7 Unto whom the prince of the eunuchs gave names: for he gave unto Daniel *the name* of Belteshazzar; and to Hananiah, of Shadrach; and to Mishael, of Meshach; and to Azariah, of Abednego.

Dan 1:8 But Daniel purposed in his heart that he would not defile himself with the portion of the king's meat, nor with the wine which he drank: therefore he requested of the prince of the eunuchs that he might not defile himself.

Deu 1:16 And I charged your judges at that time, saying, Hear *the causes* between your brethren, and judge righteously between *every* man and his brother, and the stranger *that is* with him.

Dan 3:17 If it be *so*, our God whom we serve is able to deliver us from the burning fiery furnace, and he will deliver *us* out of thine hand, O king.

Dan 3:18 But if not, be it known unto thee, O king, that we will not serve thy gods, nor worship the golden image which thou hast set up.

Deu 4:2 Ye shall not add unto the word which I command you, neither shall ye diminish *ought* from it, that ye may keep the commandments of the LORD your God which I command you.

Dan 7:25 And he shall speak *great* words against the most High, and shall wear out the saints of the most High, and think to change times and laws: and they shall be given into his hand until a time and times and the dividing of time.

Dan 9:5 We have sinned, and have committed iniquity, and have done wickedly, and have rebelled, even by departing from thy precepts and from thy judgments:

Dan 9:6 Neither have we hearkened unto thy servants the prophets, which spake in thy name to our kings, our princes, and our   fathers, and to all the people of the land.

Dan 9:7 O Lord, righteousness *belongeth* unto thee, but unto us confusion of faces, as at this day; to the men of Judah, and to the inhabitants of Jerusalem, and unto all Israel, *that are* near, and *that are* far off, through all the countries whither thou hast driven them, because of their trespass that they have trespassed against thee.

Dan 9:8 O Lord, to us *belongeth* confusion of face, to our kings, to our princes, and to our fathers, because we have sinned against thee.

Dan 9:9 To the Lord our God *belong* mercies and forgivenesses, though we have rebelled against him;

Dan 9:10 Neither have we obeyed the voice of the LORD our God, to walk in his laws, which he set before us by his servants the prophets.

Dan 9:11 Yea, all Israel have transgressed thy law, even by departing, that they might not obey thy voice; therefore the curse is poured upon us, and the oath that *is* written in the law of Moses the servant of God, because we have sinned against him.

Dan 9:12 And he hath confirmed his words, which he spake against us, and against our judges that judged us, by bringing upon us a great evil: for under the whole heaven hath not been done as hath been done upon Jerusalem.

Dan 10:3 I ate no pleasant bread, neither came flesh nor wine in my mouth, neither did I anoint myself at all, till three whole weeks were fulfilled.

Deu 4:19 And lest thou lift up thine eyes unto heaven, and when thou seest the sun, and the moon, and the stars, *even* all the host of heaven, shouldest be driven to worship them, and serve them, which the LORD thy God hath divided unto all nations under the whole heaven.

Deu 5:31 But as for thee, stand thou here by me, and I will speak unto thee all the commandments, and the statutes, and the judgments, which thou shalt teach them, that they may do *them* in the land which I give them to possess it

Deu 6:5 And thou shalt love the LORD thy God with all thine heart, and with all thy soul, and with all thy might.

Deu 7:6 For thou *art* an holy people unto the LORD thy God: the LORD thy God hath chosen thee to be a special people unto himself, above all people that *are* upon the face of the earth.

Deu 7:7 The LORD did not set his love upon you, nor choose you, because ye were more in number than any people; for ye *were* the fewest of all people:

Deu 10:11 And the LORD said unto me, Arise, take *thy* journey before the people, that they may go in and possess the land, which I sware unto their fathers to give unto them.

Deu 10:17 For the LORD your God *is* God of gods, and Lord of lords, a great God, a mighty, and a terrible, which regardeth not persons, nor taketh reward:

Deu 12:8 Ye shall not do after all *the things* that we do here this day, every man whatsoever *is* right in his own eyes

Deu 12:13 Take heed to thyself that thou offer not thy burnt offerings in every place that thou seest:

Deu 13:2 And the sign or the wonder come to pass, whereof he spake unto thee, saying, Let us go after other gods, which thou hast not known, and let us serve them;

Deu 13:3 Thou shalt not hearken unto the words of that prophet, or that dreamer of dreams: for the LORD your God proveth you, to know whether ye love the LORD your God with all your heart and with all your soul.

Deu 13:4 Ye shall walk after the LORD your God, and fear him, and keep his commandments, and obey his voice, and ye shall serve him, and cleave unto him.

Deu 14:7 Nevertheless these ye shall not eat of them that chew the cud, or of them that divide the cloven hoof; *as* the camel, and the hare, and the coney: for they chew the cud, but divide not the hoof; *therefore* they *are* unclean unto you.

Deu 17:3 And hath gone and served other gods, and worshipped them, either the sun, or moon, or any of the host of heaven, which I have not commanded;

Deu 17:4 And it be told thee, and thou hast heard *of it*, and enquired diligently, and, behold, *it be* true, *and* the thing certain, *that* such abomination is wrought in Israel:

Deu 17:5 Then shalt thou bring forth that man or that woman, which have committed that wicked thing, unto thy gates, *even* that man or that woman, and shalt stone them with stones, till they die.

Deu 21:18 If a man have a stubborn and rebellious son, which will not obey the voice of his father, or the voice of his mother, and *that*, when they have chastened him, will not hearken unto them:

Deu 17:18 And it shall be, when he sitteth upon the throne of his kingdom, that he shall write him a copy of this law in a book out of *that which is* before the priests the Levites:

Deu 21:19 Then shall his father and his mother lay hold on him, and bring him out unto the elders of his city, and unto the gate of his place;

Deu 21:20 And they shall say unto the elders of his city, This our son *is* stubborn and rebellious, he will not obey our voice; *he is* a glutton and a drunkard.

Deu 21:21 And all the men of his city shall stone him with stones, that he die: so shalt thou put evil away from among you and all Israel shall hear and fear.

Deu 21:22 And if a man have committed a sin worthy of death, and he be to be put to death, and thou hang him on a tree:

Deu 23:5 Nevertheless the LORD thy God would not hearken unto Balaam; but the LORD thy God turned the curse into a blessing unto thee, because the LORD thy God loved thee.

Deu 23:24 When thou comest into thy neighbour's vineyard, then thou mayest eat grapes thy fill at thine own pleasure; but thou shalt not put *any* in thy vessel.

Deu 23:25 When thou comest into the standing corn of thy neighbour, then thou mayest pluck the ears with thine hand; but thou shalt not move a sickle unto thy neighbour's standing corn.

Deu 28:58 If thou wilt not observe to do all the words of this law that are written in this book, that thou mayest fear this glorious and fearful name, THE LORD THY GOD;

Deu 29:13 That he may establish thee to day for a people unto himself, and *that* he may be unto thee a God, as he hath said unto thee, and as he hath sworn unto thy fathers, to Abraham, to Isaac, and to Jacob.

Deu 29:14 Neither with you only do I make this covenant and this oath;

Deu 29:15 But with *him* that standeth here with us this day before the LORD our God, and also with *him* that *is* not here with us this day:

Deu 29:20 The LORD will not spare him, but then the anger of the LORD and his jealousy shall smoke against that man, and all the curses that are written in this book shall lie upon him, and the LORD shall blot out his name from under heaven.

Deu 31:19 Now therefore write ye this song for you, and teach it the children of Israel: put it in their mouths, that this song may be a witness for me against the children of Israel.

Deu 31:20 For when I shall have brought them into the land which I sware unto their fathers, that floweth with milk and honey; and they shall have eaten and filled themselves, and waxen fat; then will they turn unto other gods, and serve them, and provoke me, and break my covenant.

Deu 31:21 And it shall come to pass, when many evils and troubles are befallen them, that this song shall testify against them as a witness; for it shall not be forgot ten out of the mouths of their seed: for I know their imagination which they go about, even now, before I have brought them into the land which I sware.

Deu 31:24 And it came to pass, when Moses had made an end of writing the words of this law in a book, until they were finished,

Deu 31:26 Take this book of the law, and put it in the side of the ark of the covenant of the LORD your God, that it may be there for a witness against thee.

Eph 3:17 That Christ may dwell in your hearts by faith; that ye, being rooted and grounded in love,

Eph 4:28 Let him that stole steal no more: but rather let him labour, working with *his* hands the thing which is good, that he may have to give to him that needeth.

Eph 5:9 (For the fruit of the Spirit *is* in all goodness and righteousness and truth;)

Eph 6:12 For we wrestle not against flesh and blood, but against principalities, against powers, against the rulers of the darkness of this world, against spiritual wickedness in high *places*.

Est 3:2 And all the king's servants, that *were* in the king's gate, bowed, and reverenced Haman: for the king had so commanded concerning him. But Mordecai bowed not, nor did *him* reverence.

Est 3:3 Then the king's servants, which *were* in the king's gate, said unto Mordecai, Why transgressest thou the king's commandment?

Est 3:4 Now it came to pass, when they spake daily unto him, and he hearkened not unto them, that they told Haman, to see whether Mordecai's matters would stand: for he had told them that he *was* a Jew.

Est 3:5   And when Haman saw that Mordecai bowed not, nor did him reverence, then was Haman full of wrath.

Est 6:1   On that night could not the king sleep, and he commanded to bring the book of records of the chronicles; and they were read before the king.

Est 9:26   Wherefore they called these days Purim after the name of Pur. Therefore for all the words of this letter, and *of that* which they had seen concerning this matter, and which had come unto them,

Exo 3:7   And the LORD said, I have surely seen the affliction of my people which *are* in Egypt, and have heard their cry by reason of their taskmasters; for I know their sorrows;

Exo 4:25   Then Zipporah took a sharp stone, and cut off the foreskin of her son, and cast *it* at his feet, and said, Surely a bloody   husband *art* thou to me.

Exo 4:26   So he let him go: then she said, A bloody husband *thou art*, because of the circumcision.

Exo 7:2   Thou shalt speak all that I command thee: and Aaron thy brother shall speak unto Pharaoh, that he send the children of Israel out of his land.

Exo 12:5   Your lamb shall be without blemish, a male of the first year: ye shall take *it* out from the sheep, or from the goats:

Exo 12:8   And they shall eat the flesh in that night, roast with fire, and unleavened bread; *and* with bitter *herbs* they shall eat it.

Exo 12:14 And this day shall be unto you for a memorial; and ye shall keep it a feast to the LORD throughout your generations; ye shall keep it a feast by an ordinance for ever.

Exo 12:17 And ye shall observe *the feast of* unleavened bread; for in this selfsame day have I brought your armies out of the land of Egypt: therefore shall ye observe this day in your generations by an ordinance for ever.

Exo 12:19 Seven days shall there be no leaven found in your houses: for whosoever eateth that which is leavened, even that soul shall be cut off from the congregation of Israel, whether he be a stranger, or born in the land.

Exo 12:24 And ye shall observe this thing for an ordinance to thee and to thy sons for ever.

Exo 12:48 And when a stranger shall sojourn with thee, and will keep the passover to the LORD, let all his males be circumcised, and then let him come near and keep it; and he shall be as one that is born in the land: for no uncircumcised person shall eat thereof.

Exo 12:49 One law shall be to him that is homeborn, and unto the stranger that sojourneth among you.

Exo 15:1   Then sang Moses and the children of Israel this song unto the LORD, and spake, saying, I will sing unto the LORD, for he hath triumphed gloriously: the horse and his rider hath he thrown into the sea.

Exo 15:25 And he cried unto the LORD; and the LORD shewed him a tree, *which* when he had cast into the waters, the waters were made sweet: there he made for them a statute and an ordinance, and there he proved them,

Exo 16:4 Then said the LORD unto Moses, Behold, I will rain bread from heaven for you; and the people shall go out and gather a certain rate every day, that I may prove them, whether they will walk in my law, or no.

Exo 16:5 And it shall come to pass, that on the sixth day they shall prepare *that* which they bring in; and it shall be twice as much as they gather daily.

Exo 16:5 And it shall come to pass, that on the sixth day they shall prepare *that* which they bring in; and it shall be twice as much as they gather daily.

Exo 16:28 And the LORD said unto Moses, How long refuse ye to keep my commandments and my laws?

Exo 17:6 Behold, I will stand before thee there upon the rock in Horeb; and thou shalt smite the rock, and there shall come water out of it, that the people may drink. And Moses did so in the sight of the elders of Israel.

Exo 17:14 And the LORD said unto Moses, Write this *for* a memorial in a book, and rehearse *it* in the ears of Joshua: for I will utterly put out the remembrance of Amalek from under heaven.

Exo 19:13 There shall not an hand touch it, but he shall surely be stoned, or shot through; whether *it be* beast or man, it shall not live: when the trumpet soundeth long, they shall come up to the mount.

Exo 20:1 And God spake all these words, saying,

Exo 20:2 I *am* the LORD thy God, which have brought thee out of the land of Egypt, out of the house of bondage.

Exo 20:3 Thou shalt have no other gods before me.

Exo 20:4 Thou shalt not make unto thee any graven image, or any likeness *of any thing* that *is* in heaven above, or that *is* in the earth beneath, or that *is* in the water under the earth:

Exo 20:5 Thou shalt not bow down thyself to them, nor serve them: for I the LORD thy God *am* a jealous God, visiting the iniquity of the fathers upon the children unto the third and fourth *generation* of them that hate me;

Exo 20:6 And shewing mercy unto thousands of them that love me, and keep my commandments.

Exo 20:7 Thou shalt not take the name of the LORD thy God in vain; for the LORD will not hold him guiltless that taketh his name in vain.

Exo 20:8 Remember the Sabbath day, to keep it holy.

Exo 20:9 Six days shalt thou labour, and do all thy work:

Exo 20:10 But the seventh day *is* the Sabbath of the LORD thy God: *in it* thou shalt not do any work, thou, nor thy son, nor thy daughter, thy manservant, nor thy maidservant, nor thy cattle, nor thy stranger that *is* within thy gates:

Exo 20:11 For *in* six days the LORD made heaven and earth, the sea, and all that in them *is*, and rested the seventh day: wherefore the LORD blessed the Sabbath day, and hallowed it.

Exo 20:12 Honour thy father and thy mother: that thy days may be long upon the land which the LORD thy God giveth thee.

Exo 20:13 Thou shalt not kill.

Exo 20:14 Thou shalt not commit adultery.

Exo 20:15 Thou shalt not steal.

Exo 20:16 Thou shalt not bear false witness against thy neighbour.

Exo 20:17 Thou shalt not covet thy neighbour's house, thou shalt not covet thy neighbour's wife, nor his manservant, nor his maidservant, nor his ox, nor his ass, nor any thing that *is* thy neighbour's.

Exo 23:7 Keep thee far from a false matter; and the innocent and righteous slay thou not: for I will not justify the wicked.

Exo 23:14 Three times thou shalt keep a feast unto me in the year.

Exo 23:16 And the feast of harvest, the firstfruits of thy labours, which thou hast sown in the field: and the feast of ingathering, *which is* in the end of the year, when thou hast gathered in thy labours out of the field.

Exo 23:19 The first of the firstfruits of thy land thou shalt bring into the house of the LORD thy God. Thou shalt not seethe a kid in his mother's milk.

Exo 24:7 And he took the book of the covenant, and read in the audience of the people: and they said, All that the LORD hath said will we do, and be obedient.

Exo 24:12 And the LORD said unto Moses, Come up to me into the mount, and be there: and I will give thee tables of stone, and a law, and commandments which I have written; that thou mayest teach Exo 25:14 And thou shalt put the staves into the rings by the sides of the ark, that the ark may be borne with them.

Exo 29:36 And thou shalt offer every day a bullock *for* a sin offering for atonement: and thou shalt cleanse the altar, when thou hast made an atonement for it, and thou shalt anoint it, to sanctify it.

Exo 29:39 The one lamb thou shalt offer in the morning; and the other lamb thou shalt offer at even:

Exo 32:19 And it came to pass, as soon as he came nigh unto the camp, that he saw the calf, and the dancing: and Moses' anger waxed hot, and he cast the tables out of his hands, and brake them beneath the mount.

Exo 32:26 Then Moses stood in the gate of the camp, and said, Who *is* on the LORD'S side? *let him come* unto me. And all the sons of Levi gathered themselves together unto him.

Eze 8:14 Then he brought me to the door of the gate of the LORD'S house which *was* toward the north; and, behold, there sat women weeping for Tammuz.

Eze 8:15 Then said he unto me, Hast thou seen *this*, O son of man? turn thee yet again, *and* thou shalt see greater abominations than these.

Eze 8:16 And he brought me into the inner court of the LORD'S house, and, behold, at the door of the temple of the LORD, between the porch and the altar, *were* about five and twenty men, with their backs toward the temple of the LORD, and their faces toward the east; and they worshipped the sun toward the east.

Eze 14:20 Though Noah, Daniel, and Job, *were* in it, *as* I live, saith the Lord GOD, they shall deliver neither son nor daughter; they shall *but* deliver their own souls by their righteousness.

Eze 16:24 *That* thou hast also built unto thee an eminent place and hast made thee a high place in every street. v16:25 Thou hast built thy high place at every head of the way, and hast made thy beauty to be abhorred, Eze 16:26 Thou hast also committed fornication with the Egyptians thy neighbours, great of flesh; and hast increased thy whoredoms, to provoke me to anger.

Eze 18:20 The soul that sin, it shall die. The son shall not bear the iniquity of the father, neither shall the father bear the iniquity of the son: the righteousness of the righteous shall be upon him, and the wickedness of the wicked shall be upon him.

Eze 13:3 Thus saith the Lord GOD; Woe unto the foolish prophets, that follow their own spirit, and have seen nothing!

Eze 22:25 *There is* a conspiracy of her prophets in the midst thereof, like a roaring lion ravening the prey; they have devoured souls; they have taken the treasure and precious things; they have made her many widows in the midst thereof.

Eze 22:26 Her priests have violated my law, and have profaned mine holy things: they have put no difference between the holy and profane, neither have they shewed *difference* between the unclean and the clean, and have hid their eyes from my sabbaths, and I am profaned among them.

Eze 28:3 Behold, thou *art* wiser than Daniel; there is no secret that they can hide from thee:

Eze 33:13 When I shall say to the righteous, *that* he shall surely live; if he trust to his own righteousness, and commit iniquity, all his righteousnesses shall not be remembered; but for his iniquity that he hath committed, he shall die for it.

Eze 33:14 Again, when I say unto the wicked, Thou shalt surely die; if he turn from his sin, and do that which is lawful and right;

Eze 33:15 *If* the wicked restore the pledge, give again that he had robbed, walk in the statutes of life, without committing iniquity; he shall surely live, he shall not die.

Eze 33:16 None of his sins that he hath committed shall be mentioned unto him: he hath done that which is lawful and right; he shall surely live.

Eze 33:19 But if the wicked turn from his wickedness, and do that which is lawful and right, he shall live thereby.

Eze 36:1 Also thou son of man, prophesy unto the mountains of Israel and say Ye mountains of Israel, hear the word of the LORD

Eze 36:2 Thus saith the Lord GOD; Because the enemy hath said against you, Aha, even the ancient high places are ours in possession:

Eze 36:3 Therefore prophesy and say, Thus saith the Lord GOD; Because they have made *you* desolate, and swallowed you up on every side, that ye might be a possession unto the residue of the heathen, and ye are taken up in the lips of talkers, and *are* an infamy of the people:

Eze 36:4 Therefore, ye mountains of Israel, hear the word of the Lord GOD; Thus saith the Lord GOD to the mountains, and to the hills, to the rivers, and to the valleys, to the desolate wastes, and to the cities that are forsaken, which became a prey and derision to the residue of the heathen that *are* round about;

Eze 45:14 Concerning the ordinance of oil, the bath of oil, *ye shall offer* the tenth part of a bath out of the cor, *which is* an homer of ten baths; for ten baths *are* an homer:

Eze 46:9 But when the people of the land shall come before the LORD in the solemn feasts, he that entereth in by the way of the north gate to worship shall go out by the way of the south gate; and he that entereth by the way of the south gate shall go forth by the way of the north gate: he shall not return by the way of the gate whereby he came in, but shall go forth over against it.

Ezr 2:62 These sought their register *among* those that were reckoned by genealogy, but they were not found: therefore were they, as polluted, put from the priesthood.

Ezr 4:15 That search may be made in the book of the records of thy fathers: so shalt thou find in the book of the records, and know that this city *is* a rebellious city, and hurtful unto kings and provinces, and that they have moved sedition within the same of old time: for which cause was this city destroyed.

Ezr 6:2 And there was found at Achmetha, in the palace that *is* in the province of the Medes, a roll, and therein *was* a record thus written:

Gal 2:1 Then fourteen years after I went up again to Jerusalem with Barnabas, and took Titus with *me* also.

Gal 2:3 But neither Titus, who was with me, being a Greek, was compelled to be circumcised:

Gal 2:8 (For he that wrought effectually in Peter to the apostleship of the circumcision, the same was mighty in me toward the Gentiles:)

Gal 2:12 For before that certain came from James, he did eat with the Gentiles: but when they were come, he withdrew and separated himself, fearing them which were of the circumcision.

Gal 3:24 Wherefore the law was our schoolmaster *to bring us* unto Christ, that we might be justified by faith.

Gal 3:25 But after that faith is come, we are no longer under a schoolmaster.

Gal 6:12 As many as desire to make a fair shew in the flesh, they constrain you to be circumcised; only lest they should suffer persecution for the cross of Christ.

Gal 6:13 For neither they themselves who are circumcised keep the law; but desire to have you circumcised, that they may glory in your flesh.

Gen 1:3 And God said, Let there be light: and there was light.

Gen 1:4 And God saw the light, that *it was* good: and God divided the light from the darkness.

Gen 1:5 And God called the light Day, and the darkness he called Night. And the evening and the morning were the first day.

Gen 1:8 And God called the firmament Heaven. And the evening and the morning were the second day.

Gen 1:14 And God said, Let there be lights in the firmament of the heaven to divide the day from the night; and let them be for signs, and for seasons, and for days, and years:

Gen 1:15 And let them be for lights in the firmament of the heaven to give light upon the earth: and it was so.

Gen 1:16 And God made two great lights; the greater light to rule the day, and the lesser light to rule the night: *he made* the stars also.

Gen 2:3 And God blessed the seventh day, and sanctified it: because that in it he had rested from all his work which God created and made.

Gen 4:3 And in process of time it came to pass, that Cain brought of the fruit of the ground an offering unto the LORD.

Gen 4:4 And Abel, he also brought of the firstlings of his flock and of the fat thereof. And the LORD had respect unto Abel and to his offering:

Gen 7:2 Of every clean beast thou shalt take to thee by sevens, the male and his female: and of beasts that *are* not clean by two, the male and his female.

Gen 7:12 And the rain was upon the earth forty days and forty nights.

Gen 8:20 And Noah builded an altar unto the LORD; and took of every clean beast, and of every clean fowl, and offered burnt offerings on the altar.

Gen 9:2 And the fear of you and the dread of you shall be upon every beast of the earth, and upon every fowl of the air, upon all that moveth *upon* the earth, and upon all the fishes of the sea; into your hand are they delivered.

Gen 9:3 Every moving thing that liveth shall be meat for you; even as the green herb have I given you all things.

Gen 9:4 But flesh with the life thereof, *which is* the blood thereof, shall ye not eat.

Gen 9:5 And surely your blood of your lives will I require; at the hand of every beast will I require it, and at the hand of man; at the hand of every man's brother will I require the life of man.

Gen 9:6 Whoso sheddeth man's blood, by man shall his blood be shed: for in the image of God made he man

Gen 9:7 And you, be ye fruitful, and multiply; bring forth abundantly in the earth, and multiply therein.

Gen 9:8 And God spake unto Noah, and to his sons with him, saying,

Gen 9:9 And I, behold, I establish my covenant with you, and with your seed after you;

Gen 9:10 And with every living creature that *is* with you, of the fowl, of the cattle, and of every beast of the earth with you; from all that go out of the ark, to every beast of the earth.

Gen 9:11 And I will establish my covenant with you; neither shall all flesh be cut off any more by the waters of a flood; neither shall there any more be a flood to destroy the earth.

Gen 9:12 And God said, This *is* the token of the covenant which I make between me and you and every living creature that *is* with you, for perpetual generations:

Gen 9:13 I do set my bow in the cloud, and it shall be for a token of a covenant between me and the earth.

Gen 9:14 And it shall come to pass, when I bring a cloud over the earth, that the bow shall be seen in the cloud:

Gen 9:15 And I will remember my covenant, which *is* between me and you and every living creature of all flesh; and the waters shall no more become a flood to destroy all flesh.

Gen 9:16 And the bow shall be in the cloud; and I will look upon it, that I may remember the everlasting covenant between God and every living creature of all flesh that *is* upon the earth.

Gen 9:17 And God said unto Noah, This *is* the token of the covenant, which I have established between me and all flesh that *is* upon the earth.

Gen 10:5 By these were the isles of the Gentiles divided in their lands; every one after his tongue, after their families, in their nations.

Gen 12:19 Why saidst thou, She *is* my sister? so I might have taken her to me to wife: now therefore behold thy wife, take *her*, and go thy way.

Gen 16:9 And the angel of the LORD said unto her, Return to thy mistress, and submit thyself under her hands.

Gen 17:11 And ye shall circumcise the flesh of your foreskin; and it shall be a token of the covenant betwixt me and you.

Gen 17:12 And he that is eight days old shall be circumcised among you, every man child in your generations, he that is born in the house, or bought with money of any stranger, which *is* not of thy seed.

Gen 17:12 And he that is eight days old shall be circumcised among you, every man child in your generations, he that is born in the house, or bought with money of any stranger, which *is* not of thy seed.

Gen 18:19 For I know him, that he will command his children and his household after him, and they shall keep the way of the LORD, to do justice and judgment; that the LORD may bring upon Abraham that which he hath spoken of him.

Gen 19:19 Behold now, thy servant hath found grace in thy sight, and thou hast magnified thy mercy, which thou hast shewed unto me in saving my life; and I cannot escape to the mountain, lest some evil take me, and I die:

Gen 19:26 But his wife looked back from behind him, and she became a pillar of salt

Gen 20:6 And God said unto him in a dream, Yea, I know that thou didst this in the integrity of thy heart; for I also withheld thee from sinning against me: therefore suffered I thee not to touch her.

Gen 22:3 And Abraham rose up early in the morning, and saddled his ass, and took two of his young men with him, and Isaac his son, and clave the wood for the burnt offering, and rose up, and went unto the place of which God had told him.

Gen 26:5 Because that Abraham obeyed my voice, and kept my charge, my commandments, my statutes, and my laws.

Gen 26:10 And Abimelech said, What *is* this thou hast done unto us? one of the people might lightly have lien with thy wife, and thou shouldest have brought guiltiness upon us.

Gen 27:8 Now therefore, my son, obey my voice according to that which I command thee.

Gen 35:10 And God said unto him, Thy name *is* Jacob: thy name shall not be called any more Jacob, but Israel shall be thy name: and he called his name Israel.

Gen 35:14 And Jacob set up a pillar in the place where he talked with him, *even* a pillar of stone: and he poured a drink offering thereon, and he poured oil thereon.

Gen 35:22 And it came to pass, when Israel dwelt in that land, that Reuben went and lay with Bilhah his father's concubine: and Israel heard *it*. Now the sons of Jacob were twelve:

Gen 35:23 The sons of Leah; Reuben, Jacob's firstborn, and Simeon, and Levi, and Judah, and Issachar, and Zebulun:

Gen 35:24 The sons of Rachel; Joseph, and Benjamin:

Gen 35:25 And the sons of Bilhah, Rachel's handmaid; Dan, and Naphtali:

Gen 35:26 And the sons of Zilpah, Leah's handmaid; Gad, and Asher: these *are* the sons of Jacob, which were born to him in Padanaram.

Gen 39:9 *There is* none greater in this house than I; neither hath he kept back any thing from me but thee, because thou *art* his wife: how then can I do this great wickedness, and sin against God?

Gen41:40 Thou shalt be over my house, and according unto thy word shall all my people be ruled: only in the throne will I be greater than thou.

Heb 1:2 Hath in these last days spoken unto us by *his* Son, whom he hath appointed heir of all things, by whom also he made the worlds;

Heb 4:4 For he spake in a certain place of the seventh *day* on this wise, And God did rest the seventh day from all his works.

Heb 4:9 There remaineth therefore a rest to the people of God.

Heb 5:9 And being made perfect, he became the author of eternal salvation unto all them that obey him;

Heb 7:11 If therefore perfection were by the Levitical priesthood, (for under it the people received the law,) what further need *was there* that another priest should rise after the order of Melchisedec, and not be called after the order of Aaron?

Heb 7:12 For the priesthood being changed, there is made of necessity a change also of the law

Heb 8:7 For if that first *covenant* had been faultless, then should no place have been sought for the second.

Heb 8:8 For finding fault with them, he saith, Behold, the days come, saith the Lord, when I will make a new covenant with the   house of Israel and with the house of Judah:

Heb 8:9 Not according to the covenant that I made with their fathers in the day when I took them by the hand to lead them out of the land of Egypt; because they continued not in my covenant, and I regarded them not, saith the Lord.

Heb 8:10 For this *is* the covenant that I will make with the house of Israel after those days, saith the Lord; I will put my laws into   their mind, and write them in their hearts: and I will be to them a God, and they shall be to me a people:

Heb 8:11 And they shall not teach every man his neighbour, and every man his brother, saying, Know the Lord: for all shall know me, from the least to the greatest.

Heb 8:12 For I will be merciful to their unrighteousness, and their sins and their iniquities will I remember no more.

Heb 8:13 In that he saith, A new *covenant*, he hath made the first old. Now that which decayeth and waxeth old *is* ready to vanish away.

Heb 9:1 Then verily the first *covenant* had also ordinances of divine service, and a worldly sanctuary.

Heb 9:2 For there was a tabernacle made; the first, wherein *was* the candlestick, and the table, and the shewbread; which is called the sanctuary.

Heb 9:3 And after the second veil, the tabernacle which is called the Holiest of all;

Heb 9:12 Neither by the blood of goats and calves, but by his own blood he entered in once into the holy place, having obtained eternal redemption *for us.*

Heb 9:22 And almost all things are by the law purged with blood; and without shedding of blood is no remission.

Heb 10:1 For the law having a shadow of good things to come, *and* not the very image of the things, can never with those sacrifices which they offered year by year continually make the comers thereunto perfect

Hos 6:6 For I desired mercy, and not sacrifice; and the knowledge of God more than burnt offerings.

Isa 1:15 And when ye spread forth your hands, I will hide mine eyes from you: yea, when ye make many prayers, I will not hear: your hands are full of blood.

Isa 51:4 Hearken unto me, my people; and give ear unto me, O my nation: for a law shall proceed from me, and I will make my judgment to rest for a light of the people. Isa 56:3 Neither let the son of the stranger, that hath joined himself to the LORD, speak, saying, The LORD hath utterly separated me from his people: neither let the eunuch say, Behold, I *am* a dry tree.

Isa 8:2 And I took unto me faithful witnesses to record, Uriah the priest, and Zechariah the son of Jeberechiah.

Isa 26:3 Thou wilt keep *him* in perfect peace, *whose* mind *is* stayed *on thee*: because he trusteth in thee.

Isa 29:13 Wherefore the Lord said, Forasmuch as this people draw near *me* with their mouth, and with their lips do honour me, but have removed their heart far from me, and their fear toward me is taught by the precept of men:

Isa 29:14 Therefore, behold, I will proceed to do a marvellous work among this people, *even* a marvellous work and a wonder: for the wisdom of their wise *men* shall perish, and the understanding of their prudent *men* shall be hid.

Isa 33:16 He shall dwell on high: his place of defence *shall be* the munitions of rocks: bread shall be given him; his waters *shall be* sure.

Isa 43:21 This people have I formed for myself; they shall shew forth my praise.

Isa 49:6 And he said, It is a light thing that thou shouldest be my servant to raise up the tribes of Jacob, and to restore the preserved of Israel: I will also give thee for a light to the Gentiles, that thou mayest be my salvation unto the end of the earth.

Isa 51:4 Hearken unto me, my people; and give ear unto me, O my nation: for a law shall proceed from me, and I will make my judgment to rest for a light of the people.

Isa 55:10 For as the rain cometh down, and the snow from heaven, and returneth not thither, but watereth the earth, and maketh it bring forth and bud, that it may give seed to the sower, and bread to the eater:

Isa 56:3 Neither let the son of the stranger, that hath joined himself to the LORD, speak, saying, The LORD hath utterly separated me from his people: neither let the eunuch say, Behold, I *am* a dry tree.

Isa 56:6 Also the sons of the stranger, that join themselves to the LORD, to serve him, and to love the name of the LORD, to be his servants, every one that keepeth the Sabbath from polluting it, and taketh hold of my covenant;

Isa 56:7 Even them will I bring to my holy mountain, and make them joyful in my house of prayer: their burnt offerings and their sacrifices *shall be* accepted upon mine altar; for mine house shall be called an house of prayer for all people.

Isa 56:8 The Lord GOD which gathereth the outcasts of Israel saith, Yet will I gather *others* to him, beside those that are gathered unto him.

Isa 58:13 If thou turn away thy foot from the Sabbath, *from* doing thy pleasure on my holy day; and call the Sabbath a delight, the holy of the LORD, honourable; and shalt honour him, not doing thine own ways, nor finding thine own pleasure, nor speaking *thine own* words:

Isa 58:13 If thou turn away thy foot from the Sabbath, *from* doing thy pleasure on my holy day; and call the Sabbath a delight, the holy of the LORD, honourable; and shalt honour him, not doing thine own ways, nor finding thine own pleasure, nor speaking *thine own* words:

Isa 58:14 Then shalt thou delight thyself in the LORD; and I will cause thee to ride upon the high places of the earth, and feed thee with the heritage of Jacob thy father: for the mouth of the LORD hath spoken *it*.

Isa 60:3 And the Gentiles shall come to thy light, and kings to the brightness of thy rising.

Isa 61:9 And their seed shall be known among the Gentiles, and their offspring among the people: all that see them shall acknowledge them, that they *are* the seed *which* the LORD hath blessed.

Jam 1:17 Every good gift and every perfect gift is from above, and cometh down from the Father of lights, with whom is no variableness, neither shadow of turning.

Jam 2:10 For whosoever shall keep the whole law, and yet offend in one *point*, he is guilty of all.

Jam 2:11 For he that said, Do not commit adultery, said also, Do not kill. Now if thou commit no adultery, yet if thou kill, thou art become a transgressor of the law.

Jam 2:12 So speak ye, and so do, as they that shall be judged by the law of liberty.

Jer 4:6   Set up the standard toward Zion: retire, stay not: for I will bring evil from the north, and a great destruction.

Jer 4:7   The lion is come up from his thicket, and the destroyer of the Gentiles is on his way; he is gone forth from his place to make thy land desolate; *and* thy cities shall be laid waste, without an inhabitant.

Jer 4:14 O Jerusalem, wash thine heart from wickedness, that thou mayest be saved. How long shall thy vain thoughts lodge within thee?

Jer 7:18 The children gather wood, and the fathers kindle the fire, and the women knead *their* dough, to make cakes to the queen of heaven, and to pour out drink offerings unto other gods, that they may provoke me to anger.

Jer 23:1 Woe be unto the pastors that destroy and scatter the sheep of my pasture! saith the LORD.

Jer 23:2 Therefore thus saith the LORD God of Israel against the pastors that feed my people; Ye have scattered my flock, and driven them away, and have not visited them: behold, I will visit upon you the evil of your doings, saith the LORD.

Jer 23:11 For both prophet and priest are profane; yea, in my house have I found their wickedness, saith the LORD.

Jer 23:13 And I have seen folly in the prophets of Samaria; they prophesied in Baal, and caused my people Israel to err.

Jer 23:14 I have seen also in the prophets of Jerusalem an horrible thing: they commit adultery, and walk in lies: they strengthen also the hands of evildoers, that none doth return from his wickedness: they are all of them unto me as Sodom, and the inhabitants thereof as Gomorrah.

Jer 23:21 I have not sent these prophets, yet they ran: I have not spoken to them, yet they prophesied.

Jer 23:28 The prophet that hath a dream, let him tell a dream; and he that hath my word, let him speak my word faithfully. What *is* the chaff to the wheat? saith the LORD.

Jer 23:31 Behold, I *am* against the prophets, saith the LORD, that use their tongues, and say, He saith.

Jer 23:32 Behold, I *am* against them that prophesy false dreams, saith the LORD, and do tell them, and cause my people to err by their lies, and by their lightness; yet I sent them not, nor commanded them: therefore they shall not profit this people at all, saith the LORD.

Jer 31:31 Behold, the days come, saith the LORD, that I will make a new covenant with the house of Israel, and with the house of Judah:

Jer 31:32 Not according to the covenant that I made with their fathers in the day *that* I took them by the hand to bring them out of the land of Egypt; which my covenant they brake, although I was an husband unto them, saith the LORD:

Jer 31:33 But this *shall be* the covenant that I will make with the house of Israel; After those days, saith the LORD, I will put my law in their inward parts, and write it in their hearts; and will be their God, and they shall be my people.

Jer 31:34 And they shall teach no more every man his neighbour, and every man his brother, saying, Know the LORD: for they shall all know me, from the least of them unto the greatest of them, saith the LORD: for I will forgive their iniquity, and I will remember their sin no more.

Jer 31:35 Thus saith the LORD, which giveth the sun for a light by day, *and* the ordinances of the moon and of the stars for a light by night, which divideth the sea when the waves thereof roar; The LORD of hosts *is* his name:

Jer 31:36 If those ordinances depart from before me, saith the LORD, *then* the seed of Israel also shall cease from being a nation before me for ever.

Jer 42:6   Whether *it be* good, or whether *it be* evil, we will obey the voice of the LORD our God, to whom we send thee; that it may be well with us, when we obey the voice of the LORD our God.

Jer 43:1   And it came to pass, *that* when Jeremiah had made an end of speaking unto all the people all the words of the LORD their God, for which the LORD their God had sent him to them, *even* all these words,

Jer 43:2   Then spake Azariah the son of Hoshaiah, and Johanan the son of Kareah, and all the proud men, saying unto Jeremiah, Thou speakest falsely: the LORD our God hath not sent thee to say, Go not into Egypt to sojourn there:

Jer 43:3   But Baruch the son of Neriah setteth thee on against us, for to deliver us into the hand of the Chaldeans, that they might   put us to death, and carry us away captives into Babylon.

Jer 43:4   So Johanan the son of Kareah, and all the captains of the forces, and all the people, obeyed not the voice of the LORD, to dwell in the land of Judah.

Jer 44:15   Then all the men which knew that their wives had burned incense unto other gods, and all the women that stood by, a great multitude, even all the people that dwelt in the land of Egypt, in Pathros, answered Jeremiah, saying,

Jer 44:16   *As for* the word that thou hast spoken unto us in the name of the LORD, we will not hearken unto thee.

Jer 44:17   But we will certainly do whatsoever thing goeth forth out of our own mouth, to burn incense unto the queen of heaven, and to pour out drink offerings unto her, as we have done, we, and our fathers, our kings, and our princes, in the cities of Judah, and in the streets of Jerusalem: for *then* had we plenty of victuals, and were well, and saw no evil.

Jer 44:18   But since we left off to burn incense to the queen of heaven, and to pour out drink offerings unto her, we have wanted all *things*, and have been consumed by the sword and by the famine.

Job 22:7   Thou hast not given water to the weary to drink, and thou hast withholden bread from the hungry.

Joh 1:1   In the beginning was the Word, and the Word was with God, and the Word was God.

Joh 1:2   The same was in the beginning with God.

Joh 1:3   All things were made by him; and without him was not any thing made that was made.

Joh 3:16   For God so loved the world, that he gave his only begotten Son, that whosoever believeth in him should not perish, but have everlasting life.

Joh 4:23   But the hour cometh, and now is, when the true worshippers shall worship the Father in spirit and in truth: for the Father seeketh such to worship him.

Joh 7:22   Moses therefore gave unto you circumcision; (not because it is of Moses, but of the fathers;) and ye on the Sabbath day circumcise a man.

Joh 7:39   (But this spake he of the Spirit, which they that believe on him should receive: for the Holy Ghost was not yet *given*; because that Jesus was not yet glorified.)

Joh 8:1   Jesus went unto the mount of Olives.

Joh 8:2　And early in the morning he came again into the temple, and all the people came unto him; and he sat down, and taught them.

Joh 8:3　And the scribes and Pharisees brought unto him a woman taken in adultery; and when they had set her in the midst,

Joh 8:4　They say unto him, Master, this woman was taken in adultery, in the very act.

Joh 8:5　Now Moses in the law commanded us, that such should be stoned: but what sayest thou?

Joh 8:6　This they said, tempting him, that they might have to accuse him. But Jesus stooped down, and with *his* finger wrote on the ground, *as though he heard them not.*

Joh 8:7　So when they continued asking him, he lifted up himself, and said unto them, He that is without sin among you, let him   first cast a stone at her.

Joh 8:8　And again he stooped down, and wrote on the ground.

Joh 8:9　And they which heard *it*, being convicted by *their own* conscience, went out one by one, beginning at the eldest, *even*   unto the last: and Jesus was left alone, and the woman standing in the midst.

Joh 8:10　When Jesus had lifted up himself, and saw none but the woman, he said unto her, Woman, where are those thine accusers? hath no man condemned thee?

Joh 8:11　She said, No man, Lord. And Jesus said unto her, Neither do I condemn thee: go, and sin no more.

Joh 8:12　Then spake Jesus again unto them, saying, I am the light of the world: he that followeth me shall not walk in darkness, but shall have the light of life.

Joh 8:35　And the servant abideth not in the house for ever: *but* the Son abideth ever.

Joh 8:58　Jesus said unto them, Verily verily I say unto you, Before Abraham was I am.

Joh 10:30　I and *my* Father are one.

Joh 14:6　Jesus saith unto him, I am the way, the truth, and the life: no man cometh unto the Father, but by me.

Joh 14:17　*Even* the Spirit of truth; whom the world cannot receive, because it seeth him not, neither knoweth him: but ye know him; for he dwelleth with you, and shall be in you.

Joh 15:10　If ye keep my commandments, ye shall abide in my love; even as I have kept my Father's commandments, and abide in his love.

Joh 20:1　The first *day* of the week cometh Mary Magdalene early, when it was yet dark, unto the sepulchre, and seeth the stone taken away from the sepulchre.

Joh 20:19　Then the same day at evening, being the first *day* of the week, when the doors were shut where the disciples were assembled for fear of the Jews, came Jesus and stood in the midst, and saith unto them, Peace *be* unto you.

Joh 14:15　If ye love me, keep my commandments.

Joh 15:26　But when the Comforter is come, whom I will send unto you from the Father, *even* the Spirit of truth, which proceedeth from the Father, he shall testify of me:

Joh 16:13　Howbeit when he, the Spirit of truth, is come, he will guide you into all truth: for he shall not speak of himself; but whatsoever he shall hear, *that* shall he speak: and he will shew you things to come.

1Jo 3:4   Whosoever committeth sin transgresseth also the law: for sin is the transgression of the law.

1Jo 4:1   Beloved, believe not every spirit, but try the spirits whether they are of God: because many false prophets are gone out into the world.

1Jo 5:2   By this we know that we love the children of God, when we love God, and keep his commandments.

1Jo 5:3   For this is the love of God, that we keep his commandments: and his commandments are not grievous.

1Jo 5:7   For there are three that bear record in heaven, the Father, the Word, and the Holy Ghost: and these three are one.

1Jo 5:21   Little children, keep yourselves from idols. Amen.

Jos 5:2   At that time the LORD said unto Joshua, Make thee sharp knives, and circumcise again the children of Israel the second time.

Jos 5:3   And Joshua made him sharp knives, and circumcised the children of Israel at the hill of the foreskins.

Jos 5:4   And this *is* the cause why Joshua did circumcise: All the people that came out of Egypt, *that were* males, *even* all the men of war, died in the wilderness by the way, after they came out of Egypt.

Jos 5:5   Now all the people that came out were circumcised: but all the people *that were* born in the wilderness by the way as they came forth out of Egypt, *them* they had not circumcised.

Jos 6:17   And the city shall be accursed, *even* it, and all that *are* therein, to the LORD: only Rahab the harlot shall live, she and all   that *are* with her in the house, because she hid the messengers that we sent.

Jos 6:18   And ye, in any wise keep *yourselves* from the accursed thing, lest ye make *yourselves* accursed, when ye take of the accursed thing, and make the camp of Israel a curse, and trouble it.

Jos 6:19   But all the silver, and gold, and vessels of brass and iron, *are* consecrated unto the LORD: they shall come into the treasury of the LORD.

Jos 7:12   Therefore the children of Israel could not stand before their enemies, *but* turned *their* backs before their enemies, because they were accursed: neither will I be with you any more, except ye destroy the accursed from among you.

Jos 7:15   And it shall be, *that* he that is taken with the accursed thing shall be burnt with fire, he and all that he hath: because he hath transgressed the covenant of the LORD, and because he hath wrought folly in Israel.

Jos 7:21   When I saw among the spoils a goodly Babylonish garment, and two hundred shekels of silver, and a wedge of gold of   fifty shekels weight, then I coveted them, and took them; and, behold, they *are* hid in the earth in the midst of my tent, and the silver under it.

Jos 7:25   And Joshua said, Why hast thou troubled us? the LORD shall trouble thee this day. And all Israel stoned him with stones, and burned them with fire, after they had stoned them with stones.

Jos 20:9   These were the cities appointed for all the children of Israel, and for the stranger that sojourneth among them, that whosoever killeth *any* person at unawares might flee thither, and not die by the hand of the avenger of blood, until he stood before the congregation.

Jos 24:10 But I would not hearken unto Balaam; therefore he blessed you still: so I delivered you out of his hand.

Jud 1:4 For there are certain men crept in unawares, who were before of old ordained to this condemnation, ungodly men, turning the grace of our God into lasciviousness, and denying the only Lord God, and our Lord Jesus Christ.

Jud 1:11 Woe unto them! for they have gone in the way of Cain, and ran greedily after the error of Balaam for reward, and perished in the gainsaying of Core

Jud 1:17 But, beloved, remember ye the words which were spoken before of the apostles of our Lord Jesus Christ;

1Ki 13:8 And the man of God said unto the king, If thou wilt give me half thine house, I will not go in with thee, neither will I eat bread nor drink water in this place:

1Ki 13:33 After this thing Jeroboam returned not from his evil way, but made again of the lowest of the people priests of the high places: whosoever would, he consecrated him, and he became *one* of the priests of the high places.

2Ki 5:9 So Naaman came with his horses and with his chariot, and stood at the door of the house of Elisha.

2Ki 5:10 And Elisha sent a messenger unto him, saying, Go and wash in Jordan seven times, and thy flesh shall come again to thee, and thou shalt be clean.

2Ki 5:11 But Naaman was wroth, and went away, and said, Behold, I thought, He will surely come out to me, and stand, and call on the name of the LORD his God, and strike his hand over the place, and recover the leper.

2Ki 5:15 And he returned to the man of God, he and all his company, and came, and stood before him: and he said, Behold, now I know that *there is* no God in all the earth, but in Israel: now therefore, I pray thee, take a blessing of thy servant.

2Ki 5:16 But he said, *As* the LORD liveth, before whom I stand, I will receive none. And he urged him to take *it*; but he refused.

2Ki 5:20 But Gehazi, the servant of Elisha the man of God, said, Behold, my master hath spared Naaman this Syrian, in not receiving at his hands that which he brought: but, *as* the LORD liveth, I will run after him, and take somewhat of him.

2Ki 5:27 The leprosy therefore of Naaman shall cleave unto thee, and unto thy seed for ever. And he went out from his presence a leper *as white* as snow.

2Ki 17:13 Yet the LORD testified against Israel, and against Judah, by all the prophets, *and by* all the seers, saying, Turn ye from your evil ways, and keep my commandments *and* my statutes, according to all the law which I commanded your fathers, and which I sent to you by my servants the prophets.

2Ki 17:16 And they left all the commandments of the LORD their God, and made them molten images, *even* two calves, and made a grove, and worshipped all the host of heaven, and served Baa2Ki 21:3 For he built up again the high places which Hezekiah his father had destroyed; and he reared up altars for Baal, and made a grove, as did Ahab king of Israel; and worshipped all the host of heaven, and served them.

2Ki 17:41 So these nations feared the LORD, and served their graven images, both their children, and their children's children: as did their fathers, so do they unto this day.

2Ki 21:3 For he built up again the high places which Hezekiah his father had destroyed; and he reared up altars for Baal, and made a grove, as did Ahab king of Israel; and worshipped all the host of heaven, and served them.

2Ki 21:4 And he built altars in the house of the LORD, of which the LORD said, In Jerusalem will I put my name.

2Ki 21:4 And he built altars in the house of the LORD, of which the LORD said, In Jerusalem will I put my name.

2Ki 21:5 And he built altars for all the host of heaven in the two courts of the house of the LORD.

2Ki 21:5 And he built altars for all the host of heaven in the two courts of the house of the LORD.

2Ki 21:6 And he made his son pass through the fire, and observed times, and used enchantments, and dealt with familiar spirits and wizards: he wrought much wickedness in the sight of the LORD, to provoke *him* to anger.

2Ki 22:8 And Hilkiah the high priest said unto Shaphan the scribe, I have found the book of the law in the house of the LORD. And Hilkiah gave the book to Shaphan, and he read it.

2Ki 22:11 And it came to pass, when the king had heard the words of the book of the law, that he rent his clothes.

2Ki 22:12 And the king commanded Hilkiah the priest, and Ahikam the son of Shaphan, and Achbor the son of Michaiah, and Shaphan the scribe, and Asahiah a servant of the king's, saying,

2Ki 22:13 Go ye, enquire of the LORD for me, and for the people, and for all Judah, concerning the words of this book that is found: for great *is* the wrath of the LORD that is kindled against us, because our fathers have not hearkened unto the words of this book, to do according unto all that which is written concerning us.

2Ki 22:14 So Hilkiah the priest, and Ahikam, and Achbor, and Shaphan, and Asahiah, went unto Huldah the prophetess, the wife of Shallum the son of Tikvah, the son of Harhas, keeper of the wardrobe; (now she dwelt in Jerusalem in the college;) and they communed with her.

2Ki 22:15 And she said unto them, Thus saith the LORD God of Israel, Tell the man that sent you to me,

2Ki 22:16 Thus saith the LORD, Behold, I will bring evil upon this place, and upon the inhabitants thereof, *even* all the words of the book which the king of Judah hath read:

2Ki 22:17 Because they have forsaken me, and have burned incense unto other gods, that they might provoke me to anger with all the works of their hands; therefore my wrath shall be kindled against this place, and shall not be quenched.

2Ki 20:5   Turn again, and tell Hezekiah the captain of my people, Thus saith the LORD, the God of David thy father, I have heard thy prayer, I have seen thy tears: behold, I will heal thee: on the third day thou shalt go up unto the house of the LORD.

2Ki 23:5   And he put down the idolatrous priests, whom the kings of Judah had ordained to burn incense in the high places in the cities of Judah, and in the places round about Jerusalem; them also that burned incense unto Baal, to the sun, and to the moon, and to the planets, and to all the host of heaven.

2Ki 24:17 And the king of Babylon made Mattaniah his father's brother king in his stead, and changed his name to Zedekiah.

Lev 4:1   And the LORD spake unto Moses, saying,

Lev 4:2   Speak unto the children of Israel, saying, If a soul shall sin through ignorance against any of the commandments of the LORD *concerning things* which ought not to be done, and shall do against any of them:

Lev 4:3   If the priest that is anointed do sin according to the sin of the people; then let him bring for his sin, which he hath sinned, a young bullock without blemish unto the LORD for a sin offering.

Lev 4:4   And he shall bring the bullock unto the door of the tabernacle of the congregation before the LORD; and shall lay his hand upon the bullock's head, and kill the bullock before the LORD.

Lev 4:5   And the priest that is anointed shall take of the bullock's blood, and bring it to the tabernacle of the congregation:

Lev 5:2   Or if a soul touch any unclean thing, whether *it be* a carcase of an unclean beast, or a carcase of unclean cattle, or the carcase of unclean creeping things, and *if* it be hidden from him; he also shall be unclean, and guilty.

Lev 5:15 If a soul commit a trespass, and sin through ignorance, in the holy things of the LORD; then he shall bring for his trespass unto the LORD a ram without blemish out of the flocks, of silver, after the shekel of the sanctuary, for

Lev 6:9   Command Aaron and his sons, saying, This *is* the law of the burnt offering: It *is* the burnt offering, because of the burning upon the altar all night unto the morning, and the fire of the altar shall be burning in it.

Lev 6:14 And this *is* the law of the meat offering: the sons of Aaron shall offer it before the LORD, before the altar.

Lev 6:25 Speak unto Aaron and to his sons, saying, This *is* the law of the sin offering: In the place where the burnt offering is killed shall the sin offering be killed before the LORD: it *is* most holy.

Lev 7:1   Likewise this *is* the law of the trespass offering: it *is* most holy.

Lev 7:11 And this *is* the law of the sacrifice of peace offerings, which he shall offer unto the LORD.

Lev 7:37 This *is* the law of the burnt offering, of the meat offering, and of the sin offering, and of the trespass offering, and of the consecrations, and of the sacrifice of the peace offerings;

Lev 10:1 And Nadab and Abihu, the sons of Aaron, took either of them his censer, and put fire therein, and put incense thereon, and offered strange fire before the LORD, which he commanded them not.

Lev 11:46 This *is* the law of the beasts, and of the fowl, and of every living creature that moveth in the waters, and of every creature that creepeth upon the earth:

Lev 11:46 This *is* the law of the beasts, and of the fowl, and of every living creature that moveth in the waters, and of every creature that creepeth upon the earth:

Lev 12:7 Who shall offer it before the LORD, and make an atonement for her; and she shall be cleansed from the issue of her blood. This *is* the law for her that hath born a male or a female.

Lev 12:7 Who shall offer it before the LORD, and make an atonement for her; and she shall be cleansed from the issue of her blood. This *is* the law for her that hath born a male or a female.

Lev 13:59 This *is* the law of the plague of leprosy in a garment of woollen or linen, either in the warp, or woof, or any thing of skins, to pronounce it clean, or to pronounce it unclean.

Lev 14:2 This shall be the law of the leper in the day of his cleansing: He shall be brought unto the priest:

Lev 14:32 This *is* the law *of him* in whom *is* the plague of leprosy, whose hand is not able to get *that which pertaineth* to his cleansing.

Lev 14:54 This *is* the law for all manner of plague of leprosy, and scall,

Lev 14:57 To teach when *it is* unclean, and when *it is* clean: this *is* the law of leprosy.

Lev 15:32 This *is* the law of him that hath an issue, and *of him* whose seed goeth from him, and is defiled therewith;

Lev 16:34 And this shall be an everlasting statute unto you, to make an atonement for the children of Israel for all their sins once a year. And he did as the LORD commanded Moses.

Lev 18:6 None of you shall approach to any that is near of kin to him, to uncover *their* nakedness: I *am* the LORD.

Lev 18:7 The nakedness of thy father, or the nakedness of thy mother, shalt thou not uncover: she *is* thy mother; thou shalt not uncover her nakedness.

Lev 18:22 Thou shalt not lie with mankind, as with womankind: it *is* abomination.

Lev 18:22 Thou shalt not lie with mankind, as with womankind: it *is* abomination.

Lev 18:30 Therefore shall ye keep mine ordinance, that *ye* commit not *any one* of these abominable customs, which were committed before you, and that ye defile not yourselves therein: I *am* the LORD your God.

Lev 19:23 And when ye shall come into the land, and shall have planted all manner of trees for food, then ye shall count the fruit thereof as uncircumcised: three years shall it be as uncircumcised unto you: it shall not be eaten of.

Lev 19:34 *But* the stranger that dwelleth with you shall be unto you as one born among you, and thou shalt love him as thyself; for ye were strangers in the land of Egypt: I *am* the LORD your God.

Lev 20:2 Again, thou shalt say to the children of Israel, Whosoever *he be* of the children of Israel, or of the strangers that sojourn in Israel, that giveth *any* of his seed unto Molech; he shall surely be put to death: the people of the land shall stone him with stones.

Lev 20:13 If a man also lie with mankind, as he lieth with a woman, both of them have committed an abomination: they shall surely be put to death; their blood *shall be* upon them.

Lev 22:9 They shall therefore keep mine ordinance, lest they bear sin for it, and die therefore, if they profane it: I the LORD do sanctify them.

Lev 23:1 And the LORD spake unto Moses, saying,

Lev 23:2 Speak unto the children of Israel, and say unto them, *Concerning* the feasts of the LORD, which ye shall proclaim *to be* holy convocations, *even* these *are* my feasts.

Lev 23:2 Speak unto the children of Israel, and say unto them, *Concerning* the feasts of the LORD, which ye shall proclaim *to be* holy convocations, *even* these *are* my feasts.

Lev 23:3 Six days shall work be done: but the seventh day *is* the Sabbath of rest, an holy convocation; ye shall do no work *therein*: it *is* the Sabbath of the LORD in all your dwellings.

Lev 23:3 Six days shall work be done: but the seventh day *is* the Sabbath of rest, an holy convocation; ye shall do no work *therein*: it *is* the Sabbath of the LORD in all your dwellings.

Lev 23:10 Speak unto the children of Israel, and say unto them, When ye be come into the land which I give unto you, and shall reap the harvest thereof, then ye shall bring a sheaf of the firstfruits of your harvest unto the priest:

Lev 23:16 Even unto the morrow after the seventh Sabbath shall ye number fifty days; and ye shall offer a new meat offering unto the LORD.

Lev 23:33 And the LORD spake unto Moses, saying, v34 The fifteenth day of this seventh month *shall be* the feast of tabernacles *for* seven days unto the LORD. v35 On the first day *shall be* an holy convocation:... v36 ... on the eighth day shall be an holy convocation unto you; ... it *is* a solemn assembly; v37 These *are* the feasts of the LORD, which ye shall proclaim *to be* holy convocations

Lev 23:38 Beside the sabbaths of the LORD

Lev 24:16 And he that blasphemeth the name of the LORD, he shall surely be put to death, *and* all the congregation shall certainly stone him: as well the stranger, as he that is born in the land, when he blasphemeth the name *of the LORD*, shall be put to death.

Lev 24:22 Ye shall have one manner of law as well for the stranger, as for one of your own country: for I *am* the LORD your God

Lev 26:12 And I will walk among you, and will be your God, and ye shall be my people.

Lev 26:14 But if ye will not hearken unto me, and will not do all these commandments;

Lev 26:15 And if ye shall despise my statutes, or if your soul abhor my judgments, so that ye will not do all my commandments, *but* that ye break my covenant:

Lev 26:16 I also will do this unto you; I will even appoint over you terror consumption, and the burning ague, that shall consume the eyes, and cause sorrow of heart: and ye shall sow your seed in vain, for your enemies shall eat it.

Luk 1:67 And his father Zacharias was filled with the Holy Ghost, and prophesied, saying, Luk 9:57 And it came to pass, that, as they went in the way, a certain *man* said unto him, Lord, I will follow thee whithersoever thou goest.

Luk 4:14 And Jesus returned in the power of the Spirit into Galilee: and there went out a fame of him through all the region round about.

Luk 4:21 & he began to say unto them, This day is this scripture fulfilled in your ears.

Luk 6:26 Woe unto you, when all men shall speak well of you! for so did their fathers to the false prophets.

Luk 9:57 And it came to pass, that, as they went in the way, a certain *man* said unto him, Lord, I will follow thee whithersoever thou goest.

Luk 9:58 And Jesus said unto him, Foxes have holes, and birds of the air *have* nests; but the Son of man hath not where to lay *his* head.

Luk 9:59 And he said unto another, Follow me. But he said, Lord, suffer me first to go and bury my father.

Luk 9:60 Jesus said unto him, Let the dead bury their dead: but go thou and preach the kingdom of God.

Luk 9:61 And another also said, Lord, I will follow thee; but let me first go bid them farewell, which are at home at my house.

Luk 9:62 And Jesus said unto him, No man, having put his hand to the plough, and looking back, is fit for the kingdom of God.

Luk 10:25 And, behold, a certain lawyer stood up, and tempted him, saying, Master, what shall I do to inherit eternal life?

Luk 10:26 He said unto him, What is written in the law? how readest thou?

Luk 10:27 And he answering said, Thou shalt love the Lord thy God with all t thy heart, and with all thy soul, and with all thy strength, and with all thy mind; and thy neighbour as thyself.

Luk 10:28 And he said unto him, Thou hast answered right: this do, and thou shalt live.

Luk 11:39 And the Lord said unto him, Now do ye Pharisees make clean the outside of the cup and the platter; but your inward part is full of ravening and wickedness.

Luk 13:1 There were present at that season some that told him of the Galilaeans, whose blood Pilate had mingled with their sacrifices.

Luk 13:2 And Jesus answering said unto them, Suppose ye that these Galilaeans were sinners above all the Galilaeans, because they suffered such things?

Luk 13:3 I tell you, Nay: but, except ye repent, ye shall all likewise perish.

Luk 13:4 Or those eighteen, upon whom the tower in Siloam fell, and slew them, think ye that they were sinners above all men that dwelt in Jerusalem?

Luk 13:5 I tell you, Nay: but, except ye repent, ye shall all likewise perish.

Luk 13:16 And ought not this woman, being a daughter of Abraham, whom Satan hath bound, lo, these eighteen years, be loosed from this bond on the Sabbath day?

Luk 13:24 Strive to enter in at the strait gate: for many, I say unto you, will seek to enter in, and shall not be able.

Luk 18:20 Thou knowest the commandments, Do not commit adultery, Do not kill, Do not steal, Do not bear false witness, Honour thy father and thy mother.

Luk 22:19 And he took bread, and gave thanks, and brake *it*, and gave unto them, saying, This is my body which is given for you: this do in remembrance of me.

Luk 22:20 Likewise also the cup after supper, saying, This cup *is* the new testament in my blood, which is shed for you.

Luk 22:31 And the Lord said, Simon, Simon, behold, Satan hath desired *to have* you, that he may sift *you* as wheat:

Luk 22:32 But I have prayed for thee, that thy faith fail not: and when thou art converted, strengthen thy brethren.

Luk 24:1 Now upon the first *day* of the week, very early in the morning, they came unto the sepulchre, bringing the spices which they had prepared, and certain *others* with them.

Luk 24:36 And as they thus spake, Jesus himself stood in the midst of them, and saith unto them, Peace *be* unto you.

Luk 24:37 But they were terrified and affrighted, and supposed that they had seen a spirit.

Luk 24:38 And he said unto them, Why are ye troubled? and why do thoughts arise in your hearts?

Mal 1:7 Ye offer polluted bread upon mine altar; and ye say, Wherein have we polluted thee? In that ye say, The table of the LORD *is* contemptible.

Mal 1:8 And if ye offer the blind for sacrifice, *is it* not evil? and if ye offer the lame and sick, *is it* not evil? offer it now unto thy governor; will he be pleased with thee, or accept thy person? saith the LORD of hosts.

Mar 2:21 No man also seweth a piece of new cloth on an old garment: else the new piece that filled it up taketh away from the old, and the rent is made worse.

Mar 2:22 And no man putteth new wine into old bottles: else the new wine doth burst the bottles, and the wine is spilled, and the bottles will be marred: but new wine must be put into new bottles.

Mar 2:27 And he said unto them, The Sabbath was made for man, and not man for the Sabbath:

Mar 2:28 Therefore the Son of man is Lord also of the Sabbath.

Mar 8:36 For what shall it profit a man, if he shall gain the whole world, and lose his own soul?

Mar 9:46 Where their worm dieth not, and the fire is not quenched.

Mar 12:30 And thou shalt love the Lord thy God with all thy heart, and with all thy soul, and with all thy mind, and with all thy strength: this *is* the first commandment.

Mar 13:22 For false Christs and false prophets shall rise, and shall shew signs and wonders, to seduce, if *it were* possible, even the elect.

Mar 14:24 And he said unto them, This is my blood of the new testament, which is shed for many.

Mar 15:34 And at the ninth hour Jesus cried with a loud voice, saying, Eloi, Eloi, lama sabachthani? which is, being interpreted, My God, my God, why hast thou forsaken me?

Mar 15:35 And some of them that stood by, when they heard *it*, said, Behold, he calleth Elias.

Mar 15:36 And one ran and filled a spunge full of vinegar, and put *it* on a reed, and gave him to drink, saying, Let alone; let us see whether Elias will come to take him down.

Mar 15:37 And Jesus cried with a loud voice, and gave up the ghost.

Mar 16:1 And when the Sabbath was past, Mary Magdalene, and Mary the *mother* of James, and Salome, had bought sweet spices, that they might come and anoint him.

Mar 16:2 And very early in the morning the first *day* of the week, they came unto the sepulchre at the rising of the sun.

Mar 16:9 Now when *Jesus* was risen early the first *day* of the week, he appeared first to Mary Magdalene, out of whom he had cast seven devils.

Mar 16:11 And they, when they had heard that he was alive, and had been seen of her, believed not.

Mar 16:12 After that he appeared in another form unto two of them, as they walked, and went into the country.

Mar 16:13 And they went and told *it* unto the residue: neither believed they them.

Mar 16:14 Afterward he appeared unto the eleven as they sat at meat, and upbraided them with their unbelief and hardness of heart, because they believed not them which had seen him after he was risen.

Mar 16:19 So then after the Lord had spoken unto them, he was received up into heaven, and sat on the right hand of God.

Mar 16:20 And they went forth, and preached every where, the Lord working with *them*, and confirming the word with signs following. Amen.

Mat 3:6 And were baptized of him in Jordan, confessing their sins.

Mat 3:16 And Jesus, when he was baptized, went up straightway out of the water: and, lo, the heavens were opened unto him, and he saw the Spirit of God descending like a dove, and lighting upon him:

Mat 4:1 Then was Jesus led up of the Spirit into the wilderness to be tempted of the devil.

Mat 4:1 Then was Jesus led up of the Spirit into the wilderness to be tempted of the devil. Mat 7:22 Many will say to me in that day, Lord, Lord, have we not prophesied in thy name? and in thy name have cast out devils? and in thy name done many wonderful works?

Mat 12:18 Behold my servant, whom I have chosen; my beloved, in whom my soul is well pleased: I will put my spirit upon him, and he shall shew judgment to the Gentiles.

Mat 4:2 And when he had fasted forty days and forty nights, he was afterward an hungred.

Mat 4:3 And when the tempter came to him, he said, If thou be the Son of God, command that these stones be made bread.

Mat 4:4   But he answered and said, It is written, Man shall not live by bread alone, but by every word that proceedeth out of the mouth of God.

Mat 4:5   Then the devil taketh him up into the holy city, and setteth him on a pinnacle of the temple,

Mat 4:6   And saith unto him, If thou be the Son of God, cast thyself down: for it is written, He shall give his angels charge concerning thee: and in *their* hands they shall bear thee up, lest at any time thou dash thy foot against a stone.

Mat 4:7   Jesus said unto him, It is written again, Thou shalt not tempt the Lord thy God.

Mat 4:8   Again, the devil taketh him up into an exceeding high mountain, and sheweth him all the kingdoms of the world, and the   glory of them;

Mat 4:9   And saith unto him, All these things will I give thee, if thou wilt fall down and worship me.

Mat 4:9   And saith unto him, All these things will I give thee, if thou wilt fall down and worship me.

Mat 4:10 Then saith Jesus unto him, Get thee hence, Satan: for it is written, Thou shalt worship the Lord thy God, and him only shalt thou serve.

Mat 4:10 Then saith Jesus unto him, Get thee hence, Satan: for it is written, Thou shalt worship the Lord thy God, and him only shalt thou serve.

Mat 4:11 Then the devil leaveth him, and, behold, angels came and ministered unto him.

Mat 4:12 Now when Jesus had heard that John was cast into prison, he departed into Galilee;

Mat 5:3   Blessed *are* the poor in spirit: for theirs is the kingdom of heaven.

Mat 5:4   Blessed *are* they that mourn: for they shall be comforted.

Mat 5:5   Blessed *are* the meek: for they shall inherit the earth.

Mat 5:6   Blessed *are* they which do hunger and thirst after righteousness: for they shall be filled.

Mat 5:7   Blessed *are* the merciful: for they shall obtain mercy.

Mat 5:8   Blessed *are* the pure in heart: for they shall see God.

Mat 5:9   Blessed *are* the peacemakers: for they shall be called the children of God.

Mat 5:10 Blessed *are* they which are persecuted for righteousness' sake: for theirs is the kingdom of heaven.

Mat 5:11 Blessed are ye, when *men* shall revile you, and persecute *you*, and shall say all manner of evil against you falsely, for   my sake.

Mat 5:12 Rejoice, and be exceeding glad: for great *is* your reward in heaven: for so persecuted they the prophets which were before you.

Mat 5:17 Think not that I am come to destroy the law, or the prophets: I am not come to destroy, but to fulfil.

Mat 5:18 For verily I say unto you, Till heaven and earth pass, one jot or one tittle shall in no wise pass from the law, till all be fulfilled.

Mat 5:19 Whosoever therefore shall break one of these least commandments, and shall teach men so, he shall be called the least in the kingdom of heaven: but whosoever shall do and teach *them*, the same shall be called great in the kingdom of heaven.

Mat 5:32 But I say unto you, That whosoever shall put away his wife, saving for the cause of fornication, causeth her to commit adultery: and whosoever shall marry her that is divorced committeth adultery.

Mat 6:19 Lay not up for yourselves treasures upon earth, where moth and rust doth corrupt, and where thieves break through and steal:

Mat 6:20 But lay up for yourselves treasures in heaven, where neither moth nor rust doth corrupt, and where thieves do not break through nor steal: Mat 7:21 Not every one that saith unto me, Lord, Lord, shall enter into the kingdom of heaven; but he that doeth the will of my Father which is in heaven.

Mat 6:21 For where your treasure is, there will your heart be also.

Mat 6:24 No man can serve two masters: for either he will hate the one, and love the other; or else he will hold to the one, and despise the other. Ye cannot serve God and mammon.

Mat 6:33 But seek ye first the kingdom of God, and his righteousness; and all these things shall be added unto you.

Mat 7:21 Not every one that saith unto me, Lord, Lord, shall enter into the kingdom of heaven; but he that doeth the will of my Father which is in heaven.

Mat 7:22 Many will say to me in that day, Lord, Lord, have we not prophesied in thy name? and in thy name have cast out devils? and in thy name done many wonderful works?

Mat 7:23 And then will I profess unto them, I never knew you: depart from me, ye that work iniquity.

Mat 10:35 For I am come to set a man at variance against his father, and the daughter against her mother, and the daughter in law against her mother in law.

Mat 10:36 And a man's foes *shall be* they of his own household.

Mat 10:37 He that loveth father or mother more than me is not worthy of me: and he that loveth son or daughter more than me is not worthy of me.

Mat 10:38 And he that taketh not his cross and followeth after me is not worthy of me.

Mat 11:14 And if ye will receive *it*, this is Elias, which was for to come.

Mat 13:44 Again, the kingdom of heaven is like unto treasure hid in a field; the which when a man hath found, he hideth, and for joy thereof goeth and selleth all that he hath, and buyeth that field.

Mat 13:45 Again, the kingdom of heaven is like unto a merchant man, seeking goodly pearls:

Mat 13:46 Who, when he had found one pearl of great price, went and sold all that he had, and bought it.

Mat 13:47 Again, the kingdom of heaven is like unto a net, that was cast into the sea, and gathered of every kind:

Mat 15:6 And honour not his father or his mother, *he shall be free*. Thus have ye made the commandment of God of none effect by your tradition.

Mat 15:6 And honour not his father or his mother, *he shall be free*. Thus have ye made the commandment of God of none effect by your tradition.

Mat 26:18 And he said, Go into the city to such a man, and say unto him, The Master saith, My time is at hand; I will keep the passover at thy house with my disciples.

Mat 10:34   Think not that I am come to send peace on earth: I came not to send peace, but a sword.

Mat 16:3   And in the morning, *It will be* foul weather to day: for the sky is red and lowering. O *ye* hypocrites, ye can discern the face of the sky; but can ye not *discern* the signs of the times?

Mat 17:11   And Jesus answered and said unto them, Elias truly shall first come, and restore all things.

Mat 18:11   For the Son of man is come to save that which was lost.

Mat 19:8   He saith unto them, Moses because of the hardness of your hearts suffered you to put away your wives: but from the beginning it was not so.

Mat 19:17   And he said unto him, Why callest thou me good? *there is* none good but one, *that is*, God: but if thou wilt enter into life, keep the commandments.

Mat 19:17   And he said unto him, Why callest thou me good? *there is* none good but one, *that is*, God: but if thou wilt enter into life, keep the commandments.

Mat 19:18   He saith unto him, Which? Jesus said, Thou shalt do no murder, Thou shalt not commit adultery, Thou shalt not steal, Thou shalt not bear false witness,

Mat 19:19   Honour thy father and *thy* mother: and, Thou shalt love thy neighbour as thyself.

Mat 22:17   Tell us therefore, What thinkest thou? Is it lawful to give tribute unto Caesar, or not?

Mat 22:40   On these two commandments hang all the law and the prophets.

Mat 25:32   And before him shall be gathered all nations: and he shall separate them one from another, as a shepherd divideth *his* sheep from the goats:

Mat 25:33   And he shall set the sheep on his right hand, but the goats on the left.

Mat 26:27   And he took the cup, and gave thanks, and gave *it* to them, saying, Drink ye all of it;

Mat 26:28   For this is my blood of the new testament, which is shed for many for the remission of sins.

Mat 26:28   For this is my blood of the new testament, which is shed for many for the remission of sins.

Mat 27:21   The governor answered and said unto them, Whether of the twain will ye that I release unto you? They said Barabbas.

Mat 27:51   And behold the veil of the temple was rent in twain from the top to the bottom and the earth did quake and the rocks rent

Mic 4:2   And many nations shall come, and say, Come, and let us go up to the mountain of the LORD, and to the house of the God of Jacob; and he will teach us of his ways, and we will walk in his paths: for the law shall go forth of Zion, and the word of the LORD from Jerusalem.

Mic 6:8   He hath shewed thee, O man, what *is* good; and what doth the LORD require of thee, but to do justly, and to love mercy, and to walk humbly with thy God?

Mic 7:18   Who *is* a God like unto thee, that pardoneth iniquity, and passeth by the transgression of the remnant of his heritage? he retaineth not his anger for ever, because he delighteth *in* mercy.

Neh 8:8   So they read in the book in the law of God distinctly, and gave the sense, and caused *them* to understand the reading.

Neh 8:14 And they found written in the law which the LORD had commanded by Moses, that the children of Israel should dwell in booths in the feast of the seventh month:

Neh 9:13 Thou camest down also upon mount Sinai, and spakest with them from heaven, and gavest them right judgments, and true laws, good statutes and commandments:

Neh 9:14 And madest known unto them thy holy Sabbath, and commandedst them precepts, statutes, and laws, by the hand of Moses thy servant:

Neh 9:29 And testifiedst against them, that thou mightest bring them again unto thy law: yet they dealt proudly, and hearkened not unto thy commandments, but sinned against thy judgments, (which if a man do, he shall live in them;) and withdrew the shoulder, and hardened their neck, and would not hear.

Neh 10:31 And *if* the people of the land bring ware or any victuals on the Sabbath day to sell, *that* we would not buy it of them on the Sabbath, or on the holy day: and *that* we would leave the seventh year, and the exaction of every debt.

Neh 9:32 Now therefore, our God, the great, the mighty, and the terrible God, who keepest covenant and mercy, let not all the trouble seem little before thee, that hath come upon us, on our kings, on our princes, and on our priests, and on our prophets, and on our fathers, and on all thy people, since the time of the kings of Assyria unto this day.

Num 11:25 And the LORD came down in a cloud, and spake unto him, and took of the spirit that *was* upon him, and gave *it* unto the seventy elders: and it came to pass *that*,when the spirit rested upon them, they prophesied and did not cease

Neh 13:15 In those days saw I in Judah *some* treading wine presses on the Sabbath, and bringing in sheaves, and lading asses; as also wine, grapes, and figs, and all *manner of* burdens, which they brought into Jerusalem on the Sabbath day: and I testified *against them* in the day wherein they sold victuals.

Neh 13:16 There dwelt men of Tyre also therein, which brought fish, and all manner of ware, and sold on the Sabbath unto the children of Judah, and in Jerusalem.

Neh 13:17 Then I contended with the nobles of Judah, and said unto them, What evil thing *is* this that ye do, and profane the Sabbath day?

Neh 13:18 Did not your fathers thus, and did not our God bring all this evil upon us, and upon this city? yet ye bring more wrath upon Israel by profaning the Sabbath.

Neh 13:19 And it came to pass, that when the gates of Jerusalem began to be dark before the Sabbath, I commanded that the gates should be shut, and charged that they should not be opened till after the Sabbath: and *some* of my servants set I at the gates, *that* there should no burden be brought in on the Sabbath day.

Neh 13:20 So the merchants and sellers of all kind of ware lodged without Jerusalem once or twice.

Neh 13:21 Then I testified against them, and said unto them, Why lodge ye about the wall? if ye do *so* again, I will lay hands on you. From that time forth came they no *more* on the Sabbath.

Neh 13:22 And I commanded the Levites that they should cleanse themselves, and *that* they should come *and* keep the gates, to sanctify the Sabbath day.
Remember me, O my God, *concerning* this also, and spare me according to the greatness of thy mercy.

Num 6:21 This *is* the law of the Nazarite who hath vowed, *and of* his offering unto the LORD for his separation, beside *that* that his hand shall get: according to the vow which he vowed, so he must do after the law of his separation.

Num 9:14 And if a stranger shall sojourn among you, and will keep the passover unto the LORD; according to the ordinance of the passover, and according to the manner thereof, so shall he do: ye shall have one ordinance, both for the stranger, and for him that was born in the land.

Num 10:8 And the sons of Aaron, the priests, shall blow with the trumpets; and they shall be to you for an ordinance for ever throughout your generations.

Num 12:13 And Moses cried unto the LORD saying Heal her now OGod I beseech thee

Num 15:28 And the priest shall make an atonement for the soul that sinneth ignorantly, when he sinneth by ignorance before the LORD, to make an atonement for him; and it shall be forgiven him.

Num 15:32 And while the children of Israel were in the wilderness, they found a man that gathered sticks upon the Sabbath day.

Num 15:33 And they that found him gathering sticks brought him unto Moses and Aaron, and unto all the congregation.

Num 15:34 And they put him in ward, because it was not declared what should be done to him.

Num 15:35 And the LORD said unto Moses, The man shall be surely put to death: all the congregation shall stone him with stones without the camp.

Num 19:2 This *is* the ordinance of the law which the LORD hath commanded, saying, Speak unto the children of Israel, that they bring thee a red heifer without spot, wherein *is* no blemish, *and* upon which never came yoke:

Num 21:14 Wherefore it is said in the book of the wars of the LORD, What he did in the Red sea, and in the brooks of Arnon,

Num 22:6 Come now therefore, I pray thee, curse me this people; for they *are* too mighty for me: peradventure I shall prevail, *that* we may smite them, and *that* I may drive them out of the land: for I wot that he whom thou blessest is blessed, and he whom thou cursest

Num 22:17 For I will promote thee unto very great honour, and I will do whatsoever thou sayest unto me: come therefore, I pray thee, curse me this people.

Num 22:18 And Balaam answered and said unto the servants of Balak, If Balak would give me his house full of silver and gold, I cannot go beyond the word of the LORD my God, to do less or more.

Num 22:22 And God's anger was kindled because he went: and the angel of the LORD stood in the way for an adversary against him. Now he was riding upon his ass, and his two servants *were* with him.

Num 23:8   How shall I curse, whom God hath not cursed? or how shall I defy, *whom* the LORD hath not defied?

Num 25:6   And, behold, one of the children of Israel came and brought unto his brethren a Midianitish woman in the sight of Moses, and in the sight of all the congregation of the children of Israel, who *were* weeping *before* the door of the tabernacle of the congregation.

Num 25:7   And when Phinehas, the son of Eleazar, the son of Aaron the priest, saw *it*, he rose up from among the congregation, and took a javelin in his hand;

Num 25:8   And he went after the man of Israel into the tent, and thrust both of them through, the man of Israel, and the woman through her belly. So the plague was stayed from the children of Israel.

Num 25:9   And those that died in the plague were twenty and four thousand.

Num 27:11   And if his father have no brethren, then ye shall give his inheritance unto his kinsman that is next to him of his family, and he shall possess it: and it shall be unto the children of Israel a statute of judgment, as the LORD commanded Moses.

Num 31:8   And they slew the kings of Midian, beside the rest of them that were slain; *namely*, Evi, and Rekem, and Zur, and Hur, and Reba, five kings of Midian: Balaam also the son of Beor they slew with the sword.

Num 31:16   Behold, these caused the children of Israel, through the counsel of Balaam, to commit trespass against the LORD in the matter of Peor, and there was a plague among the congregation of the LORD.

Num 31:21   And Eleazar the priest said unto the men of war which went to the battle, This *is* the ordinance of the law which the LORD commanded Moses;

Num 35:17   And if he smite him with throwing a stone, wherewith he may die, and he die, he *is* a murderer: the murderer shall surely be put to death.

1Pe 1:23   Being born again, not of corruptible seed, but of incorruptible, by the word of God, which liveth and abideth for ever.

1Pe 4:8   And above all things have fervent charity among yourselves: for charity shall cover the multitude of sins.

1Pe 4:18   And if the righteous scarcely be saved, where shall the ungodly and the sinner appear?

1Pe 5:8   Be sober, be vigilant; because your adversary the devil, as a roaring lion, walketh about, seeking whom he may devour:

2Pe 2:3   And through covetousness shall they with feigned words make merchandise of you: whose judgment now of a long time lingereth not, and their damnation slumbereth not.

2Pe 3:8   But, beloved, be not ignorant of this one thing, that one day *is* with the Lord as a thousand years, and a thousand years as one day.

2Pe 3:10   But the day of the Lord will come as a thief in the night; in the which the heavens shall pass away with a great noise, and the elements shall melt with fervent heat, the earth also and the works that are therein shall be burned up.

Phi 2:3   *Let* nothing *be done* through strife or vainglory; but in lowliness of mind let each esteem other better than themselves

Phi 3:18 (For many walk, of whom I have told you often, and now tell you even weeping, *that they are* the enemies of the cross of Christ:

Pro 1:7 The fear of the LORD *is* the beginning of knowledge: *but* fools despise wisdom and instruction.

Pro 1:8 My son, hear the instruction of thy father, and forsake not the law of thy mother:

Pro 2:1 My son, if thou wilt receive my words, and hide my commandments with thee;

Pro 3:11 My son, despise not the chastening of the LORD; neither be weary of his correction:

Pro 3:12 For whom the LORD loveth he correcteth; even as a father the son *in whom* he delighteth.

Pro 6:23 For the commandment *is* a lamp; and the law *is* light; and reproofs of instruction *are* the way of life:

Pro 7:2 Keep my commandments, and live; and my law as the apple of thine eye.

Pro 16:25 There is a way that seemeth right unto a man, but the end thereof *are* the ways of death.

Pro 9:17 Stolen waters are sweet, and bread *eaten* in secret is pleasant.

Pro 16:25 There is a way that seemeth right unto a man, but the end thereof *are* the ways of death.

Pro 13:7 There is that maketh himself rich, yet *hath* nothing: *there is* that maketh himself poor, yet *hath* great riches.

Pro 19:16 He that keepeth the commandment keepeth his own soul; *but* he that despiseth his ways shall die.

Pro 28:9 He that turneth away his ear from hearing the law, even his prayer *shall be* abomination.

Psa 19:7 The law of the LORD *is* perfect, converting the soul: the testimony of the LORD *is* sure, making wise the simple.

Psa 40:8 I delight to do thy will, O my God: yea, thy law *is* within my heart.

Psa 81:1 To the chief Musician upon Gittith, *A Psalm* of Asaph. Sing aloud unto God our strength: make a joyful noise unto the God of Jacob.

Psa 81:2 Take a psalm, and bring hither the timbrel, the pleasant harp with the psaltery.

Psa 81:3 Blow up the trumpet in the new moon, in the time appointed, on our solemn feast day.

Psa 81:4 For this *was* a statute for Israel, *and* a law of the God of Jacob.

Psa 89:30 If his children forsake my law, and walk not in my judgments;

Psa 89:31 If they break my statutes, and keep not my commandments;

Psa 95:11 Unto whom I sware in my wrath that they should not enter into my rest.

Psa 111:7 The works of his hands *are* verity and judgment; all his commandments *are* sure.

Psa 111:8 They stand fast for ever and ever, *and are* done in truth and uprightness.

Psa 119:6 Then shall I not be ashamed, when I have respect unto all thy commandments.

Psa 119:7 I will praise thee with uprightness of heart, when I shall have learned thy righteous judgments.

Psa 119:8 I will keep thy statutes: O forsake me not utterly.

Psa 119:9 BETH. Wherewithal shall a young man cleanse his way? by taking heed *thereto* according to thy word.

Psa 119:10 With my whole heart have I sought thee: O let me not wander from thy commandments.

Psa 119:11 Thy word have I hid in mine heart, that I might not sin against thee.

Psa 119:66 Teach me good judgment and knowledge: for I have believed thy commandments.

Psa 119:142 Thy righteousness *is* an everlasting righteousness, and thy law *is* the truth.

Psa 119:172 My tongue shall speak of thy word: for all thy commandments *are* righteousness.

Rev 1:10 I was in the Spirit on the Lord's day, and heard behind me a great voice, as of a trumpet,

Rev 2:8 And unto the angel of the church in Smyrna write; These things saith the first and the last, which was dead, and is alive;

Rev 3:9 Behold, I will make them of the synagogue of Satan, which say they are Jews, and are not, but do lie; behold, I will make them to come and worship before thy feet, and to know that I have loved thee.

Rev 6:11 And white robes were given unto every one of them; and it was said unto them, that they should rest yet for a little season, until their fellow servants also and their brethren, that should be killed as they *were*, should be fulfilled.

Rev 12:17 And the dragon was wroth with the woman, and went to make war with the remnant of her seed, which keep the commandments of God, and have the testimony of Jesus Christ.

Rev 13:3 And I saw one of his heads as it were wounded to death; and his deadly wound was healed: and all the world wondered after the beast.

Rev 13:4 And they worshipped the dragon which gave power unto the beast: and they worshipped the beast, saying, Who *is* like unto the beast? who is able to make war with him? .

Rev 13:12 And he exerciseth all the power of the first beast before him, and causeth the earth and them which dwell therein to worship the first beast, whose deadly wound was healed.

Rev 13:13 And he doeth great wonders, so that he maketh fire come down from heaven on the earth in the sight of men,

Rev 13:14 And deceiveth them that dwell on the earth by *the means of* those miracles which he had power to do in the sight of the beast; saying to them that dwell on the earth, that they should make an image to the beast, which had the wound by a sword, and did live.

Rev 14:4 These are they which were not defiled with women; for they are virgins. These are they which follow the Lamb whithersoever he goeth. These were redeemed from among men, *being* the firstfruits unto God and to the Lamb.

Rev 14:6 And I saw another angel fly in the midst of heaven, having the everlasting gospel to preach unto them that dwell on the earth, and to every nation, and kindred, and tongue, and people,

Rev 14:12 Here is the patience of the saints: here *are* they that keep the commandments of God, and the faith of Jesus.

Rev 18:4 And I heard another voice from heaven, saying, Come out of her, my people, that ye be not partakers of her sins, and that ye receive not of her plagues.

Rev 20:12 And I saw the dead, small and great, stand before God; and the books were opened: and another book was opened, which is *the book* of life: and the dead were judged out of those things which were written in the books, according to **their works**.

Rev 20:13 And the sea gave up the dead which were in it; and death and hell delivered up the dead which were in them: and they were judged every man according to their works.

Rev 22:12 And, behold, I come quickly; and my reward *is* with me, to give every man according as his work shall be.

Rev 22:13 I am Alpha and Omega, the beginning and the end, the first and the last.

Rev 22:14 Blessed *are* they that do his commandments, that they may have right to the tree of life, and may enter in through the gates into the city.

Rev 22:18 For I testify unto every man that heareth the words of the prophecy of this book, If any man shall add unto these things, God shall add unto him the plagues that are written in this book:

Rev 22:19 And if any man shall take away from the words of the book of this prophecy, God shall take away his part out of the book of life, and out of the holy city, and *from* the things which are written in this book.

Rom 2:9 Tribulation and anguish, upon every soul of man that doeth evil, of the Jew first, and also of the Gentile;

Rom 2:10 But glory, honour, and peace, to every man that worketh good, to the Jew first, and also to the Gentile:

Rom 2:12 For as many as have sinned without law shall also perish without law: and as many as have sinned in the law shall be judged by the law;

Rom 2:13 (For not the hearers of the law *are* just before God, but the doers of the law shall be justified.

Rom 2:14 For when the Gentiles, which have not the law, do by nature the things contained in the law, these, having not the law, are a law unto themselves:

Rom 2:15 Which shew the work of the law written in their hearts, their conscience also bearing witness, and *their* thoughts the mean while accusing or else excusing one another;)

Rom 3:25 Whom God hath set forth *to be* a propitiation through faith in his blood, to declare his righteousness for the remission of sins that are past, through the forbearance of God;

Rom 6:6 Knowing this, that our old man is crucified with *him*, that the body of sin might be destroyed, that henceforth we should not serve sin.

Rom 6:23 For the wages of sin *is* death; but the gift of God *is* eternal life through Jesus Christ our Lord.

Rom 7:7 What shall we say then? *Is* the law sin? God forbid. Nay, I had not known sin, but by the law: for I had not known lust, except the law had said, Thou shalt not covet.

Rom 7:12 Wherefore the law *is* holy, and the commandment holy, and just, and good.

Rom 8:1 *There is* therefore now no condemnation to them which are in Christ Jesus, who walk not after the flesh, but after the Spirit.

Rom 8:6 For to be carnally minded *is* death; but to be spiritually minded *is* life and peace.

Rom 9:25 As he saith also in Osee, I will call them my people, which were not my people; and her beloved, which was not beloved.

Rom 11:19 Thou wilt say then The branches were broken off that I might be graffed in.

Rom 12:2 And be not conformed to this world: but be ye transformed by the renewing of your mind, that ye may prove what *is* that good, and acceptable, and perfect, will of God.

Rom 13:2 Whosoever therefore resisteth the power, resisteth the ordinance of God: and they that resist shall receive to themselves damnation.

Rom 13:9 For this, Thou shalt not commit adultery, Thou shalt not kill, Thou shalt not steal, Thou shalt not bear false witness, Thou shalt not covet; and if *there be* any other commandment, it is briefly comprehended in this saying, namely, Thou shalt love thy neighbour as thyself.

Rom 14:2For one believeth that he may eat all things: another who is weak eateth herbs

Rom 14:3 Let not him that eateth despise him that eateth not; and let not him which eateth not judge him that eateth: for God hath received him.

Rom 14:4 Who art thou that judgest another man's servant? to his own master he standeth or falleth. Yea, he shall be holden up: for God is able to make him stand.

Rom 14:12 So then every one of us shall give account of himself to God.

Rom 15:18 For I will not dare to speak of any of those things which Christ hath not wrought by me, to make the Gentiles obedient, by word and deed,

1Sa 13:9 And Saul said, Bring hither a burnt offering to me, and peace offerings. And he offered the burnt offering.

1Sa 13:10 And it came to pass, that as soon as he had made an end of offering the burnt offering, behold, Samuel came; and Saul went out to meet him, that he might salute him.

1Sa 13:11 And Samuel said, What hast thou done? And Saul said, Because I saw that the people were scattered from me, and *that* thou camest not within the days appointed, and *that* the Philistines gathered themselves together at Michmash;

1Sa 15:13 And Samuel came to Saul: and Saul said unto him, Blessed *be* thou of the LORD: I have performed the commandment of the LORD.

1Sa 15:20 And Saul said unto Samuel, Yea, I have obeyed the voice of the LORD, and have gone the way which the LORD sent me, and have brought Agag the king of Amalek, and have utterly destroyed the Amalekites.

1Sa 15:21 But the people took of the spoil, sheep and oxen, the chief of the things which should have been utterly destroyed, to sacrifice unto the LORD thy God in gilgal

1Sa 15:22 **And Samuel said, Hath the LORD *as great* delight in burnt offerings and sacrifices, as in obeying the voice of the LORD? Behold, to obey *is***